Praise for *Slavery and Freedom in Black Thought in the Early Spanish Atlantic*

"This book is an astounding, sweeping, and beautifully written intellectual exploration of the rich, complicated, and worldly lives of people of African descent as they negotiated experiences of enslavement and emancipation in the early modern Iberian Atlantic. It charts an extraordinary intellectual cartography of early modern Black living that upends how scholars think of Black movement and agency at the dawn of and decades into the Atlantic slave trade."

Yesenia Barragan, Rutgers University

"Ireton guides the reader through the early modern archive pointing to sources that bring into focus themes long held to be unimaginable. The narrative before us is a testament to archival presence engendered by the thoughts and actions of enslaved Africans and their early modern descendants. Ireton charts new ground in this brilliant study of slavery and freedom."

Herman Bennett, author of *African Kings and Black Slaves: Sovereignty and Dispossession in the Early Modern Atlantic*

"If there was ever a body of early modern Hispanic Black Atlantic thought, as the archive of ideas on freedom, rights, and livelihood, Ireton provides its fullest account through the examination of the lives and thoughts of myriads of Black people born in Africa, Europe, and the Americas. Behind the letters, trials, and petitions examined in this book, readers can piece together the lives of these Black men and women in both metropolitan Spain and the colonies, in tandem, as never before."

Alex Borucki, University of California, Irvine

"In her masterful exploration of a 'lettered Black public sphere' in the Spanish Atlantic, Ireton traces how Black subjects mobilized a transatlantic web of information to enact freedom. Her subjects gossip, litigate, acquire wealth, and theorize freedom as they circulate, spreading knowledge in surprising ways. Beautifully written, deeply researched, and centered in life stories, Ireton provocatively expands upon our knowledge of freedom and unfreedom."

Karen Graubart, author of *Republics of Difference: Religious and Racial Self-Governance in the Spanish Atlantic World*

"*Slavery and Freedom in Black Thought* is a marvel of methodological inventiveness and scholarly rigor. Drawing on expansive archival material, Ireton grounds readers in the 'thick spheres of communication' that enslaved and free people of African descent engaged in to shape ideas and debates about slavery and freedom across the Spanish Empire."

Tamara Walker, author of *Exquisite Slaves:
Race, Clothing and Status in Colonial Lima*

"Extensively researched and creatively argued, this groundbreaking study is replete with richly detailed vignettes featuring the voices of Africans and people of African descent in sixteenth-century Sevilla and Spanish America. Ireton reminds us of Black individuals' agency and dynamism within the early modern Iberian world, mustering a wealth of new evidence to document their multiform efforts to safeguard their liberties and loved ones."

David Wheat, author of *Atlantic Africa and
the Spanish Caribbean, 1570–1640*

Slavery and Freedom in Black Thought in the Early Spanish Atlantic

Weaving together thousands of archival fragments, this study explores a shared Black Atlantic world where the meanings of slavery and freedom were fiercely contested and claimed. It recreates the worlds of extraordinary individuals and communities in the long sixteenth century, while mapping the development of early modern Black thought about slavery and freedom. From a free Black mother's embarkation license to cross the Atlantic Ocean, to an enslaved Sevillian woman's epistles to her freed husband in New Spain, to an enslaved man's negotiations with prospective buyers on the auction block in Mexico City, to a Black man's petition to reclaim his liberty after his illegitimate enslavement, Chloe L. Ireton explores how Africans and their descendants reckoned with laws and theological discourses that legitimized the enslavement of Black people and the varied meanings of freedom across legal jurisdictions. Their intellectual labor reimagined the epistemic worlds of slavery and freedom in the early modern Atlantic.

Chloe L. Ireton is Lecturer in the History of Iberia and the Iberian World 1500–1800 in the Department of History at University College London and a current British Academy Wolfson Fellow. This is her first book.

Afro-Latin America

Series editors
George Reid Andrews, *University of Pittsburgh*
Alejandro de la Fuente, *Harvard University*

This series reflects the coming of age of the new, multidisciplinary field of Afro-Latin American Studies, which centers on the histories, cultures, and experiences of people of African descent in Latin America. The series aims to showcase scholarship produced by different disciplines, including history, political science, sociology, ethnomusicology, anthropology, religious studies, art, law, and cultural studies. It covers the full temporal span of the African Diaspora in Latin America, from the early colonial period to the present and includes continental Latin America, the Caribbean, and other key areas in the region where Africans and their descendants have made a significant impact.

A full list of titles published in the series can be found at: www.cambridge.org/afro-latin-america

Slavery and Freedom in Black Thought in the Early Spanish Atlantic

CHLOE L. IRETON
University College London

CAMBRIDGE
UNIVERSITY PRESS

CAMBRIDGE
UNIVERSITY PRESS

Shaftesbury Road, Cambridge CB2 8EA, United Kingdom

One Liberty Plaza, 20th Floor, New York, NY 10006, USA

477 Williamstown Road, Port Melbourne, VIC 3207, Australia

314–321, 3rd Floor, Plot 3, Splendor Forum, Jasola District Centre,
New Delhi – 110025, India

103 Penang Road, #05–06/07, Visioncrest Commercial, Singapore 238467

Cambridge University Press is part of Cambridge University Press & Assessment,
a department of the University of Cambridge.

We share the University's mission to contribute to society through the pursuit of
education, learning and research at the highest international levels of excellence.

www.cambridge.org
Information on this title: www.cambridge.org/9781009533485

DOI: 10.1017/9781009533461

© Chloe L. Ireton 2025

This publication is in copyright. Subject to statutory exception and to the provisions
of relevant collective licensing agreements, no reproduction of any part may take
place without the written permission of Cambridge University Press & Assessment.

When citing this work, please include a reference to the DOI
10.1017/9781009533461

First published 2025

A catalogue record for this publication is available from the British Library

Library of Congress Cataloging-in-Publication Data
NAMES: Ireton, Chloe L., author.
TITLE: Slavery and freedom in Black thought in the early Spanish Atlantic /
Chloe L. Ireton.
DESCRIPTION: Cambridge, United Kingdom ; New York, NY : Cambridge
University Press, 2025. | Series: Afro-Latin America | Includes bibliographical
references and index.
IDENTIFIERS: LCCN 2024021485 | ISBN 9781009533485 (hardback) |
ISBN 9781009533461 (ebook)
SUBJECTS: LCSH: Slavery – Latin America. | Enslaved persons – Intellectual life. |
Spain – Colonies – Intellectual life.
CLASSIFICATION: LCC HT1052.5 .I74 2025 | DDC 306.3/62098–dc23/eng/20240607
LC record available at https://lccn.loc.gov/2024021485

ISBN 978-1-009-53348-5 Hardback
ISBN 978-1-009-53349-2 Paperback

Cambridge University Press & Assessment has no responsibility for the persistence
or accuracy of URLs for external or third-party internet websites referred to in this
publication and does not guarantee that any content on such websites is, or will
remain, accurate or appropriate.

Contents

List of Figures	*page* ix
Acknowledgments	xiii
Introduction	1
1 Proving Freedom: Documenting *Alhorría*	22
2 Imagining Freedom: Black Atlantic Communities in Sevilla	65
3 Purchasing Freedom: Economics of Liberty in New Spain	117
4 Defining Freedom: Infrastructures of Black Political Knowledge between Sevilla and Mexico City	151
5 Reclaiming Freedom: The Illegitimacy of Slavery in Black Thought	189
6 Practicing Freedom: Documenting Capital	228
Coda: Felipa de la Cruz's World and Letters	252
Bibliography	265
Index	309

Figures

1.1 Abraham Ortelius, "Regni Hispaniae post omnium editiones locumplessima Descriptio" (detail of "Guadalquivir River [printed in illustration as *Guadalquivir Rio*] to Sevilla"). In *Hispaniae illustratæ seu Rerum vrbiumq. Hispaniæ, Lusitaniæ, Æthiopiæ et Indiæ scriptores varii. Partim editi nunc primum, partim aucti atque emendati.* Francofurti: Apud Claudium Marnium, & Hæredes Iohannis Aubrij, 1603. John Carter Brown Map Collection, b22212917. Courtesy of the John Carter Brown Library. *page* 32
1.2 Map of shipping routes in the sixteenth-century Spanish and Portuguese Atlantic world, principally depicting the Spanish crown's *Carrera de Indias* routes, including the *Flota de la Nueva España* and the *Flota de Tierra Firme*, as well as broadly representing the principal shipping routes of European ships that forcibly displaced enslaved people from West Africa and West-Central Africa to Spanish and Portuguese Americas and Europe (often described as the "Middle Passage"). Map drawn by Cath D'Alton, Drawing Office, University College London. 33
2.1 Photograph of the present-day facade of the palace in Sevilla where Felipa de la Cruz was enslaved; known in the late sixteenth century as Casa-Palacio Fernández de Santillán, and presently known as Palacio del Marqués de la Motilla. Photograph by Miguel Ángel Rosales, 2024. Reproduced with permission from Miguel Ángel Rosales. 68

x   *List of Figures*

2.2 Location of the palace where Felipa de la Cruz was enslaved and an approximate outline of the parish where she resided (San Salvador), overlaid on Tomás López de Vargas Machuca, "Plano geométrico de la ciudad de Sevilla...." Tomás López: Madrid, 1788. David Rumsey Map Collection, List no. 10717.000, David Rumsey Map Center, Stanford Libraries. Adaptation of the map by Cath D'Alton, Drawing Office, University College London.   70

2.3 Map of a fifteen-minute walk from Felipa de la Cruz's dwelling to the House of Trade, overlaid onto Tomás López de Vargas Machuca, "Plano geométrico de la ciudad de Sevilla...." (detail). Tomás López: Madrid, 1788. David Rumsey Map Collection, List no. 10717.000, David Rumsey Map Center, Stanford Libraries. Adaptation of the map by Cath D'Alton, Drawing Office, University College London.   72

2.4 Alonso Sánchez de Coello, "Vista de la ciudad de Sevilla," late sixteenth century, oil on canvas, width: 295 cm, height: 146 cm (P004779). Prado Museum, Madrid. © Photographic Archive Museo Nacional del Prado.   84

2.5 Alonso Sánchez de Coello, "Vista de la ciudad de Sevilla," (detail), late sixteenth century, oil on canvas, width: 295 cm, height: 146 cm (P004779). Prado Museum, Madrid. © Photographic Archive Museo Nacional del Prado.   86

2.6 Alonso Sánchez de Coello, "Vista de la ciudad de Sevilla," (detail), late sixteenth century, oil on canvas, width: 295 cm, height: 146 cm (P004779). Prado Museum, Madrid. © Photographic Archive Museo Nacional del Prado.   87

3.1 Approximate routes along which Margarita de Sossa was forcibly displaced as an enslaved woman and latterly as a free woman. Map drawn by Cath D'Alton, Drawing Office, University College London, based on a map drawn by Alex Killough in Ball et al., *As If She Were Free*, 31.   120

3.2 Map of two royal trading routes in sixteenth-century New Spain between San Juan de Ulúa and Mexico City, known as *Camino de Veracruz* and *Camino Nuevo*. Map drawn by Cath D'Alton, Drawing Office, University College London, based on "Archipelague du Mexique où sont les isles de Cuba, Espagnole [Haïti], Jamaïque, etc. [Document cartographique]." Jean Covens et Corneille

	Mortier, Amsterdam, 1741. Bibliothèque Nationale de France, FRBNF40739006.	122
3.3	Juan Gómez de Trasmonte, "Forma y Levantado de La Ciudad de México." A. Ruffoni: Florence, 1628. David Rumsey Map Collection, list no. 13213.000. David Rumsey Map Center, Stanford Libraries.	136
3.4	Juan Gómez de Trasmonte, "Forma y Levantado de La Ciudad de México" (detail). A. Ruffoni: Florence, 1628. David Rumsey Map Collection, list no. 13213.000. David Rumsey Map Center, Stanford Libraries.	136
4.1	Locations of Black and *mulato* brotherhoods and other sites where Black people gathered and worshiped in late sixteenth-century Sevilla, overlaid onto Tomás López de Vargas Machuca, "Plano geométrico de la ciudad de Sevilla…" (detail). Tomás López: Madrid, 1788. David Rumsey Map Collection, List no. 10717.000, David Rumsey Map Center, Stanford Libraries. Adaptation of the map by Cath D'Alton, Drawing Office, University College London.	166
4.2	"Pleito entre la Hdad de Ntra Sra de la Antigua y la de los Ángeles que llaman la de los morenos con sede en San Roque extramuros" (detail of in-text edits to the declaration that the Black confraternity members made before their procurator, Bartolomé de Celada, on June 22, 1604), in Archivo General del Arzobispado de Sevilla (AGAS), Fondo Arzobispal, Sección III, Hermandades, sign. 09885, expte 1, fols. 14^{r-v}. © Cabildo Catedral de Sevilla.	170
4.3	"Pleito entre la Hdad de Ntra Sra de la Antigua y la de los Ángeles que llaman la de los morenos con sede en San Roque extramuros" (detail of in-text edits to the declaration that the Black confraternity members made before their procurator, Bartolomé de Celada, on June 22, 1604), in AGAS, Fondo Arzobispal, Sección III, Hermandades, sign. 09885, expte 1, fols. 14^{r-v}. © Cabildo Catedral de Sevilla.	170
4.4	Spanish transcription of Figures 4.2 and 4.3. Author's illustration.	171
5.1	Map of the Southern Atlantic, with lines showing the enslavement and forcible displacements across the Atlantic of Domingo de *Gelofe*, Pedro de Carmona, and Francisco Martín. Map drawn by Cath D'Alton, Drawing Office, University College London.	191

C.1.1 Map of the social ties of a generation of free and liberated Black Sevillians in the late sixteenth century (c. 1569–1626). Map drawn by Cath D'Alton, Drawing Office, University College London. With thanks to Antonio Collantes de Terán Sánchez and Víctor Pérez de Escolano for granting me permission to redraw a map of Sevilla based on the maps that they each published in the following publications: Víctor de Pérez Escolano and Fernando Villanueva Sandino, eds., *Ordenanzas de Sevilla, facsímil de la edición de 1632*, impresa en Sevilla por Andrés Grande. Sevilla: OTAISA, 1975; Antonio Collantes de Terán Sánchez, *Sevilla en la baja Edad Media: La ciudad y sus hombres*. Sevilla: Sección de Publicaciones del Excmo. Ayuntamiento, 1977. Please note that the parish lines in the redrawn map are based on research by Antonio Collantes de Terán Sánchez into parish boundaries in sixteenth-century Sevilla and published in the above-mentioned publication. 254
C.1.2 Extended key for Figure C.1.1. 256

Acknowledgments

During the final stages of writing this book in January 2024, I happened to visit the monumental exhibition in London by Ghana-born, Nigeria-based sculptor El Anatsui, titled *Behind the Red Moon* that flooded floor to ceiling of the vast Turbine Hall at the Tate Modern. In this installation, El Anatsui offers a powerful contemplation on the histories of European imperialism and the violent history of the enslavement, dispossession, and displacement of millions of people from the shores of West Africa into the Atlantic world. Staged in three Acts, *Behind the Red Moon* is composed of thousands of metal bottle tops and fragments of plastic waste from the West that washes up on the shores of West Africa. Crumpling, crushing, and stitching these fragments of waste, El Anatsui composed three sculptures that evoke the sails of a slave ship and the horrors of the Middle Passage, while signaling the creativity and resilience of the global African diasporas across time. I would like to thank El Anatsui for his generosity in allowing me to reproduce a fragment of this magnificent artwork on the cover of this book.

The ideas and arguments for this book emerged slowly and in fragmentary form as I wrote and conducted archival research in different cities – I have thought about, researched, discussed, and written parts of this book in Austin, Sevilla, Mexico City, Bogotá, and London. In each site, I accrued debts in friendship and intellectual fellowship that I cannot hope to capture in these brief acknowledgments. I would, however, like to acknowledge the early emergence of this project while I conducted research for my PhD at the University of Texas at Austin. As an international student in the USA, I am indebted to this public university for funding my graduate education and professional training as a historian.

I am also indebted to Jorge Cañizares-Esguerra for serving as the director of my dissertation committee, and for our innumerable intellectual exchanges and friendship over the last thirteen years. In Austin, I made many lifelong friends whose friendships I cherish, including Ahmad Agbaria, Dharitri Bhattacharjee, Arup Chakraborty, Sandy Chang, Roni Chelben, Josh Denslow, Chris Brian Duncan, Kristie Flannery, Nicolás Alejando González Quintero, Christopher Heaney, Altina Hoti, Jack Loveridge, Adrian Masters, Ernesto Mercado-Montero, Alex Mustafa, Nicholas Roland, Elizabeth O'Brien, Juan Carlos de Orellana, Edward Shore, Cameron Strang, Sonquo Tapia†, James Vaughn, Eyal Weinberg, Henry Weincek, and Pete Weiss. I am also grateful to my PhD dissertation committee for their support and guidance during my graduate studies: Susan Deans-Smith, Alison K. Frazier, Julie Hardwick, Jane G. Landers, and Erin K. Rowe.

Over the last six years, I have been privileged to conceptualize this book project while working in the Department of History at University College London. My debts within my department are too many to list here – I have innumerable colleagues who have offered friendship and fellowship – but I would like to thank Nicola Miller, in particular, for her continual support, encouragement, and mentorship of this book project, and the following departmental colleagues for their friendship and fellowship: Alessandro de Arcangelis, Jane Dinwoodie, Margot Finn, Alex Goodall, Angus Gowland, Rebecca Jennings, Ben Kaplan, Peter Jones, Patrick Lantschner, Jagjeet Lally, Elaine Leong, Anna Maguire, Thom Rath, María Ángeles Martín Romera, Jason Peacey, Benedetta Rossi, John Sabapathy, Will Selinger, Florence Sutcliffe-Braithwaite, Peter Schroeder, and Matthew J. Smith, as well as Eleanor Robson, and Antonio Sennis for their support as department chairs. I have also been intellectually enriched by working alongside Hannah Murphy, Liesbeth Corens, Zoltán Biedermann, and John Henderson as co-convenors of a vibrant IHR seminar on early modern history. In Sevilla, I am grateful to friends and colleagues, including Amalia Almorza Hidalgo, José Luis Belmonte Postigo, Enrique Camacho, Manuel Francisco Fernández Chávez, Esther González, Manuel Herrero Sánchez, José Manuel Manzano González, Rafael Mauricio Pérez García, Inés María Santos, Francisco Javier Molinero Rodríguez, and Bartolomé Yun Casalilla; and at the Archivo General de Indias, I thank Antonio Sánchez de Mora and the archivists for their assistance with the digitization of documents. In Mexico City, I thank the following friends for their fellowship during my stays in the city: Sarah Bak-Geller Corona, Rafael Castañeda García, Susan

Deeds, Santiago Echeverri Gómez, Francisco Iván Escamilla González, Tracie Goode, Andrés Mendizabal, and Luis Fernando Tolentino García at the Archivo General de la Nación for his assistance during my various research trips. In Bogotá, I am particularly thankful to: Miguel Ángel Abadia, Liliana Aponte, John Bernal, Nelson Fernando González Martínez, Daniel Gutiérrez Ardila, Sergio Andrés Mejía Macia, Santiago Muñoz Arbeláez, Carlos Alberto Murgueito Manrique, Mauricio Nieto Olarte, Diana Peláez, Esteban Puyo, Carlos Luis Torres, Andrés Vargas, Lady Viviana Veloza Martínez, and María Uribe.

This work represents a symphony of discussions with scholars near and far whose generous and generative engagements with my research over the last ten years have shaped the questions and arguments that are threaded throughout this book. In particular, I thank the following scholars for their reading and incisive comments during a book manuscript workshop in January 2023: Herman L. Bennett, Zoltán Biedermann, Manuel Francisco Fernández Chaves, Pablo F. Gómez, Karen Graubart, Angus Gowland, Elaine Leong, Montaz Marché, Giuseppe Marcocci, Nicola Miller, Miles Ogborn, Jason Peacey, Benedetta Rossi, and Matthew J. Smith. Innumerable scholars have also generously engaged with my research throughout the cacophony of academic life by offering formal and informal comments on papers that I have presented, organizing panels, and inviting me to share my work in different settings. In particular, I thank: Ignacio Aguilo, George Reid Andrews, Berta Ares Queija, Francisco Bethencout, Diana Berruezo-Sánchez, John Beusterein, Matthew Brown, Trevor Burnard†, Rina C. Cáceres, Pedro Cardim, Luis Castellví Laukamp, Stephanie M. Cavanaugh, Adriana Chira, José Eduardo Cornelio, Jesse Cromwell, Jo Crow, Andrew Devereux, María Camila Díaz, Paulo Drinot, Francisco A. Eissa-Barroso, Manuel Francisco Fernández Chaves, Laura Fernández-González, Bethan Fisk, Baltasar Fra-Molinero, Barbara Fuchs, Alejandro de la Fuente, Rafael García Castañeda, Martin van Gelderen, Carrie Gibson, Ximena Gómez, Nelson Fernando González Martínez, Toby Green, Tamar Herzog, Mark Hutchinson, Alejandra María Irigoin, Sebastian Kroup, Cezary Kucewicz, Marc Lerner, Antonella Liuzzo Scorpo, Paul Lovejoy, Giuseppe Marcocci, Sinead McEneaney, Michelle A. McKinley, Erika Melek Delgado, Leonardo Moreno Álvarez, Jennifer L. Morgan, Andrea Mosquera-Guerrero, Santiago Muñoz Arbeláez, Lila O'Leary Chambers, Manuel Olmedo Gobante, Ana María Otero Claves, Rachel Sarah O'Toole, Jennifer L. Palmer, Adolfo Polo y la Borda, Miguel Ángel Rosales, Jesús Ruíz, Tatiana Seijas, Mark Thurner, Imaobong Umoren, Miguel A. Valerio, Peter Wade, Tamara Walker, David Wheat, Phil Whithington, Elizabeth Wright, and Jean-Paul Zuñiga.

Acknowledgments

Various funding bodies provided grants for archival research for this project. In particular, a British Academy Wolfson Fellowship (2023–2026) provided me with crucial time and resources to complete final research and revisions for this book. In addition, a British Academy/Leverhulme Small Research Grant and the interdisciplinary network, "The Making of Blackness in Early Modern Spain: A Process of Cultural and Social Negotiation from the Bottom-Up" (financed by Ministerio de Ciencia e Innovación de España, Project ID PID2021-124893NA-I00, P.I. Diana Berruezo-Sánchez), provided funding for archival research. I also thank the Institute of Advanced Studies and Department of History at University College London for financial support towards a book manuscript workshop. During my graduate training, I also benefited from generous funding to undertake archival research from the following organizations: The Leverhulme Trust Study Abroad Studentship; Social Science Research Council, Andrew W. Mellon International Dissertation Research Fellowship; American Historical Association, Albert J. Beveridge Grant for Research in the Western Hemisphere; John Carter Brown Library, Helen Watson Bucker Memorial Fellowship; The Huntington Library, W. M. Keck Foundation Fellowship; Renaissance Society of America Research Grant; The James R. Scobie Memorial Award, Conference on Latin American History; and the Department of History and the Graduate School at University of Texas at Austin.

I would like to thank my editor at Cambridge University Press, Cecelia Cancellaro, and her editorial assistant, Victoria Phillips, and the three anonymous reviewers of the manuscript for their generous engagement with the work and valuable suggestions and critiques for final revisions. I am also grateful to Simon Fletcher for his careful work copy-editing the manuscript. I also thank John Beusterein and Baltasar Fra-Molinero who each offered helpful suggestions to improve my initial translations into English of the two letters that appear in the Coda, and to José María Álvarez Hernández for joining a separate coauthorship project to cotranscribe the two letters in Spanish. I also thank Cath D'Alton from the Department of Geography's Drawing Office at University College London for her careful work illustrating eight maps for this book. Finally, a few parts of this work have also appeared in print elsewhere. The third section of Chapter 3 appeared as "Margarita de Sossa, Sixteenth-Century Puebla de los Ángeles, New Spain (Mexico)," in *As If She Were Free: A Collective Biography of Black Women and Emancipation in the Americas*, edited by Erica L. Ball, Tatiana Seijas, and Terri L. Snyder (Cambridge University Press, 2020), 27–42. Sections 1 and 3 of Chapter 5 have been adapted and revised from my article "Black Africans' Freedom Litigation Suits to Define Just War and Just Slavery in the Early Spanish Empire," *Renaissance Quarterly*, 73(4), 1277–1319 (2020).

Finally, my family have been a source of continuous support during this project and have withstood many of my long absences. I would like to thank, in particular, my mum and dad, Tim and Pippa, and my siblings, Scarlet and Felix, and their families. I also thank Vinay for bringing so much joy, light, and love to my life while I wrote this book.

Introduction

In the early modern era, millions of people were enslaved, dispossessed, and forcibly displaced from sites in West Africa and West-Central Africa to European imperial realms where the meanings of slavery and freedom were codified into distinct rules of law. These laws and traditions often differed from legal cultures about slavery in enslaved peoples' places of origin or the sites where they or their ancestors were first enslaved. *Slavery and Freedom in Black Thought* traces how West Africans and West-Central Africans and their descendants reckoned with the violent world of Atlantic slavery that they were forced to inhabit, and traces how they conceptualized two strands of political and legal thought – freedom and slavery – in the early Spanish empire. In their daily lives, Black Africans and their descendants grappled with laws and theological discourses that legitimized the enslavement of Black people in the early modern Atlantic world and the varied meanings of freedom across legal jurisdictions. They discussed ideas about slavery and freedom with Black kin, friends, and associates in the sites where they lived and across vast distances, generating thick spheres of communication in the early modern Atlantic world. Discussions about freedom and its varied meanings moved from place to place through diverse exchanges of information, fractured memories, and knowledge between Black communities and kin across the Atlantic Ocean.

Slavery and freedom were two concepts and legal categories that regulated the lives of every person of African descent in continental Europe and in the Americas in the early modern era. European empire-building projects in the Americas from the sixteenth century onwards and ambitious plans to extract and exploit the region's natural resources led to insatiable demand for unfree labor to sustain these projects. In response,

European traders and colonists created intense demand for the enslavement, dispossession, and forcible displacement of people from West Africa and West-Central Africa.[1] Armed with slave-trading licenses granted by the crowns of Spain, Portugal, England, France, and other European kingdoms (and, later, nations), merchants, investors, and ship captains who operated in sixteenth-century West Africa and West-Central Africa attempted to transform people into commodities, who they would later trade as inanimate property. This acute European demand for enslaved labor displaced over 12.5 million people from their kin and homelands over the course of three centuries, barring them from property ownership and free will, and causing cycles of devastating warfare and displacement across West African and West-Central African polities and kingdoms.[2] European merchants and slave-ship captains subjected their victims to grueling and violent crossings of the vast Atlantic, a voyage known contemporaneously as the Middle Passage.[3] Ship captains presided over such dangerous, violent, and cramped conditions on their ships that the mortality rate among enslaved people on these crossings was approximately 20 percent prior to 1600.[4] When slave ships arrived in the Americas, merchants sought to trade their enslaved embargo in the marketplaces of emerging slave societies on the continent. In doing so, they condemned those who survived the horrors of the Middle Passage to a life of harsh and dangerous unfree labor in slave societies where their enslavement was codified in laws (especially in the Spanish and Portuguese monarchies), and where the emergence of racial thinking tended to equate people who were racialized as Black as slaves or enslaveable.[5] In this violent early modern Atlantic world, European legal codes and prevalent

---

[1] Eltis, "A Brief Overview."
[2] Brown, *The Reaper's*; Candido, *Wealth* and *an African*; Green, *a Fistful* and *the Rise*; Heywood and Thornton, *Central Africans*; Konadu, *Many Black Women*; Law, *Ouidah*; Lingna Nafafé, *Lourenço*; Northrup, *Africa's Discovery*; Patterson, *Slavery*; Rediker, *The Slave Ship*; Smallwood, *Saltwater Slavery*; Thornton, "African Political."
[3] Morgan, "Accounting" and *Reckoning*; Rupprecht, "Middle Passage."
[4] Rupprecht, "Middle Passage."
[5] For selected scholarship and debates on meanings of Blackness and emergence of racial thinking in Iberia, see Böttcher, Hausberger, and Hering Torres, *El peso*; Bryant, *Rivers of Gold Bondage*; Camba Ludlow, *Imaginarios ambiguos*; Gómez, "El estigma"; Gonzalbo Aizpuru, "La trampa"; Hering Torres, "Purity"; Herring Torres et al., *Race*; Herzog, *Defining Nations*; Ireton, "They Are"; Lewis, "Between," 113–114; Lowe and Earle, *Black Africans*; Martínez, *Genealogical Fictions*; Milton and Vinson III, "Counting Heads"; Nemser, "Triangulating Blackness" and *Infrastructures of Race*; Schwaller, *Géneros de Gente*; Sweet, "Iberian Roots"; Velázquez Gutiérrez, *Mujeres de orígen africano*; Vinson III, *Before Mestizaje*.

attitudes of intolerance towards people racialized as Black rendered the lives of Africans and their descendants as highly vulnerable to unquantifiable harm, trauma, and violence. In this context, it is no surprise that enslaved and freeborn Black people sought to grapple with the diverse juridical meanings and rules of law concerning slavery and freedom in European empires, and understand how these differed from those in their places of origin in West Africa and West-Central Africa.

Freedom was often the most important concept that governed the preoccupations and day-to-day lives of enslaved, liberated, and freeborn people who were racialized as Black in the early modern Atlantic world. Some sought freedom from slavery on their own terms through precarious flights from enslavement and the establishment of self-governing communities, often known as *palenques*.[6] Fugitives from slavery built *palenque* communities across the sixteenth-century Spanish Americas (and in the broader Atlantic world), particularly in the Spanish Caribbean. The Spanish crown often waged war against such communities, perceiving their establishment as an act of aggression, while occasionally negotiating peace when politically expedient. Black people discussed freedom across legal jurisdictions too, as enslaved people learned about laws of slavery and freedom in other imperial realms where they might be able to obtain freedom or live with greater degrees of liberty within enslavement. One example is how enslaved Black people in late seventeenth-century British Jamaica and other Caribbean sites sometimes fled plantation slavery by aiming for Spanish territories where they understood slavery and freedom as being distinct legal categories in Castilian law that might improve their precarious lived experiences. For example, after the Spanish crown introduced sanctuary policies in the 1680s, enslaved people in English and French imperial realms soon learned that they could claim liberty under Spanish law if they touched foot in Spanish territories, and they

---

[6] Brewer-García, *Beyond Babel*, 116–163; Córdova Aguilar, "Cimarrones"; Dawson, "A Sea"; de Avilez Rocha, "Maroons," 15–35; Díaz Ceballos, "Cimarronaje"; Fra-Molinero, "A Postcard"; García de León, *Tierra adentro*, 555–563; Hidalgo Pérez, *Una historia* and "Volviendo"; Kauffman, *Black Tudors*; Landers, "The African" and "Cimarrón"; Laviña et al., "La localización"; McKnight, "Confronted Rituals"; Navarrete Peláez, "De reyes," "Por haber," and *Cimarrones*; Naveda Chavez-Hita, "De San Lorenzo" and *Esclavos negros*; Obando Andrade, *De objeto*; Sánchez Jiménez, "Raza"; Schwaller, *African Maroons*, "Contested," and "The Spanish Conquest"; Serna, *Los cimarrones*; Sorrell, "They Acknowledge Themselves Soldiers and Subjects of the King: Afro Spanish Maroons Negotiating Freedom and Belonging in English Jamaica 1655–1688" (manuscript in progress shared with author in private correspondence); Tardieu, *Cimarrones*; Wheat, *Atlantic Africa*, 1–4.

shared this precious information with other enslaved people to encourage them to join the flight.[7] Other enslaved Black people in the Spanish empire navigated diverse legal ecologies of freedom by litigating for their entire or partial freedom in royal, ecclesiastical, and inquisitorial courts, while sharing the broad aim of pressing for a freedom (or fraction of freedom) that was codified in law and could be proven through official paperwork issued by a court.[8] Whatever means Black people deployed to seek degrees of freedom in their lives, discussions about freedom and its varied meanings moved across the Atlantic world.

Slavery and Freedom in Black Thought traces how Black communities and kin exchanged ideas about slavery and freedom across the long sixteenth century (1520–1630) in the Spanish Atlantic world. The book sketches the emergence of thick spheres of communication among free and enslaved Black people between key port towns through relays of word of mouth, epistolary networks, and legal powers. In particular, everyday lives and experiences in the ports that constituted the maritime trading routes in the late sixteenth-century Spanish Atlantic (known as the Carrera de Indias), namely Cartagena de Indias, Havana, Nombre de Dios (and later Portobelo), Sevilla, and Veracruz, and the towns dotted along trading routes between key ports and the viceregal capitals, especially Lima and Mexico City (the capitals of the viceroyalties of Peru and New Spain, respectively), were often intertwined with events across the Atlantic, as ship passengers and port-dwellers trafficked in mundane and noteworthy information about people and events in faraway places

---

[7] "Felipa, negra, libertad," Archivo General de Indias, (cited as AGI), Escribanía 48A, libro 13, no. 2; Bretones Lane, "Free to Bury"; Dawson, "A Sea"; Fisk, "Transimperial Mobilities"; "Hoonhout and Mareite," "Freedom"; Landers, *Black Society* and "Spanish Sanctuary"; Rupert, *Creolization*, "Seeking the Water," and "Curaçaoan Maroons"; Schneider, "A Narrative"; Singleton and Landers, "Maritime Marronage."

[8] For selected scholarship of freedom through litigation, see Bennett, *Colonial Blackness*; Bryant, *Rivers of Gold*; Chira, "Affective Debts," "Freedom with Local Bonds," and *Patchwork Freedoms*; Diaz, *The Virgin*; de la Fuente, *Havana* and "Slave Law"; de la Fuente, and Gross, *Becoming Free*; Fernández Martín, "Entra las" and "La esclavitud"; Graubart, "*Pesa más*"; Helg, *Slave No More*; Ireton, "Black African's"; McKinley, *Fractional Freedoms*; Navarrete Peláez, "Consideraciones en Torno"; Obando Andrade, *De objeto*; Owensby, "How Juan"; Salazar Rey, *Mastering*. For selected scholarship on clothing as expressions of freedom, see Dawson, "The Cultural"; Walker, *Exquisite Slaves*. For ideas about freedom through intimacy, safety, and security, see Johnson, *Wicked Flesh*. For ideas about freedom and changing meanings of freedom in later periods, see Barragan, *Freedom's Captives*; de la Torre, *The People of the River*; Eller, "Rumors of Slavery"; Landers, *Atlantic Creoles*; Oliveira, *Slave Trade*; Reis et al., *Oalufá Rufino*; Rossi, "Beyond the Atlantic" and "Global Abolitionist"; Scott and Hébrard, *Freedom Papers*; Scott and Venegas Fornias, "María Coleta." Smith, *Liberty, Fraternity*.

(Figure 1.1). *Slavery and Freedom in Black Thought* explores how relays of word of mouth – stitched together through itinerant merchant communities, mariners, and passengers – bridged vast distances across the Spanish empire and allowed Black dwellers to send and receive messages from kin and associates from afar. Tapping official and informal messengers also allowed Black people to partake in a lettered world of communication by sending and receiving missives that traveled across the Atlantic. Rare surviving letters penned by enslaved Black people to their distant kin also reveal conversations about their hopes and expectations of freedom.

Slavery and Freedom in Black Thought argues that these vast spheres of communication shaped Black individuals' and communities' legal consciousness about the laws of slavery and freedom in the early Spanish empire. This builds on foundational work by scholars who have explored the emergence of a Black legal consciousness in colonial Latin America, as well as scholarship that has explored how Indigenous Americans developed knowledge of plural legal jurisdictions and petitioning in the Spanish and Portuguese empires.[9] For example, Alejandro de la Fuente has posited that scholars working on the history of slavery should acknowledge that it was not laws that had a social agency, but instead that enslaved people gave meaning to laws through their work as litigants.[10] Herman L. Bennett has also explored how free Black people residing in New Spain developed a creole legal consciousness and an understanding of how to navigate legal structures. With a focus on the eighteenth

---

[9] For selected studies of Black legal consciousness in the Spanish empire, see Belmonte Postigo, "La vida improbable"; Bennett, *Colonial Blackness* and *Africans in Colonial*; Bryant, *Rivers of Gold*; Cardim, "Mulheres negras"; Chira, "Affective Debts," "Freedom with Local Bonds," and *Patchwork Freedoms*; de la Fuente, *Havana* and "Slave Law"; de la Fuente and Gross, *Becoming Free*; Fernández Martín, "La esclavitud"; Graubart, "*Pesa más*" and *Republics of Difference*; Ireton, "Black African's"; McKinley, *Fractional Freedoms*; Navarrete Peláez, "Consideraciones en Torno"; Obando Andrade, *De objeto*. For selected studies of Indigenous Americans' legal consciousness, see Ares Queija, "Un borracho"; Cunille, "El uso indígena," "Etnicidad en clave," "Justicia e interpretación," "La negociación," *Los defensores*, "Los intérpretes," and "Philip II"; Cunill, et al., *Actores, redes*; Cunill and Glave Testino, *Las lenguas*; Deardorff, *A Tale*; de la Puente Luna, *Andean Cosmopolitans*, "En lengua de" and "That Which Belongs"; de la Puente Luna and Honores, "Guardianes"; Domingues et al., *Os indígenas*. Graubart, *Republics of Difference*, "Shifting Landscapes," and *With Our Labor*; Mumford, "Aristocracy" and "Litigation as Ethnography"; Owensby, *Empire of Law*, "Pacto entre rey," and "The Theatre"; Owensby and Ross, *Justice*; Premo, "Custom Today" and *The Enlightenment*; Ruan, "The *Probanza*"; Yannakakis, "Allies or Servants?," "Indigenous People," *Since Time Immemorial*, and *The Art of Being*; Yannakakis and Schrader-Kniffki, "Between the."
[10] de la Fuente, "Slave Law."

century, Bianca Premo has explored how Indigenous Americans, enslaved Africans, and colonial women pressed for royal justice in colonial courts and composed legal arguments about the secularization of law, formalism, rights, freedom, and historicism, and conceptualized ideas in their legal arguments that scholars often associate with a lettered European Enlightenment.[11] Michelle A. McKinley has studied how enslaved Black women sought to negotiate fractions of their freedom within enslavement in ecclesiastical courts in seventeenth-century Lima.[12] Similarly, Adriana Chira has explored how Afro-descendants in nineteenth-century Cuba engaged with colonial legal frameworks that allowed custom and manumission in order to gradually wear down the institution of slavery through litigation, self-purchase, and the collection of fragmentary legal papers.[13]

Slavery and Freedom in Black Thought reveals how the speed of communication flows across the late sixteenth-century Spanish Atlantic shaped the lives, ideas, and legal consciousness of enslaved and free Black people who lived in key trading entrepôts. The intensity and fast pace of maritime communication between key port towns in this period meant that news in Sevilla about an enslaved person's litigation for freedom against their owner in a royal court, or of how an owner had sold one of their domestic slaves and displaced them from Sevilla, or news about an enslaved person's liberation from slavery may have reached friends and acquaintances in the ports of Veracruz or Cartagena de Indias more quickly than the same news traveled to kin living in other parts of Castilla. For instance, enslaved and free Black residents of late sixteenth-century Sevilla could send a letter or a message through word of mouth to an associate or kin in the Spanish Caribbean and reasonably expect a response with the arrival of the fleet the following year.[14] This constant movement of people, information, and news about freedom in particular sites served as crucial infrastructure for certain Black individuals and communities to exchange ideas about the laws and customs of slavery and freedom. Partaking in these flows of communication allowed free and enslaved Black people to gather requisite information, knowledge, and strategies to seek or defend their own freedom before royal courts dotted across Spanish imperial realms.

---

[11] Premo, *The Enlightenment*.
[12] McKinley, *Fractional Freedoms*.
[13] Chira, *Patchwork Freedoms*.
[14] González Martínez, "Comunicarse a pesar" and "Communicating an Empire."

These spheres of communication also shaped the legal consciousness and political strategies of Black religious brotherhoods and confraternities on both sides of the Atlantic. This book is influenced by recent historiographical debates about the applicability of the concept of the "public sphere" to contexts beyond a European lettered and "enlightened" elite, and works that have explored how enslaved and free Black people's movement across spaces (both voluntary and involuntary) led to the emergence of new forms of knowledge, including ideas about subjecthood, medicine and healing, and Black Catholicism.[15] For example, it traces how Black confraternities sometimes maintained contact with Black brotherhoods in other sites and shared legal strategies. Take the case of the leader of a prominent Black confraternity in late sixteenth-century Lima, Francisco de Gamarra, who formerly resided in Sevilla where he had been enslaved.[16] Upon his liberation from slavery, he crossed the Atlantic and settled in Lima where he became a sought-after builder (*albañil*). In Lima, Gamarra drew on a lifetime of experiences and memories from Sevilla as well as his ongoing ties to the city, especially as his enslaved daughter languished there while he sought to raise funds to pay for the price of her liberty and her voyage to Lima.[17] Similarly, leaders of Black religious brotherhoods in Mexico City and Sevilla in the early seventeenth century likely communicated with each other in the aftermath of severe political persecution and repression that was instigated by religious and royal authorities in their respective cities. This book traces their strategies for royal justice and the locations from where they organized their petitions, and suggests that the leaders of the Black brotherhoods in Sevilla and Mexico City likely communicated and shared political strategies to build their legal petitions to press for royal justice.

Slavery and Freedom in Black Thought also analyzes how free and enslaved Black people attempted in their daily lives to forge a sense of belonging in an empire that was hostile to them. Existing scholarship

---

[15] For debates about "public sphere," see Garnham, "Habermas"; Goodman, *The Republic*; Habermas, *The Structural Transformation*; Hoexter et al., *The Public Sphere*; Shami, *Publics, Politics*; Ogborn, *The Freedom*. For scholarship on significance of movement on knowledge in Black Atlantic, see Gómez, *The Experiential*; Fisk, "Black Knowledge" and "Transimperial Mobilities"; O'Toole, *Bound Lives*; Wheat, *Atlantic Africa* and "Tangomãos." See also, Scott, *The Common Wind*.
[16] "Ana," AGI, Indiferente, 2098, no. 18. See also Apodaca Valdez, *Cofradías Afrohispánicas*, 90–91; Graubart, "So color"; Hayes, "They Have Been United"; Jiménez Jiménez, "A mayor culto," 354.
[17] "Ana," AGI, Indiferente, 2098, no. 18.

has explored how enslaved and free Black people sought to build political ideas of belonging in the Spanish Americas through clothing, economic activities, property ownership, and participation in festive rituals and Black confraternity life.[18] *Slavery and Freedom in Black Thought* builds on these studies by exploring how Black people attempted to forge belonging through their participation in colonial bureaucracy (and especially in the creation of paperwork) to build evidentiary thresholds that would improve or defend their legal status.[19] In particular, the study traces how enslaved and free Black people understood that ideas and practices of belonging in the Spanish empire were often determined by an individual's local ties, namely the ability to command credible witness testimonies within a community, and the resources to document ties and biographies through paperwork, often before a public notary that would result in a legally binding notarial document known as an *escritura*.[20] They learned how to access royal justice and engage in royal petitioning, and understood the significance of gathering relevant paperwork and creating community ties to build evidentiary thresholds in legal spheres. They participated in legal cultures of belonging by enlisting diverse witnesses to testify about their biographies, including friars, friends, former owners, neighbors, merchants, members of the nobility, messengers, priests, servants, slaves, tradespeople, treasurers, and officials in city governance. Those who lacked community ties invested copious resources in generating supplementary paperwork to prove their belonging, in particular to protect and duplicate their freedom papers.

[18] For select examples, see Bennett, *Colonial Blackness*; Bryant, *Rivers of Gold*; Fromont, *Afro-Catholic*; Graubart, "Los *lazos*," *Republics of Difference*, and "The Bonds"; Jaque Hidalgo and Valerio, *Indigenous and Black*; Jouve Martín, *Esclavos* and "Public Ceremonies"; McKinley, *Fractional Freedoms*; O'Toole, *Bound Lives*, "The Bonds," and "(Un)Making"; Terrazas Williams, *The Capital*; Valerio, *Sovereign Joy*; Walker, *Exquisite Slaves*; Wheat, *Atlantic Africa* and "Catalina."

[19] The idea of forging belonging through participation in colonial bureaucracy (and especially paperwork) builds on various works, including Chira, *Patchwork Freedoms*; Deardorff, *A Tale*; de la Puente Luna, *Andean Cosmopolitans*; Sartorius, *Ever Faithful*; Scott, *Freedom Papers*, Yannakakis, *The Art*. For broader history of colonial subjects and the law, see references in note 11, and also Benton, *Law and Colonial*; Brendecke, *Imperio e información*; Coleman, *Creating Christian*; Díaz Rementería, "La formación"; Escudero, *Felipe II*; Gómez Gómez, "Libros de gestión"; Harris, *From Muslim*; Herzog, *Defining Nations* and *Frontiers*; Luque Talaván, *Un universo*; Manzorro Guerrero, "Prácticas documentales"; Masters, "A Thousand," and *We, the King*; Rosenmüller, *Corruption*; Schäfer, *Las rúbricas*; Sellers-García, *Distance and Documents*; Starr-Lebeau, *In the Shadow*; Tau Anzoátegui, *El poder* and *La ley*.

[20] My argument here is inspired by Gonzalbo Aizpuru, "La trampa."

Freeborn and liberated Black people also forged belonging in the Spanish empire by defining and expanding the privileges and rights of freedom. They did so through their day-to-day lives across different sites in the Spanish Atlantic, including their participation in economic life and commerce, labor, property ownership, litigation in royal and ecclesiastical courts, applications for royal licenses to cross the Atlantic as passengers on ships, and petitions to the crown for royal justice in response to local authorities' attempts to limit the inclusion of free Black men and women in society. Freeborn and liberated Black people also negotiated the meanings of freedom through carefully crafted petitions to the crown requesting justice or grace (privileges) for themselves or their communities. In their petitions, they often envisioned the meanings of freedom and belonging in the Spanish empire in expansive terms. These free Black political actors deftly negotiated various, and often overlapping, legal jurisdictions, and deployed political discourses of belonging to broaden the meanings of Black freedom in the Spanish empire.

As enslaved and free Black people conceptualized and pressed the crown to broaden the meanings and privileges of freedom through their daily practices and petitions in courts, they sought to shape an Iberian rule of law and Catholic tradition that would include Black people in society. An apt example of this discourse of belonging emerges from the defense presented by a Black confraternity in early seventeenth-century Sevilla, in which the Black brothers rejected their proposed exclusion from public religious life in the city by arguing that "Christ put himself on the Cross for everyone, and our Mother of the Church does not exclude us, and she adored us, and many other things more than white people, for we proceed from gentiles and Old Christians, and Black people are not excluded from priesthood as there are today many Black priests and prebendaries in our Spain."[21] The intellectual work in this line of defense, and among those deployed by many others who petitioned the crown in this period, sought to reject Iberian ideas that coalesced in the late sixteenth century that regarded Black people's purity of blood as permanently tainted by slavery and as irredeemably stained, thereby preventing their full inclusion into the Iberian community of Old Christians (a term used for people who could claim at least four generations of Christianity in their family).[22]

---

[21] "Pleito, Nuestra Señora de los Angeles," Archivo General del Arzobispado de Sevilla (cited as AGAS), 1.III.1.6, L.9885, no. 1. For a discussion of this statement, see Chapter 4.

[22] See note 5.

In other words, their intellectual work to define the meanings of slavery and freedom in the early Atlantic world rejected ideas about blood lineage that sought to exclude Black Africans and their descendants from Iberian societies and render all Black people as slaves and enslaveable. Instead, through their petitions to the crown, free Black people attempted to expand the meanings of political belonging in the Spanish empire to be inclusive of free Black people. Black people's intellectual work around political belonging in the Spanish empire had profound implications for the history of ideas about race, Blackness, exclusion, and inclusion in the Spanish Atlantic world, and the meanings and legal customs of slavery and freedom.

FROM ARCHIVAL ABSENCES TO KALEIDOSCOPIC ARCHIVES OF EXCESS: METHODOLOGICAL REFLECTIONS ON INTELLECTUAL HISTORIES OF THE BLACK ATLANTIC

This study of how enslaved, liberated, and free Black people reckoned with the legal meanings of slavery and freedom builds on foundational scholarship in African American intellectual history and the long Black intellectual tradition that has sought to broaden the definitions of intellectual work, in particular, by positioning enslaved and free Black people as intellectual actors in the early modern Atlantic world.[23] For example, the notion of reckoning deployed in this book builds on Jennifer Morgan's landmark *Reckoning with Slavery*.[24] Morgan traced how enslaved Black women understood economic value during the violent commodification of their own bodies, and how they assessed and measured economic value in their day-to-day lives and decisions. *Slavery and Freedom in Black Thought* positions enslaved and free Black men and women as intellectual actors, while deploying the notion of "reckoning" to study how people conceptualized juridical concepts of slavery and freedom and the diverse ways in

---

[23] On African American intellectual history, see Baldwin, "Foreword"; Bay et al., *Toward An*; Byrd, "The Rise"; Byrd et al., *Ideas in Unexpected*; Blain et al., *New Perspectives*; Gaglo Dagbovie, "African American Intellectual History"; Ramey Berry and Harris, *Sexuality and Slavery*. For select examples of Black intellectual history in era of Atlantic slavery, see Brown *Tacky's Revolt*; Hartman, "Venus in Two Acts"; Morgan, *Reckoning*; Scott, *The Common Wind*. For influence of African American Intellectual History and Black Studies in early modern Hispanic studies, see Branche, *Trajectories*; Smith, Jones, and Grier, "Introduction: The Contours."

[24] Morgan, *Reckoning*.

which they plotted potential paths towards obtaining their liberation from enslavement and protecting their liberty. This history of ideas about slavery and freedom also builds on scholarship in other traditions, especially Indigenous studies, subaltern studies, and postcolonial studies, that have sought to broaden the meanings of intellectual work beyond a focus on those who put pen to paper, especially historians who deploy an entangled lens to explore the roles of Indigenous actors as producers of knowledge and technology.[25]

The existence of spheres of communication between Black communities across the Atlantic world has been invisible in most historical accounts of the era owing to the various methodological challenges that arise when researching these histories in archives. With a few notable exceptions of lettered Black men in the early Iberian world who penned and published texts, the histories of monarchs and political leaders in West Africa and West-Central Africa who exchanged diplomatic correspondence with Iberian monarchs, and Black Catholic holy people in the Atlantic world whose words were recorded by their confessors, the vast majority of the history of Black thought in early modern Europe is etched into the historical record through archival fragments within documents produced by institutions of colonial administration and justice, or ecclesiastical and religious courts, all of which tended to be hostile towards enslaved and free Black people.[26] Yet scholarship that has explored how West African

---

[25] For selected scholarship on broadening intellectual history in the Spanish empire, see Acree Jr, "Jacinto Ventura"; Adorno and Boserup, *Unlocking the Doors*; Bennett, *Colonial Blackness*; Benton, *The Lords*; Berruezo-Sánchez, "Negro poeta"; Borucki, *From Shipmates*; Borucki and Acree, *Los caminos*; Cañizares-Esguerra, "The Imperial"; Clendinnen, *Ambivalent Conquests*; Dawson, "A Sea" and *Undercurrents of Power*; de la Puente Luna, *Andean Cosmopolitans*; Delmas, "Introduction"; Fisk, "Black Knowledge" and "Transimperial Mobilities"; Flannery, "Can the Devil Cross"; Fracchia, "Black but Human"; Gómez, *The Experiential*; Graubart, *Republics of Difference*, "*Pesa más*," "Shifting Landscapes," and *With Our Labor*; Jones, *Staging*; Jouve Martín, *Esclavos* and "Public Ceremonies"; Martín Casares, *Juan Latino*; Miller and Munday, *Painting a Map*; Morgan, *Reckoning*; Munday, "Indigenous Civilization"; Norton, *The Tame*; O'Toole, *Bound Lives*; Owensby, *Empire of Law*; Ramos and Yannakakis, *Indigenous Intellectuals*; Rappaport, *The Disappearing*; Rappaport and Cummins, *Beyond the*; Rowe, *Black Saints*; Terraciano, "Three Views"; Valerio, *Sovereign Joy*; van Deusen, *Global Indios* and *The Souls*; Wheat, *Atlantic Africa*; Wright, *The Epic*; Yannakakis, "Allies or Servants?," "Indigenous People," *Since Time Immemorial*, and *The Art of Being*. On Entangled History, see Bauer and Norton, "Introduction: Entangled"; Cañizares-Esguerra, "*Entangled Empires*" and "Entangled Histories"; Gould, "Entangled Histories"; Norton, "Subaltern Technologies" and "The Chicken."
[26] Bristol, "Although I Am Black"; Heywood, *Njinga of Angola*; Martín Casares, *Juan Latino*; Thornton, "African Political Ethics"; Wright, *The Epic*; van Deusen, *The Souls*.

and West-Central African cultural and political ideas, practices, and legacies survived in the Americas despite the violence of enslavement, forced displacement, and dispossession in the Atlantic world offer important examples for broadening historical methodologies to confront the challenges of archival absences.[27]

The methodological work in this study also emerges in dialogue with scholars working within Black feminist traditions who have developed foundational methods to read and grapple with the archival silences and the violent erasures of the private and intellectual lives of enslaved and free Black women from the historical record.[28] In particular, Saidiya Hartman has paved an important path by coining "critical fabulation" as a historical method that pieces together the possible experiences of people whose lives were etched in the archive through violence or who were absent and dispossessed in the historical record.[29] Marisa Fuentes has also developed methodologies to respond to the absence of enslaved Black women's voices in historical archives of late eighteenth-century Barbados.[30] Fuentes deploys the tools of critical fabulation, reasonable speculation, and reading along the bias grain within "a microhistory of urban Caribbean slavery" that explores enslaved Black women's lives through the urban geographies and environments where they lived.[31] With a more expansive geographical frame, Jessica Marie Johnson has asked us to consider the possibilities of writing histories of Black women's practices of freedom in their intimate spaces across the Atlantic world through an "accountable historical practice that challenges the known and unknowable, particularly when attending to the lives of black women and girls."[32] Johnson assembled diverse historical fragments of daily life across vast spaces of the French Atlantic, namely

---

[27] Select scholarship on West African and West-Central African cultures and political ideas in the Americas, see Ferreira, *Cross-Cultural*; Green, *A Fistful*, "Baculamento or Encomienda?," "Beyond," "Pluralism," and *The Rise*; Smallwood, *Saltwater Slavery*; Heywood and Thornton, *Central Africans*; O'Toole, *Bound Lives*; Palmié, *The Cooking*; Sobel, *The World*; Sweet, *Recreating Africa*; Thornton, *Africa and Africans*; Valerio, *Sovereign Joy*; Wheat, *Atlantic Africa*.

[28] Ball et al., *As If She*; Brown, *The Reaper's*, *Tacky's*; Fuentes, *Dispossessed Lives*; Hartman, "Venus"; Helton et al., "The Question"; Johnson, *Wicked Flesh*; Kars, *Blood on the River*; Kazanjian, *The Brink*; Morgan, *Reckoning*; Ramey Berry and Harris, *Sexuality and Slavery*; Sweeney, "Black Women" and "Market Marronage."

[29] Hartman, "Venus."

[30] Fuentes, *Dispossessed Lives*.

[31] Fuentes, *Dispossessed Lives*, 1.

[32] Johnson, *Wicked Flesh*, 1–15.

Senegambia, the Middle Passage, and New Orleans, and reads these fragments alongside each other, noting how "although it is critical to respect the limits of each document, by bringing material together in careful and creative ways, snippets of black women's lives begin to unfold."[33] Finally, in *Reckoning with Slavery*, Jennifer Morgan explores the coherence between ideas about economic value and race in order to unearth the "lived experiences and analytic responses to enslavement of these whose lives have most regularly and consistently fallen outside the purview of the archive."[34] Collectively, this scholarship invites us to consider silences in the archive as crucial pieces of historical evidence about enslaved Black women's lives, and to deploy an array of research methods to reimagine the possible experiences and ideas of enslaved women.

Inspired by these methodological discussions about archival absences and tasked with a separate challenge of writing a history of ephemeral conversations and exchanges of ideas about slavery and freedom between Black kin, friends, and associates across the sixteenth-century Spanish Atlantic, I began to assemble thousands of fragmentary testimonies about Black life and ideas across four urban sites in the Spanish Atlantic. These sites include the ports of Cartagena de Indias, Nombre de Dios, Sevilla, and Veracruz, and their respective hinterlands, over the long sixteenth century. The book assembles these fragments of historical evidence about Black life and thought to create a deliberate sense of kaleidoscopic archival excess that occasionally reveals aspects of the history of Black people's ideas about slavery and freedom. The study layers these kaleidoscopic strands of archival excess into discrete spatial frames of analysis, such as life and gossip among neighbors in a compact parish in a city, everyday life and legal knowledge in towns along a key trading route in an American colony, or the conversations between an enslaved man with strangers during multiple forced displacements across the Atlantic while he was trying to gather enough legal knowledge to launch an appeal against his illegitimate enslavement, or when assessing the significance of the employment of free and liberated Black men as town criers to convey news and to administer public auctions of enslaved people. Each of these spatial frames relies on a diverse methodological toolset, for example, drawing inspiration from foundational works in microhistory, cultural history, and histories of ideas and intellectual history.

---

[33] Johnson, *Wicked Flesh*, 5.
[34] Morgan, *Reckoning*, 7.

The methodological work in this study is also shaped by spatial turns in the history of ideas, cultural history, and historical geography. In particular, my conceptualization of public spaces as key sites for exchanges of ideas has been influenced by reading scholars of Arab intellectual history who pinpoint the movement of people across and between political spaces and public sites as important components for the exchange and disputation of ideas.[35] For example, Muhsin J. Al-Musawi argued that historians must consider an active sphere of discussion and disputation within the history of ideas, arguing that "the 'street,' as opposed to scholars and other elites, has always been part of its own opposite poetics or discourse, while in other instances its case may be played out against innovations in theological discussion."[36] Scholars working in historical geography of Black life in the colonial Americas have also developed methodologies to explore how environmental elements shaped Black life and society.[37] These readings helped me to visualize the spaces where enslaved and free Black people might have exchanged ideas in the early Atlantic world, whether exploring conversations playing out across the Atlantic on fleets crisscrossing the ocean, in port cities of the Caribbean, on street corners and squares of bustling cities, at inns and canteens along key trading routes, through relays of word of mouth among travelers in port towns, in church congregations, in markets, or in other spaces where meetings and conversations emerged amid the bustle of daily life. My approach to the orality of these diverse histories of ideas about slavery and freedom also reflects the influence of historians working on the history of communication in cities in the early modern period, such as John Paul Ghobrial, Giuseppe Marcocci, Christian de Vito, and Felipo de Vivo, who have played with scales of analysis to write histories of news in the everyday life of early modern cities, revealing urban landscapes and diverse soundscapes as key pieces of historical evidence.[38]

---

[35] al-Musawi, *The Medieval*. See also Di Capua, *No Exit*; Shami, *Publics, Politics*.
[36] al-Musawi, *The Medieval*, 9.
[37] Selected examples: Barragan, *Freedom's Captives*; Bonil-Gómez, "Free People of African," and "Las movilidades"; Dawson, *Undercurrents of Power*; Fisk, "Black Knowledge on the Move"; García, *Beyond the Walled City*; Schwartz, *Sea of Storms*.
[38] Cossar et al., "Introduction"; Ghobrial, "Introduction," "Moving Stories," and *The Whispers*; Marcocci, "Portuguese Mercenary Networks"; de Vivo, *Information and Communication*, "Microhistories," and "Walking"; de Vito, "History without"; Withers, "Place." For soundscapes in Black Atlantic, see also Brewer Garcia, *Beyond Babel*; Jones, *Staging*; Ogborn, *The Freedom*; Santos Morillo, "Quién te lo vezó a dezir". For the urban labor in these communication networks, see also Lowe, "Visible Lives."

Nicholas R. Jones has also invited us to consider how theatrical stages in this era might mirror the soundscape of cities, particularly the vernacular language and accents of different imperial subjects that a playwright might mimic in scripts and stage directions.[39] Finally, works in historical geography have also visualized how ideas moved and were exchanged across various sites. For example, in a study of slave revolts in eighteenth-century Jamaica, Vincent Brown maps the history of Black political thought about slavery and rebellion onto diverse geographical terrains and traces how these ideas were exchanged among enslaved laborers toiling on plantations as well as dwellers in towns.[40]

Thinking spatially about the history of ideas also requires us to consider whether the history of Black thought about slavery and freedom in this period was a uniquely urban phenomenon. Certainly, dwellers of port towns and viceregal capitals of the Atlantic world were often at the forefront of relays of communication, especially those who lived in ports that served as key destinations on maritime or overland trading routes.[41] In addition, archival evidence tends to be more plentiful in towns and cities as urban dwellers accessed courts of royal and ecclesiastical justice and the services of public notaries more often than their rural counterparts.[42] However, the greater volume of imprints of urban dwellers' lives and ideas in historical archives does not mean that the history of slavery and freedom in Black thought was a uniquely urban phenomenon. As Vincent Brown demonstrates in *Tacky's Revolt*, ideas about slavery and rebellion among enslaved Black people in eighteenth-century Jamaica spread across rural plantations as well as towns, as enslaved and free people on plantations taught recently arrived enslaved West Africans about the histories of previous revolts on the island. *Slavery and Freedom in Black Thought* focuses on urban landscapes because this is where a concentration of archival fragments exists to write this history. Yet the study also considers how conversations and ideas about slavery and freedom moved across vast spaces in the Spanish Atlantic world and connected rural and urban populations, as people discussed and debated these ideas with friends, kin, and associates, and plotted their hopes to obtain their liberty or greater degrees of freedom in their lives. Where possible, the

---

[39] Jones, *Staging*. See also Beusterein, *An Eye on Race*; Fra-Molinero, "Black Pride"; Fra-Molinero et al., "Antón's Linguistic Blackface."
[40] Brown, "Mapping a Slave Revolt" and *Tacky's*.
[41] Cañizares-Esguerra et al., *The Black Urban*.
[42] For importance of cities as sites of power, see Díaz Ceballos, *Poder compartido*.

book explores particular lives and lived experiences on urban and rural landscapes to make visible the shared spaces where people from different backgrounds converged and shaped one another's ideas, be it in congregations, as passengers on ships, on street corners, or through word of mouth or hearsay in urban life. The study also explores the significance of travel between places – whether over land or sea – to the history of slavery and freedom in Black thought.

SLAVERY AND FREEDOM IN BLACK THOUGHT IN THE EARLY SPANISH ATLANTIC

This study is an intellectual exploration of the rich, complicated, and worldly lives of people of African descent as they negotiated experiences of enslavement and liberation from slavery in the early modern Spanish empire. Criss-crossing multiple scales of analysis, from micro to macro, from the formal to the intimate, and from individuals' engagement with institutional processes to their spatial cosmographies, the book charts an intellectual cartography of early modern Black life that upends our understanding of Black movement across spaces, Black intellectual history, and Black agency at the dawn of and decades into the Atlantic trade in enslaved Black people. In disparate, but intimately tied sites in the early Spanish empire (from Sevilla and Mexico City to Nombre de Dios and Lima, among other key ports and towns), West Africans, West-Central Africans, and their descendants not only traveled between such spaces and constructed a Black Iberian world, but actively assembled a dynamic Black public sphere across oceans, seas, and overland trading routes, and offered their own competing intellectual visions of slavery and freedom.

In this shared Black Iberian Atlantic world, the meanings of slavery and freedom were fiercely contested and claimed. Weaving together thousands of archival fragments, the study recreates the worlds and dilemmas of extraordinary individuals and communities while mapping the development of early modern Black thought about slavery and freedom. From a free Black mother's embarkation license to cross the Atlantic as a passenger on a ship, or an enslaved Sevillian woman's letters to her freed husband in New Spain, or an enslaved man's negotiations for credit arrangements with prospective buyers on the auction block in Mexico City, to a Black man's petition to a royal court in an attempt to reclaim his liberty after his illegitimate enslavement, Africans and their descendants were important intellectual actors in the early modern

Atlantic world who reckoned with ideas about slavery and freedom in their daily lives. Their intellectual labor invites us to reimagine the epistemic worlds of the early modern Atlantic. Through fragments of personal letters, depositions in trials, commercial agreements, and petitions to the crown, the study pieces together the lives of Black men and women both in metropolitan Spain and the colonies, how people moved from one place to another, and, more importantly, how ideas and information moved and operated in different contexts. Free and enslaved people who moved freely or by force across the Atlantic shared information and legal knowledge with those they met along the way.

The study is divided into six chapters and a coda. Chapter 1 explores how free and liberated Black individuals responded to institutional processes that increased bureaucratization in the Spanish empire to understand freedom as a legal category that could be proven or unproven through paperwork. Chapter 2 plays with micro and macro scales and a spatial approach to a history of ideas by collating kaleidoscopic fragments about freedom as part of disjointed collective memories and the emotional histories of freedom, tracing how enslaved people held out hope for their liberation from slavery and the myriad ways in which they discussed and plotted for their liberty. Chapter 3 charts an economic history to document how enslaved people fought against all the odds to raise capital to purchase their freedom and the liberty of their loved ones. Chapter 4 explores how free Black people conceptualized freedom politically as they sought to make sense of repression and persecution against free Black people in the Spanish empire. Charting a history of Black petitioning for royal justice, the chapter traces how free Black people and communities across the Spanish Atlantic sought to reshape the political meanings of Black freedom and political belonging in the Spanish empire. Chapter 5 traces how enslaved and free Black people regarded freedom as an item that people possessed and that had to be carefully guarded, for it could be stolen from them. Tracing legal cases in which enslaved people argued that this had occurred, this chapter approaches freedom from a juridical point of view, tracing discussions among enslaved and free people about the laws of slavery and freedom and the strategies they shared about how to retrieve the freedom they had lost. Finally, Chapter 6 explores how free people, especially women, invested copious resources to live and practice freedom in their daily lives so that they could be seen to be living with freedom, namely by becoming active economic actors who judiciously recorded their economic activities and their practices of freedom by engaging in cultures of paperwork. The Coda introduces readers to two rare surviving epistles that constitute the earliest known private letters written by an enslaved Black woman in the Atlantic world. Owing to their immense historical value, these letters are printed in Spanish and English translation. As I have managed to locate the precise location where the author of these letters dwelt in Sevilla, I have drawn a map to visualize her possible social ties among her Black neighbors who were alive in her lifetime (Figures C.1.1–2). Readers will note that I also refer to these letters and Figure C.1.1 throughout earlier chapters in the book.

TERMS AND OMISSIONS

The book explores the intellectual legacies of people whom the Spanish monarchy racialized in the sixteenth and seventeenth century as Black. Some of the people studied in this book were born in West Africa or West-Central Africa where they were enslaved and forcibly displaced to Europe or the Americas. Others were born enslaved or free in Castilla or the Americas. The ethnonyms that appear throughout this study represent different political and linguistic communities in West Africa (*Bañol, Biafara, Bran, Casanga, Cocoli, Jolofe, Mandinga, Valunka, Yalonga, Zape*) and in West-Central Africa (*Angola, Congo*), but are only a fraction of the ethnonyms used to describe African diasporic peoples in the early modern Atlantic world.[43] Most often, these ethnonyms appear in historical documents when an enslaved or free person was referred to (or referred to themselves) by a first name followed by an ethnonym that indicated the person's place of birth or where their parents descended from. As this is not a study of the diverse meanings of ethnonyms and their survival and transformation in the Americas, the ethnonyms are presented in the text with minimal translation or interpretation. Similarly, because this study focuses on ideas about slavery and freedom in Black thought, and not the history of ideas about race in Iberian thought and the diverse and often contested meanings of racial markers and how these meanings varied across different sites, I have also retained the vocabulary of racial markers deployed in the historical documents without translating the varied and often contradictory meanings of these terms.[44] Instead of offering interpretations of these terms, when scribes, notaries, or enslaved or free people used the terms such

---

[43] For an overview, see Kelley, and Lovejoy, "Oldendorp's 'Amina': Ethnonyms." See also Wheat, *Atlantic Africa*.
[44] For scholarship on these debates, see note 5.

as *atezado* (description of someone as very Black), *bozal* (often used to indicate an enslaved person who could not speak Spanish), *mulata* (usually referring to a person of Afro-European heritage), *negra* (Black), and more ambiguous terms sometimes used to describe people of Black heritage, such as *lora* and *morena*, I have used these same terms on the first occasion when introducing the person in the text to indicate to the reader the ways that the person under discussion was being racialized in their own lifetime. In those instances, I have translated *negro/negra* through the text to the English word, Black, while I have retained the original Spanish terms for *atezada*, *lora*, *mulata*, and *morena*. In the cases where the same person was referred to with more than one racial marker, or where they themselves used a different term, I have made this difference clear in the text. When I use the term *horro* or *horra* it is to signify to the reader that the person under discussion has been liberated from slavery under Castilian laws of slavery within their lifetime in a legal act known as *alhorría*, and usage of the term usually follows the language of the sources – although sometimes I have added the term to indicate or clarify that the person has been liberated from slavery. When referring to an *alhorría* that resulted from an enslaved person or a third party furnishing sufficient funds to pay the market price of the enslaved person's value to an enslaver with the purpose of liberating the enslaved person from slavery, this payment is referred to throughout the text as a *rescate*, following the legal meaning of the term and common usage across testimonies in the sixteenth century.

Throughout the text, I have also used the terms "Spanish empire," "imperial context," "imperial institutions," and "colonial society," even though I am aware that contemporaneous political thinkers and the Habsburg crown and its deputies did not define or envision the Spanish Americas as a colony of the crown, but rather as a series of dependent viceroyalties, and nor did they see the crown as an empire.[45] Nonetheless, for people whose lives were violently ruptured by slavery, dispossession, and physical extraction from their homelands, and who bore generational trauma as they were forced to live in societies where their enslavement was justified and codified in law, the difference between a kingdom composed of viceroyalties or an empire was perhaps irrelevant. Instead, they

---

[45] Cardim, et al., *Polycentric Monarchies*. For Portugal, see Cardim, "Reassessing the Portuguese"; Marcocci and Keshvani, "Contested Legacies"; Martins Marcos, "White Innocence" and "Blackness Out of Place." For contemporary debates on the legacies of empires and slavery, see Villacañas Berlanga, *Imperiofilia* Spain, and Araujo, *Reparations*, and *Slavery* for politics of memory of slavery.

knew and understood that a conquering state in the name of the Spanish crown had conquered, waged wars, and devastated existing Indigenous societies across the Americas, while participating in and legitimizing – through legal codes and customs – the forced removal of millions of enslaved Africans to fill labor shortages resulting from the crown's ambition to extract natural resources from the newly conquered lands and build imperial societies. The use of the terms "empire," "imperial," and "colonial" are purposeful reminders to the author and the readers of the violence experienced by the subjects of this book, rather than an assessment of the nature of the polity or state in the period under study.

Any frame of analysis inevitably excludes important histories, and this study is no exception. In this book, the focus on African Diasporic people and their ideas across vast spaces in the Spanish Atlantic world in the long sixteenth century excludes the histories of many other people who inhabited these sites and who were engaged in similar reckonings with ideas about slavery and freedom. For example, from the early sixteenth century onwards, hundreds of thousands of Indigenous people were enslaved, dispossessed, and displaced by Spanish colonists. Indigenous communities played a key role in rebelling against their enslavement by Spanish colonists, and in contributing to debates about the illegitimacy of enslaving Indigenous Americans led by Dominican friar Bartolomé de las Casas (1484–1586). These debates eventually led to the crown's introduction of the New Laws in 1542, which outlawed the enslavement of Indigenous Americans, with the exception of people captured in a just war.[46] Similarly, this study also omits the lives and ideas of diverse subaltern people in Castilla who pressed royal courts for the expansion of their rights and privileges.[47] Such omissions include the vast and important history of non-Christians who were captured in what the Spanish termed as "just wars," as well as the histories of Jewish and Muslim people whom the Spanish crown expelled from its kingdoms in successive waves of repression and intolerance throughout the late fifteenth and late sixteenth century, as well as the lives of those who agreed to convert to Christianity and remain in Castilla as New Christians, namely *conversos* (converts from Judaism to Christianity and their descendants) and *moriscos* (converts from Islam to Christianity and their descendants).[48]

---

[46] Lewis, *All Mankind*.
[47] Select examples include Cavanaugh, "Litigating for Liberty"; Fernández Martín, "La esclavitud"; Hershenzon, *The Captive Sea*; Israel, "Petition and Response," "The Requerimiento," and "The Politics; Schwartz, *Blood*."
[48] Ibid.

Introduction

Finally, in a significant, yet inevitable omission, the study does not include any sites in the Lusophone Atlantic world within the key frames of analysis. During the period of this study, the Portuguese crown established colonial entrepôts and settlements in islands near West Africa, including Madeira (1420), the Azores (1439), Cape Verde (1462), and further south along the coastline towards Central Africa, the island of São Tomé (1486), and in mainland West Africa, including in Upper Guinea (Cacheu, 1588) and on the Gold Coast (São Jorge da Mina, in 1482), and later also in West-Central Africa, present-day Angola, including in Luanda (1576) and Benguela (1617). Scholars of slavery in Brazil and West-Central Africa, especially in later periods, have traced the emergence of cultural and political corridors between Brazil and West-Central Africa.[49] In addition, between 1580 and 1581, the Spanish and Portuguese crowns became unified through the Iberian Union and Philip II of Spain became the ruler of Portugal and the Portuguese empire, an arrangement that lasted until 1640.[50] The fragmentary archival work undertaken for this project meant it was not feasible to include Spanish and Portuguese cities and their respective rules of law and legal customs in the study. However, Black people who dwelt in Portuguese polities appear throughout the study, often sharing ideas about slavery and freedom that they accrued in each polity.

---

[49] Candido and Jones, *African Women*; de Carvalho Soares, "African Barbeiros" and *People of Faith*; Hébrard, "L'esclavage"; Liberato et al., *Laços Atlânticos*; Ferreira, *Cross-Cultural*; Reis, "African Nations," *Divining Slavery*, and *Slave Rebellion*. For scholarship on Black mobility and environmental knowledge in the early sixteenth century Lusophone world, see also de Avilez Rocha, "Maroons in the Montes" and "The Azorean"; Cardim, "Mulheres negras."

[50] Cardim, "Portugal unido, y separado"; Marcocci, "Too Much to Rule"; Subrayaman, "Holding the World."

I

Proving Freedom

Documenting Alhorría

Antón Segarra invested significant resources to document, protect, and assure his liberty after enduring enslavement throughout most of his life. He may have been born enslaved in the city of Sevilla to an enslaved Black mother or he may have been enslaved in West Africa and forcibly displaced to Castilla as a child. By the late sixteenth century, Antón Segarra was the property of Francisco Segarra, a member of a distinguished noble family in Sevilla. On his deathbed in 1596, Francisco Segarra included a provision in his will to liberate Antón from slavery. However, Antón's liberation would not be immediate. Instead, Francisco Segarra specified that Antón must serve his niece, Doña Juana Segarra de Saavedra, for six years prior to obtaining his liberty. During this time, Antón was displaced from Sevilla to the nearby town of Écija – where Segarra de Saavedra resided – and he intermittently traveled with his new owner to Sevilla. Upon completing the six years of additional enslaved labor, Segarra de Saavedra initiated a legal process of *alhorramiento* (liberation from slavery) under Castilian laws and issued Antón Segarra with a freedom paper, known as a *carta de alhorría* or a *carta de libertad*. Armed with this legally binding document that spelled out his liberty, Antón Segarra took further measures to protect his freedom. He invited three friends in Sevilla to serve as witnesses before a royal official who could confirm that they knew him and could attest to the veracity of his freedom paper. As a result of this process, Antón Segarra generated a supplementary document issued by a royal authority that confirmed his freedom.

Antón Segarra's actions form part of a broader history of how liberated Black people engaged in legal cultures of paperwork to document, protect, and assure their liberty across the Spanish Atlantic in the sixteenth century and beyond. Those who possessed liberty in the Spanish empire invested significant resources to protect their freedom. Although liberty was a legal term in the Spanish empire, it was also physical. Free and liberated people often documented their liberty with paperwork. Lack of paperwork documenting their legal status could endanger a liberated person, making them vulnerable to the theft of their freedom by enslavers. For this reason, liberated and free people engaged in juridical cultures of paperwork to assure and protect their liberty and sometimes deployed creative measure to generate new and supplementary freedom papers by gathering witness testimonies or seeking a certificate from a royal authority that confirmed their freedom. This history reveals a Black intellectual tradition in which enslaved and liberated people engaged with Castilian rules of law pertaining to slavery and freedom (namely the thirteenth-century legal codes known as the *Siete Partidas*) and possessed knowledge of legal customs of slavery and freedom.[1] Their participation in cultures of documentation in the Spanish empire also reveals how enslaved, free, and liberated Black people sought to protect and shape the meanings of freedom in the sixteenth-century Spanish Atlantic.[2]

Archival traces of this history span notarial contracts, probate investigations, final wills and testaments, and petitions to varied royal courts. In addition, records generated by free and liberated Black people who petitioned for royal permits to move between sites in the Spanish empire – especially when crossing the Atlantic as passengers on ships – also reveal fragmentary evidence about the emergence of cultures of freedom papers, in particular how liberated people kept their *cartas de alhorría* safe, and sometimes bolstered their freedom certificate by investing time and resources to generate additional and supplementary paperwork that confirmed their status as free people.

---

[1] *Las Siete partidas del Sabio Rey don Alfonso*, "Quarta Partida, Titulo XXII, De la Libertad," 39–40.

[2] This approach builds on scholarship that explores enslaved and free people's engagement with diverse legal cultures of paperwork to build evidentiary thresholds of their freedom in different imperial realms across the Atlantic world: in particular, Candido, "African freedom suits," and *An African Slaving Port*; Chira, *Patchwork Freedoms*; Curto, "Experiences of Enslavement," "Struggling Against," "The Story of Nbena"; Dias Paes, *Esclavos y tierras* and "Shared Atlantic Legal Culture"; Scott and Hébrard, *Freedom Papers*; McKinley, *Fractional Freedoms*.

ARCHIVES OF FREEDOM PAPERS:
METHODOLOGICAL REFLECTIONS

Liberated Black people's actions to protect and safeguard their *cartas de alhorría* reveal their participation in – and knowledge of – the Spanish laws underpinning slavery and freedom and the juridical processes that might be available to protect their freedom. Enslaved people in the Spanish Atlantic often sought a liberty that could be documented in a *carta de alhorría* because they understood the privileges and rights of an *horro* status within Castilian legal codes. The Castilian rule of law concerning freedom from enslavement derived from the thirteenth-century *Siete Partidas*, specifically the chapter on freedom in *Quarta Partida, Titulo XXII*.[3] These laws made provisions for slave-owners to liberate their slaves in an act of *alhorramiento* (manumission/liberation from slavery) in various settings, such as "in a church, in front of a judge, or in another place, through a testament, or without a testament or by a letter (*carta*)," while any oral pronouncements of freedom required the presence of five witnesses.[4] In theory, these legal codes protected a liberated person from being resubjected to slavery (or "returned" to slavery) and ensured the free status of the future progeny of liberated or freeborn women.

Freedom by *alhorramiento* as specified in the *Siete Partidas* differed in important ways from the freedoms sought by those who endured precarious flights from enslavement and joined self-governing communities, often known as *palenques*.[5] Although the Spanish crown attempted to destroy these communities through force and war, Spanish royal officials sometimes negotiated with Black fugitive communities – particularly when the crown was vulnerable to interimperial conflicts or in times of internal wars – to grant their members freedom if they agreed to be "reduced" to semiautonomous Black towns in exchange for declarations of loyalty to the Spanish crown.[6] English colonial authorities would later reach similar agreements with Black fugitives when politically expedient, such as in eighteenth-century Jamaica when authorities on the island granted legal pronouncements of freedom to runaway communities in return for their commitment to quell future slave uprisings on the island.[7] Such agreements notwithstanding, living in a state of war with the

[3] Ibid.
[4] Ibid.
[5] See note 6 in Introduction.
[6] Ibid.
[7] Brown, *Tacky's*.

Spanish crown and in the hope of eventually reaching a negotiated freedom in return for loyalty was a risky strategy. The chapter about slavery in the *Siete Partidas* specified that owners could legitimately return any enslaved fugitives to slavery.[8] And slave-owners and royal officials regularly employed agents to locate and return enslaved people who had escaped from slavery and, where possible, to destroy Black *palenques*.[9] Those dwelling in autonomous *palenque* communities therefore faced the constant prospect of persecution and forced returns to slavery.

In contrast, freedom by *alhorramiento* offered juridical protection to a liberated person from being resubjected to slavery (or "returned to slavery"), at least in theory, and ensured the free status of liberated women's future children. The *Siete Partidas* described how liberated people could be returned to slavery in limited circumstances, for example, when a former owner who had previously liberated their slave sought to undo an *alhorramiento*.[10] Such a rule of law did not prevent corrupt slave-owners from illegitimately enslaving liberated Black people by stealing their liberty or claiming freeborn children as their slaves, but these Castilian legal codes and legal customs meant that illegitimately reenslaved people had recourse – at least in theory – to structures of royal justice to appeal against their illegal captivity. Access to justice often depended on whether the victim lived in the vicinity of a royal or ecclesiastical court and whether they possessed paperwork that confirmed their freedom, such as their *carta de alhorría*. Their chance of a successful resolution in the courts also depended on whether litigators possessed community ties that would translate into compelling witness testimonies about their status as a liberated person, whether their new owners had the power to corrupt any judicial process, and whether local authorities were sympathetic to their tribulation.

This history of how liberated Black people understood the legal meanings of their liberty and how they protected their freedom papers across Spanish imperial realms is inscribed in fragmentary evidence across diverse historical archives. For example, notarial records in towns and cities across Castilla and the Spanish Americas reveal the bureaucratic process involved in the act of an *alhorramiento* or *ahorramiento*. Such acts involved an owner issuing their slave with a *carta de alhorría* that

---

[8] *Las Siete partidas del Sabio Rey don Alfonso*, "Quarta Partida, Titulo XXI, De los Siervos," 38–39.
[9] For example, see Brewer Garcia, *Beyond Babel*; McKnight, "Confronted rituals."
[10] *Las Siete partidas del Sabio Rey don Alfonso*, "Quarta Partida, Titulo XXII, De la Libertad," 39–40.

listed the reasons for their liberation and any terms in the presence of witnesses and before a public notary (*escribano publico*), who would issue a certified *escritura* (notarized document with legal validity) of the proceedings and would record the signed documents in a permanent register of notarial acts (*protocolos notariales*). Examples of this document, known as a *carta de alhorría* or *carta de libertad*, are housed in notarial archives across the Spanish Americas and Castilla. For example, Antón Segarra's *carta de alhorría* was issued in the town of Écija in December 1602 after Segarra de Saavedra approached a public notary and began proceedings for an *alhorramiento*.[11] Antón Segarra was absent from the notary's office as he was living in Sevilla at the time of the *alhorramiento*, but enslaved people were usually present during these acts. Antón Segarra's recent marriage to an enslaved Black woman named Felipa de la Cruz in Sevilla sometime between 1591 and 1601 may explain his absence from Écija, as he may have negotiated with his owner to operate as a slave-for-hire in Sevilla so that he could live a married life with his wife, or he may have been tasked by his owner to carry out duties on her behalf in Sevilla.[12] In Antón Segarra's case, Segarra de Saavedra entrusted a servant whom she knew from a prominent Sevilla household to transport Antón Segarra's *carta de alhorría* from Écija to Sevilla and to deliver the precious document to her former slave by hand.

Cartas de alhorría nestled in the voluminous registers of notarial acts across Castilla and the Spanish Americas catalog various reasons why owners chose or agreed to liberate their slaves.[13] Some scholars have concluded that slave-owners usually liberated their slaves as a calculated economic act, liberating enslaved people who were ill or elderly and who were no longer productive to avoid the financial responsibility for their care later in life.[14] However, the variety of reasons given for *alhorramientos* across *cartas de alhorría* also point to the diverse ways that enslaved people fought for and negotiated paths to freedom with their owners. These documents reveal how enslaved people accumulated or borrowed sufficient funds or credit to pay for the price of their liberty (known as a *rescate*), and how owners liberated their slaves for other reasons, including for their loyal services, by previous agreement, or because they claimed

---

[11] "Antonio Segarra," AGI, Contratación 303, no. 2, fols. 10^r, 18^v–20^v.

[12] See Chapter 2, note 8.

[13] For a recent overview of sixteenth-century Sevilla, see Fernández Chaves, "Amas, esclavas, y libertad," and Pérez García, "Matrimonio, Vida Familiar."

[14] Phillips, *Slavery*, 122–145.

to feel a charitable impulse towards their slave.[15] Such documents also outlined whether the *horro* would owe their former owner any sum or labor for the price of their liberty, or whether an owner had chosen to gift the *horro* any money or property.

Less commonly, notarized *cartas de alhorría* sometimes reflected the outcome of an enslaved person's litigation in a royal court for their freedom. Their reasons for petitioning for their freedom could include their illegitimate enslavement under the existing laws of slavery, their owner's excessive cruelty, their owner's rescinding of a former promise of liberation, or their loyalty to or bravery offered for the crown (especially during times of war). Typically, however, judges' decisions would result in a judgment issued by a court (*auto*) or a royal decree (in the case of petitions to the highest royal court in Castilla for issues pertaining to the Americas, the Council of the Indies) that outlined a person's freedom, rather than a notarial *escritura*.[16] The exception is that some *horros* who were liberated by a court order then presented the favorable *auto* or royal decree to a public notary to request that he certify that they were the person named in the judgment. Notarial registers thus reveal a variety of reasons why slave-owners or the courts liberated enslaved people from slavery in this period and, to a certain extent, some of the strategies deployed by enslaved people to negotiate a path to freedom with their owners.

Notarial documents, however, rarely indicate the varied meanings of *cartas de alhorría* to those being liberated from slavery nor how *horros* protected these documents throughout their lifetimes. Details about the significance of freedom papers in liberated people's lives sometimes emerge in their testimonies in royal courts when they litigated against former owners or corrupt notaries for withholding their *carta de alhorría* or liberation clauses in their owners' testaments. These litigations reveal how *horros* often prioritized obtaining copies of their *carta de alhorría*. In particular, the withholding of a *carta de alhorría* endangered Black *horros* who were at risk of illegitimate reenslavement when not in possession of their freedom certificate. The importance of possessing freedom papers to reduce the risk of reenslavement differs from later periods during the long and gradual abolition of slavery, and historian Yesenia Barragán has found

---

[15] Example of *alhorría* owing to loyal service to an owner: "Alhorría," December 2, 1578, Archivo General de la Nación, Peru (cited as AGN, Peru), Notarias, 1 CYH1, 28,402, 188v–189. See also Phillips, *Slavery*, 122–145, and note 13 in this chapter.
[16] "Domingo Gelofe," AGI, Indiferente 1205, no. 21; "Real Cedula, Domingo Gelofe," AGI, Indiferente 422, libro 17, fols. 114^r–115^r; "Domingo Gelofe," AGI, Contratación 5536, libro 5, fol. 156$^{r(1)}$.

evidence of liberated people not obtaining their freedom papers for many years after their liberation from slavery in nineteenth-century Colombia.[17]

An example of the risks of not possessing freedom papers for liberated people in the sixteenth century emerges after a public notary in Puerto Rico refused in the early 1540s to provide an enslaved Black man named Pedro de Carmona with a copy of his late owner's will, which reportedly liberated him and his Black wife from slavery.[18] As a result of the withholding of this document, the heirs of Carmona's late owner sold husband and wife and displaced them from Puerto Rico to Santo Domingo.[19] A decade earlier, a Black man named Rodrigo López was snatched from Cabo Verde, the Portuguese-controlled archipelago near West Africa, even though López's deceased owner had included a delayed liberation clause for López in his final will and testament.[20] After various years of López being subjected to illegitimate enslavement and displacement across the Atlantic, López's sister sent him a cache of his freedom papers through a relay of merchants sailing between Cabo Verde and the Spanish Caribbean. Upon receipt of this paperwork, López was able to prove his freedom in a Spanish royal court.[21] Similarly, enslaved people whose owners promised to liberate them, but did not formalize such agreements through paperwork, might later struggle to prove that they were free.[22] These examples drawn from petitions for freedom in royal courts reveal the importance of Black *horros* possessing copies of their *cartas del alhorría* as a means to document and protect their freedom.

Records of freedom certificates among lists of Black *horros'* personal belongings also point to how they kept these documents safe throughout their lives. Such lists were often produced in the context of probate investigations, especially for those who perished far from where their heirs resided. These records reveal how Black *horros* kept their freedom papers safe many years after their liberation from slavery, and how some carried multiple freedom certificates on their person. For example, liberated Black people traveling as passengers on ships that crossed the Atlantic tended to keep a copy of their *carta de alhorría* in a locked box or casket among their belongings. For instance, a Black *horra* named Inés de Rebenga perished on board a

---

[17] Barragan, *Freedom's Captives*. For freedom across legal jurisdictions, see Scott and Venegas Fornias, "María Coleta."

[18] "Pedro de Carmona," AGI, Justicia 978, no. 2, ramo 1.

[19] Ibid.

[20] "Rodrigo López," AGI, Justicia 11, no. 4. See also Cortés Alonso, "La Liberacion," 533–568; Liddell, "Social Networks"; Turits, "Slavery."

[21] Ibid.

[22] For an example, see "Gonzalo Miguel Moreno," AGI, Escribanía 1012A, años 1601–1603.

ship (*galeon*) in 1550 near the town of Veragua in present-day Panama.[23] Among Rebenga's belongings was her freedom certificate, which had been issued thousands of kilometers away in the city of Lima. Rebenga was likely a small-scale merchant of precious jewels as she traveled with numerous pieces of fine jewelry, worth 102 *reales*.[24] Half a century later, a recently liberated mulato from Lisbon in Portugal named Juan Limón was on board a ship sailing through the Gulf of Panamá in the Pacific in the early months of 1607. On the ship, Limón reportedly carried a casket where he kept his treasured freedom papers that spelled out how he had purchased his freedom from his owner in Portugal. Although formerly enslaved, Limón had accrued significant capital since his liberation from slavery. On the ship, he was travelling as a passenger and he had brought his own slave, a twenty-eight-year-old man described as "Black *Angola*," to serve him on the journey. Limón also carted over 880 pesos and thirty patacones and a half in silver, a significant amount of money, given that he lent half of this sum to the owner of the ship to pay for necessary repairs to the vessel.[25] Other lists of belongings were produced within the bureaucracy of the Holy Offices of the Inquisition when arresting officers inventoried arrestees' property before auctioning their belongings to raise funds for the cost of their pending imprisonment. Scribes compiling lists of arrestees' effects would often include a description of the contents of any of their papers.[26] Lists of belongings compiled by Inquisitors also confirm how *horros* kept their freedom papers safe throughout their lives. For example, four *cartas de alhorría* were listed among the belongings of three Black *horras* named Barbola de Albornoz, Ana Suárez, and Luissa Domínguez (who had two freedom papers) among sixteen women arrested by Inquisitors between 1632 and 1633 in Cartagena de Indias.[27]

Petitions to Real Audiencias (the highest royal appellate courts that were established across the Americas throughout the sixteenth century) and to other royal authorities in the Spanish Americas also reveal fragmentary elements of the history of freedom papers. This is because some freeborn and formerly enslaved people petitioned royal courts to issue judicial rulings confirming their freedom after presenting evidence of their liberty.

---

[23] "Inés de Rebenga," AGI, Contratación 5709, no. 7.
[24] Ibid., fol. 3^r: "*a ciento y dos reales de a treinta y cuatro maravedíes cada uno.*"
[25] "Juan Limón," AGI, Contratación 5581, no. 72, fols. 4^r–7^v.
[26] "Hacienda secuestrada Cartagena 1632–1637," Archivo Histórico Nacional de España (cited as AHN, España), Inquisición 4822, exp. 2. See also Silva Campo, "Fragile Fortunes"; von Germeten, "African Women's Possessions."
[27] "Hacienda secuestrada Cartagena 1632–1637," AHN, España, Inquisición 4822, exp. 2.

Black *horros* and freeborn people often took such precautions on the eve of lengthy and uncertain journeys. But other *horros* and freeborn people with no immediate intentions to travel sometimes petitioned the courts to confirm their freedom as a preventative measure to protect their freedom when fearing an illegitimate enslavement. For example, in 1574, Catalina sent a petition to the Real Audiencia in Santa Fé (present-day Bogotá) explaining that she was a freeborn *mulata* who had been born to a free Indigenous woman and a Black man. Catalina petitioned judges to issue a ruling confirming her status as a freeborn woman. Catalina explained that she and her two sons were "Black people (*negros atezados*)" and that because of the "color Black that we are, people might now or in time aggrieve us, and even though we are free, we might be imprisoned as slaves." To avoid this dreadful fate, Catalina had gathered witnesses in Santa Fé who described her status as a freeborn woman. Catalina requested that the judges review this evidence and issue a judicial confirmation of her and her sons' status as freeborn people. Catalina envisioned that such a ruling would "assure and protect my liberty and that of Juan Bonifico and Balthasar Bonifico, my sons" and ensure that "our freedom is not disturbed."[28]

Finally, Black people's petitions for royal licenses to cross the Atlantic as passengers and wage-earning servants on ships also reveal how Black people sought to protect and prove their status as free people. These records show how liberated Black people often invested significant resources to generate supplementary freedom certificates to protect and safeguard their freedom prior to a journey. The most common strategy for this was when *horros* requested a second public notary to certify their existing *carta de alhorría*. These strategies to supplement freedom papers are often difficult to trace in historical archives as *horros* approached public notaries in different locales and over various years. However, fragments of this history were sometimes recorded in petitions for royal licenses to travel across the Spanish Atlantic. Records of the paperwork that Black *horros* presented to support their petitions reveal how liberated people often invested significant resources and social capital to accumulate additional freedom papers, sometimes notarizing their freedom certificate with more than one notary. Records of petitions for royal licenses to cross the Atlantic therefore reveal fragmentary details about how Black people sought to protect and prove their status as free people after enduring lifetimes of enslavement and precarious and often lengthy routes to legal manumission.

---

[28] "Catalina, mulata, petición," Archivo General de la Nación de Colombia (cited as AGN, Colombia), Sección Colonia (cited as SC), Negros y esclavos (cited as NE), 43, 9, doc. 13.

FREEDOM PAPERS AND TRAVEL LICENSES IN THE SIXTEENTH CENTURY

Records of Black people's petitions for royal licenses to cross the Atlantic to the Spanish Americas are worth exploring in detail as they provide valuable insights into how liberated and freeborn people sought to protect and prove their free status in the sixteenth-century Spanish Atlantic. In the first instance, petitions for travel licenses reveal how hundreds of free and liberated Black people obtained royal permits to sail across the Atlantic to the Spanish Americas and shed light on the phenomenon of Black migration. But these records also reveal how enslaved, liberated, and freeborn Black people engaged in a culture of freedom papers in the sixteenth century and became adept at navigating an increasingly complicated bureaucratic system of petitioning for royal travel licenses.

The center of this history is the city of Sevilla, the inland port on the Guadalquivir River in southwest Castilla (Figures 1.1 and 1.2). From the early sixteenth century onwards, the crown ensured that Sevilla would serve as the center of trade and communication in the sprawling Spanish empire. The crown established key institutions in Sevilla to govern tax, trade, and travel to the Americas, such as the House of Trade (Casa de la Contratación), which was tasked with collecting tax and controlling the flow of passengers to the Americas. Throughout the sixteenth century, every ship sailing from the Spanish Americas was required to traverse the Guadalquivir River and anchor in Sevilla for inspections and tax payments, while every ship departing to the Indies had to be inspected in Sevilla for the requisite licenses for goods and passengers on board.

These policies resulted in a demographic boom in Sevilla, which came to rival some of Europe's most populous cities. In 1534, Sevilla had approximately 50,000 residents; by 1561, the population had doubled to 100,000, fueled by internal migration patterns within Castilla as people moved to Sevilla in search of economic or labor opportunities or to prepare for voyages to the Spanish Americas.[29] Sevilla also became the

---

[29] For passengers in the sixteenth century, see Almorza Hidalgo, *No se hace pueblo*; Altman, *Emigrants and Society*; Boyd-Bowman, *Índice geobiográfico de más de cuarenta mil*, and *Índice geobiográfico de más de 56 mil*; Cook, *Forbidden Passages*; Durán López, "Pasajes a Indias"; Fernández López, *La Casa*; Gil-Bermejo García, "Pasajeros a Indias"; Hernández González, "Ronda y la Emigración"; Ireton, "They Are"; Jacobs, *Los movimientos*; Martínez, *Pasajeros de Indias*; Martínez Shaw, *La emigración*; Mörner and

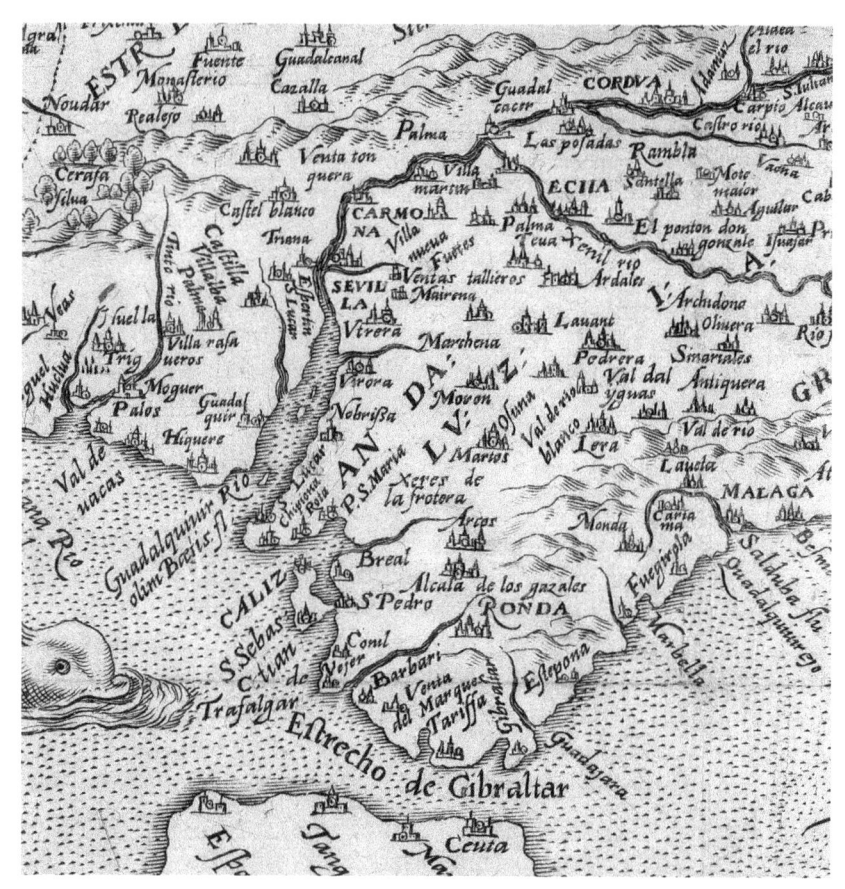

FIGURE 1.1 Abraham Ortelius, "Regni Hispaniae post omnium editiones locuplessima Descriptio" (detail of "Guadalquivir River [printed in illustration as *Guadalquivir Rio*] to Sevilla"). In *Hispaniae illustratæ seu Rerum vrbiumq. Hispaniæ, Lusitaniæ, Æthiopiæ et Indiæ scriptores varii. Partim editi nunc primum, partim aucti atque emendati*. Francofurti: Apud Claudium Marnium, & Hæredes Iohannis Aubrij, 1603. John Carter Brown Map Collection, b22212917. Courtesy of the John Carter Brown Library.

mercantile heartbeat of the distribution of natural resources extracted from the Americas, leading to a constant stream of visitors and mercantile activity and travel, while foreign merchant communities from Italy, England, Holland, and other European regions also settled in Sevilla in

Sims, *Aventureros*, 20; Otte, *Cartas Privadas*; Porro Girardi, "Criados en Indias"; Rey Castelao, *El vuelo corto*; Rodríguez Lorenzo, "El contrato," "'El mar se mueve," *La Carrera de Indias*, and "Sevilla y la carrera"; Sainz Varela, "Los pasajeros."

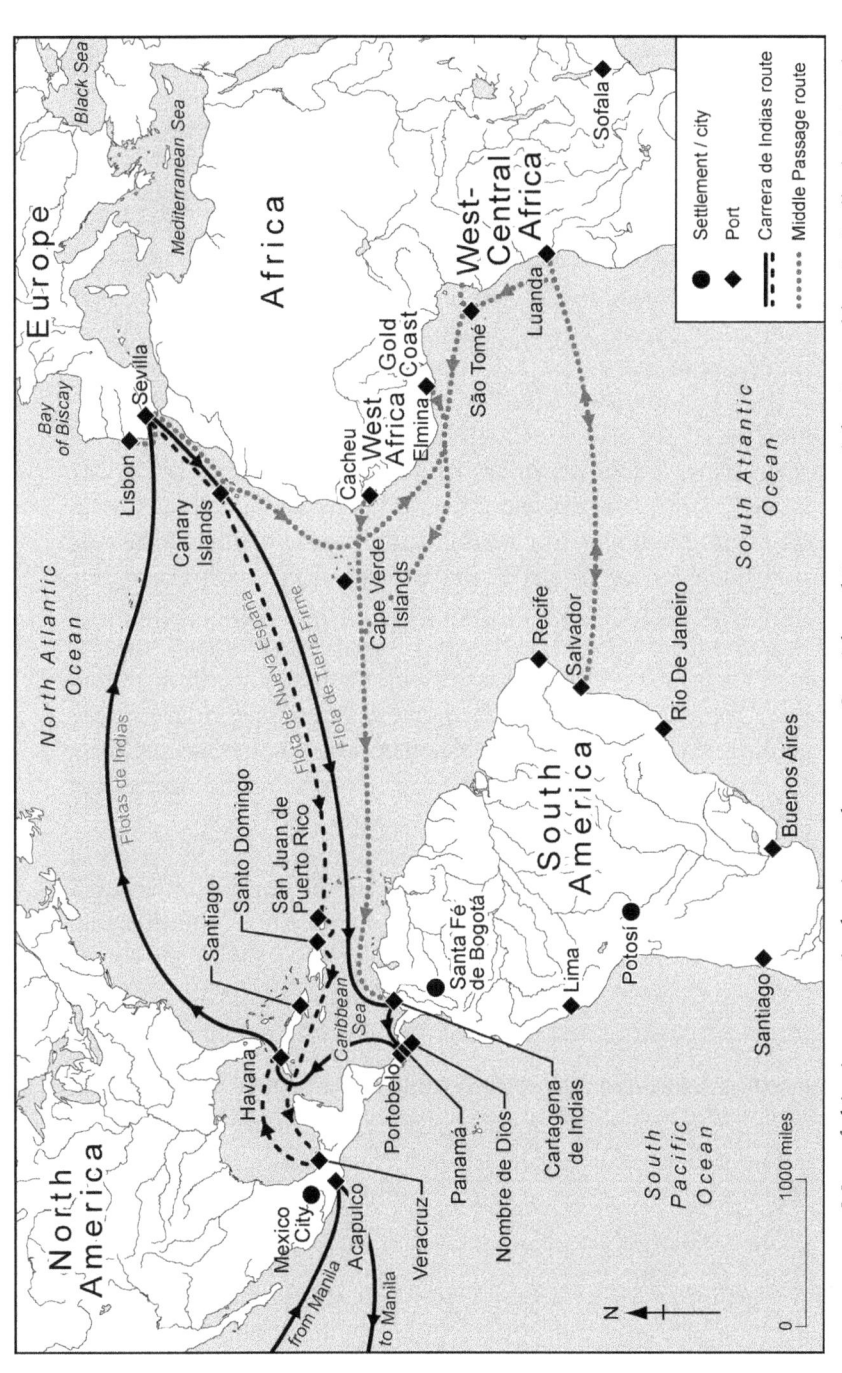

FIGURE 1.2 Map of shipping routes in the sixteenth-century Spanish and Portuguese Atlantic world, principally depicting the Spanish crown's *Carrera de Indias* routes, including the *Flota de la Nueva España* and the *Flota de Tierra Firme*, as well as broadly representing the principal shipping routes of European ships that forcibly displaced enslaved people from West Africa and West-Central Africa to Spanish and Portuguese Americas and Europe (often described as the "Middle Passage"). Map drawn by Cath D'Alton, Drawing Office, University College London.

this period. The pace of population growth in the city continued into the late sixteenth century; the number living there rose to 140,000 by 1588 and to 150,000 by 1599.[30] While Sevilla was not the most populous city in late sixteenth-century Europe, this rapid population growth is comparable to similar increases experienced by London and Venice between the 1570s and 1590s. The population of London grew from 80,000 in the mid sixteenth century to 200,000 at the turn of the seventeenth, while Venice's population stood at 115,000 in the mid sixteenth century and rose to 170,000 by the 1570s.[31] These three cities were dwarfed by Europe's most populous sixteenth-century city, Paris, which had approximately 294,000 residents in 1565; this declined to 220,000 in 1590 and then doubled to 440,000 by 1636.[32] After a century of unprecedented population growth in Sevilla, the seventeenth century witnessed a plateau, followed by a steep decline. Plague swept the city between 1599 and 1601, causing a slowdown in demographic growth, while the expulsion of *moriscos* from Castilla in 1610 resulted in at least 7,500 of them departing Sevilla. As the seventeenth century wore on, the population of Sevilla entered a period of moderate decline owing to a growing economic crisis and the crown's increasing favoritism towards the port of Cádiz as the center of trade with the Indies, so much so that by 1649 the population of Sevilla had gradually declined from its peak of 150,000 to 130,000 people. The plague returned in devastating form between 1647 and 1652 and claimed 60,000 lives in Sevilla, accounting for approximately 45 percent of the city's population.[33]

Amid the fast-paced demographic changes in Sevilla in the sixteenth century, there was also a significant increase in the number of enslaved and free Black people dwelling in the city. Contemporary chroniclers suggested that the Black population constituted at least 10 percent of the city's residents.[34] Such a growth in the Black population stems from the

---

[30] Domínguez Ortíz, *La población de Sevilla en la baja Edad Media*, and "La población de Sevilla a mediados."

[31] Harding, "The Population"; Newton and Smith, "Convergence"; Vivo, "Walking."

[32] Blanchet and Biraben, "Essay on the Population."

[33] Domínguez Ortíz, "La población de Sevilla a mediados del siglo XVII," and *Orto y ocaso*, 132–133.

[34] For history of slavery and Black presence in Sevilla, and Spain more broadly, see Ares Queija and Stella, *Negros, Mulatos*; Berruezo-Sanchez et al., *Iberia Negra*; Blumenthal, *Enemies and Familiars*; Martín Casares, *La esclavitud*, and *Juan Latino*; Martín Casares and García Barranco, *La Esclavitud*; Martín Casares and Periáñez Gómez, *Mujeres*; Corona Pérez, "Aproximación," and *Trata Atlántica*; Cortés Alonso, *La esclavitud*, and "La población"; Domínguez Ortíz, *La esclavitud*, and *La población de Sevilla en la*

insatiable demand among Sevilla's private households for enslaved Black laborers, as Sevillians began to favor ownership of Black people from West Africa and West-Central Africa and their descendants for enslaved labor in private households over enslaved people from other regions and religious backgrounds. In addition, prospective passengers for the Americas often hoped to purchase enslaved Black people in Sevilla prior to their departure to the Americas owing to reports of the higher sale prices demanded for enslaved Black people in the Indies.[35] Despite the significant demand for enslaved Black people in Sevilla, sales tended to be modest affairs between private individuals or small-scale merchants, rather than the lot-type auction sales that later became more common in the Spanish Caribbean. In this period, a significant free Black population also emerged in Sevilla owing to existing Castilian laws and practices of slavery and freedom, namely the practice among owners to liberate slaves for specific reasons and the laws that stipulated that free women would bear freeborn children. The growth of a free Black population in Sevilla mirrors similar patterns across other towns and cities in the Spanish imperial realms in this period and beyond.

Like the 450,000 Castilians who emigrated from Castilla to the Americas in the sixteenth century, freeborn and liberated Black people residing in Castilla also regarded the Indies as a site for economic opportunity and sought royal licenses to cross the Atlantic as passengers and wage-earning laborers on ships.[36] Research for this project has uncovered over 435 documents that catalog how at least 370 free Black men and women obtained royal licenses to cross the Atlantic between 1511 and 1630, comprising ninety-nine petitions to the Council of the Indies and/or royal decrees granting passenger licenses, and ninety-three records of petitions for embarkation licenses at the

---

baja Edad Media; Fernández Chaves, "Amas, esclavas, y libertad"; Fernández Chaves and Pérez García, *Tratas atlánticas*; Franco Silva, *La Esclavitud*, and "La Esclavitud en Sevilla entre 1526 y 1550"; Grove Gordillo, "Una aproximación"; Ireton, "They Are"; Izquierdo Labrado, "La esclavitud"; Jarana Vidal, "Lebrija"; Lobo Cabrera, *Los libertos*, and "Los libertos y la emigración"; Lowe and Earle, *Black Africans*; Morgado García, "Los libertos," and *Una metrópoli*; Ortega y Sagrista, "La Cofradía"; Pérez García, "Matrimonio, Vida Familiar," and "Metodología"; Pérez García and Fernández Chaves, "La cuantificación"; Pérez García et al., *Tratas, esclavitudes*; Pike, "Sevillian Society"; Sancho de Sopranis, *Las cofradias*; Stella, *Amours et désamours*, *Histoires d'esclaves*, and *Ser esclavo*; Valverde Barneto, "La esclavitud"; van Deusen, *Global Indios*; Vaseur Gamez et al., *La esclavitud*; Vincent, "L'esclavage," and "San Benito"; Wheat, "Catalina," and "Tangomãos"; Wheat and Eagle, "The Early Iberian."

[35] Otte, *Cartas Privadas*.
[36] Mörner and Sims, *Aventureros*, 20. See also note 26.

House of Trade in Sevilla, which recorded Black applicants' biographical details, proof of freedom and religious lineage, community ties, and varied personal cartographies, in addition to 200 records of passenger lists (*asientos de pasajeros*).[37] In addition, a further thirty-five probate records (*bienes de difuntos*/assets of the deceased) administered by the House of Trade detail the transoceanic biographies and personal effects of free Black people who perished in the Americas after leaving Castilla. Collectively, these records reveal how free and liberated Black men and women engaged in legal cultures of paperwork to document and protect their liberty.

Free Black people preparing to cross the Atlantic from Sevilla to the Spanish Americas in the sixteenth century had to prove that they were not of the "prohibited people," and this included proving that they were not enslaved. These prohibitions arose because the Spanish monarchy became increasingly concerned throughout the sixteenth century about the quality of people permitted to cross the Atlantic to the Americas, with a particular concern to protect Indigenous communities in the Spanish Americas from the influence of groups of people whom the crown perceived as "undesirable" and "dangerous." In particular, the crown sought to prevent "prohibited" categories of people from crossing the Atlantic, namely anyone who was newly converted to the Catholic faith or their descendants, which included *moriscos* and *conversos*, anyone who was deemed to be a criminal or a vagrant, and anyone who had been pursued or arrested by the Holy Office of the Inquisition for crimes against the Catholic faith.[38] Enslaved people were also included in the group of "prohibited people" unless their owners had obtained licenses and paid relevant taxes to take specified numbers of enslaved people to the Americas. Freeborn and liberated Black people who wished to cross the Atlantic had to prove that they were not of the prohibited people, principally that they were Old Christians and that they were free people who were not subjected to slavery.[39] Elsewhere, I have explored how

---

[37] For other scholars who have also explored how free Black people crossed the Atlantic with royal licenses, see Domínguez Domínguez, "Circulaciones imperiales," and "Veracruz"; Garofalo, "Afro-Iberians in the Early," "Afro-Iberian Subjects," and "The Shape"; Ireton, "They Are"; Lobo Cabrera, "Los libertos."

[38] A number of these royal edicts from throughout the sixteenth century are cited in Cook, *Forbidden Passages*, 53–79.

[39] For a discussion on discourses of Christianity among Black petitioners, see Garofalo, "Afro-Iberians in the Early," "Afro-Iberian Subjects," and "The Shape"; Ireton, "They Are."

free and liberated Black people positioned themselves as Old Christians in these travel petitions, but their strategies to prove their liberty remain understudied.[40]

In the first half of the sixteenth century, royal officials at the House of Trade in Sevilla sought to prevent people from the "prohibited" groups from traveling to the Indies by inspecting passengers on ships poised to set sail across the Atlantic and recording their names and destinations in the books of Passenger Lists (*Asientos de Pasajeros*).[41] Black *horros* on board ships had to prove their status as free people to royal inspectors. Formerly enslaved Black individuals would often board a ship in possession of their treasured *carta de alhorría* in which their previous owner confirmed their freedom before a public notary or a certified copy of a clause of a late owner's will that set out the terms of their liberation. House of Trade officials would record the names of passengers and their destinations in the Passenger Lists, noting the date when and location where their freedom papers had been issued.

The often-brief Passenger Lists for the first half of the sixteenth century reveal how Black *horros* resided in various locales in Castilla prior to embarking to the Americas. Between 1500 and 1550, at least ninety men and women recorded as Black or *mulato* are named in the Passenger Lists.[42] Of those, at least forty-two were formerly enslaved people who presented their *cartas de alhorría* or other freedom papers to inspectors on ships. Approximately sixteen of forty-two Black *horros* had received their freedom papers in Sevilla, while others had been liberated from slavery in towns across the broader Andalucía region and beyond, including Baena, Córdoba, Jerez de la Frontera, Montemolin, Sanlúcar la Mayor,

---

[40] Ireton, "They Are."
[41] See note 26 for existing scholarship on these passenger records.
[42] Travel records for passengers labeled as Negro, Mulato, Loro, Moreno between Castilla and New Spain 1500–1550, include the following caches: AGI, Contratación 5536, libro 1: fols. 6$^{(1)}$, 11$^{(3)}$, 150$^{(1)}$, 206$^{(3)}$, 153$^{(4)}$, 203$^{(7)}$, 125$^{(3)}$, 344$^{(4)}$, 227$^{(1)}$, 315$^{(5)}$, 253$^{(2)}$, 276$^{(2)}$, 293$^{(3)}$, 284$^{(5)}$, 330$^{(6)}$, 473$^{(7)}$, 417$^{(4)}$, 438$^{(15)}$, 469$^{(12)}$, 469$^{(12)}$, 473$^{(8)}$, 474$^{(1)}$, 474$^{(2)}$, 507$^{(8)}$, 473$^{(7)}$; AGI, Contratación 5536, libro 2, fols. 32$^{(2)}$, 63$^{(5)}$, 64$^{(1)}$, 75$^{(3)}$, 74$^{(10)}$, 112$^{(1)}$ 220$^{(1)}$; AGI, Contratación 5536, libro 3, fols. 5$^{(2)}$, 37$^{(6)}$, 130$^{(2)}$, 135$^{(4)}$, 157$^{(1)}$, 165$^{(4)}$, 214$^{(6)}$, 215$^{(6)}$, 257$^{(4)}$, 358$^{(6)}$; AGI, Contratación 5536, libro 5, fols. 35$^{v(2)}$, 57^{v}, 60$^{v(1)}$, 73$^{v(3)}$, 78$^{v(4)}$, 80$^{v(6)}$, 81$^{v(5)}$, 84$^{r(3)}$, 113$^{v(2)}$, 124$^{r(3)}$, 156$^{r(1)}$, 169$^{r(1)}$, 197$^{r(5)}$, 197$^{r(6)}$, 199$^{v(1)}$, 202$^{r(3)}$, 203$^{r(2)}$, 204$^{v(7)}$, 215$^{r(1)}$, 231$^{r(1)}$, 238$^{r(5)}$, 241$^{v(5)}$, 283$^{v(9)}$, 285$^{v(3)}$, 295$^{r(3)}$, 312$^{r(4)}$, 321$^{v(4)}$, 360$^{r(2)}$, 340$^{r(1)}$, 364R$^{(2)}$; AGI, Indiferente 424, libro 21, fols. 124^{r}–124^{v}; AGI, Indiferente 1961, libro 3, fols. 324^{r}–324^{v}; AGI, Indiferente 1964, libro 10, fols. 88, 351^{v}–352, 354^{v}; AGI, Indiferente 2048, no. 4; AGI, Indiferente 2059, no. 97; Archivo Histórico Provincial de Sevilla (cited as AHPS), Protocolos Notariales, Libro del año 1529, Oficio V, Libro I, Escribania de Francisco de Castellanos, fol. 604.

Talavera, Úbeda, Valencia de Alcántara, and Zafra.[43] In other cases, *horros* presented paperwork that documented how their freedom had been granted by a royal court. For example, Domingo *Gelofe* boarded a ship armed with a royal decree that outlined his freedom in 1537. Domingo had received this royal decree following his successful petition for liberty at the Council of the Indies in 1536 on the basis that his enslavement in Upper Guinea had been illegitimate as per Castilian laws of slavery.[44]

Tracing the locations where Black *horros* notarized their freedom papers reveals that many *horros* in the first half of the sixteenth century moved to Sevilla upon obtaining their liberty and prior to embarking to the Americas. For example, seven years had elapsed between a Black man named Antón de Zafra receiving his freedom papers in the town of Morilla in 1531 and his eventual Atlantic voyage in 1538.[45] Zafra lived as an *horro* in Castilla for seven years, likely either in Morilla or Sevilla, prior to embarking on a ship to the Americas. In 1536, a Black woman named Isabel de Zafra was listed in the Passenger Lists as a *natural* of Zafra (in present-day Extremadura, Spain) and a *vecina* of Sevilla.[46] In general, *naturaleza* referred to a person's place of birth and community of belonging, while *vecino* meant that someone was considered as a free person who resided in a city for several years, often equaling five (although this varied between sites).[47] While some scholars have traced how the label of *vecindad* was reserved for heads of households (and certainly may have appeared as such in censuses), in everyday speech, witness testimonies, colonial bureaucracy, and in petitions to the crown, the term *vecino/a* was used more broadly to describe people who resided in a town or city permanently. This practice also reflects how individuals from diverse ethnic backgrounds across the Spanish empire often sought to position themselves as *vecinos* of the cities where they dwelt as a way of expanding their political belonging and rights. Inspectors' description of Isabel de Zafra as a *vecina* of Sevilla suggests that she resided in Sevilla for some time, after she had received her freedom papers thirteen

---

[43] Ibid.
[44] "Domingo Gelofe," AGI, Indiferente 1205, no. 21; "Domingo Gelofe," AGI, Indiferente 422, libro 17, fols. 114^r–115^r; "Domingo Gelofe," AGI, Contratación 5536, libro. 5, fol. 156$^{r(1)}$. For further discussion of this case, see Chapter 5.
[45] "Antón de Zafra," AGI, Contratación 5536, libro 5, fol. 78$^{v(4)}$.
[46] "Isabel de Zafra," AGI, Contratación 5536, libro 5, fol. 35$^{v(2)}$.
[47] For a study on the meanings of *vecindad* and *naturaleza* in the Spanish empire, see Herzog, *Defining Nations*. For the term *vecino* in sixteenth-century censuses, see Kagan, "Contando Vecinos." For a study on how indigenous and mestizo people forged *vecindad* in New Granada, see Deardorff, *A Tale*.

years earlier in Zafra. Another Black *vecina* of Sevilla named Leonor de Espinosa was recorded in the Passenger Lists in 1535 when she was preparing to sail to Veragua in Panama.[48] Espinosa presented freedom papers that she had notarized in Jerez de la Frontera in 1534. Royal officials' description of her as a *vecina* of Sevilla implies that she resided in Sevilla in the year between obtaining her liberty in Jerez and embarking on an Atlantic voyage. Finally, Francisca Hernández de Cola and her husband, Jorge, traveled to the Americas in 1527 and were described as Black *horros*.[49] Hernández de Cola proved her freedom by presenting a notarized freedom certificate from the town of Alcalá de Guadaira (southwest of Sevilla, between Dos Hermanas and Carmona) dated two years earlier on April 3, 1525. Her husband, Jorge, had been enslaved to the archbishop of Tarragona, who had liberated him from slavery in Sevilla.[50] These records therefore reveal where and when Black *horros* were liberated from slavery and the places where they notarized their *cartas de alhorría*. The Passenger Lists also confirm evidence from the lists of belongings compiled by judges of the assets of deceased that point to how Black *horros* carried these precious documents on their person as they crossed the Atlantic.

Black *horros* due to depart Castilla in this era sometimes notarized their freedom papers more than once to ensure their freedom in the bureaucracy of the Spanish empire. Such an act reflects a lack of trust in the reliability of public notaries and an attempt to generate various certified copies of their freedom papers. This could take various forms, including seeking the services of a public notary in a different town or a second notary in the same town, usually by providing new witness testimonies to prove that the individual was the same as the person named in a *carta de alhorría*.[51] Isabel de Zafra, for example, had notarized her *carta de alhorría* with two different notaries in the town of Zafra in 1522 and 1523, and she presented both documents to prove her freedom when she embarked on an Atlantic voyage thirteen years later.[52]

Passenger Lists dating from the first half of the sixteenth century sometimes reveal arduous histories of years-long battles for delayed freedom,

---

[48] "Leonor," AGI, Contratación 5536, libro 3, fol. 215$^{(6)}$.
[49] "Francisca Hernández de Cola," AGI, Contratación 5536, libro 2, fol. 63$^{(5)}$.
[50] "Jorge," AGI, Contratación 5536, libro 2, fol. 64$^{(1)}$.
[51] This may also reflect a broader practice among liberated people to protect freedom papers by making secondary freedom papers. See Fernández Chaves, "Amas, esclavas, y libertad."
[52] "Isabel de Zafra," AGI, Contratación 5536, libro 5, fol. 35$^{v(2)}$.

as enslaved people completed long terms of labor specified in their owner's testaments before they were liberated from slavery. Such was the case of Ana, described as "of *lora* color," who traveled to New Spain in 1538, after a decade-long period waiting for her promised freedom in Sevilla.[53] On the ship, Ana presented inspectors with various freedom papers that attested to this arduous journey towards freedom. Her late owner's testament had specified that she could be free after serving Pedro de Pineda for ten years, and she notarized this testament clause on December 7, 1526, in Sevilla, but Pedro de Pineda later transferred the use of Ana's enslaved labor to his uncle, Juan de Pineda. To reflect this change in arrangements, all parties signed another notarial contract in Sevilla in June 1529 and drew up another contract that same year to clarify that Ana had already completed the initial years of labor as specified in the original testament. Finally, on December 11, 1537, Juan de Pineda liberated Ana, as she had completed eight years of service, and issued a *carta de alhorría* before a public notary of Sevilla. Since the death of her first owner, Ana had signed four notarial contracts associated with her path to freedom with three slave-owners and three different notaries in 1526, 1529, and 1537. After this decade of enslaved labor for her promised freedom, Ana crossed the Atlantic to New Spain in 1538 carrying copies of these four notarized contracts that documented her long path to liberty.[54]

Over the course of the sixteenth century, the crown introduced new layers of bureaucracy for prospective passengers seeking permits to travel to the Spanish Americas. A two-tier system of petitions for passenger and embarkation licenses was introduced to exert greater control over the flow of people to the Indies. In theory from the mid-1530s, and in practice from the 1550s, most potential Atlantic passengers were supposed to petition the Council of the Indies for a royal decree that would grant them a passenger license (*licencia de pasaje*).[55] Throughout the sixteenth century, the Council of the Indies was an itinerant court that followed the king and the Council of Castilla to various locations across Castilla, but after 1561, these courts were located in Madrid. Supplicants for passenger licenses could present petitions in person to the Council of the Indies or by sending written representations to the court. After obtaining a royal decree with a passenger license, prospective passengers then had to attend the House of Trade in Sevilla to request an embarkation

---

[53] "Ana," AGI, Contratación 5536, libro 5, fol. 80$^{v(6)}$.
[54] Ibid.
[55] Fernández López, *La Casa*; Hernández González, "Ronda y la Emigración."

license (*licencia de embarque*). The House of Trade's principal remit was to establish that the supplicant was not of the prohibited peoples and to identify that the person presenting themselves at the House of the Trade was the same as the person named in the royal decree. To prevent fraud and to establish the veracity of supplicants' claims, judges at the House of Trade in Sevilla interviewed all supplicants for embarkation licenses in person.[56] Judges also required that any Sevilla-based witnesses appear at the House of Trade for their testimonies to be taken in person. This meant that a petitioner seeking an embarkation license would arrange to meet their three or four witnesses at the House of Trade in Sevilla, where they would seek to prove that they were not "of the prohibited people," namely that they were Old Christians and that they were not criminals and had not been pursued by the Holy Office of the Inquisition, and in the case of Black people that they were also free people.

The crown's attempts to prohibit large swathes of the population in Castilla from traveling to the Americas rarely succeeded, as colonial subjects learned how to navigate or bypass the stringent requirements. For many inhabitants of Castilla, proving that they were not New Christians or that they had never been the subject of an Inquisitorial investigation could prove difficult. Much like the purchase of desirable Catholic religious lineages that emerged for wealthier residents in sixteenth-century Castilla, a shadowy trade in the falsification of travel licenses also developed in the city.[57] From the mid-sixteenth century onwards, the crown became particularly concerned with – and prosecuted – cottage industries in Sevilla and Madrid dedicated to falsifying passenger licenses.[58] Similarly, judges at the House of Trade routinely prosecuted Sevillian residents for providing false testimonies in support of supplicants' applications for embarkation licenses.[59] The growing demand for – and production of – false royal decrees and embarkation licenses in Sevilla highlights a know-how among city-dwellers of legitimate and illegitimate routes to cross the Atlantic.

Throughout the sixteenth century, the crown continued to issue royal decrees that instructed officials in the ports of the Indies to prohibit

---

[56] Fernández López, *La Casa*.
[57] For royal responses to forgeries of travel licenses, see AGI, Justicia 1177, no. 1; AGI, Contratación 5218, no. 88; AGI, Indiferente 1965, libro 13, fol. 432ᵛ; AGI, Contratación 5283, no. 82bis; AGI, Contratación 5289, no. 36; Autos de Prisión, 1605; AGI, Contratación 5280, no. 11.
[58] Ibid.
[59] For an example of a conviction for providing false testimony about a passenger, see "Melchor de Figueroa," AGI, Justicia 940, no. 10.

passengers from disembarking if they arrived on a ship without a passenger and embarkation license.[60] For example, in 1551, King Charles I insisted that the governor of Tierra Firme "visit all the ships that arrive in that land and ensure that only the persons listed in the ship's register are on board."[61] In the event that "any of them is found to be carrying passengers without licenses, make them return and compile a report of the people who passed through, if there were more who had disembarked in another port, and of the ship, pilots and captain of the ship, and send this report to the House of Trade so that they could be punished." In addition, the monarch insisted that "this decree be sung in the Gradas of the city of Sevilla," suggesting that this message was also aimed at prospective passengers in Sevilla, as Gradas was the principal site of mercantile activity in the city (Figure 2.3, no. 4).[62]

Prospective Black passengers who were unable to locate witnesses to testify about their freedom and biography found it almost impossible to obtain an embarkation license at the House of Trade. Instead, they may have resorted to crossing the ocean on a ship without a royal license – either by reaching another port of departure or midway port, such as the Canary Islands or Azores – or by finding a captain who would agree to hide them.[63] Others might seek to pass to the Indies by laboring as mariners or soldiers. Black mariners on ships rarely had to petition for embarkation licenses. Instead, they appeared inscribed in the registers of ships in the ranks of divers, gunners, mariners, pages (*paje de nao*), ship laborers (*grumete*), and soldiers, where House of Trade officials noted brief biographical information.[64] For example, the register of the San Francisco ship at the head of the Armada and Fleet of New Spain in 1596 listed four Black or *mulato* mariners who do not appear in records of embarkation licenses or Passenger Lists, including Mateo Cañete, "Black, mariner," Alonso Suárez, "Black, mariner," Francisco, "Black, mariner, and *natural* of Sevilla," and Sebastián Rodríguez, "*mulato, grumete, natural* of Sevilla."[65] These Black maritime laborers worked on ships between

---

[60] "Real Cedula," AGI, Panama, 235, libro 8, fols, 347ᵛ–348ᵛ; "Real Cedula," AGI, Panama, leg. 229, libro 2, fols. 74ᵛ–75bisʳ.
[61] "Real Cedula," AGI, Panama, 235, libro 8, fols. 347ᵛ–348ᵛ, and all quotes in this paragraph.
[62] For a discussion of Gradas, see Chapter 2.
[63] de Avilez Rocha, "The Azorean." See also Wheat, "'Global Transit Points," "Catalina," "Tangomãos."
[64] For more on mariners and men of the sea in late sixteenth-century Sevilla, see Pérez-Mallaína Bueno, *Spain's Men of the Sea*.
[65] "Alarde," AGI, Contratación 5252, no. 1, ramo 75. For more on Black mariners, see also Domínguez Domínguez, "Veracruz"; Garofalo, "The Shape."

Castilla and the Americas, as well as on vessels that transported enslaved cargoes from West Africa or West-Central Africa to the Americas.[66] When Black laborers from Castilla perished at sea or in the Spanish Americas, their kin or slave-owners often petitioned for their wages.[67] Such was the case of a young ten-year old *mulato* named José Vásquez who died in the port of Veracruz in 1634. Young Vásquez had labored as a ship page and had reportedly proven his freedom to royal officials inspecting the craft in Sevilla.[68] His father was a free Black *vecino* of Sevilla named Francisco de Torres who likely oversaw the arrangements for Vásquez's maritime labor contract and guided Vásquez to prove his freedom to any royal inspectors. In other cases, the histories of Black mariners were recorded in testimonies and trials prosecuted by the Holy Office of the Inquisition when free Black people claimed to have worked on ships that crossed the Atlantic before they settled in the New World.[69]

Other free Black people partially circumvented the requirements for passenger licenses by contracting their labor as *criados* (wage-earning servants) to passengers who already possessed royal decrees that granted the bearer a license to travel with wage-earning servants. As historian Fernández López has explored, ambivalent royal decrees that granted passengers a license to travel and take a specified number of *criados* created a market for wage-earning servants in Castilla, providing ample opportunities for people to cross the ocean without their own royal decrees.[70] Instead, such wage-earning servants only needed to obtain an embarkation license at the House of Trade. In addition to the convenience of bypassing the requirements for applying for a passenger license at the Council of the Indies, contracting one's labor as a servant to another passenger often

---

[66] On Black and *mulato* freeborn Castilians laboring on slave ships, see "Antonio de Arenas," Archivo General de la Archivo General de la Nación, México (cited as AGN, México), GD61 Inquisición, vol. 107, exp. 4.

[67] For example, "Alonso Hernández Manzano," AGI, Contratación 476, no. 1, ramo 5; "Pedro Pablo," AGI, Contratación 5577, no. 65; "Pedro de Montesdeoca," AGI, Contratación 485, no. 4, ramo 5; "Juan de Aroche," AGI, Contratación 5578, no. 51, item. 6 (a free *mulato* who left Castilla as a young boy (*muchacho*) and had become a *vecino* of the city of Truxillo in Honduras); "Antón Sardina," AGI, Contratación 941B, no. 32; "Baltasar de los Reyes," AGI, Contratación 5709, no. 211, ramo 24; "Pedro de la Torre," AGI, Contratación 5709, no. 218, ramo 27; "Cristóbal Rosado," AGI, Contratación 5709, no. 218, ramo 21; "Juan Rosell, Mateo, and Anton," AGI, Contratación 5709, no. 218, ramo 23; "Cristóbal López Riquel," AGI, Contratación 963, no. 2, ramo 11.

[68] "José Vázquez," AGI, Contratación 962A, no. 3.

[69] "Antonio de Arenas," Archivo General de México, GD61 Inquisición, vol. 107, exp. 4.

[70] Fernández López, *La Casa*. See also Porro Girardi, "Criados en Indias," 1245.

meant crossing the ocean without incurring the hefty cost of the voyage and sustenance.[71] Notarial records in Sevilla document the contractual nature of many of these arrangements, as each party specified the renumeration for the labor, the extent of maintenance costs during the voyage, and the exact time period for the employment contract.[72]

Approximately one-third of free and formerly enslaved Black people who sought embarkation licenses in the second half of the sixteenth century crossed the Atlantic as wage-earning servants on an employer's royal decree. Some of these individuals worked within a household and continued laboring for the same employers, while others entered the marketplace for wage-earning servants on Atlantic crossings, often serving various employers on different ships and sometimes settling in the Spanish Americas after an initial journey as a servant. For example, a freeborn *mulato* from Sevilla named Cristóbal de Castroverde crossed the Atlantic at least four times in the late sixteenth century, each time laboring for a different employer, before he finally settled in New Spain.[73] Testimonies about wage-earning servants also indicate that some Black people who resided in port towns of the Spanish Caribbean sometimes spent their working lives laboring

---

[71] For information on contracts for passage, maintenance costs and food on Atlantic crossings, see Rodríguez Lorenzo, "El contrato." For discussion of free Black *criados*, see also Ireton, "They Are."

[72] For contracts between free Black criados and employers for Atlantic crossings, see "Escritura de concierto," May 31, 1535, AHPS, Libro de Protocolos, signatura P-5856, libro del año 1535, oficio 10, Escribanía de Pedro de Coronado, ramos 24–26, fols. 82ᵛ–83ʳ; "Francisco Pérez," October 7, 1535, AHPS, signatura P-53, libro del año 1536, oficio 1, libro 2, Escribanía de Alonso de la Barrera, fols. 908ʳ–9ʳ; "Perdono," February 16, 1503, AHPS, signatura P-2163, libro del año 1503, oficio 4, libro 2, Escribanía Manuel Segura, fol. 333; "Poder," March 23, 1509, AHPS, signatura P-2183, libro del año 1509, oficio 4, libro 2, Escribanía Manuel Segura, fol. 895; "Compañía," February 19, 1509, AHPS, signatura P-2182, libro del año 1509, oficio 4, libro 1, Escribanía Manuel Segura, fol. 597; "Poder," March 23, 1509, AHPS, signatura P-2183, libro del año 1509, oficio 4, libro 2, Escribanía Manuel Segura, fol. 895ᵛ; "Asunto: Juan de Zafra," March 23, 1509, AHPS, signatura P-2183, libro del año 1509, oficio 4, libro 2, Escribanía Manuel Segura, fols. 899ʳ–900ʳ; "Diego Álvarez Chanca," July 28, 1511, AHPS, signatura P-2195, libro del año 1511, oficio 4, libro 4, Escribanía Manuel Segura, fol. 2465. 70; "Registros de naos correspondientes al tesorero Andrés de Haro," 1516–1517, AGI, Contaduría 1072, no. 1, ramo 3, fols. 381ʳ–91ᵛ (I thank David Wheat for sharing this reference with me); "Asunto: Alonso del Algaba," October 21, 1517, AHPS, signatura P-1518, libro del año 1517, oficio 3, libro 2, Escribanía Juan Ruiz de Porras, fols. 29ʳ–30ᵛ; "Compañía," February 19, 1509, AHPS, signatura P-2182, libro del año 1509, oficio 4, libro 1, Escribanía Manuel Segura, fol. 597. See also Ireton, "They Are."

[73] "Cristóbal De Castroverde," Archivo General de la Nación, México, GD61 Inquisición, vol. 310, exp. 7, fols. 32–32ᵛ.

as servants for different passengers on Atlantic crossings.[74] For example, in 1595, witnesses described how a free Black woman from the town of Panamá named Angelina Díaz had come to Castilla because "she is free and she serves whoever she wishes (*quien le parezca*) and she earns to eat in this way,"[75] while another witness explained how many women "similar to" Díaz came to Castilla on ships serving passengers for wages.[76] A third witness reported that "similar people to her [Díaz] have their trade and work (*granjería*) of coming [to Castilla] serving passengers on the ships who pay them and that she [Díaz] also came to earn her living as a *criada* and now it is necessary for her to return to her *natural* [Panamá]."[77] Some Black women who served as wage-earning servants on Atlantic crossings remained in Castilla for longer periods. Such was the case of a *mulata horra* named Isabel de Bustos, who had traveled to Castilla from Cartagena as a wage-earning servant at the turn of the seventeenth century, and who spent ten years residing in Sevilla prior to returning to Cartagena in 1612, this time embarking as a wage-earning servant for a different employer.[78]

DOCUMENTING AND DISCUSSING LIBERTY IN LATE SIXTEENTH-CENTURY SEVILLA

Black *horros*' engagement with the bureaucratization of petitions for passenger and embarkation licenses to cross the Atlantic in the second half of the sixteenth century has generated a rich archive that documents how liberated people sought to prove and protect their freedom through paperwork. Formerly enslaved Black individuals who sought coveted embarkation licenses at the House of Trade from the 1550s onwards tended to adopt a two-pronged approach to proving their freedom that relied on paperwork and witness testimony. After petitioning the Council of the Indies for a passenger license (or after having secured a potential employer who had a royal decree with permission to take servants), Black

---

[74] For select examples, see "Felipa Pérez," AGI, Indiferente 2105, no. 32; "Felipa Pérez," AGI, Contratación 5266, no. 1, ramo 59; "Dominga Díaz," AGI, Indiferente 2100, no. 3; "Dominga Díaz de Cea," AGI, Contratación 5245, no. 1, ramo 41; "Dominga Díaz de Sea," AGI, Contratación 5538, libro 3, fol. 207ᵛ; Galbis Díez, *Catálogo de Pasajeros*, vol. VII, 3254; "Isabel de Bustos," AGI, Contratación 5327, no. 83.
[75] "Angelina Díaz," AGI, Indiferente 2102, no. 166; "Angelina Díaz," AGI, Contratación 5251B, no. 2, ramo 42, fols. 2ʳ–2ᵛ.
[76] Ibid.
[77] Ibid.
[78] "Isabel de Bustos," AGI, Contratación 5327, no. 83. See also Coronado as discussed later in this chapter.

supplicants would attend the House of Trade in Sevilla and present an array of documents to prove their eligibility to travel to Americas, namely that they were not of the prohibited peoples and that they were free. The documents that Black *horros* presented to prove their freedom included notarized *cartas de alhorría* written by former owners, extracts of particular clauses in their owners' testaments that set out the terms of liberation, confirmation by a local royal official such as an *alcalde* or local judge of an individual's free status after manumission (and usually after provision of witness statements), a judgment in a Real Audiencia that confirmed an individual's freedom from slavery, or royal decrees issued after a Black supplicant's petition to the Council of the Indies or the Council of Castilla. In addition to presenting these documents, liberated Black petitioners would also bring three or four witnesses to the House of Trade who would attest to the petitioner's status as a liberated person.[79]

The following two Black *horras*, for example, applied for embarkation licenses at the House of Trade in Sevilla in the late sixteenth century. In 1592, twenty-four-year-old Lucía de Mendoza applied for an embarkation license to travel to Peru as a wage-earning servant.[80] Mendoza showed a copy of her 1574 *carta de alhorría* and she brought three witnesses who attested to her status as a free person.[81] Each witness assured that they had known Mendoza since she was a very young child in Sevilla and that her parents, Antón and Paula, were "Black people *atezados bozales* from Guinea," and described how Mendoza had been liberated in her owner's will fourteen years earlier.[82] Also in 1592, a Black *horra* from Sevilla named Juana Bautista, who was described as the daughter of "Black people from Guinea," sought an embarkation license to travel to Honduras as a wage-earning servant.[83] As supporting evidence to prove her freedom, Mendoza presented her *carta de alhorría* written by her former owner, in addition to three witnesses who also described her liberty.

Sevilla-based Black *horros* who petitioned for embarkation licenses often had varied social and economic ties across the city. This is evidenced by the parishes of residence of the witnesses who testified on behalf of a generation of free Black people who applied for such travel permits between 1569

---

[79] Fernández López, *La* Casa.
[80] "Lucía de Mendoza," AGI, Contratación 5240, no. 1, ramo 31.
[81] Ibid., fol. 3^r.
[82] Ibid., fols. 4^r–5^v.
[83] "Juana Bautista," AGI, Contratación 5237, no. 2, ramo 47, fols. 2^r–3^r, 4^r–5^r; "Juana Bautista," AGI, Contratación 5538, libro, 3, fol. 127^v; Galbis Díez, *Catálogo de Pasajeros*, vol. VII. Catalogo no. 2153.

and 1621, as illustrated in Figures C.1.1-2 (see Coda). People who served as their witnesses included friars, friends, former owners, neighbors, merchants, messengers (*correos*), members of the city nobility, pilots, priests, sailors, servants, shoemakers, slaves, tradespeople, and treasurers and other officials in the governing body of the city (*cabildo de Sevilla*). Witnesses also often resided in different parishes to the Black supplicants, reflecting the varied social relations that emerged across public and private spheres of the city. Labour arrangements and participation in commercial activities inevitably led to people's lives colliding on a regular basis, reflecting the common usage across witness testimonies of the following phrases to describe their relationships with Black supplicants: *trato y comúnicacion* (trade and communication); *los conoció y trató mucho tiempo* (met and traded with them over a long time); and *por el mucho trato y conversación que con ella y sus padres tuvo mucho tiempo* (the great trade and conversation that the witness had with the supplicant and her parents over a long time). Sometimes witnesses were Black residents of the city who lived in different parishes from the supplicant, and who testified to decades-long relationships with the petitioners across various ports and towns of the Spanish Atlantic. Such was the case of Catalina de Tapia's 1622 application for an embarkation license, when two free Black sisters named María and Barbola Ybarra testified to knowing Tapia from "sight, dealings, and communication" for thirty and forty years, respectively, in the cities of Santo Domingo, Cartagena de Indias, and Sevilla, and to knowing Tapia both as an enslaved Black woman and latterly as a free person (Figure C.1.1, nos. 12a–12c).[84]

City dwellers across the socioeconomic spectrums also partook in the soundscapes of cities where news flowed through whispers, songs, and conversations among friends and strangers. Individuals might hear or exchange news through word of mouth in public or domestic settings, through conversations in public squares and marketplaces, or from town criers in public squares who conveyed formal news. Ambivalent private spheres, especially in the lower and higher socioeconomic echelons of society, also led individuals to develop ties across the city. Economically precarious populations in cities in this period also ate, bathed, cooked, and washed clothes in a variety of communal or semiprivate spaces, sites that were often pregnant with murmurs, whispers, and conversations about daily life and comings and goings.[85] Those who endured

---

[84] "Catalina de Tapia," AGI, Contratación 5380, no. 41. fols. 2ʳ–3ʳ.
[85] "Cristóbal de Castroverde," AGN, México, GD61 Inquisición, vol. 310, exp. 7, fols. 41ʳ (538ʳ)–41ᵛ (538ᵛ).

life in the lower socioeconomic spectrums often experienced precarious residential arrangements, as they rented cheap rooms or beds wherever available and moved various times across the city over the course of their lives.[86] Relationships born through daily life among and between neighbours could transform into ties across different parishes of the city when the respective parties relocated owing to insecure housing.

The diversity of witnesses who testified on behalf of Black *horros* about their liberty at the House of Trade reveal everyday conversations about slavery and freedom on the streets of Sevilla. Witnesses would often assert Black supplicants' freedom by commenting on their reputation as free people, describing how an individual's liberty was common knowledge across the city. Other testimonies described precise moments of liberation from slavery. In 1570, Jerónima petitioned the Council of the Indies for a royal decree to travel to Peru to join her free Black husband, Pablo, who had left for Peru some years earlier.[87] To supplement her petition, on August 28, 1570, Jerónima asked three witnesses to attest to her history of liberation.[88] Her former owner's brother testified that Jerónima had been liberated from slavery and had been given her *carta de alhorría*, while a servant in her former owner's household explained that he knew that Jerónima was free because he had witnessed Jerónima obtaining her liberty and receiving her *carta de alhorría*. Finally, a Black slave named Felipe Ramos testified that he had known Jerónima for twelve years and had also attended her marriage vows. Ramos described how he knew that Jerónima was a free woman because "she is seen and treated like a free woman," while describing how he had also heard from others that Jerónima's former owner had liberated her from slavery. None of the witnesses elaborated on Jerónima's – or her husband Pablo's – Guinean *naturaleza*, nor the whereabouts of her parents. This silence about her parents suggests that Jerónima might have been enslaved in West Africa and forcibly displaced to Castilla.

Some witnesses' descriptions of a Black supplicants' reputation as a freeborn person stood at odds with their actual history of enslavement and liberation, as described in a *carta de alhorría*. Such inaccurate public opinion about an enslaved individual's status as a free person may point towards the Black supplicant having lived semiautonomously during a period of their enslavement. For example, María de la O was liberated at

---

[86] Ibid.
[87] "Jerónima," AGI, Indiferente 2084, no. 98. See also Figure C.1.1, nos. 2a–2d.
[88] Ibid., fols. 2^r–4^v.

the age of thirty six in her owner's testament in 1596 in San Salvador parish in Sevilla.[89] She sought an embarkation license to travel to Peru with her husband in 1600.[90] The couple arrived at the House of Trade with six witnesses who hailed from a diverse array of socioeconomic social milieus and who lived across five parishes of the city, ranging from a shoemaker from Santa Marina, to a member of Sevillian nobility named Doña Isabel Xuárez from San Vicente parish, and an agricultural laborer (*hortelano*) who was a resident in the economically precarious neighborhood of San Bernardo located outside the city walls (Figure C.1.1, nos. 10a–g).[91] Her six witnesses claimed that she had always been free because her parents were also free. Doña Isabel Xuárez stated that María de la O was "a free woman and not subject to any captivity and because of this she is treated (*avida y tenida*) as [free] because her parents were also free."[92] Diego de Morales testified that he had heard that "María de la O was born of a free womb," implying that she was free because her mother was a free woman.[93] These witnesses perceived María de la O as a freeborn woman, even though she had actually been enslaved during most of the time that they had known her. Perhaps their perceptions of her freedom stemmed from an arrangement between O and her owner that she could work as a slave-for-hire and operate as an independent laborer who would pay a proportion of her wages to her owner while living with her husband, whom she had married in 1586. Such an arrangement might explain why her six witnesses believed that she had always been free, even though only four years had elapsed between her liberation from slavery in 1596 and their witness testimonies in 1600.

Black *horros*' attempts to prove and document their status as free people before judges at the House of Trade stands in contrast to freeborn Black people who rarely presented physical documents to prove their liberty when applying for an embarkation license. This difference suggests that various visual and aural markers, beyond how officials racialized certain people as Black, may have alerted judges to a person's past status as an enslaved person. Such signals could include permanent scarring and markings on a petitioner's skin that betrayed a history of enslavement. Formerly enslaved Black people often lived with letters scarred and carved onto their faces and chests owing to slave merchants' and

---

[89] "María de la O," AGI, Contratación 5262A, no. 55, fol. 10^v.
[90] Ibid.
[91] Ibid., fols. 2^r–8^v. Figure C.1.1, nos. 10a–g.
[92] Ibid., fols. 2^r–8^v.
[93] Ibid.

slave-owners' practices of branding enslaved subjects' skin with scorching irons to engrave their initials on an enslaved person's body. For example, Margarita de Sossa, who was born enslaved in Porto (Portugal) and was later sold in Sevilla and forcibly displaced to New Spain, reportedly had "some letters on her face (*rostro*)" from when a former owner burned his initials on her skin to mark her status as a slave.[94] Similarly, a free *mulata* from Sevilla named Ana de Carvajal, who was the daughter of an enslaved Black woman from Guinea, reportedly had a "mark on the face on her right cheek," as described by one of her witnesses in 1576.[95] Similarly, a Black *horra* named Magdalena who resided in Sevilla described how she had an iron mark on her right chest in 1594, while in 1611, a thirty-four-year-old Black *horro* named Luis de Espinosa was described in his *carta de alhorría* as having a "scar of a wound below the left eyebrow."[96] On the other side of the Atlantic in 1594, a notary in Mexico City described a Black woman named Catalina from the land of *Zape* as having letters marked on her face that spelled the name "Maestro de Roa," while in 1614, a free *mulato* merchant named Sebastián Barroso in Cartagena de Indias described how an enslaved Black man from Upper Guinea had a "mark of fire on his chest."[97] Other signals of a history of enslavement might include aural markers, such as a supplicant's register of speech, accent, or linguistic dexterity in the Spanish language.[98] These physical and sonic markers of slavery may have provoked judges at the House of Trade or those assisting petitioners with their paperwork to inscribe a history of enslavement and informally request that formerly enslaved Black supplicants provide their freedom papers.[99]

In contrast, freeborn Black people from Sevilla rarely provided any physical proof of their freedom when requesting embarkation licenses. They may have donned visual markers of freedom. For example, they

---

[94] "Margarita Sossa," AGN, México, GD61 Inquisición, vol. 208, exp. 3, fols. 31–32.
[95] "Ana de Carvajal," AGI, Contratación 5225A, no. 1, ramo 35.
[96] "Magdalena," AGI, Contratación 5252, no. 1, ramo 11; "Luis de Espinosa," AGI, Contratación 5323, no. 53.
[97] "Alhorría," in Mijares *Catálogo de Protocolos del Archivo General de Notarías de la Ciudad de México, Fondo Siglo XVI* (hereafter Mijares *CPAGNXVI*), Protocolos Notariales, "Luis de Basurto" (Escribano real), México, January 21, 1594, Notaría 1, vol. 20, foliación 1 177–180 (89–90ᵛ), foliación 2 92–93ᵛ. Ficha 99; "Francisco Martín," AGN, SC, NE 43, legajo 13, doc. 9, fols. 27ʳ–36ᵛ.
[98] For scholarship on soundscapes in Black Atlantic, see note 40 in Introduction.
[99] For an example of an authority judging someone to be enslaved based on branding, see Fernández Chaves, "Amas, esclavas, y libertad," and Pérez García, "Matrimonio, Vida Familiar."

may have appeared at the House of Trade wearing fine clothing, such as cloaks and silks, and expensive jewelry.[100] Occasionally, Black *horros* did not need to prove their freedom through paperwork at the House of Trade, as credible witness testimony and the appearance of social standing sufficed. For example, a free Black man named Francisco González petitioned the Council of the Indies on two occasions for a passenger license to move to New Spain with his free Black wife in 1569 and 1577.[101] In his second petition, González suggested that he had been formerly enslaved and that he was an *horro*, as he described how he had been "free for many years and *vecino* of the city of Sevilla."[102] In spite of González's claim that he would prove that he had been free for many years, he did not present any paperwork that documented his freedom. Instead, three sailors and men of the sea, who served as his witnesses at the House of Trade in 1569 and three others who testified a decade later in 1577, merely confirmed that he was a free wage-earning Black mariner and a celebrated diver who criss-crossed the Atlantic employed on ships, that he was married to a free Black woman named Juana Rodríguez in Sevilla, and that they were both *vecinos* of Sevilla.[103]

GENERATING AND PROTECTING FREEDOM PAPERS

The bureaucratic processes that the crown established for petitions for passenger and embarkation licenses from the mid-sixteenth century onwards have resulted in the archiving of varied strategies deployed by Black *horros* to safeguard their liberty by generating new and confirmatory freedom papers. With a *carta de alhorría* in hand that spelled out their liberation from slavery, some sought to bolster the authority of this document by generating additional freedom papers. Most commonly, this would involve gathering witnesses before a public notary to swear that the individual was a free person. The notary would then issue a new *escritura* attesting to the *horro's* freedom. This practice responded to the

---

[100] On clothing as expressions of freedom, see Dawson, "The Cultural"; Walker, *Exquisite Slaves*. For an example of clothing shaping perceptions of freedom, see "Diego Suárez," AGI, Contratación 255, no. 1, ramo 5.

[101] "Francisco González," AGI, Indiferente 2052, no. 14; "Francisco González," AGI, Indiferente 2058, no. 6; "Francisco González," AGI, Contratación 5538, libro I, fol. 427ᵛ; "Francisco González," AGI, Indiferente 1968, libro 21, fol. 131ᵛ; "Francisco González," AGI, Contaduría 241, no. 117.

[102] "Francisco González," AGI, Indiferente 2058, no. 6, fol. 2ʳ: "*digo que yo soy libre muchos años y que soy vecino de esta ciudad de Sevilla.*"

[103] Ibid. See also Figure C.1.1, nos. 1a–1g.

importance placed on witness testimony in the Spanish empire, or, as Gonzalbo Aizpuru describes the phenomena of *"testigos memoriosos,"* whereby individuals with higher social capital, social standing, or honor in the community were more likely to have the social cache to enlist witnesses from their community who could attest to their status.[104] While formerly enslaved Black supplicants for embarkation licenses regularly leant on other Sevillians to testify about their freedom at the House of Trade, such testimonies did not necessarily generate paperwork that the supplicant could keep on their person and use at a later date. Rather, scribes at the House of Trade transformed oral witness testimonies into paperwork destined for the archives of the House of Trade or the Council of the Indies. Many formerly enslaved Black people chose the more secure route of employing the services of a public notary in Sevilla to document witness testimony about their freedom and therefore ensure that they could keep a copy of the notarized statements on their person. They would ask their friends, neighbors, and acquaintances to provide sworn statements before a public notary about the supplicants' freedom. This was the course of action taken by Magdalena in 1590 when she gathered witnesses before a Sevilla notary to testify about her status as a liberated Black woman, six years before she eventually requested an embarkation license at the House of Trade in 1596.[105]

Black *horros* who had notarized witness testimonies about their liberation from slavery in Sevilla or elsewhere would present this physical document – that they had generated and that affirmed their freedom – as evidence of their freedom in a petition to the Council of the Indies for a passenger license or at the House of Trade for an embarkation license. Arriving at the House of Trade with notarized witness statements was not unusual as passengers who were *naturales* of regions beyond Sevilla had to compile a notarized *escritura* of witness statements about their biography in the places in Castilla where they were born or resided. Nonetheless this preemptive act by Black *horros* in Sevilla to notarize witness testimonies about their freedom highlights one way in which *horros* invested in a legal culture of paperwork to generate a supplementary set of freedom papers.

As a further measure, some formerly enslaved Black people would take the copy of these sworn testimonies and their *carta de alhorría* to request that a royally appointed chief justice of a city, often known as an *alcalde, alcalde ordinario, asistente, corregidor,* or *governador,* or their

---

[104] Gonzalbo Aizpuru, "La trampa."
[105] "Magdalena," AGI, Contratación 5252, no. 1, ramo 11.

deputies (*tenientes*), issue a certificate confirming the petitioner's freedom. An example of this effort to generate additional freedom papers is the aforementioned case of Antón Segarra, who invested significant resources to create a trail of freedom papers that would assure his legal status as a free man before he crossed the Atlantic from Sevilla to New Spain at the turn of the seventeenth century.[106] Within three months of obtaining his *carta de alhorría* and anticipating that he might travel to other regions of the Spanish empire, on February 3, 1603, Segarra petitioned the *teniente* (deputy) of the *Asistente de Sevilla* (a role similar to *alcalde* or *corregidor* in other cities, and appointed by the king to oversee matters of civil justice and to supersede the authority of the city *cabildo*), doctor Alonso de Liévana, to confirm his status as a free man.[107] Segarra was not unique in requesting that a *teniente* of the *asistente de Sevilla* confirm his freedom papers, as the aforementioned Jerónima had petitioned the same figure to confirm her freedom thirty years earlier.[108]

Segarra explained in his petition that he wished to protect his freedom anywhere that he might be in the present or the future, both within and outside Castilla, as he wished to "protect my right and wherever in these kingdoms that I might be or where I might go that my freedom be proved and that no conditions be imposed and that I can freely use my liberty."[109] Segarra requested that the *teniente* of the *asistente* review his *carta de alhorría* issued in the town of Écija and receive witness testimonies from people in Sevilla about his freedom.[110] For his witnesses, Segarra chose three servants who labored in the Sevilla-household where he had previously stayed with his former owner.[111] In the process of eliciting and notarizing witness testimonies about his freedom and requesting that the city authority confirm his freedom so that he could "freely use my liberty ... wherever in these kingdoms that I might be," Segarra generated new paperwork in the form of a four-folio notarized document that affirmed the most important document of his life, his *carta de alhorría*.

---

[106] "Antonio Segarra," AGI, Contratación 303, no. 2, fols. 11ᵛ–13ʳ.
[107] For replication of the Asistente de Sevilla position in the governance of America colonies, see Hampe Martínez, "Esbozo." See also "Cédula," Archivo General de Simancas, PTR, LEG, 87, 38; "Cédula," Archivo General de Simancas, PTR, LEG, 87, 39; "Real Cédula," AGI, Indiferente 427, libro 31, fols. 185r–185ᵛ; "Real Cédula," AGI, Indiferente 427, libro 31, fols. 184ᵛ–185ʳ.
[108] "Jerónima," AGI, Indiferente 2084, no. 98.
[109] "Antonio Segarra," AGI, Contratación 303, no. 2, fols. 11ᵛ–13ʳ. Antón Segarra's cache of freedom papers are transcribed in Ireton and Álvarez Hernández, "Epístolas."
[110] Ibid.
[111] For analysis of these witness testimonies, see Chapter 2.

Segarra crossed the Atlantic to New Spain a few months later as a wage-earning servant for a Dominican friar armed with both his *carta de alhorría* and the certified document that contained the witness statements and the pronouncement of his liberty by the city authority in Sevilla. Segarra spent six years living in the port town of Veracruz, where he eventually became an independent laborer; he rented a small parcel of land and owned some livestock.[112] Throughout these years, Segarra safeguarded these documents, along with two letters that he received from his enslaved Black wife, and a record of his sacraments of confession in a box of papers in his residence in Veracruz.[113] In 1609, Antón Segarra suffered a fatal stab wound. Royal officials who inventoried his belongings found a locked "old box with old papers" that contained his treasured freedom papers. These documents revealed Segarra's long history of enslavement and delayed liberation from slavery in Castilla, and the history of how he invested time and resources to certify his freedom papers in Sevilla prior to his journey across the Atlantic.[114]

Such attempts to generate confirmatory freedom papers through city officials were especially common for those who resided or were liberated from slavery in towns outside Sevilla. For example, prior to embarking to Peru as a wage-earning servant in 1579, thirty-five-year-old Isabel de Flandes requested that the *alcalde* of the town of Lepe in Huelva certify her freedom.[115] Flandes specifically requested that the *alcalde* issue a document certifying her freedom that contained notarized transcriptions of the testimonies of four witnesses and that he ensure that his document be valid wherever she may be so that she could prove her freedom elsewhere.[116] Her witnesses were *vecinos* of Lepe who hailed from a variety of social strata, including a Presbyterian priest.[117] The witnesses described how Isabel de Flandes was born enslaved as the daughter of "Antón and Beatris, Black people from Guinea," and explained that they knew that Isabel de Flandes "is free and free of all subjection and captivity and servitude and that she is a free woman" because they had known her since she was born and had often conversed with Flandes and her parents over the previous

---

[112] Ibid.
[113] Ibid., fols. 10ʳ, 18ᵛ–20ᵛ.
[114] "Antonio Segarra," AGI, Contratación 303, no. 2, fols. 10ʳ, 18ᵛ–20ᵛ.
[115] "Isabel de Flandes," AGI, Contratación 5227, no. 2, ramo 36.
[116] Ibid., fol. 3ᵛ: "*ynterponga su autoridad y decreto judicial para que valga y haga fee y juysio fuera del [donde] quiera que pareciere para lo qual.*"
[117] Ibid., fols. 3ᵛ–7ᵛ.

thirty-five years.[118] In response, the *alcalde* of Lepe issued Flandes with a thirteen-folio document that certified her freedom and included the transcriptions of witness testimonies and the copy of the undated clause from her former owner's testament that set out the terms of her liberation from slavery. Flandes presented this document as proof of her freedom to the House of Trade when requesting an embarkation license to travel to Peru in 1579 as a wage-earning servant.[119]

Such strategies to create supplementary freedom papers were not limited to those seeking embarkation licenses at the House of Trade. Black *horros* engaged in similar practices across the Spanish empire, especially when poised to embark on lengthy journeys. For example, in 1577, a Black *horra* named Ana de Jesús appeared before the *alcalde ordinario* of the *cabildo* of Lima in Peru to request that he certify her *carta de alhorría*.[120] Her freedom certificate documented how Jesús had liberated herself from slavery through a *rescate* thirteen years earlier in the city of Sevilla by paying the price of her freedom to the nuns of the Monastery of Jesus in that city. In the interim, Jesús had crossed the Atlantic in 1569, and had shown her *carta de alhorría* to inspectors on the ship.[121] Ana de Jesús likely spent the subsequent decade residing in the viceregal capital of Lima, until 1577, when she prepared for a journey to the silver boomtown of Potosí, located over 2,000 km away from Lima.[122] The wording of Jesús' petition to the *alcalde ordinario* in Lima reveals how she sought to protect her treasured freedom certificate from any dangers during the lengthy journey ahead, explaining how "because she was on the journey to the town of Potosí, and she had her *carta de libertad*, and she could lose it," she wished for the *alcalde ordinario* to review her freedom certificate and make a copy of the document before a public notary in Lima.[123] By copying the document with a notary, Jesús ensured that her treasured document would be archived in Lima should the original be misplaced.

Black *horros* such as Antón Segarra, Isabel de Flandes, and Ana de Jesús, sought every means possible to document and protect their

---

[118] Ibid.
[119] "Isabel de Flandes," AGI, Contratación 5538, libro 1, fol. 197ᵛ.
[120] "Ana de Jesús," Archivo General de la Nación, Peru (hereafter AGNP), Notarias, 1 CYH1, 28, 70, fols. 103–106.
[121] "Ana de Jesús," AGI, Contratación 5537, libro 3, fol. 299ᵛ.
[122] "Ana de Jesús," AGNP, Notarias, 1 CYH1, 28,70, fols. 103–106.
[123] Ibid.: "*dado que ella estaba de camino para la villa de Potosi, y que ella tenya su carta de libertad y podria se le perder.*"

freedom.[124] They understood the enduring power of paperwork in the Spanish empire, and invested significant resources and time to certify and copy their freedom certificates with city and town authorities, hoping that these supplementary documents would bolster the original one, or serve as a protection in the event that they misplaced their freedom certificate or that they were illegitimately enslaved. In doing so, they also generated new documents that they could keep on their person throughout their lives.

Other Black *horros* who petitioned for embarkation licenses sought to generate additional freedom papers through their interactions with the bureaucratic procedures at the House of Trade. For example, a Black *horra* named Lorenza de Valladolid, whose owner had promised that he would liberate Valladolid and her son if they accompanied him on a voyage from Lima to Castilla, sought an embarkation license in 1611.[125] She appeared at the House of Trade with her young son, along with three witnesses who were residents of Sevilla. They attested that Valladolid was a free liberated woman, as she and her son had been promised their liberty on the condition that she serve her owner on the Atlantic crossing to Sevilla.[126] Knowing the importance of possessing physical copies of freedom papers that would attest to and assure her freedom throughout the Spanish empire, Valladolid requested that the scribe copy her freedom certificate and return the original document to her. She pled that "a copy be made of my *carta de libertad* and that the original be returned to me."[127] Valladolid also insisted that the scribe issue a second document attesting that she had shown the House of Trade her treasured freedom certificate.[128] These requests show that Valladolid understood the importance of paperwork – and her possession of physical documents – to safeguard her freedom. She hoped to enter the House of Trade with one document attesting to her freedom, her *carta de alhorría*, and leave with two. However, perhaps owing to the economic precarity that she

---

[124] "Antonio Segarra," AGI, Contratación 303, no. 2. "Isabel de Flandes," AGI, Contratación 5227, no. 2, ramo 36. See also "Jerónima," AGI, Indiferente 2084, no. 98.

[125] "Lorenza de Valladolid," AGI, Contratación 5323, no. 54. For other enslaved women who were brought to Castilla and then liberated from slavery, see "Catalina," AGI, Contratación 5401, no. 23, and "Leonor de Espinosa," AGI, Indiferente 2093, no. 181. For evidence of this practice in notarial records, see Fernández Chaves, "Amas, esclavas, y libertad."

[126] "Lorenza de Valladolid," AGI, Contratación 5323, no. 54, fols. 1^v–3^r.

[127] Ibid., fol. 1^r.

[128] Ibid., fol. 1^r.

was experiencing, Valladolid had not yet petitioned the Council of the Indies for a passenger license. The surviving documents are ambivalent as to whether judges granted Valladolid permission to embark to Lima without a royal decree or whether Valladolid subsequently obtained a royal decree.

Lorenza de Valladolid was one of many Black *horros* who were *naturales* of the Americas and who had been brought to Castilla as enslaved people by their owners before being liberated from slavery.[129] Black individuals who were *naturales* of the Spanish Americas and who were liberated from slavery in Castilla were highly vulnerable to abuse in due process, as they often lacked sufficient community ties in Castilla or resources to mount a legal defense when facing injustices. For example, Gaspar Juan was critically aware of the vulnerabilities of being a recently liberated person far from his birthplace.[130] He had been born in Santo Domingo and brought to Sevilla as a slave in the 1570s. Juan had been freed in his owner's testament, but his owner's heirs had reportedly refused to honour the liberation clause and continued to subject him to enslavement. Juan took his plight for justice from illegitimate enslavement to the highest royal court of the city, the Real Audiencia in Sevilla, where he instigated a petition against his owners' heirs.[131] The court ruled in Juan's favor in 1584, declaring him a free man as long as he paid *treinta ducados* to his owner's heirs.

Although Juan's freedom was conferred by the royal court in 1584, he did not return to Santo Domingo until 1598. In the intervening fourteen years, Juan established life in Sevilla as a free Black man. In this time, he developed relationships with other city dwellers whom he would rely on in his subsequent petition for an embarkation license to cross the Atlantic. During those years, Juan had collected an array of paperwork that constituted his cache of freedom papers. When Juan requested an embarkation license at the House of Trade in 1594, he presented his owner's testament, his freedom certificate, the record of his petition to the Real Audiencia of Sevilla, and the result of judges' deliberations on his case, in addition to calling on a host of witnesses who attested to the facts of the case heard by the Real Audiencia and his status as a free

---

[129] "Faustina," AGI, Contratación 5260B, no. 1, ramo 44; "Faustina," AGI, Contratación 5538, libro III, 50–53^v (see also Galbis Díez, *Catálogo de Pasajeros*, vol. VII. no. 5.368); "María de Cota," AGI, Contratación 5222, no. 4, ramo 70; "María de Cota," AGI, Indiferente 2060, no. 10.
[130] "Gaspar Juan," AGI, Contratación 5248, no. 1, ramo 17.
[131] Ibid., fols. 3^r–7^v.

man in Sevilla.[132] Juan subsequently boarded a ship destined to Santo Domingo on May 11, 1594.[133]

Black individuals from the Spanish Americas who were born free sometimes generated certificates of their *vecindad* and freedom before an impending departure to another region of the Spanish imperial realms. These precautions stemmed from their understanding of the vulnerability of leaving a place where they were known as free people to travel to regions where they may lack sufficient community ties to prove their status as freeborn people. For example, a Black man named Pero Hernández crossed the ocean with his Indigenous wife and four children for unspecified business matters in the 1550s. Prior to his voyage, Hernández took preventative measures in Mexico City to protect his freedom by generating freedom papers. In 1538, Hernández had requested that the *cabildo* of Mexico City issue a certificate of his *vecindad* in the city, which confirmed that he was a free man and a *vecino* who enjoyed the same freedoms and privileges of other *vecinos* of the city.[134] Pero Hernández crossed the Atlantic with his wife and four children in possession of this physical document issued by the *cabildo* in Mexico City, anticipating that he would require such proof of freedom when requesting a license to return to New Spain. Just four months after arriving in Castilla, Pero Hernández sent a petition to the Council of the Indies requesting a passenger license to return to New Spain, and presented this document and witness testimony at the House of Trade in 1556.[135] A Black *horro* named Sebastián de Toral obtained a similar certificate of *vecindad* by petitioning the *alcalde* of Mérida (Yucatán, New Spain) on January 21, 1568. He also drew on this certificate of *vecindad* a decade later when he crossed the ocean to Madrid in 1577 to present a petition to the Council of the Indies, and when he subsequently requested an embarkation license at the House of Trade.[136]

Free Black women from the Spanish Americas who embarked on Atlantic voyages as wage-earning servants sometimes also sought confirmatory documents of their *vecindad* and status as freeborn people. For example, a fourteen-year-old Black woman named Melchora de los Reyes from the port of Veracruz obtained two different types of documents in New Spain that confirmed her freedom prior to embarking on a voyage

---

[132] Ibid., fols. 1^r–7^v.
[133] "Gaspar Juan," AGI, Contratación 5538, libro 3, fol. 230.
[134] "Pero Hernández," AGI, Indiferente 2049, no. 54, fols. 2^v–3^r.
[135] "Pero Hernández," AGI, Indiferente 2049, no. 54.
[136] "Sebastián de Toral," AGI, Indiferente 2059, no. 108, fol. 3^v.

Proving Freedom

to Castilla as a wage-earning servant.[137] In 1583, Melchora de los Reyes requested that the Holy Office of the Inquisition in Mexico City issue a certificate to confirm her freedom and that she had not been punished for any crimes against the Catholic faith.[138] She subsequently requested that the royal office of *Real Hacienda* in the port of Veracruz issue a second document stating that she was a free woman who was permitted to travel to Castilla as a wage-earning servant.[139] Melchora de los Reyes crossed the Atlantic as the servant of a Sevilla-native *boticario* (trader of medicinal drugs) named Baltasar Ruíz who resided in the port of Veracruz. The retinue of Baltasar Ruíz's servants who departed Veracruz in 1583 also included Melchora de los Reyes' mother, who was a Black woman named Juana Ruíz (Díaz), a young Black boy named Diego, and a young Black *vecina* of Veracruz named Magdalena de Coronado who had been born in Mexico City.[140] Magdalena de Coronado had also sought to assure her freedom prior to her voyage, but had built a different set of documentary evidence. In Veracruz, Coronado had gathered witnesses before a public notary to attest to her freedom and then presented these to the office of the *Real Hacienda* when her employer sought a license to travel and take wage-earning servants to Castilla.[141] One of the witnesses was a merchant who testified to having known Coronado for fifteen years, and described that he knew that Coronado was a free Black woman who lived in a house in Veracruz with her mother and sisters, while another *vecino* of Veracruz testified to knowing Coronado for ten years as a free woman in the town.[142] Melchora de los Reyes and Magdalena de Coronado therefore gathered various certificates attesting to their status as freeborn Black women and *vecinas* prior to embarking on an Atlantic voyage as servants of the same employer.

These Black women – Melchora de los Reyes and Magdalena de Coronado – who served in Baltasar Ruíz's retinue on the 1583 voyage from Veracruz to Sevilla, drew on these freedom papers in the following years as they traversed the Atlantic. The next year, in 1584, Baltasar Ruíz petitioned the Council of the Indies for a license to return to Veracruz from Castilla with his servant, Magdalena de Coronado, who by that

---

[137] "Melchora de los Reyes," AGI, Indiferente 2065, no. 60.
[138] Ibid., fols. 2^r–2^v.
[139] Ibid.
[140] Ibid. "Magdalena de Coronado," AGI, Indiferente 2061, no. 134 (fol. 2: "*Un negrillo nombrado Diego*"); "Magdalena Coronado," AGI, Indiferente 1952, libro 2, fol. 208.
[141] "Magdalena de Coronado," AGI, Indiferente 2061, no. 134, fols. 3^r–5^v.
[142] "Melchora de los Reyes," AGI, Indiferente 2065, no. 60.

time had given birth to a daughter.[143] Coronado presented the freedom papers that she had generated in New Spain to support her petition.[144] Neither Melchora de los Reyes, nor her mother Juana Díaz, nor the young Black boy named Diego appeared in the documentation pertaining to that return voyage. Instead, Melchora de los Reyes established residency in Sevilla after the 1583 Atlantic crossing. Seven years later, in 1590, Melchora de los Reyes petitioned the Council of the Indies for a passenger license to return to Veracruz and presented a string of paperwork to prove her freedom, which included the two certificates of her freedom that she had obtained in New Spain seven years earlier.[145] Within two months of obtaining a royal decree in her name, Melchora de los Reyes took two witnesses to the House of Trade in Sevilla to request an embarkation license on July 3, 1590.[146] Her witnesses claimed to have known Melchora de los Reyes on both sides of the Atlantic in the ports of Veracruz and Sevilla.

Pero Hernández, Sebastián de Toral, Melchora de los Reyes, and Magdalena de Coronado's calculated actions to collect confirmatory paperwork of their freedom from city authorities in New Spain on the eve of their departures from the viceroyalty highlights how formerly enslaved and freeborn Black people in the Spanish Atlantic world valued paperwork. This was especially so for those who were leaving the sites where they were known by a community as free people and who were unsure whether they would have sufficient networks and ties to rely on witness testimony in other sites when requesting a license to return to their places of *naturaleza*.

Formerly enslaved Black people also invested in generating trails of paperwork to prove and assure their freedom when original documents, such as *cartas de alhorría*, were irretrievable. The following case of a Black woman who tragically lost her freedom papers on a ship shows the importance of this practice. Onboard a ship sailing from Sevilla to Tavira in Portugal, a free Black woman named María Gómez lost her most valuable possession, her freedom papers.[147] Arriving in Tavira in 1572, she gathered four witnesses from the ship to confirm that she had indeed been in possession of her freedom papers and that she had lost them on the voyage.[148] María Gómez was a free Black woman from the island of Santiago in the

---

[143] "Magdalena de Coronado," AGI, Indiferente 2061, no. 134, fols. 3^r–5^v.
[144] Ibid.
[145] "Melchora de los Reyes," AGI, Indiferente 2065, no. 60.
[146] "Melchora de los Reyes," AGI, Contratación 5232, no. 25.
[147] "María Gómez," AGI, Contratación 5226, no. 2, ramo 28, fols. 1^v, 5^r–6^v.
[148] Ibid.

West African archipelago of Cabo Verde. Vasco Fernández, a mariner and resident of Tavira, attested that María Gómez had lost her freedom papers on a ship from Sevilla to Tavira, while Jorge Viegas, a merchant who also hailed from the island of Santiago in the Cabo Verde archipelago, stated that he knew María Gómez from Cabo Verde and that he was aware that María Gómez had come to Castilla with her *carta de alhorría* and had subsequently lost the precious document during her return journey.[149] These hastily gathered witness statements in the port of Tavira in 1572 after a turbulent journey that described how María Gómez had lost her freedom papers on the ship, became her de facto freedom papers.

These de facto freedom papers were the evidentiary centerpiece of María Gómez's liberty in her application for an embarkation license five years later in the House of Trade. María Gómez did not return to Cabo Verde from Tavira in 1572 after she lost her freedom papers. Instead, she reappeared in Sevilla five years later, when she applied for an embarkation license to travel to Nicaragua as the wage-earning servant of the newly-appointed treasurer of the region.[150] In 1577, María Gómez was one of four wage-earning servants to travel in the treasurer's retinue, along with another free Black woman named Inés Díaz.[151] The Passenger Lists described Gómez as, "María Gómez Black, *natural* of Cabo Verde, Black *atezada*."[152] To support her petition for an embarkation license, María Gómez presented copies of the notarized witness testimonies that she had gathered in 1572 in Tavira to attest that she had been in possession of her *carta de alhorría* before losing it.[153] She also brought witnesses who were residents of Sevilla.[154] Her witnesses attested to having known Gómez for approximately ten years in Sevilla and to knowing that she had been born in Guinea (as opposed to Cabo Verde), where she had been brought up by her parents and with her sister. They explained that they knew that María Gómez was free from captivity because they had seen her living with her liberty in Sevilla, a description that implied that Gómez had some agency as a free Black woman over her employment and life in Sevilla. Gómez's efforts in Tavira to generate new paperwork that attested to the physical existence – and subsequent loss – of her freedom papers by transforming

---

[149] "María Gómez," AGI, Contratación 5226, no. 2, ramo 28, fols. 1ᵛ, 5ʳ–6ᵛ.
[150] "Juan Moreno Alvarez de Toledo," AGI, Contratación 5792, libro 1, fols. 198–199.
[151] "Alonso Dorta, María Gómez, Inés Díaz, and Sebastián de Herrera," AGI, Contratación 5226, no. 2, Ramos, 27–30.
[152] "María Gómez," AGI, Contratación 5538, libro 1, fol. 10ᵛ ⁽⁸⁾.
[153] "María Gómez," AGI, Contratación 5226, no. 2, ramo 28, fols. 1ᵛ, 5ʳ–6ᵛ.
[154] Ibid., fols. 2ʳ–3ʳ.

witness statements into physical pieces of paper thus had the effect of serving as her new de facto freedom papers when she subsequently applied for a license to cross the Atlantic to the Americas. In addition, María Gómez was able to develop sufficient ties in Sevilla to call on residents to testify about her status as a free Black woman from Cabo Verde.[155]

Another strategy for developing new trails of freedom papers involved petitioning the Council of the Indies to confirm the petitioner's status as a free person while requesting a passenger license. Such *horros* either sought to prove their freedom in this superior court because they were already in Madrid or because they calculated that a royal decree confirming their freedom would assure their liberty in the eyes of judges at the House of Trade when seeking an embarkation license.[156] Owing to this practice, some royal decrees instructed judges at the House of Trade to issue embarkation licenses to specific Black men and women without obliging these passengers to provide any detailed information about themselves because they had already proven their freedom in the courts in Madrid. Black individuals often kept copies of these royal decrees on their person and presented them directly to the House of Trade. In other instances, House of Trade officials already had access to a particular royal decree that the Council of the Indies had sent directly to the institution.

Two examples of formerly enslaved Black supplicants who proved their freedom when petitioning for a passenger license at the Council of the Indies are the cases of Ana Díaz and the aforementioned Catalina de Tapia.[157] These two Black women may have been at the royal court in Madrid contemporaneously as they obtained royal decrees within a year of each other. In the first instance, in March 1620, a royal decree noted that a Black woman named Ana Díaz and her eight-year-old *mulata* daughter named Beatriz had appeared in person at the Council of the Indies, and had proven that they were free and had come from New Spain as wage-earning servants.[158] Whether Ana Díaz proved her freedom to the court by presenting copies of her freedom papers or through her own testimony is unclear. The decree granted mother and daughter permission to return to New Spain and instructed the judges at the House

---

[155] For further analysis of María Gómez's case, see Chapter 2. See also Figure C.1.1 4a–4c.
[156] "Domingo de Zúñiga," AGI, Indiferente 2054, no. 43; "Francisco Zape," AGI, Indiferente 2094, no. 144; "Elena Méndez," AGI, Indiferente 2064, no. 135.
[157] "Ana Díaz," AGI, Contratación 5370, no. 30; "Ana Díaz," AGI, Indiferente 1978, fol. 16; "Catalina de Tapia," AGI, Contratación 5380, no. 41; "Catalina de Tapia," AGI, Indiferente 1978, fol. 16.
[158] "Ana Díaz," AGI, Contratación 5370, no. 30.

Proving Freedom 63

of Trade not to request any further information from them, except to establish that they were the same people as those named in the decree. Lacking witnesses in Sevilla who could confirm her identity, Ana Díaz instead generated paperwork in Madrid that would prove that she and her daughter were the same people as those named in the royal decree. Díaz leant on a resident of Madrid who was present at the royal court to testify about their biography before a public notary in Madrid.[159] With this notarized document containing the testimony proving her biography and the royal decree with a passenger license, Ana Díaz and her daughter Beatriz appeared in the House of Trade, and the judges granted them an embarkation license without asking any further questions about their status as free people.[160]

The following year, Catalina de Tapia also savvily bolstered the power of her *carta de alhorría* and generated a second set of freedom papers by petitioning the Council of the Indies.[161] Catalina de Tapia had been born into slavery in Santo Domingo (Isla Española) in approximately 1572. In her mid-thirties, Tapia likely became the subject of a sale transaction that forcibly displaced her from Santo Domingo to Cartagena de Indias. There, at the turn of the seventeenth century, Tapia found herself dwelling in one of the highest-volume slave-trading ports of the early seventeenth-century Atlantic world toiling as a domestic slave to Alonso de Tapia y Cáceres, the treasurer (*contador*) of the city.[162] In 1618, after living in Cartagena for a decade, Catalina de Tapia crossed the Atlantic to Sevilla. Whether she obtained her freedom in Cartagena de Indias and subsequently traveled to Sevilla as a free woman, or whether Alonso de Tapia – who was a native of Castilla – forcibly displaced his slave to Sevilla and later liberated her in that city remains unclear. However, by 1621 – three years after her arrival in Sevilla and by then fifty-years old – Tapia was a free woman.

Catalina de Tapia petitioned the Council of the Indies sometime before March 1621 for a passenger license to return to Santo Domingo owing to the poverty that she was experiencing in Castilla. In her petition, Tapia presented her *carta de alhorría* to prove her freedom and received a royal decree that confirmed her status as a free Black woman. The decree explained that Tapia had presented freedom papers at the royal court, "as it [Tapia's freedom] is proven through an *escritura* of freedom that she

---

[159] Ibid., fols. 2ʳ–7ʳ.
[160] Ibid., fol. 1ʳ.
[161] "Catalina de Tapia," AGI, Contratación 5380, no. 41.
[162] "Alonso de Tapia, contador de Cartagena de Indias," AGI, Contratación 5792, libro 2, fols. 61ᵛ–62.

presented."¹⁶³ The royal decree granted Tapia permission to travel to her place of *naturaleza*, Santo Domingo, and stipulated that judges at Sevilla's House of Trade should only establish Tapia's biography and not her religious lineage or freedom.¹⁶⁴ Tapia therefore assured her freedom in the eyes of judges at the House of Trade by generating freedom papers that had been confirmed by the Council of the Indies. This royal decree also became the evidentiary centerpiece of her freedom in her 1621 petition for an embarkation license, as Tapia did not present a *carta de alhorría* within her application at the House of Trade, instead relying on the aforementioned two free Black sisters, María and Barbola Ybarra, who testified to knowing and communicating with Tapia in each of the sites where she had previously dwelt as both an enslaved subject and latterly as a free person.

CONCLUSION

Black *horros* in the sixteenth-century Spanish empire often invested time and resources in legal cultures of paperwork to protect and safeguard their *carta de alhorría* after they were liberated from slavery. Free Black people's interactions with the bureaucratic processes for travel permits in the sixteenth century reveal their strategies to protect and assure their freedom through an engagement with cultures of paperwork. Black *horros* were aware of the importance of safekeeping their *carta de alhorría*, and, where possible, sought to bolster their freedom certificate by investing resources to generate additional and supplementary paperwork that confirmed their status as free people. This history of Black *horros'* engagement with juridical cultures of paperwork is often difficult to trace as different archives hold fragmentary clues. However, the archive of petitions for embarkation and passenger licenses to cross the Atlantic reveals an unexplored history of free Black migration in this period, as well as a rare snapshot of how hundreds of Black *horros* invested significant resources to protect their liberty, especially by generating additional and supplementary freedom papers that they could keep on their person throughout their lives.

[163] "Catalina de Tapia," AGI, Contratación 5380, no. 41, fol. 3ᵛ.
[164] Ibid.

2

Imagining Freedom

Black Atlantic Communities in Sevilla

Felipa de la Cruz spent her whole life hoping to be liberated from slavery and imagining freedom.[1] Cruz grew up enslaved in a prominent household in late sixteenth-century Sevilla, where she met and married the aforementioned enslaved Black man named Antón Segarra. In 1602, Cruz witnessed how her husband was liberated from slavery and his subsequent departure from Sevilla to New Spain as a wage-earning servant for a Dominican friar. Together they had two children, who were also enslaved to Cruz's owner, following Castilian laws of slavery that determined that children inherited their mother's enslaved legal status.[2] During Segarra's absence, Cruz penned two letters to her husband that she sent to his place of dwelling in the port of Veracruz through a network of trusted messengers in 1604 and 1608. Laced with the emotional pain and heartache of missing her loved and adored husband, Cruz also kept her spouse informed about news of their children, friends, neighbors, and members of the noble family to whom Cruz was enslaved. These letters were not just loving epistles between spouses separated by vast distances, they were also reminders of an informal contract between husband and wife that Segarra would use his freedom to accumulate capital and send funds to Sevilla to liberate his wife and children from slavery. Felipa de la Cruz left a remarkable documentary trail of her multiple attempts to obtain liberty for herself and her two enslaved children, revealing her legal know-how of different paths to *alhorría* (the juridical status of liberation from slavery). These attempts

---

[1] "Antón Segarra," AGI, Contratación, 303, no. 2, fols. 10ʳ, 18ᵛ–20ᵛ. For this case and letters discussed in this chapter, see also von Germeten, *Violent Delights*, 100–101.
[2] *Las Siete partidas del Sabio Rey don Alfonso*, "Quarta Partida, Titulo XXI, De los Siervos," 38–39.

involved urging her husband to accumulate capital in Veracruz so that he could purchase the price of his family's liberty, and latterly, petitioning to inherit her late husband's property by falsifying information about her status as a free woman before judges at the House of Trade in Sevilla.

Exploring Felipa de la Cruz's various pursuits of freedom and the lives and affairs of other enslaved and liberated Black people in her generation who lived in her neighborhood brings into relief the varied conversations and fractured memories, hopes, and desires about paths to freedom among free, enslaved, and *horro* Black populations in late sixteenth-century Sevilla. The pages ahead play with various scales of analysis, shifting between micro and macro lenses to explore Cruz's world and her hopes and expectations about liberty for her and her children and a broader history of ideas about freedom and mutual aid practices in Sevilla. The microscale involves drawing on information penned by Cruz to explore the urban environment that she inhabited, her walks in the neighborhood, her community ties and neighbors, and the key institutions of the Spanish crown that she interacted with throughout her lifetime. Expanding to a macro vista of Black life in late sixteenth- and early seventeenth-century Sevilla reveals how Felipa de la Cruz's epistles to her absent husband represented a broader history of Black residents' transatlantic ties with kin and associates in the Americas. Assembling diverse archival materials that catalog how hundreds of free and liberated Black men and women crossed the Atlantic as passengers on ships also reveals fragmentary evidence of spheres of communication between Black and *mulato* residents of Sevilla with kin and associates in the Spanish Americas, especially through word of mouth and letters. Such records also document mutual aid practices across the vast Atlantic world, when Black parents in the Spanish Americas sent funds to Sevilla to liberate their kin from slavery. Such Atlantic ties and fractured community memories of liberations from slavery inevitably impacted enslaved Black Sevilla-dwellers' ideas and hopes about liberty. Felipa de la Cruz's letters and interactions with royal institutions show that even though she remained trapped in captivity for most (if not all) of her life, Cruz was also a member of an emerging lettered Black public sphere in late sixteenth-century Sevilla.

PLAYING WITH SCALES, FROM MICRO TO MACRO: WALKING THROUGH FELIPA DE LA CRUZ'S NEIGHBORHOOD IN LATE SIXTEENTH-CENTURY SEVILLA

Felipa de la Cruz's personal cartography stretched across the Atlantic world, even though she never left the city of Sevilla. Cruz's ideas about freedom and slavery were influenced by the urban environment in which she lived, in particular, the lives of free and enslaved Black neighbors, the institutions of religious and royal governance that surrounded the streets near her home, and the ubiquity of traders, passers-by, men of the sea, colonial officials, religious clerics, and many others sojourning in central Sevilla before undertaking voyages to the Americas, Asia, West Africa, West-Central Africa, and beyond.

Felipa de la Cruz grew up enslaved in a palace at the north entrance of a street known as Calle Carpinterías and Carpinteros (present-day Calle Cuna) in the San Salvador parish of the city.[3] Cruz was enslaved to a prominent family in Sevilla's aristocratic landscape whose name, Fernández de Santillán, was associated with the Catholic monarchy's reconquest of Sevilla and the subsequent governance of the city, while the clan had also fostered powerful noble alliances through generations of well-chosen marriages.[4] Cruz's owner, Francisco Fernández de Santillán (b. 1565), served as a *caballero veinticuatro de Sevilla*, one of twenty-four *regidores* (officers charged with the governance of the city) in the *cabildo* of Sevilla.[5] The Fernández de Santillán family had lived since the early fifteenth century in a palace that sprawled over a 2,000 square meter plot at the entrance of Calle Carpinterías on the northern edge of San Salvador parish.[6] Known in the sixteenth century as the Casa Palacio Francisco Fernández de Santillán, the property housed Fernández de Santillán's six children and many notable visitors, including the aforementioned Doña Juana Segarra de Saavedra (see Chapter 1) and her slave, Antón Segarra, as well as a sizable retinue of wage-earning servants and domestic slaves (Figure 2.1).[7] Felipa de la Cruz probably met Antón Segarra during one of his many visits when his owner stayed as a guest in the palace between 1596 and 1601, or possibly earlier when Antón was enslaved to another member of the Sevilla nobility.

---

[3] Ramírez de Guzmán, *Libro de algunos ricoshombres*, 509.
[4] *Origen y Descendencia de la Casa y familia de Santillán de la Ciudad de Sevilla, con otras varias noticias de los linages de ella por el enlace que tienen con la referida casa.16??*, Biblioteca de la Universidad de Sevilla, A 331/214, fol. 42^v; Cuartero y Huerta et al., *Índice de la Colección*, 103; Rivarola y Pineda, *Descripcion historica*, 381–382; Cartaya Baños, "Un listado inédito," 103.
[5] Rahn Phillips, *El tesoro*, 56.
[6] Ramírez de Guzmán, *Libro de algunos ricoshombres*, 509. I thank Juan Cartaya Baños at Universidad de Sevilla for his advice about locating information about the family's place of residence.
[7] Núñez González, *La casa sevillana*; "Antón Segarra," AGI, Contratación, 303, no. 2, fols. 10^r, 18^v–20^v.

FIGURE 2.1 Photograph of the present-day facade of the palace in Sevilla where Felipa de la Cruz was enslaved; known in the late sixteenth century as Casa-Palacio Fernández de Santillán, and presently known as Palacio del Marqués de la Motilla. Photograph by Miguel Ángel Rosales, 2024. Reproduced with permission from Miguel Ángel Rosales.

Within the palace there existed a hierarchy between enslaved laborers, and Cruz viewed herself among the most prominent enslaved servants in the household.[8] Cruz seemed to occupy a prominent role in the house, likely in the service of Fernández de Santillán's wife, whom she described in some detail in her 1608 letter. Cruz's prominent status within the palace is also apparent in her description of another enslaved woman's fate. She relayed how her enslavers had sold another enslaved Black woman in the palace, named Ana, because she had married. Even though Cruz had also exchanged marriage vows a few years earlier, her owners had not subjected her to Ana's fate. Her discussion of Ana's duties within the palace also suggests that she perceived her own position in the household as more prestigious than the one that Ana occupied. In conveying the news about Ana's forced departure, Cruz seemed relieved not to have been asked to take on Ana's cooking duties, as she wrote that "These noble people have rewarded me as I deserved, instead of throwing me in the kitchen when they sold Ana because she got married."[9] In another instance, Cruz described how her enslavers had sold "María the Black" without giving any further explanation as to the reasons for the sale. Cruz never described her enslavers

[8] Antón Segarra," AGI, Contratación, 303, no. 2, fols. 10r, 18v–20v.
[9] Ibid.

Imagining Freedom 69

as her owners, instead referring to Fernández de Santillán and his wife as *mi señor* and *mi señora* throughout. This choice of language might reflect Cruz's views on her elevated status in the palace. Certainly, Cruz's comments about her enslavers included a few witty remarks about their affairs, as she described how "My *señora* is well. She only cares about giving birth and getting pregnant soon after."

Cruz also developed relationships with her neighbors in San Salvador parish. In her 1608 letter, she sent news about neighbors and friends beyond the palace walls, informing her husband of the recent marriages, births, and deaths in the neighborhood, and relaying how "all of the rest of our other acquaintances kiss your hands with much desire to see you."[10] These lines suggest that Cruz's relationships stretched well beyond the household where she was enslaved, and that she was privy to broader know-how and relays of information in her neighborhood.

Cruz lived in the compact and strategically located parish of San Salvador. This neighborhood constituted one of the most important commercial markets for city dwellers, providing bread, fish, meat, and vegetables, as well as serving as the artisanal heartbeat of the city, while also maintaining its status as a residential neighborhood. City dwellers, laborers, and passers-by in the area might also spend time relaxing in the many taverns and *bodegas* that opened along the narrow alleys in the late sixteenth century.[11] Streets in the parish often comprised both palatial homes, such as the one where Cruz dwelt, as well as the homes and rooms of artisans and traders, whose shops lined the storefronts.[12] Figure 2.2 is a late eighteenth-century street map of Sevilla (and the earliest known street map of the city), with an overlay that indicates the location of Felipa de la Cruz's dwelling at the turn of the seventeenth century and an approximate outline of the border for the parish of San Salvador.

Cruz's ideas about freedom were inevitably impacted and shaped by her experiences in San Salvador parish, and, in particular, her discussions about slavery and freedom with other Black dwellers of the parish and beyond. Following in Cruz's footsteps on a fifteen-minute walk through her neighborhood allows us to trace her daily life in the city, her participation in spheres of communication between Black neighbors, her networks with friends and kin in the broader Atlantic world, and her know-how about freedom. This act of walking with Cruz in her

[10] Ibid.
[11] Núñez González, "Las áreas de mercado," 27–30.
[12] Núñez González, *La casa sevillana* and "Las áreas de mercado."

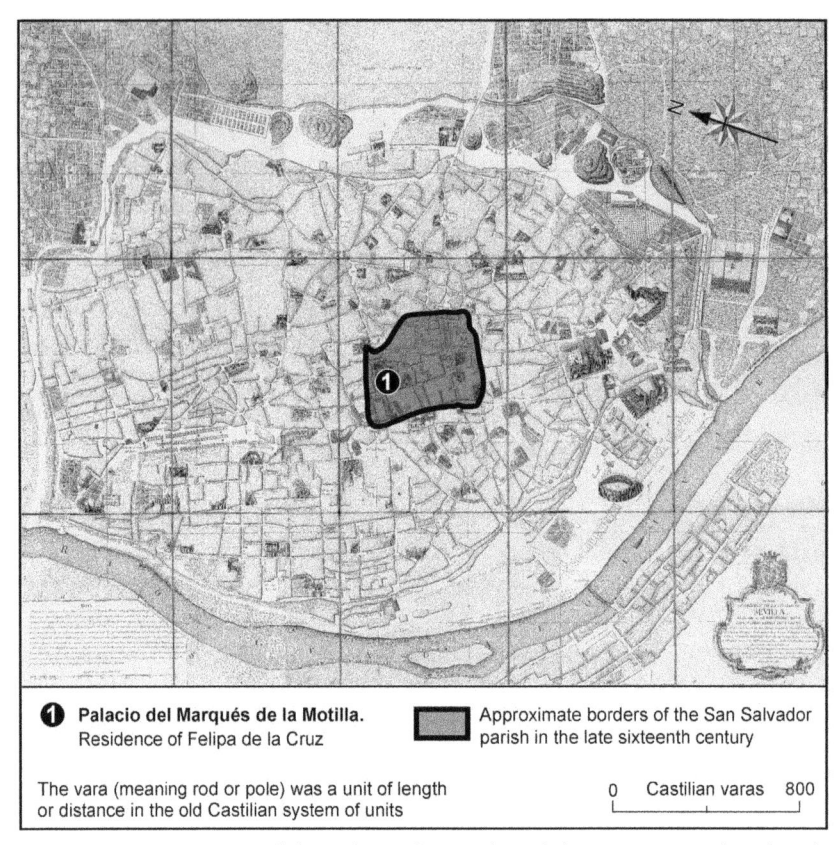

70   *Slavery and Freedom in the Early Spanish Atlantic*

FIGURE 2.2 Location of the palace where Felipa de la Cruz was enslaved and an approximate outline of the parish where she resided (San Salvador), overlaid on Tomás López de Vargas Machuca, "Plano geométrico de la ciudad de Sevilla...." Tomás López: Madrid, 1788. David Rumsey Map Collection, List no. 10717.000, David Rumsey Map Center, Stanford Libraries. Adaptation of the map by Cath D'Alton, Drawing Office, University College London.

neighborhood draws on an array of archival fragments that record elements of Black life and thought in the environs of San Salvador parish in this period, as well as information that she penned in her letters and other documents that she generated during her years-long pursuit of freedom.

Walking southbound along Calle Carpinterías from her owner's palace, Cruz would have been acquainted with the wood-artisans and carpenters whose workshops lined the narrow street.[13] City ordinances of

---

[13] Núñez González, "Las áreas de mercado," 27.

Imagining Freedom 71

Sevilla published in 1525 and 1632 prohibited any free or enslaved Black person from admittance to city examinations for the carpentry trade, and prohibited any free or liberated Black wood-artisan from opening a carpentry shop on Calle Carpinterías.[14] The existence of such rules suggest that free and enslaved Black men may have labored as wood-artisans in this area, and that some may have toiled in the shops that lined Felipa de la Cruz's street.[15]

Calle Carpinterías led to the bustling square of Plaza del Salvador (henceforth Salvador Square) (Figure 2.3, no. 2).[16] The square housed one of the most prominent and prestigious places of worship in the city, the imposing Iglesia Colegial del Divino Salvador (henceforth, Salvador Church). By the mid sixteenth century, Salvador Square and its adjoining squares and streets lay at the heart of Sevilla's commercial district for internal trade, where city dwellers purchased food and products for their own consumption.[17] Upon entering Salvador Square, Cruz might smell the putrid odor of rotting fish floating from the nearby Plaza de Arriba that housed a daily fish market or in the morning the warm aroma of baking bread wafting from the bakers on the lower square. Salvador Square was lined with shops selling candlewax and incense, and during religious festivities clouds of aroma-filled smoke engulfed the square. Nearby, Calle Sierpes and the adjoining streets that led to Salvador Square housed shops where shoemakers, saddlers, leather artisans, swordsmiths, knifesmiths, locksmiths, and printers peddled their trades.

Felipa de la Cruz's relationships with the artisans of the parish are reflected in her letters, as she reported on news from the wider neighborhood. For example, she described that "Beatriz Gómes married her niece to a capmaker, and she is pregnant," and that "Casilda de Velasco is also well. You have already heard that her daughter, Francisca de Velasco, passed away, and how she arranged for her granddaughter to marry a shoemaker from Montilla. María Jiménez arranged for her daughter Elvira to marry a silversmith."[18] Cruz also built kinship ties in the parish. For example, she enlisted a *vecino* of the parish named Luis de Aguilar to serve as her son's godfather in 1603, as she explained to her husband:

---

[14] *Recopilacion de las ordena[n]ças*, "titulo, de los Carpinteros, CXLVII," 313–315. *Ordenanças de Seuilla*, fols. 148^{r-v}.
[15] Ibid. and Núñez González, *La casa sevillana*.
[16] Collantes de Terán Sánchez et al., *Diccionario Histórico*, See entry for "Cuna."
[17] Núñez González, "Las áreas de mercado"; Collantes de Terán Sánchez, "*Los Mercados.*"
[18] "Antón Segarra," AGI, Contratación, 303, no. 2, fols. 10^r, 18^v–20^v.

72   *Slavery and Freedom in the Early Spanish Atlantic*

- - - - 15-minute walk from Felipa de la Cruz's dwelling (1), to the House of Trade (6)

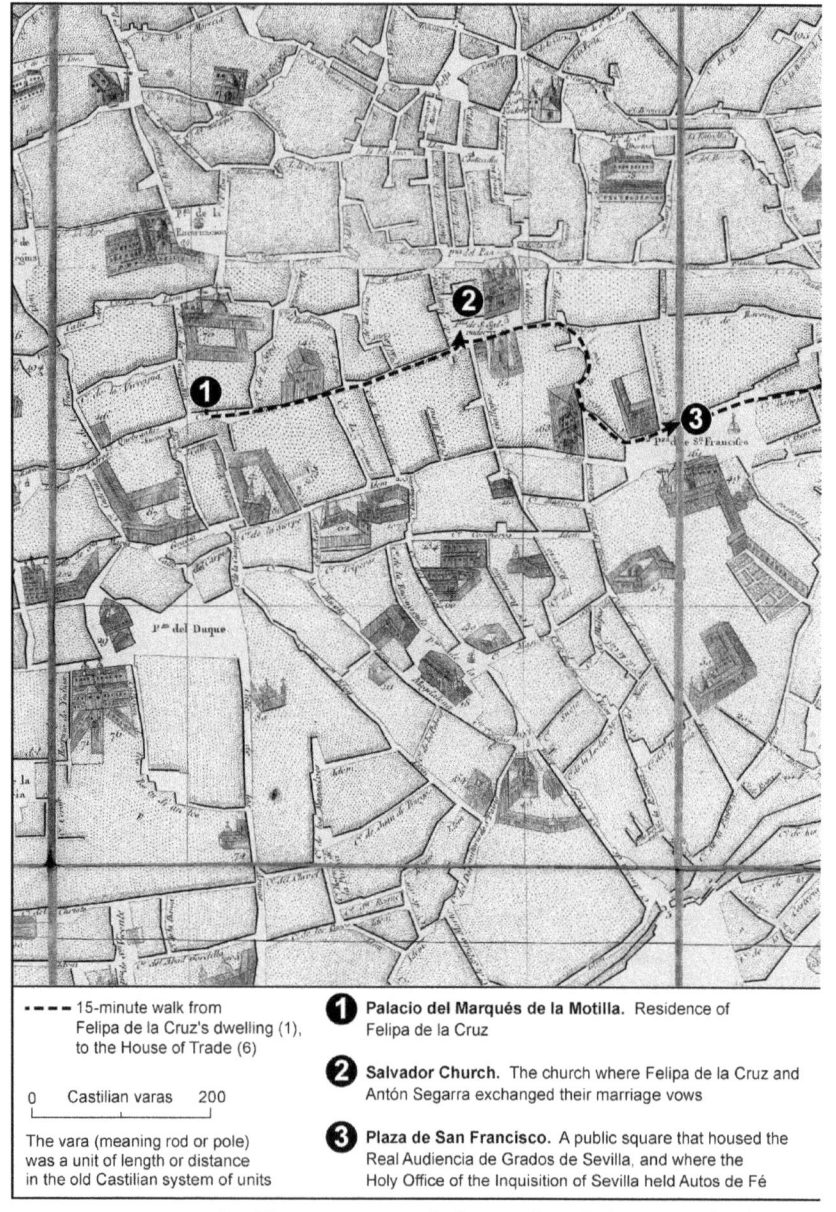

0 ⊢——————⊣ 200 Castilian varas

The vara (meaning rod or pole) was a unit of length or distance in the old Castilian system of units

❶ Palacio del Marqués de la Motilla. Residence of Felipa de la Cruz

❷ Salvador Church. The church where Felipa de la Cruz and Antón Segarra exchanged their marriage vows

❸ Plaza de San Francisco. A public square that housed the Real Audiencia de Grados de Sevilla, and where the Holy Office of the Inquisition of Sevilla held Autos de Fé

FIGURE 2.3 Map of a fifteen-minute walk from Felipa de la Cruz's dwelling to the House of Trade, overlaid onto Tomás López de Vargas Machuca, "Plano geométrico de la ciudad de Sevilla...." (detail). Tomás López: Madrid, 1788. David Rumsey Map Collection, List no. 10717.000, David Rumsey Map Center, Stanford Libraries. Adaptation of the map by Cath D'Alton, Drawing Office, University College London.

Imagining Freedom   73

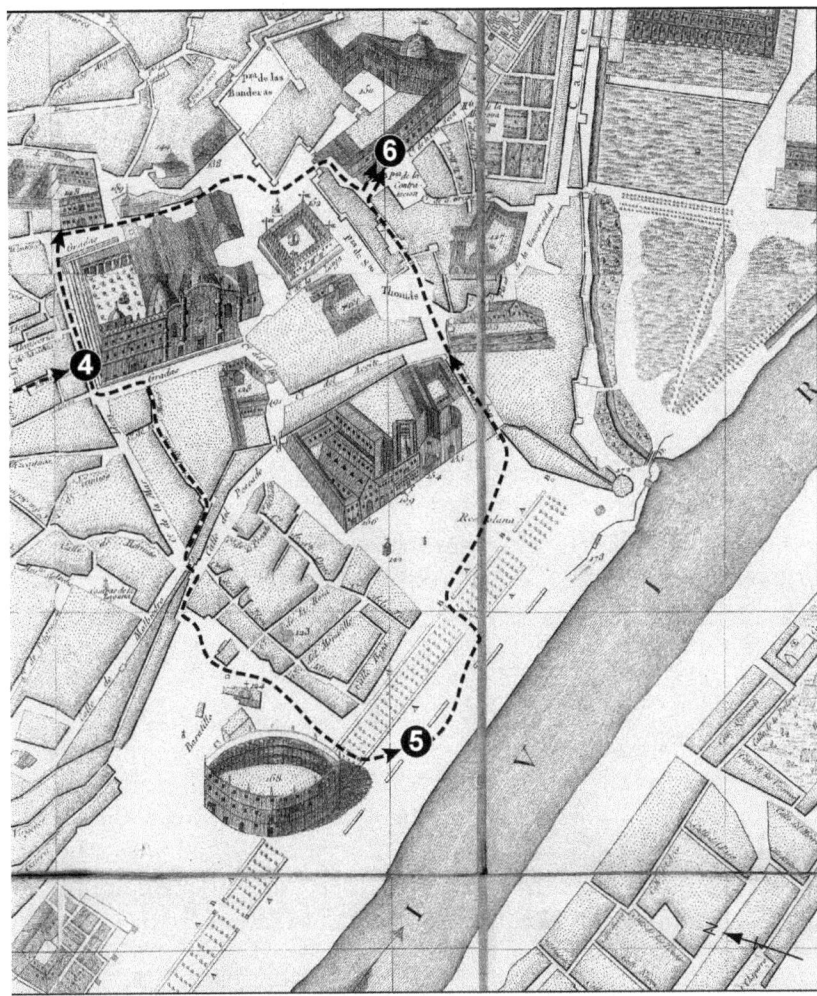

④ **Gradas.** The most important site of mercantile activity and trade in sixteenth-century Sevilla along the steps at the northern side of the Cathedral

⑤ **Riverbank/Port of Sevilla.** Site where Felipa de la Cruz may have met prospective and returning passengers on ships

⑥ **House of Trade.** A royal institution where Felipa de la Cruz petioned to inherit her deceased husband's belongings in 1612

FIGURE 2.3 (cont.)

"You have Luis de Aguilar as a godfather, who lifted Andres out of the baptismal font."[19] This kinship tie is also confirmed in the baptism records for the parish, where the following entry was recorded for a baby named Andrés on December 11, 1603: "I, Alonso Fernández del Tovar, priest of Salvador Church, baptized Andrés, slave of don Francisco de Santillán, son of Antón, Black, and of Phelipa. Luis de Aguilar, *vecino* of this parish was his godfather."[20] Cruz therefore knew some of the artisans on her street and the broader neighborhood, and would have constantly seen and met passers-by from other parishes of the city.

In Salvador Square, Felipa de la Cruz would have heard any official news from the crown or city governance, as the square was one of five sites in Sevilla where town criers were required to sing news announcing any royal decrees, local legislation, or announcements from the city *cabildo*. The other sites where city dwellers would hear such news included the nearby Plaza de San Francisco (hereafter San Francisco Square), Plaza del Alfalfa, Plaza de los Terceros, and Calle Feria. City ordinances stipulated that only fifteen people could be appointed as city criers at any time, with two senior criers (*pregoneros mayores*) who would examine and appoint thirteen junior criers (*pregoneros menores*), subject to confirmation by the *cabildo*.[21] As well as their responsibility for conveying news and official announcements, town criers also had to offer their services to private individuals wishing to organize any public sales, and to announce any lost property, including enslaved people who fled their owners. Given the proximity of her dwelling to this square, Cruz would have heard official news through the criers' songs throughout her lifetime, in particular about the absconding of any enslaved people from their owners in this compact neighborhood.

In Cruz's lifetime, San Salvador parish had a sizable Black population comprising enslaved, liberated, and freeborn dwellers.[22] Their presence is reflected in the marriage and baptism records for the parish, especially in Salvador Church. Enslaved and free Black couples exchanged marriage vows there throughout Cruz's lifetime, and most of them likely resided

---

[19] "Antón Segarra," AGI, Contratación, 303, no. 2, fols. 10[r], 18[v]–20[v].
[20] "Andrés, 11th December 1603," AGAS, Parroquia del Salvador, 3.I.1.1, "Libro de Bautismos," libro 11, 1597–1605, fol. 330.
[21] *Recopilacion de las ordena[n]ças*, "titulo, de los Pregoneros, CXXXIIII," pp. 284–288; *Ordenanças de Seuilla*, fols. 84[v]–85[v], 132[v]–133[v]; Walleit, "El oficio de pregonero."
[22] Corona Pérez, "Aproximación," and *Trata Atlántica*; Valverde Barneto, "La esclavitud."

(at least temporarily) in San Salvador parish.[23] For example, in 1564, at least thirty-one free and enslaved Black couples exchanged their vows in Salvador Church.[24] The records of these marriages reveal the entangled lives of the Salvador-elite with the lives of dispossessed enslaved Black people and free Black artisans and laborers who also resided in the parish. For example, records of marriages in 1564 reveal ties across socioeconomic strata in the parish: an enslaved Black couple, Jorge and Ana – who were each enslaved to two different *vecinos* of the parish – wed on January 4; Francisco and Leonor, the former described as Black and both as free servants to different Salvador residents, married on January 30; finally, Francisco and Francisca, both described as Black and enslaved to the same *vecino* of San Salvador named Alonso de la Pricola, exchanged their vows on July 20.[25]

Marriage records also reflect how enslaved Black people formed familial and social bonds across different parishes in the city. In Cruz's generation, various enslaved Black couples who wed in Salvador Church dwelt in different parishes from each other, suggesting that enslaved people living in San Salvador parish sometimes developed ties across different regions of the city. For example, in March 1590, an enslaved Black man named Sebastián from the parish of Santa María La Mayor exchanged marriage vows in Salvador Church with an enslaved Black woman named Catalina, who was owned by a *vecino* of San Salvador parish.[26] A decade later an enslaved Black couple named Antón and Marta wed in Salvador Church, even though Antón's owner resided in the Magdalena parish and Marta was enslaved in San Salvador parish.[27] Like other enslaved Black couples who married across parish lines, Felipa de la Cruz and Antón Segarra also exchanged vows in Salvador Church sometime between 1591 and 1601, at a time when both were enslaved to different owners and when Segarra's owner resided in the town of Écija.[28] The

---

[23] "Libro de Matrimonios de la Parroquia del San Salvador," AGAS, 3.I.2.1, libros 2–6; Valverde Barneto, "La esclavitud."
[24] Corona Pérez, *Trata Atlántica*.
[25] "Libro de Matrimonios," libro 2, 1563–1566, AGAS, 3.I.2.1, Año 1564.
[26] Ibid., March 13, 1590, May 31, 1590.
[27] "Libro de Matrimonios," libro 6 1601–1609, AGAS, 3.I.2.1, April 26, 1601.
[28] Libro 5 corresponding to the years 1591–1601 of the "Libro de Matrimonios" for San Salvador parish in AGAS has been lost and is not accessible in the archive. Felipa and Antón's marriage record does not appear in libros 2–6 spanning the years 1563–1610. This date range for the marriage dates their union between two and four years prior to the baptism of their second child, Andrés, in December 1603 (see note 20).

pair met at Salvador Church for their marriage sacrament in the presence of their friends, neighbors, and Cruz's owners, who likely walked there from the palace along Calle Carpinterías.[29]

Salvador Square was also the site of a violent encounter between a prominent Black brotherhood named Our Lady of the Angels (Nuestra Señora de los Ángeles) and a white confraternity on Maundy Thursday during Easter celebrations in 1604, one year after Segarra had departed Sevilla for New Spain.[30] Contemporary accounts often point to the frightening, confusing, and dangerous nature of the "panics" that emerged in the early hours during the long processions of Maundy Thursday in the city. This highly contested incident between the two brotherhoods took place at one of the busiest crossroads of Maundy Thursday processions, near Salvador Church. One witness described how the white confraternity's procession departed from the church towards Calle Carpinterías (Figure 2.3, no. 2) and a procession led by the Black brothers of the confraternity Our Lady of the Angels (Figure 4.1, no. 1) attempted to barge through and ambush their *paso* (a large float that dozens of confraternity brothers balance on their heads while marching in procession, upon which lies a platform with a sumptuously decorated life-size sculpture of a biblical image). Mayhem ensued, predictably so given a collision of two elaborate *pasos* in the early hours of Maundy Thursday in narrow streets packed with devout onlookers, with dozens of confraternity members holding the weight on their heads of heavy floats loaded with images and adornments. To add to the drama, the white confraternity claimed that the Black brothers were armed with swords and rocks and had proceeded to attack them with the aim of breaking up the procession and injuring the members. The *alguacil* (sheriff) of the Real Audiencia of Sevilla arrested eleven of the Black confraternity brothers that night.[31] A shoemaker who lived nearby described how he was woken by the commotion to find his wife observing the unfolding violence on Salvador Square through their window.[32] Another *vecino* of San Salvador parish testified to having seen

---

[29] "Antón Segarra," AGI, Contratación, 303, no. 2, fols. 25ʳ–30ʳ.

[30] My description is based on testimonies in "Pleito entre la Hdad de Ntra Sra de la Antigua y la de los Ángeles," AGAS, III.1.6, L.9883, Expte 2; "Pleito, Nuestra Señora de los Angeles," AGAS, 1.III.1.6, L.9885, no. 1. Other scholars who have analyzed this event and subsequent trial include Berruezo-Sánchez, *Black Voices*; Beusterien et al., "Callejeando Sevilla"; Fracchia, "*Black but Human*"; Moreno, *La Antigua*; Rowe, *Black Saints*.

[31] La Cofradia de hermanos de Nuestra Señora de la Antigua y Siete Dolores, AGAS, 1.III.1.6, legajo 9885, no. 1, fols. 4ʳ–11ʳ.

[32] Ibid., fol. 7ᵛ.

the Black brothers' nocturnal processions in the neighborhood over the previous eight years.[33] Although these witnesses attested in a charged court hearing in order to support an archbishop who was intent on prohibiting the Black confraternity from participation in Holy Week, their vivid descriptions of the violence and piercing screams imply that most people living in the vicinity would have been aware of the commotion. Cruz may not have kept abreast of their subsequent legal trials between 1604 and 1606 and the Black brothers' insistence on their right to partake in public displays of piety in the city (see Chapter 4), but she probably witnessed or heard about the conflict during Holy Week in 1604.

Another Black soundscape that Cruz may have witnessed in this square was enslaved and free Black performers singing *Villancicos de Negros* (Christmas carols of Black people). Although the first recorded instances of *Villancicos de Negros* being performed in Salvador Church and in the cathedral date to 1635 and 1625, respectively, it is possible that such traditions may have begun by the late sixteenth century.[34] Living in this area, Cruz likely also witnessed Black dancers and musicians during city festivities, such as the raucous "Black people dance" (*"negro baile"*) that the playwright Lope de Vega (1562–1635) depicted unravelling in the street below a window scene in central Sevilla in the first decade of the seventeenth century, when Black characters entered the stage singing, dancing, and playing music on guitars and jingles.[35]

Turning south-west from Salvador Church, Cruz would have reached the San Francisco Square within a few minutes (Figure 2.3, no. 3). This prominent central square housed the Real Audiencia of Sevilla. Like Real Audiencias in the Americas, subjects from lower socioeconomic spectrums and legal statuses of bondage and unfreedom sometimes managed to bring cases for justice at this court.[36] San Francisco Square was also the site where the Holy Office of the Inquisition of Sevilla

---

[33] "Pleito entre la Hdad de Ntra Sra de la Antigua y la de los Ángeles," AGAS, III.1.6, legajo 9883, Expte 2, *Sin Foliación*, Testigo, Julio López de la Cruz.

[34] Pujol i Coll, "'Els vilancets.'" See also Berruezo-Sánchez, *Black Voices*; Brewer Garcia, *Beyond Babel*; DiFranco and Labrador Herraiz, "Villancicos de negros" 163–188; Fracchia, *"Black but Human."*

[35] Lope de Vega, *La Vitoria de la Honra*. For other examples, see also Berruezo-Sánchez, *Black Voices*; Beusterien, *An Eye on Race*; de Salas Barbadillo, *The Gawkers/Los Mirones*; Fra-Molinero, "Black Pride," *La Imagen*; Fra-Molinero et al., "Antón's Linguistic Blackface"; Jones, *Staging*.

[36] Rubiales Torrejón, *La Real Audiencia*. For an example of an enslaved Black person petitioning for justice in this court, see Chapter 1, notes 126–128.

celebrated twenty three *autos-da-fé* (Acts of Faith) between 1559 and 1604.[37] Inquisitors hoped that the lavishly expensive day-long *autos-da-fé* in San Francisco Square, and the city-wide processions that preceded them, would induce fear and awe in city dwellers and prevent them from succumbing to heretical practices, especially Lutheranism, Judaism, and Islam, while indoctrinating residents in the Catholic faith.[38] The processions departed from the Castle of the Inquisition in Triana, crossing the rickety bridge balanced on a line of boats anchored across the Guadalquivir river, and then snaked through the city to celebrate the *auto-da-fé* in San Francisco Square. Those whom the Inquisition had condemned to death endured a further procession to their ghastly fates in the *Quemadero de San Diego* (Incinerator of San Diego) in the Prado San Sebastián. Inquisitors described an *auto-da-fé* in 1546 as "an extraordinarily solemn event" that lasted an entire day from ten in the morning to sunset and condemned seventy people, including the burning of twenty-one and the sentencing to perpetual jail of sixteen.[39] Inquisitors in Sevilla had a wide geographical remit, investigating transgressions in the city and other regions of Andalucía. The *auto-da-fé* of April 26, 1562, for example, condemned individuals who lived in Sevilla, Cádiz, Gibraltar, Granada, and further away.[40] News of neighbors' arrests and punishment by the Inquisition spread widely and were especially visible in local church gatherings and processions, as Inquisitors often punished the condemned by ordering that they hear the *missa mayor* in their parish on a Sunday or feast day while standing naked or walking the procession barefoot without a *bonete* and with a *soga* around their throat, while holding a wax candle. Inquisitors on occasion also imposed sentences of temporary exile and banishment from the city of Sevilla for a number of years.[41]

---

[37] "Relacion de las Causas de Autos da Fé en la Inquisición de Sevilla," AHN España, Inquisición, 2075, expedientes 1–29. See also González de Caldas, *Judíos o cristianos?*, 528.

[38] Ibid.

[39] Relacion de las Causas, Sevilla, AHN, España, Inquisición, 2075, Expediente 1, September 21, 1559, fols. 2^r–11^v.

[40] Relacion de las Causas, Sevilla, AHN, España, Inquisición, 2075, Expediente 4, April 26, 1562, fols. 1^r–11^v. For another description of an *auto-da-fé* in Sevilla, see also "Auto Publico de Fe," John Carter Brown (cited as JCB), Library, Rare Books, BA646.A446s, fol. 158^r.

[41] For an example of such punishments for free Black men and women in the 1562 *auto-da-fé*, see Relación de las Causas, Sevilla, AHN, España, Inquisición, 2075, Expediente 4, fol. 9^v.

San Francisco Square also housed a sprawling Franciscan convent known as Casa Grande de San Francisco, which served as the regional headquarters for the Franciscan order's missionary efforts for global Christian expansion. The Casa Grande's activities contributed to Sevilla feeling like a global city in the sixteenth century, as the institution provided extended hospitality for Franciscans departing and returning from the Americas and other regions of the world.[42] The compound also housed prominent confraternities that were embedded in Sevillian society. While the Casa Grande's most elite confraternity, de la Vera Cruz, did not appear to have members who were identified as Black or *mulato*, other confraternities within the Casa Grande did admit Black and *mulato* members.[43] At least one late sixteenth-century free *mulato* parishioner maintained long-standing religious ties with the Casa Grande, even from the Americas.[44] A *mulato* named Diego Suárez (d. 1589), who was born in the nearby Pajería Street (present-day Calle Zaragoza), was a member of one of the brotherhoods in the convent.[45] In Sevilla, Suárez was a stage-actor who donned extravagant military garments for his roles, while his free Black mother eked out a living by peddling sweets on the streets in the area. When Suárez traveled to the Americas in the 1570s employed as a soldier and an actor, the brotherhood of San Buenaventura and Ánimas in the Casa Grande reportedly tasked him to collect alms in the Spanish Americas on their behalf.[46] In the Indies, Suárez likely continued working as both a soldier and an actor as he named a Captain Pedro de Valencia as one of his benefactors, and he owned a horse and a saddle, while he also had scripts for plays among his personal papers. When Suárez became ill in Arequipa, he composed a will leaving money to the Casa Grande in San Francisco Square and to his mother.[47]

Wandering southeast from San Francisco Square, Cruz would reach the northern edge of the cathedral, where a bustling market of global goods sprawled across the large concrete steps that encircled this holy site of worship. This space, where competitive mercantile life often

---

[42] McClure, "Worlds within worlds."
[43] On cofradia, de la Veracruz, see McClure, "Worlds within Worlds."
[44] "Diego Suárez," AGI, Contratación 255, no. 1, ramo 5.
[45] "Diego Suárez," AGI, Contratación 255, no. 1, ramo 5. Collantes de Terán Sánchez et al., *Diccionario Histórico*, See entry for "Zaragoza," 486–487. For a detailed study on Diego Suárez, see Garofalo, "Afro-Iberians in the Early"; Ireton, "They Are." See also Figure C.1.1.
[46] Ibid.
[47] Ibid.

encroached on the holy sanctity of the interior patios of the vast edifice of the cathedral, was known as Gradas. Here, Cruz would have encountered one of the most significant sites of global mercantile activity of the late sixteenth century, as merchants peddled their wares from distant lands and signed lucrative commercial and trading contracts (Figure 2.3, no. 4). Gradas may also have been the location where Cruz sought the services of informal writers, known as *escribientes*, to pen her letters. Merchants often crowded into the cathedral's interior Patio de los Naranjos through one of the cathedral doors known as the Puerta del Perdón, especially in inclement weather, causing consternation among generations of archbishops who fretted about mercantile activity polluting a site of worship.[48] According to a sixteenth-century city chronicler named Alonso Morgado, hordes of criers congregated at Gradas every single day to auction wares that merchants or private individuals had tasked them to sell. The city ordinances ruled that the city criers should be present at Gradas every day except festivities between sunrise and ten o'clock in the morning to offer their services to potential customers wishing to organize a sale.[49] Morgado described how these daily auctions were notable for "the continual, perpetual, and great abundance of items of great value that are auctioned there, including gold, silver, expensive and luxury clothes, possessions, expensive textiles and tapestries, and many slaves, weapons, and all of the riches that can be imagined."[50] The streets that lined Gradas also overflowed with silversmith workshops.[51]

Perched at Gradas amid the commotion of sales and bartering, it is likely that Cruz witnessed a common scene in the city – the daily sales of enslaved Black people on the steps of the cathedral. Onlookers in the sixteenth century regularly witnessed enslaved Black men and women locked in chains awaiting their torturous fates after sale to the highest bidder, as criers and prospective buyers haggled over prices for their bodies and labor. Such sales tended to be organized by private individuals selling their enslaved property, rather than large-scale lot-type auctions by merchants.[52] City ordinances

[48] Eventually, the crown built a dedicated building for mercantile activity, known as the Casa de Lonja, on the south side of the cathedral in the mid seventeenth century.
[49] *Recopilacion de las ordena[n]ças*, 1527, "titulo, de los Pregoneros, CXXXIIII," pages 284–288; *Ordenanças de Seuilla*, 1632, fols. 84ᵛ–85ᵛ, 132ᵛ–133ᵛ; Walleit, "El oficio de pregonero."
[50] Morgado, *Historia de Sevilla*, 1587, libro JI, capítulo 13, 169.
[51] Núñez González, *Arquitectura, dibujo*.
[52] On the presence and importance of the slave market in Gradas among other commerce, see ibid.; see also Vaseur Gamez et al., *La esclavitud*; Chaves and Pérez García, *Tratas atlánticas*; Pérez García et al., *Tratas, esclavitudes*.

also obliged criers to organize the auctions of deceased people's belongings at Gradas to avoid fraud.⁵³ As a result, any enslaved person in Sevilla who was due to be sold as part of their late owner's estate would likely be subjected to a sale by auction there. It may well be that Felipa de la Cruz's enslaver had sent Ana and María, who had previously labored with Cruz in the palace, to be sold by public auction at this very site. Bearing witness to this common scene of economic trade that led to the inevitable destruction of kinship ties – as mothers and children were sold to different enslavers or siblings were separated by the demands of the market – would have served as a patent reminder to Felipa of her and her children's enslavement and her lack of agency over their own lives and bodies. Even though Felipa once described how her enslavers treated her well, she could never forget that her family could be ripped apart in an instant at the whims of her enslavers.

Walking a few minutes southwest from the cathedral, Cruz would have reached Arenal. This was the neighborhood that bordered the banks of the Guadalquivir River. Residents of Sevilla gathered here to meet the ships arriving from the Spanish Americas, West Africa, and beyond, and to offer services to weary passengers (Figure 2.3, no. 5). Cruz was on high alert in the years between 1604 and 1611 for any information from or about her husband. Cruz likely approached the riverbanks numerous times over the course of the summer of 1608 in the hopes of hearing news from distant shores of the Atlantic Ocean. Four long years had passed since Segarra had been liberated from slavery and had left Sevilla on a ship destined to sail to the Americas. Felipa was feeling exasperated. Segarra's long absence was even more inexplicable for Cruz as she had not heard any news from him in some time. In a letter that Cruz penned to her husband earlier in the year, she had beseeched him to contact her:

I am very upset for the great neglect that you have shown in not writing to me for so long, and I do not know what I can attribute [myself] to your great forgetfulness, except that it must be for to the little love that you have for me and your children; it [your love] is not steadfast like mine because every hour and every moment I remember you and there is never a time that I attend mass or that I am in the house that I do not entrust you to God that he protect you and bring you before my eyes and those of our children so that their great wish to see you can be fulfilled.⁵⁴

---

⁵³ *Ordenanças de Seuilla*, 1632, fols. 84ᵛ–85ᵛ, 132ᵛ–133ᵛ.
⁵⁴ "Antón Segarra," AGI, Contratación, 303, no. 2, fols. 10ʳ, 18ᵛ–20ᵛ.

Late sixteenth- and early seventeenth-century Sevilla was a key node in the annual fleets of ships that crossed the Atlantic to the Spanish Americas under the auspices of the Spanish crown, known as the Carrera de Indias (Figure 1.2). From the late 1560s onwards, two fleets consisting of hundreds of medium-sized ships departed Sevilla annually to the Americas. One fleet set sail from Sevilla in April towards the port of Veracruz, and another fleet departed Sevilla in August destined to the port of Nombre de Dios (and after 1599, to Portobelo). The respective convoys sailed to the Canary Islands, before crossing the Atlantic. After anchoring briefly in Isla Dominica, smaller ships with other destinations peeled off from the fleet, and the ships destined for New Spain sailed to the port of Veracruz, while the Tierra Firme fleet sojourned in Cartagena de Indias for a two-week stopover, before anchoring at Nombre de Dios (or Portobelo after 1599). These vessels remained in the Americas over the winter until March, when captains readied their ships by loading cargo, mostly the silver caravels transported from the mines in the mountainous peaks of the silver-boomtowns in the Americas, as well as paperwork and information, passengers, and diverse cargoes of private merchandise. The fleets set sail from Veracruz and Nombre de Dios to the port of Havana in Cuba, from whence the two fleets sailed in convoy to Sevilla, often numbering 400 ships.[55]

The arrival and departure of the fleets in Sevilla touched almost every aspect of daily life in the city. Ships brought news from afar through word of mouth, epistles, and petty trade. Relays of word of mouth stitched together through itinerant merchant communities, mariners, and passengers bridged vast distances across the Spanish empire. Everyday lives and experiences in urban sites that formed part of the Carrera de Indias ports, namely Sevilla, Havana, Veracruz, and Nombre de Dios (and, later, Portobelo) – even among those in the lowest socioeconomic spectrums of society – were often intertwined with events across the Atlantic as passengers and port-dwellers trafficked in mundane and noteworthy information about people and events in faraway places. Recollections about events that had taken place years earlier reveal a world of word of mouth about passengers that preceded most people's arrival in particular ports of embarkation.[56] Such information about passengers' places of origin, destinations,

---

[55] For studies on the socioeconomic fabric of urban life in along the Carrera de Indias routes, see Clark, *Veracruz*; de la Fuente, *Havana*. For an important study of smuggling activities and intra-imperial relations in the ports and regions where the Carrera de Indias fleets did not anchor in the Caribbean, see Ponce Vázquez, *Islanders and Empire*.

[56] For example, "Juan de Pineda," AGI, Indiferente, 2094, no. 1, fols. 3^v–7^r; "Jerónimo González," AGI, Contratación, 5238, no. 1, ramo 38, fols. 1^v–2^r.

and retinue was often gathered and exchanged in taverns and inns on the key trade and travel routes between towns and in the docks in port towns.[57]

News in Sevilla in the summer months of the impending arrival of the fleets from the Americas created a sense of excitement and trepidation among city-dwellers. Merchants and investors would soon discover whether their investments had been successful or whether they had incurred insurmountable losses. Judges at the House of Trade adjudicated on individuals' requests for embarkation licenses throughout the year, but with the impending arrival of the fleets, officials at the House also readied themselves for the bureaucratic task of cataloging and collecting taxes on imported silver and other natural resources violently extracted from the veins of the Americas with forced Black and Indigenous labor, and adjudicating between ship captains, investors, and the crown about the division of gains and losses incurred on overseas ventures. Those waiting for news from kin, friends, or associates organized their affairs to the beat of the annual arrival of the fleets. City dwellers could send news to kin and associates in ports along the Carrera de Indias with a letter or by word of mouth in the spring, knowing that the recipient would receive the message by the summer, and they would then hope to hear a response by the following year with the arrival of the fleets in the summer months. By the time that Cruz penned her second letter on March 15, 1608, she had endured an interminable four-year wait for news from or about her husband since her first letter in 1604. She may have waited a further four years until she heard news in 1612 of his untimely death.

The arrival of the annual fleet in the summer, often numbering hundreds of ships, was a visual spectacle. The scene inspired the artist Alonso Sánchez Coello (1531–1588) to paint *Vista de la ciudad de Sevilla* in the late sixteenth century (Figures 2.4–2.6). The fleets brought hundreds of passengers and maritime laborers to Sevilla, who often spent time residing in the city prior to an onward journey.[58] The lower socioeconomic rung of Sevillian society often eked out a living in trades that supported this maritime commerce by unloading the silver cargo and other precious metals from the ships and hauling the wares to the House of Trade for tax collection, laboring on ship repairs in the Reales Atarazanas or on the shores of

---

[57] For an example of these exchanges taking place in taverns and inns along key overland trading routes, see witness statements in "Juan de Rojas," AGI, Contratación, 293A, no. 1, ramo 6.
[58] For more on mariners and men of the sea in late sixteenth-century Sevilla, see Pérez-Mallaína Bueno, *Spain's Men of the Sea*.

FIGURE 2.4 Alonso Sánchez de Coello, "Vista de la ciudad de Sevilla," late sixteenth century, oil on canvas, width: 295 cm, height: 146 cm (P004779). Prado Museum, Madrid. © Photographic Archive Museo Nacional del Prado.

the river in Triana, or by providing other services at the river. Town criers crisscrossed the city announcing the arrival of news from the Americas and readied to their voices before taking up their role as auctioneers of exotic goods from distant lands at Gradas. City-dwellers crowded onto the riverbanks to watch people disembarking from the ships, and often met new acquaintances among the weary passengers reaching land for the first time in months. Sevilla residents who were plotting their own Atlantic voyages might seek out precious knowledge about the crossing by conversing with passers-by who were disembarking. Other city-dwellers arrived on the riverbanks, poised to offer much-needed services, such as beds, food, information, and healing. Tavern owners, including free *mulatas*, such as Ana Sánchez who owned a tavern in Triana in the 1590s, prepared for the arrival of an influx of customers.[59]

Some Sevillians approached the river to wait expectantly for news from afar. Many would hear about friends or family through word of mouth from passengers disembarking from the ships. Others approached the river to wait for messengers to deliver long-awaited private letters from kin and associates. Cruz may well have been on the riverbank when she tasked trusted messengers to deliver letters to her husband in 1604 and 1608. On the far-left side of Figure 2.5, Coelho depicted a Black woman in conversation with two recently arrived passengers from the Indies. Sevillians from all socioeconomic spectrums crowded the riverbanks to receive legal papers (notarial *escrituras*) drawn up and signed by kin and associates in the Americas that spelled out powers of attorney (*poderes*) that instructed them to engage in commercial transactions on their associates' behalf in Castilla.[60] Others, such as

---

[59] "Lucas Sanchez Barquero contra Christoval esclavo," AHN, España, Inquisición, 2058, exp. 17, fols. 2^v–5^v.

[60] For select examples of *poderes* issued in towns in New Spain and Lima and sent to Sevilla, see "Poder," Unidad de Servicios Bibliotecarios y de Información, Jalapa (cited as USBI Xalapa), Protocolos Notariales Jalapa, Año del protocolo: 1578–1594, April 14, 1582, no. 1, clave del acta: 22, 1578, 196, fols. 67–67^{vta}; "Poder," USBI Xalapa, Protocolos Notariales de Orizaba, Año del protocolo: 1583–1584, September 14, 1583, no. 5, clave del acta: 220, 1583, 21290, fols. 7–8; "Poder," USBI Xalapa, Protocolos Notariales Jalapa, Año del protocolo: 1600–1608, 27 de dic. 1604, no. 3, clave del acta 27, 1600, 1461, fols. 320–320^{vta}; "Poder," Archivo General de la Nación, Perú (hereafter AGNP), Protocolos Notariales de Lima (hereafter PNL), Bartolomé Gascón, Protocolo, 42.1, 19, fols. 23–25 (January 7, 1554); "Poder," AGNP, PNL, Juan Gutiérrez y Nicolás de Grado, Protocolo, 69, 827, fols. 1018–1019 (November 24, 1567); "Poder," AGNP, PNL, Juan Gutierrez, Protocolo, 71, 205, fols. 422–424^v (April 16, 1573); "Poder," AGNP, PNL, Alonso de la Cueva, Protocolo, 29,264, fols. 7^v–9 (January 9, 1580); "Poder," AGNP, PNL, Cristóbal De Aguilar Mendieta, Protocolo, 4,177, fols. 367^v–368 (April 1, 1597).

FIGURE 2.5 Alonso Sánchez de Coello, "Vista de la ciudad de Sevilla," (detail), late sixteenth century, oil on canvas, width: 295 cm, height: 146 cm (P004779). Prado Museum, Madrid. © Photographic Archive Museo Nacional del Prado.

FIGURE 2.6 Alonso Sánchez de Coello, "Vista de la ciudad de Sevilla," (detail), late sixteenth century, oil on canvas, width: 295 cm, height: 146 cm (P004779). Prado Museum, Madrid. © Photographic Archive Museo Nacional del Prado.

a free *mulata* named Catalina Rámirez, might approach the ships to hear news of whether the *poderes* that she had previously sent to Lima had been actioned.[61] Upon learning in 1605 that such instructions had not been carried out, Rámirez decided to embark on an expensive journey to Lima, along with her two freeborn *mulata* daughters, to organize her late husband's estate and ensure the integrity of her daughters' inheritance.[62] Free Black *vecinas* of Sevilla, such as Inés de Jesús, waited anxiously in the early 1600s for factors to deliver funds from their debtors in the New World.[63] Upon hearing of the death in 1615 of the factor tasked to deliver her money, Jesús petitioned to inherit the funds that she was owed from the late factor's estate at the House of Trade.[64] Family members of men and young boys from the lower socioeconomic rungs of society who labored as ship crew and mariners crisscrossing the Atlantic, might also approach the riverbanks to learn about the fate of their kin. A free *mulato vecino* of San Juan de la Palma parish named Juan de Montedeosca learned in 1591 of the death of his brother, a *mulato* soldier named Pedro de Montedeosca,

---

[61] "Catalina Ramírez," AGI, Contratación, 5313, no. 13. Catalina Ramírez, AGI, Indiferente, 2106, no. 85.
[62] Ibid.
[63] "Francisco Morales Matamoros, Inés de Jesús," AGI, Contratación, 324B, no. 1, ramo 9.
[64] Ibid.

after the latter had spent eleven years laboring on Atlantic fleets.[65] Other people readied for their own journeys, sometimes crossing the Atlantic to return to their place of birth and traveling as multigeneration families, as was the case when an elderly *morena horra* named Lucía Cordera received a license to return to Cuba with her *mulato* son, his wife, and their two children in 1576.[66]

Enslaved people in private households of Sevilla might fear the fleets, knowing that their owners could forcibly displace them to the Spanish Americas at any time. This was the case for an enslaved Black woman from Portugal named Margarita de Sossa, whose owner sent her from Sevilla to be sold in New Spain in 1580, never to return.[67] Enslaved people in private households in the city might also find themselves laboring with people from distant lands, as passengers who arrived there often brought servants, including Indigenous Americans and enslaved Black people whom they had purchased in the Americas (and elsewhere) to labor in their households. For example, an enslaved Black man named Juan Miguel was forcibly displaced by his owner from Mexico City to Sevilla in the early seventeenth century.[68] For other enslaved Black people such as Felipa de la Cruz, the arrival of the fleets might signify hopefulness, as they wondered whether their distant kin in the Spanish Americas had sent funds to liberate them from slavery.

Many Black residents of San Salvador parish in Felipa de la Cruz's generation had ties that stretched across the Atlantic, while others embarked on voyages to the New World. For example, free Black woman named Ana Gómez owned two pairs of houses on Salvador Square on the corner of Calle Torneros (known today as Calle Álvarez Quintero) (Figures C.1.1, C1 and 2.3, no. 2).[69] Ana Gómez had traveled to the Panama region in 1576 and settled in Nombre de Dios, where she cemented her status as a wealthy merchant. Gómez maintained ownership of her properties in Salvador Square during her twenty-year absence, and a Sevilla-based factor collected rent on her behalf throughout the late sixteenth

---

[65] "Pedro de Montesdeoca," AGI, Contratación, 485, no. 4, ramo 5; "Testamento de Pedro de Montesdeoca mulato libre," May 24, 1580, AHPS, signatura P-152, libro del año 1580, oficio 1, libro 2, Escribanía de Diego de la Barrera Farfán, fols. 353r–53v. I thank David Wheat for sharing a transcription of this source.

[66] "Lucía Cordera," AGI, Contaduría, 241, no. 74; "Lucía Cordera," AGI, Indiferente, 1968, libro 20, fol. 255ᵛ; "Lucía Cordera," AGI, Indiferente, 1968, libro 20, fol. 259.

[67] "Margarita de Sossa," AGN, Inquisición 208, exp. 3, 80–84,

[68] "Sebastián Robles," AGI, Contratación, 5352, no. 33.

[69] "Ana Gómez," AGI, Contratación, 257A, no. 3, ramo 12, fols. 84ʳ–115ᵛ.

century until her death in 1596.⁷⁰ Gómez's houses on Salvador Square were worth 14,500 *maravedíes* when town criers sold them in a public auction in 1600, while her remaining houses in Magdalena parish at the intersection of Calle de San Pablo and the Puerta de Triana were sold for 6,000, 7,500, and 8,000 *maravedíes* respectively, and her houses in the peripheral parish of San Gil sold for 3,000 *maravedíes* (Figure C.1.1, C1–3).⁷¹ For a sense of the approximate value of these sums, in the late sixteenth century an average mariner on a merchant ship in the *Carrera de Indias* would have earned between 18,750 and 22,500 *maravedíes* in wages per annum in addition to board and sustenance and any spoils from petty trade, while the average cost to an enslaved person to purchase their liberty in Sevilla in this period was approximately 22,720.7 *maravedíes*.⁷²

Cruz likely witnessed the liberation from slavery and the transatlantic lives and ties of some of her Black neighbors in San Salvador parish. Ana de Carvajal, a *mulata* and *natural* of Sevilla, probably also lived in the Salvador neighborhood as she enlisted two *vecinas* of the parish to testify to her freedom when applying for an embarkation license in 1576.⁷³ Other Black *vecinas* who lived in the area during Cruz's lifetime included Leonor de Alarcón, a free *mulata* who resided on Calle Carpinterías. Alarcón provided testimony about the free status of a Black woman named Juana Bautista when the latter applied for an embarkation license in 1592.⁷⁴ Another Black woman who grew up enslaved in the vicinity was Agustina de Jesús, who was born in the nearby parish of San Vicente and was liberated from slavery upon the death of her owner sometime before 1593.⁷⁵ After her liberation, Jesús embarked on a voyage to Santo Domingo as a wage-earning servant in 1593. María de la O also lived in San Salvador parish when her owner liberated her from slavery in 1596, and four years later she sought an embarkation license to travel to Peru

---

⁷⁰ Ibid.
⁷¹ Ibid., fols. 1ʳ–1ᵛ (digital image, 749–750).
⁷² Fernández Chaves, "Amas, esclavas, y libertad"; Pérez-Mallaína Bueno, *Spain's Men of the Sea*, 99. For the value of money, see Muñoz Serrulla, *La Moneda Castellana*; Serrulla calculates that 450 *maravedíes* was the equivalent of 1 *peso de oro común*.
⁷³ "Ana de Carvajal," AGI, Contratación, 5225A, no. 1, ramo 35. See also Figure C.1.1, 3a–d.
⁷⁴ "Simón López, Juana Bautista," AGI, Contratación, 5237, no. 2, ramo 47; "Juana Bautista," AGI, Contratación 5538, libro 3, fols. 127ᵛ⁽⁵⁾. See also Figure C.1.1, 6a–c.
⁷⁵ "Agustina de Jesús," AGI, Contratación, 5243, no. 2, ramo 40; "Libros de Asientos de Pasajeros," "Agustina de Jesús," AGI, Contratación 5538, libro 3, fol. 151ʳ⁽²⁾. See also Figure C.1.1, 8a–d.

with her husband.⁷⁶ A Black *horro* from Santo Domingo named Gaspar Juan (see Chapter 1) likely also lived in this neighborhood. He tasked *vecinos* from San Salvador and the nearby parish of Santa María la Mayor to provide testimony about his liberation from slavery and his successful petition for freedom at the Real Audiencia when he requested an embarkation license in 1594.⁷⁷ At the turn of the seventeenth century, an enslaved Black woman named Lucía Tenorio Palma, who resided in San Salvador parish near the convent of San Leandro, bore a daughter named Juana Tenorio with her enslaver, Gregorio Tenorio. Palma obtained her liberty and subsequently crossed the Atlantic and settled in Portobelo.⁷⁸ It is unclear whether Gregorio Tenorio also liberated their daughter, as Lucía departed from Sevilla without Juana. In Portobelo, Palma accumulated some wealth and married an enslaved Black man named Cristóbal de la Palma, whom she lent 500 pesos so that he could liberate himself from slavery. She also purchased at least six Black slaves, some houses, and a *buhío*.⁷⁹ Like Felipa de Cruz, the young Juana Tenorio – who may or may not have been enslaved, but who remained in Sevilla after her mother departed the city – may also have approached the riverbanks in the hopes of hearing news from or about her absent mother.

A final site in Felipa de la Cruz's neighborhood for possible news about her husband was the palace of the Real Alcázar where the House of Trade was located (Figure 2.3, no. 6). The walk from the Fernandéz de Santillán palace to the House of Trade would have taken approximately twelve to fifteen minutes on foot. Cruz was familiar with this institution and the strategies deployed by liberated Black people to apply for embarkation licenses, as her own husband had petitioned for one in 1603. This is also where Cruz later attempted to inherit her deceased husband's property by falsifying information about her status as a free woman.⁸⁰ In this neighborhood, she may have known another Black couple who later experienced a similar fate to her own. Isabel de Vargas was a free Black woman who labored as a servant in a distinguished household in Santa Cruz parish near the House of Trade (Figure C.1.1, G). Vargas had married an enslaved Black man in the same household, who later

---

[76] "María de la O," AGI, Contratación, 5262A, no. 55. See also Figure C.1.1, 10a–g.
[77] "Gaspar Juan," AGI, Contratación, 5248, no. 1, ramo 17; "Gaspar Juan," AGI, Contratación, 5538, libro 3, fol. 230.
[78] "Lucía Tenorio Palma," AGI, Contratación 526, no. 1, ramo 1, doc. 8, fol. 60ʳ. See also Figure C.1.1, F.
[79] Ibid. A *buhío* is a hut built with wood, branches, cane, or straw.
[80] "Antón Segarra," AGI, Contratación 303, no. 2, fols. 4ʳ–5ʳ.

obtained his liberation from slavery and departed Sevilla in 1624 to labor as a wage-earning drummer (*atambaor*) on board a ship destined for the Americas.[81] Like Felipa de la Cruz, Isabel de Vargas remained in Sevilla waiting for news about her absent husband, until she learned of his death at sea in 1627.[82]

Cruz might have approached the House of Trade in the hope of hearing news about her husband's whereabouts. This is because the crown established probate courts of assets of the deceased (*bienes de difuntos*) across the viceroyalties of the Spanish Americas to ensure the return of Castilians' orphaned property – when no heirs existed in the Indies – to the kingdom of Castilla. Such courts in the American viceroyalties dispatched officials to inventory orphaned goods and to establish biographical information about the deceased and their heirs. These courts then sent the worth of the deceased's property to the House of Trade in Sevilla to be distributed among existing heirs.[83] House officials alerted potential heirs in a three pronged effort, first by publishing written information for public viewing at the interior squares adjoining the building of the House of Trade in the Real Alcázar, then by dispatching criers to sing news of death and property in Sevilla's public squares, and finally by dispatching messengers to the deceased's places of *naturaleza* (birthplace) across Castilla.[84]

House of Trade criers announced the arrival of the assets of the deceased across public squares in Sevilla, meaning that those who lived in the city, and especially those who resided near the House of Trade, would regularly hear about the arrival of deceased Castilians' goods, including those of at least thirty-five men and women who were described by probate judges as Black or *mulato* who perished in the Indies between 1550 and 1630 and whose property was returned to the House of Trade.[85] As Cruz dwelt in or near the neighborhoods where Diego Suárez, Pedro de Montedeosca, and Luis Pinelo grew up and where Ana Gómez owned property, it is possible that she heard House of Trade criers announcing news of their respective deaths in 1590, 1591, 1596, and 1610 (Figure C.1.1, A–E).[86] Even

---

[81] "Alonso de Castro," AGI, Contratación, 526, no. 1, ramo 1, doc. 12.
[82] Ibid.
[83] Almorza Hidalgo, "*No se hace pueblo sin ellas*"; González Sánchez, *Dineros de ventura*; Mangan, *Transatlantic Obligations*; Tempère, *Vivre et mourir*.
[84] Ibid.
[85] "Real Cédula," AGI, Indiferente, 1967, libro 16, fols. 251–251ᵛ.
[86] "Ana Gómez," AGI, Contratación, 257A, no. 3, ramo 12; "Diego Suárez," AGI, Contratación 255, no. 1, ramo 5; "Pedro de Montedeosca," AGI, Contratación, 485, no. 4, ramo 5; "Luis Pinelo," AGI, Contratación, 296A, no. 2, ramo 3.

if Cruz had not personally heard the criers singing the news, she may later have heard about inheritance of their estates, as neighbors regularly discussed such details among their acquaintances. For example, in Cruz's 1608 letter to Segarra, she offered details about the property that her neighbors had inherited, describing how María Jiménez had "married her daughter, Elvira, to a silversmith. As a dowry for the marriage, she gave 400 ducats of the 1,000 that she had been given for the death of Julián González."[87] Cruz may also have heard that a twenty-two-year-old free *mulata* named María de Ribera, who resided in the Plazuela de Santa Catalina in the parish of San Pedro (a seven-minute walk from the palace where Cruz lived), inherited money in 1610 to pay for her marriage after her late brother perished in Cuba and named her as a benefactor in his will.[88] Cruz may also have heard about Ana Gómez's and Diego Suárez's posthumous endowments to local religious associations in her vicinity – in 1596, Gómez bestowed fifty *ducados* to the hospital of Nuestra Señora de la Paz that stood opposite Salvador Church where Cruz and Segarra had exchanged marriage vows, while Suárez's estate donated monies to the confraternities in the Franciscan Convent in San Francisco Square after a lengthy legal dispute between his heirs in the probate courts at the House of Trade.[89]

Tracing Cruz's footsteps and experiences along this fifteen-minute walk from the palace where she was enslaved to the House of Trade reveals how her personal cartography stretched well beyond Sevilla, even though she never left the city. Her hopes and ideas about freedom and slavery were inevitably impacted and informed by the global city that she inhabited and the relationships that she forged in the palace where she was enslaved and in her broader neighborhood.

BLACK TRANSATLANTIC TIES: WORD OF MOUTH AND EPISTLES ACROSS THE ATLANTIC

Thick spheres of communication emerged across the Spanish Atlantic between free and enslaved Black people woven through relays of word of mouth, epistolary networks, and legal powers. These ephemeral histories of nascent Black public spheres that stretched across vast distances in the

---

[87] "Antonio Segarra," AGI, Contratación, 303, no. 2, fols. 10^r, 18^v–20^v.
[88] "Luis Pinelo," AGI, Contratación, 296A, no. 2, R.3, fols. 5^r–6^v.
[89] "Ana Gómez," AGI, Contratación, 257A, no. 3, ramo 12. fols. 84^r–115^v; "Diego Suárez," AGI, Contratación 255, no. 1, ramo 5, fols. 27^r–30^r.

early Atlantic world are difficult to trace as the evidence that catalogs this history is fragmentary and scattered across diverse archives. Transatlantic conversations often became etched into archives through witness testimonies about people's biographies across various types of documents, including in trials prosecuted by Holy Offices of the Inquisition stationed across the Spanish empire, in petitions to royal and ecclesiastical courts, in criminal cases, in notarial records, and in free and liberated Black people's petitions for passenger and embarkation licenses to cross the Atlantic. In particular, Black petitioners who requested embarkation and passenger licenses responded to policies introduced by the Spanish crown to control who could migrate to the Americas by discussing their ties in the Spanish Americas (where relevant to their lives). Judges at the Council of the Indies regarded family reunification or return to place of birth as legitimate reasons for individuals to undertake journeys to the Americas from Castilla.[90] Consequently, free Black and *mulato* applicants for passenger licenses often relied, where possible, on evidence of their familial ties in the Americas. To prove such ties, supplicants would enlist witnesses in Sevilla to speak of their American *naturaleza* or family ties across the Atlantic. These testimonies mirrored broader strategies deployed by Castilians of all socioeconomic strata, as prospective passengers presented letters sent by their kin in the Americas or information that they had obtained through word of mouth to the House of Trade as evidence of their ties to America. The tendency among married Castilian women of all social strata to present letters from their absent husbands to the House of Trade has resulted in one of the richest archives of private letters and information about word of mouth in the early modern period.[91] In lieu of presenting original letters, some supplicants for licenses brought witnesses who would attest to the existence of this Atlantic correspondence. These witness testimonies catalog how Black dwellers of late sixteenth-century Sevilla often partook in epistolary networks and relays of word of mouth with kin and associates in the Americas.

Word of mouth was a powerful form of communication in this period. Trading entrepots in Castile and the Spanish Americas were often connected through hearsay, whispers, and gossip about people's lives, as passers-by trafficked in information about the whereabouts of family members. These informal whispers through word of mouth were sometimes formalized through webs of informants to the Inquisition,

---

[90] Almorza Hidalgo, "*No se hace pueblo sin ellas*"; Rey Castelao, *El vuelo corto*.
[91] Almorza Hidalgo, "*No se hace pueblo sin ellas*"; Otte, *Cartas Privadas*.

especially for suspected crimes of bigamy.[92] For example, two Iberian *mulatos* accused of bigamy in Inquisitorial trials in Mexico City in 1579 and 1622, named Antonio de Arenas and Cristóbal de Castroverde, suggested to Inquisitors that they had not committed bigamy as they had learned upon arriving in the Americas that they had become widows. They each explained that they had heard news about the deaths of their respective *mulata* wives in Cádiz and Sevilla through information relayed by travelers passing through the port of Veracruz.[93] Neither of these individuals lived in the port of Veracruz. Instead, they resided in Mexico City and the rural and mining environs of the viceregal capital. But their pinpointing of Veracruz as the site where they received news of their wives' deaths in Castilla highlights that they traveled through that port on their way to Mexico City and shows how people often heard news about loved ones in distant lands when passing through port towns.[94] Similarly, in 1575, a free Black woman named Luisa de Abrego defended herself against charges of bigamy before Inquisitorial authorities in Mexico City. The accusations had materialized because five different passers-by in Mexico City had heard rumors that Abrego had married a free Black man in Jerez de la Frontera in Castilla some years earlier. In her trial, she explained that she had not married in Jerez and instead had only received a promise of marriage and an embrace from a suitor, who later married someone else.[95] Since this episode in Jerez, Abrego had spent some years living in Sevilla, and had crossed the Atlantic onboard a ship in an Armada (a large fleet of military ships equipped for wars at sea or land) to Florida where she had married one of the soldiers on the fleet, the couple then moving to Mexico City. Despite the many years that had elapsed between the episode with her suitor in Jerez and her life in Mexico City, rumors from Abrego's affair followed her to Mexico City and resulted in Inquisitors ordering her arrest. While Inquisitors determined that both Castroverde and Arenas were guilty of bigamy as they had both married *mulata* women in Cádiz and Sevilla, respectively, and subjected them to severe punishments, in Luisa de Abrego's case, judges ruled that she was innocent of the charges, after Abrego declared that her experience in Jerez had not been a marriage as there was "no carnal

---

[92] "Cristóbal de Castroverde," AGN, México, GD61 Inquisición, vol. 310, exp. 7, fol. 53.
[93] Ibid., fols. 30ᵛ (547ᵛ), 31 (548); "Antonio de Arenas," AGN, México, GD61 Inquisición, vol. 107, exp. 4, fol. 209ᵛ.
[94] "Cristóbal de Castroverde," AGN, México, GD61 Inquisición, vol. 310, exp. 7, fols. 32 (549)–32ᵛ (549ᵛ).
[95] "Luisa de Abrego," AGN, México, GD61 Inquisición, vol. 103, exp. 6, fol. 20.

copulation or any thing else, other than holding hands, embracing, and kissing each other."[96]

Another example of how word of mouth brought news from afar appears in Juan de Pineda's 1583 petition for a passenger license to return from Sevilla to Lima to reunite with his recently liberated Black mother, María de Pineda.[97] Juan de Pineda had been brought to Sevilla when he was three years-old by a Sevilla-merchant named Pedro de Ribera, who had resided in Lima in the 1560s. Juan was reportedly the son of Ribera's Black slave, María de Pineda, and his servant named Pedro de Osorio. Pedro de Ribera had apparently promised to look after Osorio's son and bring him to Sevilla so that he could learn how to read and write, and in so doing had separated enslaved mother and child. Juan de Pineda managed to keep in touch sporadically from Sevilla with his mother in Lima. Fifteen years after arriving in Sevilla, he received news that his mother was alive and that she had accrued significant wealth in Lima after her liberation from slavery. One witness described how it is "well known that for a woman of her color, she is rich and well resourced."[98] Specifically, Pineda reported that this news had reached him via the fleet of ships that arrived from Tierra Firme in 1583. Whether María de Pineda sent a letter to her son inviting him to return to Lima via a messenger aboard this fleet or whether the news arrived through word of mouth is unclear. Nonetheless, in this connected world between Lima and Sevilla, with merchants moving between sites who testified to having personal relationships with both mother and son, it is not unfeasible that the latter was the case.

Witnesses' discussions of how Black residents of Sevilla sent and received letters reveal Black people's access to lettered cultures in this period. The cases studied here reveal Black letter writers who were either literate or were able to purchase the services of *escribientes* (individuals who knew how to read and write, but lacked the formal education or social status that would allow them to enter a writing profession, such as the notarial ranks, and instead wrote and read documents for a fee), or relied on the favors of friends or associates who possessed these skills. In the 1550s, there was at least one *mulato escribiente* in Sevilla, named Juan de Lugones; he sent a petition regarding a probate case to the Council of

---

[96] "Luisa de Abrego," AGN, México, GD61 Inquisición, vol. 103, exp. 6, fols. 263ʳ and 274ʳ.
[97] "Juan de Pineda," AGI, Indiferente, 2094, no. 1.
[98] Ibid.

the Indies.[99] The aforementioned Black confraternity of Our Lady of the Angels in Sevilla appointed a brother to the role of *escribano*; in 1604, a Black brother named Antonio de Villalobos occupied this position, signing declarations on behalf of all the Black brothers in the confraternity.[100]

Free and enslaved Black people in Sevilla and its environs were also sometimes taught how to read and write in formal settings when they were children.[101] For example, the aforementioned Cristóbal de Castroverde described how he had learned to read and write with a tutor while living with his free Black mother and white father in late sixteenth-century Carmona (a village neighboring Sevilla), while Leonor de la Isla, a Cádiz-born *mulata* arrested by the Inquisition in Veracruz in 1622, described how her father had sent her to a convent as a child to learn how to read and write.[102] Another indicator of literacy was if an individual signed documents and petitions; a signature implied that the individual did not require the document to be read to them to understand the contents.[103] Other examples of literacy emerge in the testimonies of free Black and *mulato* people who reported sending and receiving letters to their kin across the Atlantic when arrested by a Holy Office of the Inquisition. Leonor de la Isla described how she sent letters from Veracruz to her friends in Cádiz; María Gerónima, a Sevilla-native *mulata*, testified that she maintained

---

[99] "Juan de Lugones, de color mulato, loro, escribiente," AGI, Indiferente, 1207, no. 60, fol. 1.

[100] "Pleito entre la Hdad de Ntra Sra de la Antigua y la de los Ángeles que llaman la de los morenos," AGAS, III.1.6, L.9885, No. 1, fols. 14ʳ–15ʳ.

[101] For examples of Black and *mulato* people learning how to read and write as children in Sevilla, see "Juan de Pineda," AGI, Indiferente, 2094, no. 1; "Pedro," AGI, Indiferente, 2089, no. 29. For selected scholarship on Black people's access to writing and literacy in the colonial period, see Acree Jr, "Jacinto Ventura"; Berruezo-Sánchez, "Negro poeta"; Borucki, *From Shipmates*; Borucki and Acree, *Los caminos*; Cañizares-Esguerra, "The Imperial"; Dawson, "A Sea" and *Undercurrents of Power*; Fisk, "Black Knowledge" and "Transimperial Mobilities"; Fracchia, *"Black but Human"*; von Germeten, *Violent Delights*. Gómez, *The Experiential*; Graubart, *Republics of Difference*; Jouve Martín, *Esclavos* and "Public Ceremonies"; Lazzari, "A Bad Race"; Martín Casares, *Juan Latino*; Rowe, *Black Saints*; Wright, *The Epic*.

[102] "Cristóbal De Castroverde," AGN, México, GD61 Inquisición, vol. 310, exp. 7, fols. 32–32ᵛ; "Leonor de Isla," AGN, México, GD61 Inquisición. vol. 341, exp. 1, fols. 71ᵛ.

[103] Selected Black and *mulato* people who signed their name on petitions and who resided in, or passed through Sevilla, in the late sixteenth century include "Sebastián de Toral," AGI, Indiferente, 2059, no. 108, fol. 3ʳ, See also Restall, *The Black Middle*, 6–12, 15–16; "Juan Baptista de Cárdenas," AGI, Indiferente, 1233; "Jerónimo González," AGI, Contratación, 5238, no. 1, ramo 38; "Angelina Díaz," AGI, Indiferente, 2102, no. 166; "Susana Manuel," AGI, Indiferente, 2075, no. 140.

written correspondence with her Sevilla-based son intermittently every few years during the three decades she resided in Cartagena de Indias and Veracruz; Cristóbal de Castroverde attested to receiving letters in New Spain from his Sevilla-based free *mulata* wife Isabel Hernández, interpreting the absence of these letters in later years as confirmation of the news of her death; while as a final example, in 1605, an eighty-year-old liberated Black woman named Catalina Déniz, who had borne fourteen children and married three times in Tenerife (Canary Islands), testified before Inquisitorial authorities that she had received letters from two of her sons who had departed to the Indies.[104] Occasionally, probate records also revealed indicators of literacy. For example, listed among the possessions of the previously mentioned Diego Suárez were scripts of plays, namely "scripts of comedies and *autos* of comedies."[105] The fact that Suárez had "scripts of comedies" among his possessions suggests that he was literate, as actors who were given such scripts tended to be able to read and memorize complex dialogue, unlike illiterate actors who might act in a play by improvising a scene.[106] Similarly, dozens of letters listed among Ana Gómez's possessions reveal that she was also literate.[107] Other lettered enslaved and liberated Black people from this era included Juan Latino, who penned epics and epithets in Latin and taught Latin and grammar in Granada Cathedral in the late sixteenth century, and the Tangier-born free *mulato* named Gaspar de Vasconcelos who lived in various sites of the Atlantic world before eventually settling in Mexico City in the early seventeenth century, where he earned a living as an *escribiente* to high-ranking colonial officials and also taught grammar in a school.[108]

---

[104] "Leonor de Isla," AGN, Mexico, GD61 Inquisicion. vol. 341, exp. 1, fols. 154ᵛ–155ʳ; "Trial of María Gerónima [de Vallejo], mulatto, for witchcraft," Huntington Library, San Marino (cited as HLSM), Huntington Manuscripts (cited as HM), 35165, fol. 34; Catalina Déniz,' Archivo del Museo Canario, Inquisición de Canarias, INQ-142.001, Causas de fe, Libros de penitenciados, vol. 146, libro 34 de penitenciados, fols. 41ʳ–43ᵛ; Cristóbal De Castroverde,' AGN, México, GD61 Inquisición, vol. 310, exp. 7, fols. 32–32ᵛ. For analysis of Catalina Déniz, see Fra-Molinero, "'Mis padres."

[105] "Diego Suárez," AGI, Contratación 255, no. 1, ramo 5, fol. 29ʳ.

[106] I thank Baltasar Fra-Molinero for conveying this point about the significance of Suárez possessing these papers in a conversation with me.

[107] "Ana Gómez," AGI, Contratación, 257A, no. 3, ramo 12.

[108] "Proceso Contra Gaspar de Rivero Vasconcelos, Mulato Libre, Estudiante Canonista," AGN, Mexico, GD61 Inquisicion, vol. 435, exp. 248, fols. 527–528. See also, Lazzari, "A Bad Race"; Latino, *The Song of John*; Martín Casares, *Juan Latino*; Wright, *The Epic*.

Black residents of late sixteenth-century Sevilla who penned and sent letters across the Atlantic likely relied on the services of trusted messengers. Antón Segarra sent Felipa de la Cruz at least one letter from New Spain to Sevilla, as she acknowledged its receipt in the first lines of her 1604 letter, describing her elation at receiving it: "I received your letter with much happiness to learn that you are in good health and that you had a successful crossing [of the Atlantic], and I rejoiced greatly, and I plead to God that he give you [good health], and that he gives it to you entirely, which is what I wish."[109] Four years later, she explained that she had sent such a long epistle because "The messenger is trustworthy as it is *señor* Juan García." Cruz's first lines in her 1608 missive indicated to the messenger that her husband was "in the convent of Santo Domingo in San Juan de Ulúa," the religious institution where Segarra spent some years laboring as a wage-earning servant to Fray Pablo de la Magdalena.[110] This suggests that her husband would know where to collect her correspondence and that Cruz probably used a *particular* (private messenger), who may have been a trusted *vecino* of Sevilla, a merchant, or a religious figure who traveled between both sites. As historian González Martínez has shown, private messengers played an important role in delivering official mail relating to urgent royal affairs as well as private mail, the main qualification for the role being "inspiring trust in the sender" that they would deliver the letters.[111] For example, the previously mentioned Leonor de la Isla offered a detailed description of the arrival of the *navío de aviso* (a ship within the annual fleet that transported royal mail) to the port of Veracruz, and how she had sent letters to her friends in Cádiz to convey news about a recent murder in Veracruz by enlisting the help of a resident of Cádiz who was on board the *navío de aviso* and agreed to deliver letters to her friends in Cádiz.[112]

In other cases, private merchants and passengers served as informal messengers who delivered messages via word of mouth as well as precious letters. Witness testimonies in Luisa de Valladolid's petition for a passenger license reveal the interconnected world that allowed Black

---

[109] "Antón Segarra," AGI, Contratación, 303, no. 2, fols. 10ʳ, 18ᵛ–20ᵛ.
[110] Ibid. On the role of private merchants in royal mail, see González Martínez, "Comunicarse a pesar de."
[111] González Martínez, "Comunicarse a pesar de."
[112] "Leonor de Isla," AGN, México, GD61 Inquisicion. vol. 341, exp. 1, fols. 154ᵛ–155ʳ. For a discussion of systems of mail delivery in the Spanish empire in the sixteenth century, see González Martínez, "Comunicarse a pesar de" and "Communicating an Empire."

kin separated by vast distances to keep in touch via letters. Luisa de Valladolid, a sixteen- to eighteen-year-old free *mulata* who resided in Sevilla, sent a petition to the Council of the Indies in 1588 to request a passenger license to cross the Atlantic so that she could return to the port of Nombre de Dios.[113] Luisa de Valladolid employed a procurator to help deliver the petition. Speaking on her behalf, the procurator explained that Valladolid had been born free in Nombre de Dios and that her mother was a free Black woman named Sebastiana de la Sal who resided in the Caribbean port town. While dwelling in Sevilla, Luisa de Valladolid had kept in touch with her free Black mother through letters that she had sent via trusted messengers on ships that crisscrossed the ocean and via word of mouth involving merchants and other passengers who passed through both Atlantic ports. They were sufficiently in contact for Sebastiana de la Sal to hear news about the death of Valladolid's father sixteen years after their departure to Sevilla. After hearing the news, Sebastiana de la Sal wrote many letters to her daughter insisting that she return to Nombre de Dios, and she also sent money to pay for her daughter's voyage. Luisa's procurator explained how Sebastiana de la Sal "resides in the city of Nombre de Dios and she is rich, and she has written to Luisa to ask her to go there to be with her and she has sent funds for the cost of the journey."[114] Sebastiana de la Sal might have also provided funds to employ the services of a procurator to help maneuver Luisa de Valladolid's petition to the Council of the Indies for a passenger license.

In anticipation of this 1588 petition, Luisa de Valladolid and her procurator gathered four merchants to testify about her life before a public notary in Sevilla. These Sevilla-based merchants' descriptions of their acquaintance with mother and daughter in Nombre de Dios and Sevilla over the previous two decades reveal the impact of mercantile travel in connecting disparate communities across the Atlantic. These witnesses attested that they had attended Luisa's baptism in Nombre de Dios and knew that Sebastiana de la Sal had sent letters to her daughter in Sevilla. One witness explained that Sal had also written letters to him, urging that he ensure that Luisa "be made to start the journey to Nombre de Dios."[115] It is possible that these witnesses may have delivered verbal messages and letters across the Atlantic between mother and daughter

---

[113] "Luisa de Valladolid," AGI, Indiferente, 2097, no. 197.
[114] Ibid.
[115] Ibid., fols. 2^v–4^r.

during the course of the sixteen years that Luisa de Valladolid lived in Sevilla, as they testified to traveling between the two places during this period.[116] Further examples of letter writing between Black parents residing in the Americas and their progeny in Castilla, especially when a parent had accumulated sufficient capital to pay for the cost of their voyage and maintenance, are also recorded in other petitions for passenger licenses.[117]

Letter writing practices between Black kin generated a sense of public knowledge in Sevilla about family arrangements across the Atlantic. Individuals discussed letters they had sent and received in their daily life with their friends, neighbors, and associates. For example, a poverty-stricken *mulata* from Sevilla named Francisca de Figueroa petitioned for a passenger license at the Council of the Indies by providing witness testimony at the House of Trade in June 1600, and later applied for an embarkation license.[118] Figueroa positioned her impending departure as a response to a family member "calling for her" (*la ha mandado a llamar*) from the Americas, thereby attempting to prove her familial ties in the Americas, even though she was a *natural* of Castilla. She claimed that her daughter had sent her many letters from Cartagena de Indias, promising to pay for the cost of her and her twenty-year-old daughter's voyage. Figueroa's five witnesses lived across various parishes of the city (Figure C.1.1, 11a–f). They described her transatlantic family ties and letter writing, explaining that Juana de Figueroa resided in Cartagena de Indias and had sent her mother many letters inviting her to live in Cartagena, with one witness describing how "she knows that [Juana de Figueroa] called for her mother Francisca de Figueroa to relieve her of her needs and because of the poverty that she and her daughter María experience in these kingdoms."[119] Another witness explained that "she has seen the letters of Juana Figueroa in which she tells her mother to go and offering her money for the cost of the voyage and that she will help/

---

[116] Ibid., The Council of the Indies initially rejected Luisa de Valladolid's petition, noting "no ha lugar," but changed their decision upon appeal and granted the passenger license.

[117] For other examples of Black parents in the Indies writing to their children in Sevilla, see "Beatriz de Landa," AGI, Indiferente, 2095, no. 14; "Crispina de Herrera," AGI, Indiferente, 2105, no. 17; "Crispina de Herrera," AGI, Contratación, 5262A, no. 73; "Isabel de Vitoria," AGI, Indiferente, 2091, no. 24.

[118] "Francisca de Figueroa," AGI, Contratación 5268, no. 2, ramo 68; "Francisca de Figueroa," AGI, Contratación, 5261, no. 2, ramo 33. Part of this petition is transcribed in Garofalo, "Afro-Iberian Subjects."

[119] Ibid., fols. 1ᵛ–2ʳ.

relieve her."[120] Neighbors, friends, and associates therefore sometimes saw, read, or heard about transatlantic epistles between family members, leading to public awareness about the Atlantic dimensions of Black kinship networks.

Two of Figueroa's witnesses at the House of Trade were members of the professional ranks of official messengers in the city, tending to the business of delivering letters across the sprawling Spanish empire.[121] One witness was Francisca de Mendoza who described herself as the "wife of Sevastian de Saavedra, messenger by horse of our king (*correo a lla caballo del rey nuestro*)" and lived in the parish of La Magdalena. A *correo* in this period was a specialized professional who served as a messenger for institutions and private individuals, often working seasonally on different routes (based on necessity and demand), who often accumulated some capital.[122] Francisca de Mendoza testified on two occasions for Francisca de Figueroa (in 1600 and in 1601), suggesting a close friendship between the pair. A second witness was Felipe de Selpuldes, who described himself as a *correo* and as a resident of the parish of San Bartolomé. Figueroa's reliance on these witnesses implies that she was friends with, and possibly formed part of a network of, messengers in Sevilla whose trade involved delivering letters across the peninsula and the Atlantic. Historian González Martínez has traced how messengers often crossed the Atlantic with two cases of letters, one containing mail pertaining to official business of the Spanish crown and the other containing private letters.[123] It is possible that one of these witnesses delivered letters between Francisca de Figueroa and her daughter in Cartagena, or that they saw letters that other messengers delivered.

Letter writing between Black kin also generated knowledge about the Atlantic world in particular sites, as friends and neighbors sometimes participated in relays of exchanges of information by hearing about contents of letters and commenting on these with others. In a petition for an embarkation license at the House of Trade in 1607, a twenty-six-year-old *mulata vecina* of Havana (Cuba) named Francisca de Azuaga stated that she had journeyed to Sevilla five years earlier to meet and communicate with her family in the Castilian city and for other important matters that

---

[120] Ibid.
[121] González Martínez, "Comunicarse a pesar de" and "Communicating an Empire."
[122] I thank Nelson Fernando González Martínez for sharing his manuscript for an article titled "Postal Freedoms and Coverage: The Multispatial Circulation of Correspondence Between Spain and America (1492–1560)" with me in private correspondence in 2023.
[123] Ibid.

obliged her to be in Sevilla.[124] Azuaga explained that she now wished to embark on the next fleet to Havana as her mother, a free Black woman named María Bautista, had sent a message instructing her to return.

Azuaga brought three witnesses to the House of Trade. Their testimonies reveal an interconnected world of communication across key trading entrepots of the Spanish Atlantic and highlight the public dimensions of letter writing between kin.[125] A widow from the neighborhood of Triana named Catalina Ruíz described how she had met Azuaga five years earlier when Azuaga had disembarked from the ship in Sevilla. Ruíz testified that she knew that Azuaga had received letters from her mother in Havana because she had heard the letters being read aloud.[126] This description points to the aurality of written correspondence in sixteenth- and early seventeenth-century Sevilla. The exact phrase that Ruíz used leaves some ambiguity as to who exactly was reading the letters: "and she [Ruíz] has heard her [Azuaga] read letters from the said her mother in which her mother calls for her" (*y ésta le ha oydo leer cartas de la dicha su madre en q enbia a llamarla*).[127] This implies that they either lived in close quarters and Ruíz heard Azuaga reading the letters aloud, and possibly also discussed the contents of the letters, or perhaps that Azuaga sought the services of an *escribiente* in a public or private space and Ruíz was privy to hearing the letters being read. Azuaga may have enlisted two merchants who regularly crossed the Atlantic between Havana and Sevilla to deliver her correspondence with her mother, as these two witnesses each later claimed to have known and communicated with Azuaga and her mother in Havana every time they passed through that port, that they knew that María Bautista had sent her daughter to Sevilla five years earlier, and that they had communicated with Azuaga in Sevilla over the preceding five years.

Free Black women also used evidence of epistles with their distant spouses to persuade judges at the House of Trade and the Council of the Indies that their husbands had invited them to travel to the Indies to live together. Such strategies were common among women of all socioeconomic backgrounds, as married Castilian women rarely obtained a passenger license unless they traveled to join their husbands with the view to living a married life in the Indies. The phrase "he has called for her

---

[124] "Francisca de Azuaga," AGI, Contratación, 5301, no. 2, ramo 6.
[125] Ibid., fols. 2^r–3^r.
[126] Ibid., fols. 2^r–3^r.
[127] Ibid., fol. 3^r.

(*la ha mandado a llamar*)," appears frequently in petitions for licenses across all socioeconomic spectrums. In addition, some husbands in the Indies issued *poderes* to associates in Sevilla to help guide their wives and children through the process of petitioning for a passenger license and sometimes also to accompany them to the Americas. Such was the case when a carpenter from Sevilla who resided in the town of Jalapa in New Spain issued a *poder* to two associates in 1619, instructing them to organize provisions in Sevilla to bring his wife and children on the first fleet to New Spain and provided money to cover the costs.[128] Black and *mulata* women also deployed this strategy to argue in their petitions that their absent husbands had "called for them." One example is María Gutiérrez, a woman who described herself as *mulata* and *lora* and *vecina* of Cádiz. In her petition for a passenger license in 1577, Gutiérrez explained that her husband had left Cádiz for the viceregal capital of Mexico City to work as a tailor and had sent her "many letters" begging her to travel to New Spain to live a married life with him.[129] Many Black and *mulata* women who crossed the ocean to reunite with their husbands or other family members also traveled with their children, as was the case of Sofía Hernández, a free Black woman from Sevilla who traveled to New Spain with her son, Pedro, in 1578 to live with her husband, Pedro de Lunares.[130] Sometimes spouses returned to Castilla to collect their wives and children and accompany them through the process of applying for the relevant licenses for the family to move to the Indies.[131]

These archival fragments that document how free and enslaved Black dwellers of late sixteenth- and early seventeenth-century Sevilla kept

---

[128] "Poder," USBI Xalapa, Protocolos Notariales de Jalapa, Años de Protocolo, 1617–1631, no. 5, May 21, 1621, clave del acta: 27, 1617, 2644, fols. 140–140ᵛ.

[129] "María Gutiérrez," AGI, Indiferente, 2058, no. 51; "Real Cédula, María Gutiérrez," AGI, Indiferente, 1968, libro 21, fol. 1.

[130] "Sofía Hernández," AGI, Contratación 5538, libro 1, fol. 95ᵛ; "Real Cédula, Sofia Hernández," AGI, Indiferente, 1969, libro 22, fol. 130. Other selected examples of Black and *mulata* women who petitioned for licenses to cross the Atlantic to live a married life with their spouses in the Spanish Americas include "Juana," AGI, Contratación, 5537, libro 3, fol. 429ʳ; "Jeronima," AGI, Indiferente, 2084, no. 98; "Constanza Sánchez," AGI, Indiferente, 2053, no. 43; "Constanza Sánchez," AGI, Contratación, 5225B, no. 33; "Felipa de Santiago," AGI, Contratación, 5248, no. 1, ramo 1. See also Garofalo, "The Shape of a Diaspora."

[131] "Antonio Núñez," AGI, Indiferente, 2084, no. 52; "Francisco González," AGI, Indiferente, 2052, no. 14; "Francisco González," AGI, Indiferente, 2058, no. 6; "Francisco González," AGI, Contratación 5538, libro I, fol. 427ᵛ; "Francisco González," AGI, Indiferente, 1968, libro 21, fol. 131ᵛ; "Francisco González," AGI, Contaduría, 241, no. 117.

in touch with associates, kin, and friends from afar through word of mouth and written communication reveal the emergence of a nascent Black public sphere that stretched across the Spanish Atlantic world in the late sixteenth century. The history of Black thought in Sevilla in the late sixteenth and early seventeenth centuries must be studied through the prism of Black city dwellers' interactions with the broader Atlantic world, in particular through their participation in relays of word of mouth and letter writing, as well as varied experiences of movement across maritime spaces, including as a result of forced displacements as enslaved people, and departures as free and liberated people spurred by opportunities for wage-earning labor, or as fee-paying independent passengers. The diverse social and economic ties that Black dwellers of Sevilla maintained across the Atlantic as well as the impact of the arrival of news from afar inevitably shaped enslaved and free people's ideas about freedom and slavery in Sevilla.

IMAGINING FREEDOM IN SEVILLA THROUGH FRACTURED COMMUNITY MEMORIES OF *RESCATES* FROM AFAR AND TRANSATLANTIC EPISTLES

In Felipa de la Cruz's social milieu, freedom was on everybody's lips. Within the palace, enslaved laborers and servants gossiped constantly about other people's lives and status as free, *horro*, or enslaved (and under what conditions). They spoke among themselves to exchange news about the lives of their friends and acquaintances within and outside their households, and inevitably shared such news with other acquaintances.

Glimpses of such gossip within the palace walls appear in Felipa de la Cruz's letters to her absent husband.[132] Other evidence emerges from witness statements made by three palace-servants who attested on behalf of Cruz's husband, Antón Segarra, to certify his freedom in February 1603.[133] They described that they knew Segarra because he used to stay in Fernández de Santillán's Sevilla residence with his former owner, Juana Segarra de Saavedra. They explained that they had heard from other servants in the household about Segarra's impending freedom owing to result of a liberation clause in his late owner's will, with one servant testifying that he had "heard other servants in the house talk about it many

---

[132] "Antón Segarra," AGI, Contratación, 303, no. 2, fols. 10ʳ, 18ᵛ–20ᵛ.
[133] Ibid., fols. 11ᵛ–13ʳ. These testimonies are transcribed, along with Antón Segarra's cache of freedom papers, in Ireton and Álvarez Hernández, "Epístolas."

times."¹³⁴ According to their testimonies, everyone in Fernández de Santillán's household knew that Antón Segarra had been subject to a six-year delayed manumission clause and that Juana Segarra de Saavedra had liberated Segarra after he had completed the required service. Segarra's witnesses also described having seen, touched, and in some cases transported Segarra's freedom certificate. For example, Julián González explained how Saavedra had notarized Segarra's *carta de alhorría* in the town of Écija and had entrusted him to deliver the document to Antón Segarra. The testimonies of the three servants in Fernández de Santillán's palace indicate that Segarra's status, his eventual liberation from slavery, and the physicality of Segarra's *carta de alhorría* were common knowledge, and that laborers in the household shared and exchanged information about people's status and liberation from slavery. The discussions about freedom and slavery within this palace reflected broader conversations across neighborhoods in Sevilla, as residents gossiped about one another.

Felipa de la Cruz's letters to her husband reveal how enslaved Black people in Sevilla might have held out hope that distant family members would send funds to purchase their liberty from slavery. Cruz's letters envisioned Segarra's Atlantic travels as a means to accumulate wealth in order to purchase her and their children's freedom.¹³⁵ In her 1608 letter, among news about their neighbors and her enslavers, Cruz also described how the children were faring without their father and exasperatedly reminded Segarra of his family's enslaved status and that their children had no other salvation except to hope that their father would relieve them of their enslaved condition:

> Your daughter María is healthy, although in past days the poor creature was very unwell, and all she does is ask after you and when you will return, and they take great care to entrust you to God every night when they go to sleep. Your son Andrés Segarra is also pretty: all he does is play with these ladies, and in this way, fortunately, both siblings entertain themselves in this way, and they are always chirping for their father. And I am not surprised, because they do not have any other source of goodness or relief other than God, if it is not the one you will have to provide them.

The source of relief that Cruz envisioned Segarra providing their children likely reflects a previous arrangement between the married couple that Antón would use his liberty to earn enough money to send funds to pay for their liberation from slavery.

---

¹³⁴ Ibid.
¹³⁵ Ibid., fols. 10ʳ, 18ᵛ–20ᵛ.

Cruz spelled out this expectation in the final lines of her 1608 letter, when her anxiousness about Segarra's silence became unbearable. In the closing lines of that epistle, Cruz beseeched Segarra to remember how much enslaved people desired liberty:

Dear brother of my soul, remember my predicament and how I am not in my house, even though it is true that these people raised me and treat me well. You already know my [enslaved] condition and that it does not spare anyone, and so for your life's sake keep this ahead of anything else and see that your children are captive, and suffering grief and spite. You already know how much we desire freedom. Let me know about your health.

These lines reveal how Cruz envisioned Segarra's Atlantic sojourns as a means of accumulating capital to purchase their freedom.

Cruz's letters are emblematic of a host of collective and fractured memories in Sevilla of histories of liberation from slavery shared by neighbors and mutual aid practices between Black kin that sometimes spanned the Atlantic. Cruz's reminder to her husband not to forget her desire for liberty likely reflected an informal contractual agreement between husband and wife that he would use his liberty to accumulate capital and purchase his kin's freedom. Such an agreement reflects a broader practice between spouses of engaging in mutual aid to liberate their loved ones from enslavement.[136] Cruz may have been thinking of the experience of her neighbor, the aforementioned María de la O, who grew up enslaved in San Salvador parish and married a free man named Francisco Hernández in 1583. Hernández eventually purchased María de la O's freedom in 1596 for sixty *ducados en realles de plata*,[137] and the couple subsequently traveled to Peru in 1600 as free people.[138]

Cruz may also have known or heard about María Gómez, the beforementioned free Black woman who traveled to Sevilla from Cabo Verde in the early 1570s and who generated new freedom papers through witness testimonies in 1573 after losing her freedom papers on a ship.[139] Those testimonies also revealed that Gómez had traveled from Cabo Verde to Sevilla to liberate her sister from slavery in Sevilla.[140] Vasco Fernández,

---

[136] For an overview of the number and proportion of enslaved people who purchased their liberty in sixteenth-century Sevilla based on notarial records, see Fernández Chaves, "Amas, esclavas, y libertad" and Pérez García, "Matrimonio, Vida Familiar."

[137] "María de la O," AGI, Contratación, 5262A, no. 55, fols. 10^r–11^r.

[138] Ibid.

[139] See Chapter 1, notes 136–145; "María Gómez," AGI, Contratación, 5226, no. 2, ramo 28, fols. 1^v, 5^r–6^v.

[140] Ibid.

a mariner who testified about Gómez's lost *carta de alhorría* in 1573, described how she had traveled from Cabo Verde to Sevilla to liberate (*alhorrar*) her sister in Sevilla. A second witness, Jorge Viegas, described that Gómez "is from Cabo Verde, where this witness is resident and *natural* and that she [María Gómez] is *horra* and free and came to this city with a freedom certificate (*carta de alhorría*) of her own and she came to Castilla to liberate her sister."[141] In short, Gómez was a liberated Black woman who had embarked independently on a voyage from Cabo Verde to Sevilla armed with her own freedom certificate to liberate her sister who was languishing as an enslaved subject in the city of Sevilla.

Gómez's voyage to Sevilla from Cabo Verde sheds light on flows of communication through word of mouth and letters between Black populations in Cabo Verde and Castilla, and this will be of significance to those studying Sevilla-Cabo Verdean merchant communities in sixteenth-century Cabo Verde. But this epic history of a formerly enslaved Black woman traveling to Sevilla to liberate her sister from slavery may also have become etched into communal memories within late sixteenth-century Sevilla, impacting the personal cartographies and horizons of possibilities and expectations for enslaved Black people in the city, such as Felipa de la Cruz. Gómez resided in Sevilla for at least ten years before she embarked on a voyage as a wage-earning servant to Nicaragua in 1577.[142] Cruz was likely a young child during the years that Gómez resided in Sevilla, so she may have heard about this history of mutual aid between Cabo Verde and Sevilla, especially as Gómez likely resided in the parish of San Juan or San Pedro, which lay in close proximity to Cruz's abode on the northern edge of San Salvador parish (see Figure C.1.1).[143]

Cruz may also have heard about how some liberated Black people who had moved from Sevilla to the Spanish Americas later sent funds to liberate their enslaved children and pay for their journey to the Spanish Americas. Examples of mutual aid and liberation between parents and children that span the Atlantic reveal transoceanic ties and communication between Black people forcibly separated by slavery, and the existence of webs of trust that permitted absent Black parents to facilitate the fraught and delicate legal process of liberating their children from afar. Sending money and engaging in economic transactions in absentia

---

[141] Ibid.
[142] "María Gómez," AGI, Contratación, 5538, libro 1, fol. 10ʳ.
[143] "María Gómez," AGI, Contratación, 5226, no. 2, ramo 28, fols. 2ʳ–3ʳ.

involved a degree of literacy as well as access to networks of social capital and trust. These cases reveal that absent parents communicated through letters and word of mouth across the Atlantic, and also that they employed legal representatives to act on their behalf in Sevilla.

One example of a liberation from afar by an absent parent took place in 1579, when twenty-year-old Isabel de Vitoria petitioned the Council of the Indies in Madrid for a license to travel to Lima.[144] Vitoria explained that she wished to be reunited with her mother, a free Black woman named Ginesa de Sosa, who resided in Lima. Sosa was likely born enslaved in Sevilla, but had obtained her freedom and traveled to Lima. In Lima, Sosa had gathered enough capital to send money to pay for her daughter's liberation from slavery. The freedom certificate that Isabel de Vitoria presented at the House of Trade to prove that she was an *horra* outlined how Sosa had sent the funds for her daughter's liberation.[145] Sosa would have instructed an agent to take the funds for her daughter's liberation from Lima to Sevilla, and to act on her behalf in the city of Sevilla when drawing up the contract of purchase with Vitoria's owner. In this case, Ginesa de Sosa entrusted the purchasing of her daughter's liberation to a factor named Fernando Guzmán, whom she presumably also entrusted to deliver some of her letters to Vitoria. Guzmán also likely helped Vitoria with the process of petitioning for a passenger license at the Council of the Indies. Vitoria described how her mother had sent her letters requesting that she travel to Lima and had provided the money to pay for the cost of the journey. Vitoria obtained a license, as she was recorded as a passenger on a ship bound for the Americas on January 23, 1582.[146] Within a decade, Ginesa de Sosa was an active economic actor in Lima who had accumulated some wealth, signing various notarial contracts in the 1590s that cataloged commercial agreements and her purchase and sale of enslaved people.[147]

A second example of liberation from slavery by absent parents is the case of Francisco de Gamarra, described as both *mulato* and Black, who was formerly enslaved in Castilla and settled in Lima as a free man where he became a distinguished and celebrated builder (*albañil*), commanding a

---

[144] "Isabel de Vitoria," AGI, Indiferente, 2091, no. 24.
[145] Ibid., fols. 2^r–3^r, 6^r–7^v.
[146] "Isabel de Vitoria," AGI, Contratación 5538, libro 1, fol. 330^r.
[147] "Isabel de Vitoria," AGI, Indiferente, 2091, no. 24; "Isabel de Vitoria," AGI, Contratación 5538, libro 1, fol. 330^r; "Ginesa de Sosa," AGNP, Notarias, no. 1 DCM1 23,75 and 23,76, fols. 109^v–112 (November 21, 1591).

significant salary for his work.[148] He also held the position of *mayordomo* in a prominent Black confraternity that was established between 1569 and 1574, called the Cofradía de Nuestra Señora de la Antigua, at Lima Cathedral.[149] Gamarra's tenure as *mayordomo* lasted until some time between 1585 and 1598, after which subsequent *mayordomos* pursued him for embezzlement of alms.[150] He owned Black slaves and regularly signed labor, commercial, and trading contracts before Lima's notaries and won building contracts commissioned by Lima's *cabildo*. In the late 1580s, Gamarra sent funds across the Atlantic to purchase his daughter's freedom from slavery in Sevilla and to pay for her voyage to Lima. In 1589, a young Black woman named Ana explained in a petition for a passenger license that her father, Francisco Gamarra, had sent funds from Lima to Sevilla to "purchase her liberty" ("*rescatarla*"), and that she wished to travel to Lima to live with him.[151] Even though Francisco de Gamarra was comparatively wealthy for a *horro*, the cost of sending funds to Sevilla to liberate his daughter from slavery would not have been insignificant. He would have sent these funds via trusted associates given this was such a delicate matter. Ana described how the person who brought the funds that her father had sent from Lima was the same person who had paid her owner for the price of her liberty to liberate her from slavery. I have been unable to locate any further information as to whether judges at the House of Trade or the Council of the Indies granted Ana a license to cross the Atlantic to join her father in Lima, although there is no indication that her request was denied. Francisco de Gamarra later became embroiled in legal disputes with associates in the 1590s and was briefly imprisoned, but when he passed away in 1605 he had significant capital.[152]

---

[148] Francisco de Gamarra was contracted for many building projects by the *cabildo* of Lima, and appears in Bromley, *Libros de Cabildos de Lima*, 118, 163, 266, 316, 328, 363, 421, 436, 517, 584, 639, 666, 703–4, 741–742, and 757. See also AGNP, PNL, N 1, CYH1: 29,74, fols. 102ᵛ–103ᵛ; 29,397, fols. 261–261ᵛ; AGNP, PNL, N 1 RGB1 43,61 fols. 105ᵛ–106; AGNP, PNL, N 1 AYH1: 10,39, fols. 246–246ᵛ; 10,291, fols. 317–317ᵛ; AGNP, PNL, N 1 AYH1: 11,305, fols. 84–84ᵛ; 11,319, fols. 105–105ᵛ; AGNP, PNL, N 1 CAM1 3,786, fols. 1193–1193ᵛ; AGNP, PNL, N 1 CAM1: 5,730, fols. 1232–1232ᵛ; 7,151, fols. 281ᵛ–282; AGNP, PNL, N 1 JBE1 12,679, fols. 1075–1075ᵛ.

[149] Apodaca Valdez, *Cofradías Afrohispánicas*, 90–91; Graubart, "'So color de una cofradía'"; Jiménez Jiménez, "A mayor culto," 354.

[150] Campos and Sevilla, *Catálogo de Cofradías*, 117: Cat. no. 584 "Libro LXIV:3 1598/99 Lima. Autos seguidos contra Francisco Gamarra, moreno libre. Car, 32f."

[151] "Ana," AGI, Indiferente, 2098, no. 18.

[152] Francisco de Gamarra's brief imprisonment appears in Bromley, *Libros de Cabildos de Lima*, 76, 77, 97, 123, 126, 149, 181, 470, 584, 939.

Felipa de la Cruz's reminder to her husband to "remember my predicament" and to not forget "how much we desire freedom" because the condition of slavery "does not spare anyone" thus reflects a broader history of ideas and hopes about slavery, freedom, and mutual aid in Sevilla. Such ideas permeated the worlds of many of Cruz's contemporaries and the collective memories of enslaved and formerly enslaved Black people in the city.[153] While it may not be possible to discern the precise moments when individuals discussed collective memories and their knowledge about possible paths from slavery to freedom, these discussions were omnipresent as enslaved people went about their daily lives in the city, performing labor duties, tending to their affective ties, and hearing about news of their neighbors and friends, near and far. Cruz's plea to her husband formed part of a broader set of murmurs and discussions in her household and in the streets of Sevilla about people's paths to liberty, as well as the fractured communal memories about how kin might send funds across the Atlantic to pay for the price of their loved one's liberty.

LAST HOPE FOR FREEDOM: FELIPA DE LA CRUZ'S PETITION TO THE HOUSE OF TRADE

Freedom was constantly on Cruz's mind, especially when she learned in the early months of 1612 of her husband's early demise. Three years after penning her last letter – and nine years after Segarra had left Sevilla – Cruz received news that her husband had been killed in Veracruz two years earlier. Cruz's hopes that he would liberate her from slavery were dashed in an instant. Through the word-of-mouth networks that brought news of her husband's early demise, Cruz also learned that he had left some property in Veracruz. Such news also caused a dilemma. Castilian laws dictated that neither Cruz nor her two enslaved children could inherit this capital, as enslaved people could not own property.[154] Cruz's actions after learning about Segarra's death reveal her engagement with the rule of law in the Spanish empire, and the know-how she possessed to maneuver through legal cultures in the hopes of obtaining a coveted *carta de alhorría*. While enslaved her whole life in Sevilla, Cruz possessed an acute awareness of the laws of freedom, the role of

---

[153] "Antón Segarra," AGI, Contratación, 303, no. 2, fols. 10ʳ, 18ᵛ–20ᵛ.
[154] *Las Siete partidas del Sabio Rey don Alfonso*, "Quarta Partida, Titulo XXI, De los Siervos," 38–39.

Imagining Freedom   111

the House of Trade, the rights of imperial subjects to petition for royal justice at the Council of the Indies, and of the various possible routes to obtain liberation from slavery.

After hearing that Segarra had perished in Veracruz, Cruz employed the services of a procurator to send a petition to the Council of the Indies.[155] At the time of this petition, Cruz had only learned of her husband's death through informal networks and had not yet heard an announcement from the House of Trade. She therefore surmised that royal officials in New Spain had not yet sent the value of Segarra's belongings to Castilla, even though two years had already elapsed since his death. In her petition to the Council of the Indies, Cruz insisted that the crown order royal officials in New Spain to investigate her husband's death and to collect the value of his property.[156] Without a doubt, she presented herself to the crown in this petition (and perhaps also to her procurator) as a free Black woman who had the right to inherit her deceased free husband's property, and hid the fact that she was enslaved. Although I have not yet located Cruz's original petition, it is likely that she explained she had heard about Segarra's death through word of mouth: The resulting royal decree noted that "Phelipa de la Cruz, Black woman, *vecina* of the city of Sevilla, has made representations that her husband Antón Segarra was killed in New Veracruz about two years ago, and that he left certain effects and property in the power of Francisco Moreno, notary of the *cabildo* of that city."[157] These lines reveal that Cruz was able to date the time of Segarra's death and the location of his property in Veracruz before official news of his death arrived in Sevilla. Her petition also shows her awareness of the role that the House of Trade played in distributing the property of deceased Castilians to their heirs in Castilla. In her petition to the Council of the Indies, Cruz also pleaded that the crown ensure that royal officials in New Spain send Segarra's belongings to the House of Trade in order that she could then petition to inherit the property, as the resulting royal decree explained how "the property should be inherited by her."[158] Cruz's petition to the Council of the Indies resulted in the crown issuing a royal decree on May 29, 1612, instructing royal officials

---

[155] The royal decree issued in response to Cruz's petition is Real Cédula, AGI, México 1094, legajo 18, fols. 102ʳ–103ʳ. I have not yet located Cruz's petition, although so far, I have searched for it in Peticiones y Memoriales, AGI, Indiferente, 1257, 1434, and 1435, and Expedientes y Peticiones sueltas, AGI, Escribanía, 974.
[156] Ibid.
[157] Ibid.
[158] Ibid.

in New Spain to ensure the safe return of Segarra's estate to the House of Trade in Sevilla.

By early April 1612, however, Cruz had already received news that the value of Segarra's belongings had arrived at the House of Trade. Soon thereafter, she appeared in person at the House of Trade to request further information and to inform officials that she was the legitimate heir.[159] During that visit, Cruz requested that the House of Trade show her a copy of Segarra's testament and any other relevant paperwork, noting that she had the right to receive these documents as she was Segarra's wife. Such a request signals that Cruz was not yet aware that Segarra had perished intestate. Cruz may also not have known that Segarra had received her letters in Veracruz and had kept them locked in a box along with his treasured freedom papers, and that transcribed copies of her letters had arrived in Sevilla as part of his estate. She also made a statement that embellished her fictional account as a free Black woman by claiming that she and Segarra had a son named Cristóbal who had been born free, and positioned herself as the guardian of Segarra's heir:

Felipa de la Cruz, a Black woman, widow of Antón Segarra, who perished in the Indies. As I am the legitimate mother of Cristóbal, my son, and son of the said my husband, I say that the property of my husband Antón Segarra has arrived in this House [of Trade], in the value of 44,500 *maravedíes*, as is recorded, which I should be given as the administrator of the said Cristóbal my son, as there are no other heirs except me and my son.[160]

In this statement, Cruz omitted any reference to her two enslaved children, Andrés and María. Instead, she described the freeborn son as Segarra's only child. She also suggested that she resided in a different parish of the city to San Salvador, noting that the pair had married in San Magdalena parish.

Cruz's statement to the House of Trade reveals her strategies to obtain freedom, even after the tragic death of her husband. She hoped to inherit Segarra's estate and save enough capital to eventually purchase her children's liberty. The amount of money that arrived in Sevilla as Segarra's estate was 44,500 *maravedíes* (approximately 99 *pesos de oro común*). Historian Fernández Chaves has traced how the average cost to enslaved people in Sevilla of purchasing their own liberty was approximately 22,720.7 *maravedíes* in the late sixteenth century.[161] Segarra's estate

---

[159] "Antón Segarra," AGI, Contratación, 303, no. 2, fol. 2ʳ.
[160] Ibid.
[161] Corona Pérez, *Trata Atlántica*; Fernández Chaves, "Amas, esclavas, y libertad."

therefore represented a significant sum for Cruz, an amount that could help her to purchase the freedom of her children and possibly contribute towards the cost of her own liberation too.

To support her request to inherit Segarra's belongings, Cruz also presented a written petition to the House of Trade (likely through a procurator) on April 6, 1612.[162] In this, she explicitly stated that she was a free Black woman: "I Felipa de la Cruz, of Black color, widow of Antón Segarra, Black man who perished in the Indies, and as the legitimate mother of Cristóbal Cigarra my son and son of the said my husband … I declare that I am a free person and not subject to any captivity." In addition, the petition contained declarations by two witnesses who both attested to Cruz's fabricated biography as a free Black woman.[163] One of these witnesses was a free Black woman named María de la Torre, whose declaration provides tentative evidence of a community of free and enslaved Black residents of Sevilla who might act in solidarity to help liberate one another from slavery. In this case, perhaps Cruz hoped that if she managed to convince judges at the House of Trade that she was a free person, she might have the opportunity to funnel the funds to a friend or corporation that would help her to pay for the price of her liberty; perhaps to María de la Torre.

Unfortunately for Cruz, her owner discovered her ploy, and within two months of her petition, Don Francisco Fernández de Santillán sent a competing claim to the House of Trade, on June 8, 1612. Fernández de Santillán argued that while Segarra was indeed a liberated Black man, his heirs – his two children named María and Andrés (and not Cristóbal) – were his property.[164] Santillán presented three witnesses to support his claim. One was his daughter, Doña Beatriz Gómez, who had known Felipa de la Cruz as a slave in the palace her whole life, and the other two were neighbors who lived on Calle Carpinterías.[165] They described how they had known Cruz for over twenty years as Fernández de Santillán's slave and that they had witnessed Cruz and Segarra exchanging vows in Salvador Church (not Magdalena Church as Cruz had attested in her own petition that same year), and that the couple had two children named Andrés and María (and not Cristóbal) who were also enslaved to Francisco Fernández de Santillán.[166]

---

[162] "Antón Segarra," AGI, Contratación, 303, no. 2, fols. 4ʳ–5ʳ.
[163] Ibid.
[164] Ibid., fols. 25ʳ–30ʳ.
[165] Ibid.
[166] Ibid.

Without the copies of Cruz's own letters to Segarra in 1604 and 1608, which were serendipitously transcribed on the orders of the judge of the assets of the deceased in Veracruz in 1609, it might be tempting to regard the entire episode as a nefarious attempt by Fernández de Santillán to illegitimately claim Cruz as his slave. However, Cruz's descriptions of her enslaved status, her two children, and her owner's affairs in the letters that she penned and sent to her husband make it fairly certain that Cruz did fabricate her biography as a free woman in 1612 in the hope of inheriting her husband's property and then purchasing her freedom. For example, in 1608, she had relayed news about her owners and the affairs of the Sevillian nobility who had passed through the prominent palace. Cruz described her owner's recent ill-health, writing that "Don Francisco, my *señor*, is well, although before now he had a great illness that almost left him blind." Describing the children of the household, she noted that the young daughters of the noble family, including one of the witnesses who later testified against her at the House of Trade, "Doña Beatriz and Doña Luisa are very pretty," while also sending news of the birth of her owner's son, "my *señora* gave birth to a child last Christmas, a boy called Don Alonso de Santillán."[167] Here, Cruz was describing the birth in 1604 of Alonso Fernández de Santillán, a figure who would go on to cement the family's prominent status through his appointment by the Spanish monarchy as Caballero de Santiago, while his own son, Francisco Fernández de Santillán (b. 1629), elevated the family's noble status when the Spanish monarchy granted him the title of Marqués de la Motilla in 1679. Thereafter, the family's palace – where Cruz had grown up – became known as the Palacio del Marqués de la Motilla and remained in the family's ownership for the next four centuries until 2023, when the property was sold to a Córdoba-based company, reportedly for the owner's private use.[168]

Faced with these two competing claims for Segarra's inheritance, judges at the House of Trade concluded that Fernández de Santillán should inherit Segarra's property as he had proven that both of Segarra's children and their mother were his slaves.[169] Such a decision is not surprising given Cruz's enslaved status. Judges at the House of Trade did not rule against Cruz because they perceived that she was ineligible to

---

[167] Felipa uses the phrase "mi señora" and "mi señor" to refer to her owners. Ibid., 10^r, 18^v–20^v.
[168] Antolín, "Una empresa cordobesa," *Diario de Sevilla*, November 12, 2022.
[169] Ibid.

claim inheritance if she was in fact a free Black woman – other Castilla-based free Black individuals were successful at petitioning the House of Trade to inherit Black family members' property – but rather, her petition failed because judges reasoned that Castilian law stipulated that owners of slaves legally inherited any property that might transfer to their slaves (in this case, Segarra's two enslaved children), and that Cruz and her two children were indeed enslaved to Fernández de Santillán.[170] Such a logic contradicts the practice of urban slave-owners allowing their slaves to accumulate small portions of their wages as slaves for hire with the aim of eventually purchasing their liberty, thus implying a degree of legal separation of property between slaves and their owner, as Chapter 3 explores. Nonetheless, judges at the House of Trade reasoned that Cruz and her children could not inherit the estate because they were enslaved. In addition, the prominence of Francisco Fernández de Santillán in the governance of the city of Sevilla as a *venticuatro* and as he was a member of one of the city's most notable families likely swayed House judges to rule in his favor, especially as Cruz provided no further countertestimony or evidence in her petition after her owner made a claim to the property.

CONCLUSION

Although Felipa de la Cruz spent her entire life languishing in enslavement in a palace near Salvador Church in Sevilla, she maintained transatlantic ties and developed extensive legal know-how in her pursuit for freedom. Free and enslaved Black people who resided in, or passed through, Sevilla often formed part of diverse webs of transoceanic relationships that were stitched together through word of mouth on ships, letter writing, and relationships born out of the commerce that serviced annual fleets of ships in particular ports. The history of ties and communication between key urban and maritime nodes in the Atlantic world facilitated the exchange, discussion, and disputation of ideas between Black individuals and communities in urban spaces across the Atlantic world in the late sixteenth century. Felipa de la Cruz's interactions with the House of Trade after Segarra's death indicate that she possessed an acute awareness of the rule of the law in the Spanish empire and of the role of the House of Trade in administering and distributing property that belonged to

---

[170] "Alonso de Castro, Isavel de Vargas," AGI, Contratación, 526, no. 1, ramo 1, doc. 12; "Cristóbal López Riquel," AGI, Contratación, 963, no. 2, ramo 11; "Alonso Hernández Manzano," AGI, Contratación, 476, no. 1, ramo 5.

deceased members of the Castilian diaspora. Further, mirroring her husband's copious efforts to obtain two freedom certificates upon his liberation from slavery in 1602, Cruz understood the importance of freedom papers and the possible routes to obtain these coveted documents.[171] In her fabricated tale of 1612, Cruz presented herself to the House of Trade as a free Black woman who had the right to inherit her deceased husband's property. She anticipated that doing so might provide her with a marginal chance to purchase her and her children's liberty. Living in the center of Sevilla near to the House of Trade and the routes of town criers who announced recent deaths, and thus the possibilities to inherit the riches of those who perished in the Indies, inevitably informed her knowledge about how to petition for her husband's property both at the Council of the Indies and at the House of Trade. Additionally, her relationships with, or knowledge of, many other Black men and women in her neighborhood who had obtained their liberation from slavery and sometimes left Sevilla for the Americas also meant that she was privy to a constant murmur of information among Black residents about slavery and freedom.

Felipa de la Cruz, a Black woman who spent a lifetime in captivity toiling as a domestic slave, interacted with the Atlantic world and the Castilian empire with confidence and knowledge. She took pen to paper to fight for her freedom on various fronts, and in so doing left a remarkable trail of documents about her life. It is a great injustice to her and her fearless pursuit of freedom that the historical archives remain silent as to whether she and her children ever obtained their liberty, or how gravely she was punished by her owners for attempting to inherit her deceased husband's property – or by judges at the House of Trade for providing false testimony about her status as a free woman. Hopefully, scholars working on the history of enslaved and free people in Sevilla's notarial, parish, or judicial archives will in due course locate further documents about her life, and write a more comprehensive history of this remarkable woman who spent her life imagining, hoping, and fighting for liberty.

---

[171] "Antón Segarra," AGI, Contratación, 303, no. 2, fols. 11ᵛ–13ʳ. See also Chapter 1, notes 96–103.

3

Purchasing Freedom

Economics of Liberty in New Spain

In late sixteenth-century Puebla de los Ángeles (in present-day Mexico), an enslaved Black woman named Margarita de Sossa accumulated sufficient funds to pay the market price of her freedom and liberated herself from slavery. Sossa later described how she had provided healing services to residents of Puebla to raise the necessary funds to pay for her liberty, explaining how "the money with which I liberated myself was from my work and sweat."[1] Enslaved people residing across the Spanish Atlantic world often plotted paths to obtain their liberty through economic decisions that thrust them into nascent Atlantic economies as creditors, debtors, and owners of capital. Sossa likely negotiated the price of her liberty with her former owner after obtaining permission from him to hire out her labor and keep a share of the proceeds. Enslaved people's economic decisions in pursuit of their liberty also extended to raising credit through commercial agreements with friends and strangers. Notarial records often reveal how and where enslaved people and their creditors agreed the terms of loans, labor, or gifts. Such conversations took place during auctions when enslaved people sometimes negotiated with prospective owners for their freedom, in private residences between friends who had known each other for many years, in urban spaces with neighbors, associates, and employers during labor-for-hire arrangements. Loans from friends and strangers sometimes provided enslaved people with sufficient capital to liberate themselves from slavery, even though the price of their liberty might involve siphoning a vast proportion of their future wages to their creditors to repay their debts. In other

---

[1] "Margarita Sossa," AGN, México, GD61 Inquisición, vol. 208, exp. 3, fols. 102–103ᵛ. See also Ireton, "Margarita de Sossa."

words, some enslaved people managed, against all the odds, to plot paths to purchase their own liberty or the freedom of their kin by participating in early modern economic life (even when still enslaved) and developed sufficient creditworthiness in their communities or among residents and passersby in the sites where they dwelt to raise sufficient capital. And, in doing so, they made choices about the type of liberty that they sought, namely the legal status of an *horro* that could be proven through a physical *carta de alhorría* or *carta de libertad*.

The rule of law in the Castilian empire concerning slavery legitimized the enslavement of certain people and rendered them into commodities that slave-owners could buy and sell at will, while dispossessing enslaved people from their right to property ownership. Under these legal conditions, how did some enslaved people in the sixteenth-century Spanish realms accumulate their own capital and negotiate with their owners to pay the price of their liberty and become free? The answer lies in enslaved people's determined work as economic actors, their precarious and brave economic choices in pursuit of their liberty, and the broad social ties that they developed to accumulate credit or capital. Conversations between enslaved people with potential creditors as they attempted to raise capital were rarely recorded in archival documents. Yet, these ephemeral conversations shaped the history of Black thought about freedom in this period. Conversations with friends and strangers about their enslaved condition informed enslaved people about laws of slavery in the Spanish empire and the possibilities to negotiate their freedom with their owners through self-purchase agreements. And some enslaved people developed social and economic ties to raise the capital to pay for their freedom through conversations with friends and strangers. As the work of historian Yesenia Barragan and others demonstrates, enslaved and liberated people's participation in economic life and entrance into complex debt relationships continued throughout the late colonial period and into the era of abolition.[2] This chapter traces a history of conversations about purchasing freedom along a major thoroughfare in the viceroyalty of New Spain in the late sixteenth century, namely the two royal trading routes that connected the coastal fort of San Juan de Ulúa and the viceregal capital of Mexico City. The fragmentary archives that document this history include a detailed cache of records about the life of Margarita de Sossa and a

---

[2] Barragán, *Freedom's Captives*. For an analysis of similar economic activity in this period in Sevilla through notarial records, see Fernández Chaves, "Amas, esclavas, y libertad"; Pérez García, "Matrimonio, Vida Familiar."

host of commercial contracts of self-purchase, loans, and credit agreements signed by enslaved Black people before public notaries in the towns of Veracruz, Jalapa, Puebla de los Ángeles, and Mexico City, as well as records of embarkation and passenger licenses, probate records, and inquisitorial investigations into the lives of free Black dwellers in Veracruz and Puebla de los Ángeles. Collectively, these records reveal a history of Black thought about freedom constituted through enslaved and free people's discussions about their attempts to accumulate sufficient capital to purchase their liberty, and the ways that liberated people reckoned with the meanings of freedom after their liberation from slavery.

COMMUNICATION BETWEEN THE TOWNS ALONG THE CAMINOS REALES IN THE TIMES OF ECONOMIC BOOM

Tracing Margarita de Sossa's forced journey inland to Puebla de los Ángeles after her arrival in New Spain in the late sixteenth century allows us to reflect on the economic, political, and geographical conditions that shaped the lives of enslaved and free Black people in this region. The annual fleet of ships sailing from Sevilla in the Carrera de Indias usually arrived in San Juan de Ulúa in the spring. People and commodities offloaded from the fleets were often destined for towns and cities along the royal routes in New Spain that linked Sevilla with Manila (Philippines). Life in the towns dotted along these trading was characterized by a constant influx and transit of merchants, travelers, royal officials, clergymen, passengers, and local tradesmen, and significant flows of money.

Margarita de Sossa arrived at the fort of San Juan de Ulúa in 1580 on board a ship in the annual fleet that had departed from Sevilla.[3] Before then, she had endured a grueling life of slavery, violence, and sexual abuse as she forcibly displaced across the Atlantic world at the hands of various owners before she disembarked in chains from the ship (Figure 3.1). Years later, Sossa recounted in an Inquisitorial trial in Mexico City that she had been born enslaved in Porto (Portugal). Her father was a merchant named Juan de Cáceres from Porto and her mother was an enslaved Black woman named Lucía. Sossa reported that she had spent her early years enslaved in the house of Señora Lucrecia de Cisna, who sold her in Lisbon when she was twenty years old. Her second owner

---

[3] "Margarita Sossa," AGN, México, GD61 Inquisición, vol. 208, exp. 3, fols. 31–32, 80–84.

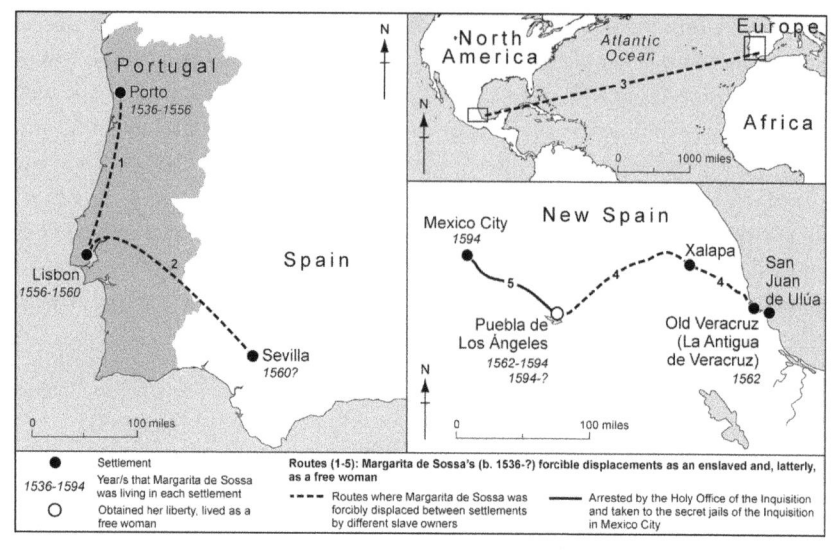

FIGURE 3.1 Approximate routes along which Margarita de Sossa was forcibly displaced as an enslaved woman and latterly as a free woman. Map drawn by Cath D'Alton, Drawing Office, University College London, based on a map drawn by Alex Killough in Ball et al., *As If She Were Free*, 31.

reportedly forced Sossa into sexual relations with him, and after a few years of enduring this sexual violence, she described how she refused any further access to her body. As a result, her owner sent her to Sevilla, where a Flemish merchant purchased her. Thereafter, in 1580, Sossa's owner sent her from Sevilla to be sold in New Spain, where she was bought and sold by three further enslavers. At some point during these years, one of Sossa's owners used scorching irons to burn his initials on her face, as witnesses later described how she had "some letters on her face (*rostro*)."[4]

Margarita de Sossa likely arrived in San Juan de Ulúa in 1580 on a medium-sized vessel with other passengers and merchandise as part of the annual fleet that departed Sevilla in the spring, her owner probably enlisting an agent or a merchant to take her to New Spain.[5] After disembarking at San Juan de Ulúa, Sossa likely spent some days in Old Veracruz, a nearby settlement that served as the de facto port town for the region until 1599, while an agent or merchant arranged onward travel. Her voyage differed from those of enslaved Black people from West Africa

[4] Ibid., fols. 31–32.
[5] Ibid., fols. 80–84.

and West-Central Africa, who were forced to disembark from slave ships in San Juan de Ulúa after surviving the torturous displacements through the Middle Passage and would then have endured a treacherous overland journey in chains through mountainous terrain along the royal trading routes to the towns of Jalapa, Puebla de los Ángeles, and Mexico City.[6] Merchants sold enslaved Black people in slave markets in each of these towns, often condemning them to a precarious and violent existence in the sugar-producing plantations that abounded in the hinterlands between Old Veracruz, Jalapa, and Puebla de los Ángeles, and in silver mines across New Spain and beyond.[7]

From San Juan de Ulúa, there were two major *caminos reales* (royal trading routes) to Mexico City, each of which veered around the highest peaks of the mountainous Sierra Madre Oriental that lay between the coast and Mexico City. The first Camino Real, later known as the Camino de Veracruz, had been built by Spanish officials in the 1520s on existing pre-Hispanic indigenous routes (Figure 3.2). From San Juan de Ulúa, the route passed through Old Veracruz, where royal officials inspected and taxed goods, and then veered to the northern edge of the Sierra Madre Oriental and to the town of Jalapa before circling the northern peak of the Cofre de Perote to the town of Puebla de los Ángeles, and then continued to Mexico City. Spanish officials ordered further construction

---

[6] Carroll, *Blacks in Colonial Veracruz*; Clark, *Veracruz*; Méndez Maín, "Apuntes para"; Sierra Silva, "The Slave Trade" and *Urban Slavery*.

[7] For a select bibliography on the histories of enslaved and free Black people in New Spain, specifically in the regions between Veracruz and Mexico City (broadly conceived), see Apodaca Valdez, *Cofradías Afrohispánicas*; Bennett, *Africans in Colonial México* and *Colonial Blackness*; Bristol, "Although I Am Black" and *Christians, Blasphemers*; Carroll, *Blacks in Colonial Veracruz*; Castañeda García, *Esclavitud africana*, "La devoción a Santa Ifigenia," "Modelos de Santidad," "Piedad y participación," and "Santos negros, devotos de color"; Castañeda García and Ruíz Guadalajara, *Africanos y afrodescendientes*; Castañeda García and Velázquez, "Introducción"; Clark, *Veracruz*; Domínguez Domínguez, "Circulaciones imperiales," "Entre resistencia," and "Veracruz"; Martínez, *Genealogical Fictions* and "The Black Blood"; Masferrer León, "Confraternities" and *Muleke*; Milton and Vinson III, "Counting Heads"; Mondragón Barrios, *Esclavos africanos*; Naveda Chávez-Hita, "De San Lorenzo" and *Esclavos negros*; Nemser, *Infrastructures of Race* and "Triangulating Blackness"; Proctor III, *Damned Notions of Liberty*; Restall, *The Black Middle*; Roselló Soberón, "Relevancia y función"; Schwaller, *Géneros de Gente*; Seijas and Sierra Silva, "The Persistence"; Sierra Silva, "Afro-Mexican Women," *Mexico, Slavery, Freedom*, "The Slave Trade," and *Urban Slavery*; Smith, "African-Descended" and "Juana Ramírez"; Terrazas Williams, "My Conscience" and *The Capital of Free Women*; Valerio, *Sovereign Joy*, "The Spanish," and "'That There Be No Black Brotherhood'"; Velázquez Gutiérrez, *Mujeres de orígen africano*; Velázquez Gutiérrez and Correa Duró, *Poblaciónes y culturas*; Vinson III, *Bearing Arms* and *Before Mestizaje*; Vinson III and Restall, *Black Mexico*; von Germeten, *Black Blood Brothers*.

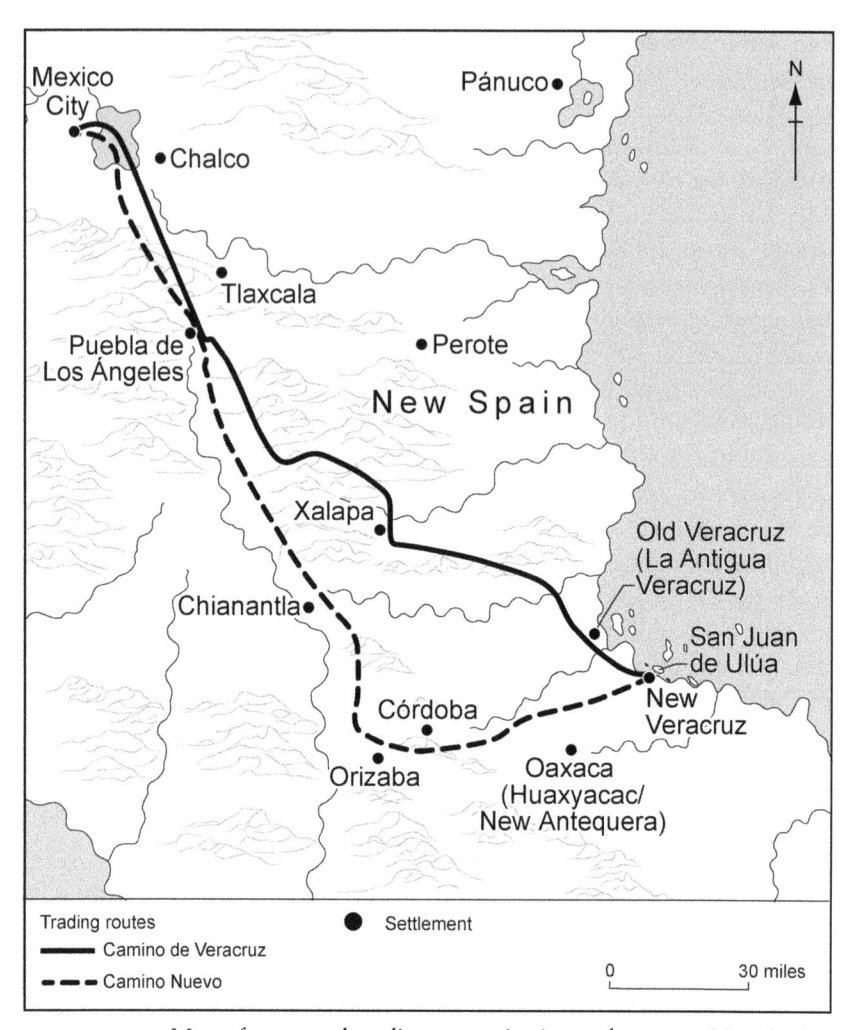

FIGURE 3.2 Map of two royal trading routes in sixteenth-century New Spain between San Juan de Ulúa and Mexico City, known as *Camino de Veracruz* and *Camino Nuevo*. Map drawn by Cath D'Alton, Drawing Office, University College London, based on "Archipelague du Mexique où sont les isles de Cuba, Espagnole [Haïti], Jamaïque, etc. [Document cartographique]." Jean Covens et Corneille Mortier, Amsterdam, 1741. Bibliothèque Nationale de France, FRBNF40739006.

work on the route between 1530 and 1532 to expand the road, allowing wagons of mule- and oxen-pulled trains to haul precious metals and other natural resources violently extracted with Black and Indigenous labor from the mountainous highlands to the coast to be loaded onto ships at San Juan de Ulúa.[8] The second half of the sixteenth century was a period of economic boom in New Spain, following key developments in technologies for silver mining in the 1550s, namely "the amalgamation process, a cheap, simple method of refining large quantities of low-grade silver ore" that led to the mass extraction, melting, and refining of silver in New Spain and Peru, and its transportation to Europe in the late sixteenth century.[9] In the 1550s, the viceroy of New Spain, Luis de Velasco (viceroy 1550–1564) authorized further construction work on the route to improve the reliability and speed of transportation, relying on forced Indigenous labor for the works. And between 1560 and 1562, royal officials again forced Indigenous laborers to toil on a construction project to improve the infrastructure, including bridges; this allowed for the introduction of large wagons with metallic wheels that could be pulled by up to sixteen mules.[10] Throughout the sixteenth century, Spanish royal officials favored this northern Camino Real for the transportation of silver caravels, other precious natural resources, and voluminous merchandise.

A second royal route also connected San Juan de Ulúa, Puebla de los Ángeles, and Mexico City, by veering south of the mountainous Sierra Madre Oriental range near the Pico de Orizaba. The two routes joined at the town of Puebla de los Ángeles, from where various routes splintered off to the metropolis of Mexico City. This southern route supported regional and intraregional commerce within the Americas for most of the sixteenth century.[11] The southern route became known as the Camino Nuevo, while the northern route was referred to as the Camino de Veracruz. The Camino Nuevo became consolidated by the mid sixteenth century with the rise of the production of grains, especially flour and wheat, as well as sugar in the Orizaba region. By the turn of the seventeenth century, royal officials had expanded the Camino Nuevo, spelling the downfall of the Camino de Veracruz.[12] As wagon drivers increasingly used the Camino Nuevo instead of the Camino de Veracruz, the town of Old Veracruz became obsolete, and in 1599 royal officials recognized the small settlement of Buitron near the fort of San Juan de Ulúa as New Veracruz (henceforth Veracruz) and encouraged residents

---

[8] del Valle Pavon, "Desarrollo" and *El camino México-Puebla-Veracruz*; Pérez González, *Los caminos reales*; Vargas Matías, "El Camino Real de Veracruz."
[9] Baskes, "The Colonial Economy"; Brading and Cross, "Colonial Silver Mining"; Guerrero Quintero, "The Environmental History"; Martínez López-Cano et al., *El crédito*.
[10] del Valle Pavon, "Desarrollo" and *El camino México-Puebla-Veracruz*.
[11] See note 8.
[12] del Valle Pavon, "Desarrollo" and *El camino México-Puebla-Veracruz*.

to move their dwellings to the new town.[13] Old Veracruz maintained a small population at the turn of the seventeenth century, as people often lived and labored in the two places.[14]

In Old Veracruz of the early 1580s, Sossa would have encountered a town where the majority of the year-round population comprised free and enslaved Black people: The coastal littoral proved inhospitable for many Spaniards, who tended to prefer to settle in the inland towns of Jalapa and Puebla de los Ángeles.[15] As a result, many Black residents of the town were enslaved to owners who lived elsewhere and endured labor-for-hire arrangements; they often lived and labored semiautonomously in the town while their distant owners resided in Jalapa, Puebla de los Ángeles, or Mexico City and received a portion of their wages.[16] Both Veracruz towns also had significant populations of free Black people who hailed from the broader region of New Spain, around the Caribbean, and other sites in the Spanish empire. Free and liberated Black people were often attracted to the Veracruz region by the economic opportunities of the annual passing trade and the relative autonomy experienced by Black residents.[17] Free Black women, in particular, developed trades that responded to the commercial demands of the port, working as seamstresses, clothes-washers, innkeepers, cooks, street sweepers, healers, hospital workers, and chocolate producers, to name just a few professions.[18]

---

[13] Clark, "Environment and the Politics" and *Veracruz*.

[14] García Quintana and Castillo Farreas, *Tratado curioso*: Antonio de Ciudad Real, "De cómo salió la flota del puerto de San Juan de Ulúa y llegó al de La Habana" pp. 409–412; Domínguez Domínguez, "Circulaciones imperiales," "Entre resistencia," and "Veracruz"; García de León, *Tierra adentro*; Thiébaut, "San Juan de Ulúa."

[15] García de León, *Tierra adentro*; Clark, *Veracruz*.

[16] García de León, *Tierra adentro*, 536–575.

[17] See, for example, "Juana Gutiérrez Jalapa," HLSM, HM 35130, Volume 36, 1650–1684, Discurso de vida, *sin foliación*; "Proceso Contra Inés de Villalobos, Mulata," AGN, México, GD61 Inquisición, vol. 206, exp. 9. "Proceso Criminal Contra Leonor de Isla, Mulata," AGN, México, GD61 Inquisición, vol. 341, exp. 1. "Proceso Contra Beatriz de León, Mulata," AGN, México, GD61 Inquisición, vol. 131, exp. 2. "Proceso Contra Ana de Herrera, Mulata, por Hechicera (Tormento)," AGN, México, GD61 Inquisición, vol. 207, exp. 1. "Proceso contra Pero Hernández Negro Horro," AGN, México, GD61 Inquisición, vol. 102. exp. 3. In a recent study, Clark has documented many Black-Veracruz residents' ties with the broader Caribbean in the seventeenth century; see Clark, *Veracruz*, 192–225.

[18] For Black female inn-keepers in the late sixteenth-century Veracruz-Mexico City region, see María Gerónima [de Vallejo], HLSM, HM 35165, sin foliación (Discurso de vida, describes how she owned many posadas); "Juana Jalapa," HLSM, HM 35130, sin foliación (Discurso de vida, describes how Adriana Cabrera offered rooms to rent in her house in Veracruz in the early seventeenth century); Margarita de Sossa also became an inn-keeper who owned at least six beds after her liberation from slavery: "Margarita Sossa," AGN, México, GD61

Testimonies in Inquisitorial trials also document how free and enslaved Black people in Veracruz often established alliances and social and economic ties with Indigenous and Spanish people residing in the town and its environs.[19] They also maintained social, economic, and kinship ties with enslaved and free friends, family, and associates who resided inland on plantations and in the towns of Jalapa, Puebla de los Ángeles, and Mexico City. For example, testimonies provided to the Holy Office of the Inquisition in Mexico City against a free Black man named Pero Hernández and a Black woman named Juana Jalapa, dating to the 1570s and 1640s respectively, reveal how they and many other Black residents of Veracruz often had social, economic, and kinship ties with Black port dwellers whose cartographies stretched the vast distances across the Atlantic world, while they maintained kinship ties with enslaved and free people who lived in inland sugar plantations, rural communities, and in the aforementioned towns.[20]

From Veracruz, Margarita de Sossa was transported to the inland town of Puebla de los Ángeles in the central highlands of New Spain; this had been founded by Castilian colonists in 1532 and served as a major commercial and communication crossroads between Veracruz, Jalapa, and Mexico City.[21] By the mid sixteenth century, Puebla's strategic location at the intersection of numerous trading routes transformed the town into a site of transit with a concentration of intense mercantile activity.[22] Given the town's strategic location, a permanent influx of temporary dwellers arrived in Puebla. Travelers, merchants, soldiers, members of religious orders, and colonial officials constantly passed through en route to other sites in New Spain, the Caribbean, the Pacific, and the Iberian Peninsula. By the 1550s, merchants established a slave market in the town by selling enslaved Black people from Upper Guinea and Indigenous people whom the Spanish monarchy believed they had captured and enslaved in a just

---

Inquisición, vol. 208, exp. 3, fols. 31–32; "Bartolomé Martín," AGI, Contratación, 938A, no. 10 (a free Black woman named Ana de Tapia from Jalapa purchased a venta on the route between Jalapa and Puebla in 1587 with her husband, a mulato named Bartolomé Martín from Castilla (Huelva); while it is unclear whether the venta served as an inn, associates regularly stayed while traveling between sites).

[19] Ibid.
[20] "Juana Gutiérrez Jalapa," HLSM, HM 35130, vol. 36, 1650–1684; "Proceso Contra Pero Hernández Negro Horro," AGN, México, GD61 Inquisición, vol. 102, exp. 3. For detailed discussion of the Juana Jalapa case, see Clark, *Veracruz*, 195–225.
[21] Sierra Silva, *Urban Slavery*.
[22] del Valle, "Desarrollo de la economía."

war, namely the Mixtón Wars (1540–1542) in New Spain.[23] Puebla also had a significant number of free Black *vecinos*; historian Pablo Sierra Silva has explored their presence in town council records in the mid sixteenth century, and by the 1570s, contemporaries estimated a Black population of some five hundred Black men and women (most of them enslaved) as well as many people of mixed African descent (*mulatos*).[24]

Living in Puebla in the early 1580s, Sossa may have obtained a slightly greater degree of freedom than when she was enslaved in the cities of Porto, Lisbon, and Sevilla. During her time in Puebla, Sossa labored in private households. Enslaved individuals in Puebla's private households had some degree of autonomy in the city, or at least more so than enslaved people who were destined to labor in mines, plantations, and textile production. For example, enslaved women washed clothes in Puebla's public streets, and had a notable presence in the city market.[25] Sossa later testified that she had maintained a labor-for-hire arrangement with her owner in Puebla.[26] In practice, she likely worked as a healer, tending to the maladies of various residents of the city who sought her services, while her owner kept a percentage of her wages. Sossa's birth in Portugal, experiences living as an enslaved woman in households in Porto, Lisbon, and Sevilla prior to her arrival in Puebla, and her ability to speak Portuguese and Spanish meant that she possessed a particular know-how of the broader Iberian world, laws, and economic life that was distinct from the knowledge possessed by enslaved people who were displaced to New Spain from sites in West Africa and West-Central Africa. Upon Sossa's arrival in Puebla, she was purchased by a clergyman named Alonso Hernández de Santiago, who was also the commissary in Puebla to the Holy Office of the Inquisition in Mexico City. She was sold twice more to other enslavers in the same city. It is possible, given the practices of slave-ownership in nearby towns, that Sossa might have lived independently from the three men who owned her during her early years in Puebla.[27] While enslaved there, Sossa was also permitted to marry a Portuguese shoemaker named Antonio Álvarez.

---

[23] Sierra Silva, *Urban Slavery*, 32.
[24] Ibid., 30, 37.
[25] Ibid., 21–44.
[26] *Jornaleras/jornaleros* were enslaved people who usually lived separately from their owners to whom they paid a regular (daily, monthly, etc.) quota from wages earned doing different kinds of work.
[27] García de León, *Tierra adentro*; Terrazas Williams, "My Conscience" and *The Capital of Free Women*.

Upon arriving in Puebla, Sossa would have developed an understanding of the importance of the town's strategic location on the trading routes in New Spain and its proximity to the viceregal capital of Mexico City, a metropolis with a significant Black urban population of enslaved and free people.[28] As a healer, Sossa would have met a range of people from other households in Puebla and also passersby who required healing services during their lengthy voyages. Indeed she would have been aware of the commercial opportunities of passing trade, as she later eked out a living as an innkeeper after liberating herself from slavery, renting up to six beds a night for weary travelers.[29] One witness noted that Sossa's "trade and way of living has been and is to provide food and beds in her house to some people."[30]

Other free Black dwellers of late sixteenth-century Puebla also developed ties with the broader region and Spanish Atlantic world. In the first instance, free Black residents of Puebla often traveled between other towns in New Spain, and sometimes across the Atlantic.[31] For example, free Black *vecinos* of Puebla are recorded in the ranks of wage-earning servants on Atlantic crossings.[32] Some residents of Puebla developed commercial ties with those who lived in the rural hinterlands, including free Black and *mulato* men and women who rented or owned land or *ventas* along the Camino de Veracruz between the towns of Jalapa and Puebla.[33] One example is Bartolomé Martín, a freeborn *mulato* who hailed from Huelva in Castilla and had arrived in New Spain in the 1570s. Martín married a free Black woman from Jalapa named Ana de Tapia and the pair purchased a *venta* and land on the route between Jalapa and Puebla in 1587. Martín maintained economic and social ties between both towns, as he used the services of notaries in Puebla and Jalapa to record his various commercial transactions.[34] A Jalapa notarial record dating from 1586 reveals how Hipólito Hernández, the owner of *Venta de Lencero*, gave power of attorney to Bartolomé

---

[28] Velázquez Gutiérrez, *Mujeres de orígen africano*.
[29] "Margarita Sossa," AGN, México, GD61 Inquisición, vol. 208, exp. 3, fols. 31–32.
[30] Ibid., fol. 40.
[31] An example is "Isabel de Cartagena," AGN, México, GD61 Inquisición, vol. 466, exp. 3, fols. 26ʳ–35ᵛ.
[32] "Isabel Ortíz, Diego," AGI, Indiferente, 2074, no. 50; "Isabel Ortíz, Diego," AGI, Contratación, 5324, no. 30. See also Garofalo, "Shape of a Diaspora."
[33] Terrazas Williams, "My Conscience" and *The Capital of Free Women*; "Bartolomé Martín," AGI, Contratación, 938A, no. 10.
[34] "Bartolomé Martín," AGI, Contratación, 938A, no. 10.

Martín, "of *mulato* color and *vecino* of Jalapa," to collect any *pesos de oro común* owed to Hernández in New Spain.[35] The following year, in 1587, Bartolomé Martín purchased two *cavallerias* of land and a *Venta de los Naranjos* for 500 pesos, both located one league away from Xalapa.[36] He signed the contract to purchase this land in Puebla de los Ángeles. Twenty years later, Martín and his wife purchased two further *cavallerias* that adjoined the Venta, and he also owned additional land in the town of Xalapa, selling a plot (*solar*) on the Calle Real of the town for 30 pesos to a free *mulata* named Beatriz de Arriaga in 1601.[37] Martín also had access to credit in both towns. He had purchased at least one of his slaves in this way, buying thirty-year-old Lucrecia, described as Black "*bozal Angola*," in Xalapa in 1600 for 430 pesos on six months' credit.[38]

The towns along these royal trading routes that connected the fort of San Juan de Ulúa and Mexico City were visited constantly by passersby who brought information and experiences from distant parts of the Spanish empire. Even those who never left the towns where they dwelt would have developed a sense of the broader regional cartographies through discussions with passersby operating in broader trading and travel networks. And constant flows of commodities, people, and information also brought capital to these urban sites. As Ana de Tapia explained in her testament in 1602, she and her husband Bartolomé Martín had accumulated significant capital after their marriage. She explained how "in the time when we married, we didn't have any property or furniture." But in the two decades since, the pair had accumulated significant property, which Tapia detailed in her will, noting that they owned

---

[35] "Poder," USBI Xalapa, Protocolos Notariales Jalapa, Año del protocolo: 1578–1594, July 20, 1586, no. 1, clave del acta: 27 1578 446, fol. 283.

[36] "Venta," USBI Xalapa, Protocolos Notariales Puebla de los Ángeles, Año del protocolo: 1578–1594, October 19, 1587, no. 1, clave del acta: 53 1578 489, fols. 320–321; "Obligación," USBI Xalapa, Protocolos Notariales Puebla de los Ángeles, Año del protocolo: 1578–1594, October 19, 1587, clave del acta, 53, 1578, 490, no. 1 fol. 321^{vta}.

[37] "Venta," USBI Xalapa, Protocolos Notariales Jalapa, Año del protocolo: 1600–1608, November 14, 1601, clave del acta, 27, 1600, 1187, n. 3, fol. 72^{vta}; "Bartolomé Martín," AGI, Contratación, 938A, no. 10, fols. 9^{v}–11^{v}.

[38] "Venta, esclava," USBI Xalapa, Protocolos Notariales Jalapa, Año del protocolo: 1600–1608, September 19, 1600, no. 3, clave del acta: 27 1600 1126, fols. 21^{v}–22; "Obligación de Pago," USBI Xalapa, Protocolos Notariales Jalapa, Año del protocolo: 1600–1608, September 19, 1600, clave del acta 27, 1600, 1127. no. 3, fols. 22–22^{vta}.

firstly a *venta* that they call of the oranges which is in the province of Xalapa with four *cavallerias* of land, and the land of the *venta* with its houses … a Black *Biafara* slave called Catalina who is thirty years old more or less who has a Black son called Felipe and a *mulata* daughter called Sesilia … another slave called Isabel, *Angola*, who is twenty years old more or less. A horse, two mattresses on which she sleeps.[39]

Arriving into this interconnected world as an enslaved Black woman from Portugal, Sossa inevitably became an economic actor within the fabric of urban dwellers who provided services for passing trade, and likely took part in gossip and whisper networks that connected these various towns.

NEGOTIATING AND RAISING FUNDS TO PURCHASE THE PRICE OF LIBERTY ALONG THE CAMINO REAL

By the mid 1580s, Sossa had accrued sufficient funds in Puebla to purchase her liberty. It is unclear how much money she raised, but on average, enslaved Black people in this region agreed to pay 300 to 600 pesos for their liberation from slavery at this time. Two of Sossa's former owners provided testimony about how she had liberated herself, each emphasizing the different ways in which Sossa had gathered the funds. Alonso de Ribas, her most recent owner and the person who had agreed to liberate her from slavery, recalled in a witness statement in 1588 that Sossa had liberated herself through money that she had earned as a healer.[40] Ribas provided this testimony in the context of Sossa's petition for an ecclesiastical divorce from her husband in order to counter her husband's claim to have liberated her from slavery. Ribas clarified that Sossa's husband was poor when the couple married, and described Sossa as a hard worker who had earned all the capital in the couple's possession and that she had liberated herself from slavery with her own money. Years later, Sossa's first owner in New Spain, Alonso Hernández de Santiago, gave an account of her liberation that placed greater emphasis on Sossa's husband, noting how "Antonio Álvarez liberated her [Sossa], having married her before."

Although Margarita de Sossa was adamant that her husband had played no role in her liberation from slavery in Puebla, notarial records

---

[39] "Bartolomé Martín," AGI, Contratación, 938A, no. 10, fols. 57^r–67^r (Ana de Tapia's testament).
[40] "Margarita Sossa," AGN, México, GD61 Inquisición, vol. 208, exp. 3, fols. 143^v–144.

from the region reveal that spouses were often involved in furnishing the capital to pay for the liberation of their kin. For example, a free Black *vecina* of Mexico City named Ana Hernández noted in her 1593 testament that she had liberated her Black husband, Cristóbal, from slavery through the "money that [I] earned in [my] labors," which most likely involved the production of *fideos* (a type of pasta) – as she owned a *fideo* grinder.[41] Similarly, Francisco de Camacho, a fifty-year-old enslaved Black man from the Canary Islands, was liberated from slavery in Jalapa in 1641 when his free Black wife, Juana de la Cruz, negotiated to pay the sum of 100 *pesos de oro común* to Camacho's owner within five months of his liberation.[42] Thereafter, the couple lived as *vecinos* in Jalapa, where they owned a small plot of land (in the Xallitic area), later moving to Old Veracruz. Once there, they maintained ties to Jalapa through ownership of their land there, until 1658, when Camacho instructed a *vecino* of Jalapa to sell the plot via an Old-Veracruz-notary.[43] Sometimes spouses lent, rather than gave, their loved ones the funds to pay for their liberty. This occurred across the Caribbean basin in the town of Portobelo, when a Black *horra* from Sevilla named Lucía Tenorio Palma (mentioned in Chapter 2) lent her enslaved husband, Cristóbal de la Palma, the sum of 500 pesos so that he could liberate himself from slavery.[44]

Margarita de Sossa was unambiguously clear that she – and not her husband – had provided the funds for the price of her liberty. In 1588, she explained that she had purchased her liberty with her own income generated from her labor as a healer, noting that "the money with which I liberated myself was from my work and sweat and not that of my husband."[45] Sossa's accumulation of sufficient capital to purchase her freedom through labor-for-hire arrangements reflected the broad trend in the

---

[41] "Testamento, Ana Hernández," Mijares CPAGNXVI, Protocolos Notariales, Escribano Andrés Moreno, July 20, 1593, notaria 374, vol. 2463, libro 2, fols. 38–39^v, ficha 158.0.

[42] "Carta de libertad, Francisco Camacho," USBI Xalapa, Protocolos Notariales de Xalapa, November 7, 1641, Año del protocolo: 1632–1645, no. 6, clave del acta: 27 1632 3297, fols. 210^{vta}–211; "Obligación de Pago," USBI Xalapa, Protocolos Notariales de Xalapa, November 7, 1641, Año del protocolo: 1632–1645, no. 6, clave del acta: 27 1632 3298, fols. 211^{vta}–212^{vta}.

[43] "Poder," USBI Xalapa, Protocolos Notariales de Veracruz Vieja, May 2, 1658, Año del protocolo: 1645–1651, no. 7, fols. 218–218^{vta}, clave del acta: 19 1645 4037; "Venta," USBI Xalapa, Protocolos Notariales de Jalapa, Año del protocolo: 1645–1651, March 22, 1658, no. 7, clave del acta: 27 1645 4033, fols. 216–217^{vta}.

[44] "Lucia Tenorio Palma," AGI, Contratación 526, no. 1, ramo 1, doc. 8.

[45] "Margarita Sossa," AGN, México, GD61 Inquisición, vol. 208, exp. 3, fols. 102–103^v.

towns along the Camino de Veracruz and the Camino Real. Enslaved people who furnished the entire sum for their liberty often raised the money through these arrangements. For example, in 1574, two enslaved Black women named Magdalena and Francisca paid 300 pesos each for their liberation to the nuns of the monastery Nuestra Señora de la Concepcion in Mexico City.[46] In Jalapa, in 1595, Felipa *Mandinga* liberated herself by paying 300 *pesos de oro común* to her owner, Alonso de Villanueva, who was also the *alcalde mayor* of Jalapa.[47] Pedro de la Cruz, a twenty-five-year-old Black *criollo* (a term used in the sixteenth century to refer to an American-born Black person, whether enslaved or free) paid 500 *pesos de oro común* for his liberty in Mexico City in 1612.[48] In Jalapa, fifty-year-old Marta *Zape* paid 350 *pesos de oro común* to a *vecino* of Jalapa for her liberty in 1600,[49] while fifty-year-old Isabel from *tierra Zape* paid 300 *pesos de oro común* for her liberty to her owners in Jalapa in 1619.[50] None of the notarial contracts of these self-purchase agreements indicated that the liberated person accrued a debt, the absence of which suggests that they accumulated the funds themselves through labor-for-hire arrangements.

Some enslaved Black people managed to negotiate with their owners to accept partial payments of their liberty in exchange for their freedom and provide a loan for the remaining amount. For example, in 1567, a *morena* named Isabel Ruíz negotiated her freedom in Mexico City on the condition that she pay her owner 500 *pesos de oro común*, which she would furnish in instalments of 30 pesos every three months, agreeing that she could be returned to servitude if eight months elapsed without her paying 60 pesos.[51] The years-long repayment plan suggests that Ruíz hoped to raise the funds incrementally through her labor as a liberated woman. Other cases of enslaved people becoming indebted to their former owners in exchange for their liberty included a Black man named

---

[46] "Alhorría," in Mijares *CPAGNXVI*, Protocoles Notariales, Pedro Sánches de la Fuente, Notaría 1, vol. 150, fols. 1401–1404, ficha 569.

[47] "Carta de libertad, Felipa *Mandinga*," USBI Xalapa, Protocolos Notariales Xalapa, December 17, 1595, Jalapa, clave del acta: 27 1600 1217, no. 3, fol. 97.

[48] "Alhorría," in Mijares *CPAGNXVI*, Protocoles Notariales, Juan Pérez de Rivera, Notaría 497, vol. 3359, fols. 106–106^v, ficha 69,

[49] "Carta de libertad, Marta Zape," USBI Xalapa, Protocolos Notariales Xalapa, January 2, 1608, clave del acta: 27 1600 1658, no. 3, fols. 541–541^{vta}.

[50] "Carta de libertad, Isabel, de tierra Zape," USBI Xalapa, Protocolos Notariales Xalapa, November 23, 1619, clave del acta: 27 1617 2761, no. 5, fols. 251–252^{vta}.

[51] "Alhorría," in Mijares, *CPAGNXVI*, Protocoles Notariales, Antonio Alonso, February 18, 1567, Notaría 1, vol. 8, legajo 7, fols. 150^v–153 (1132–1137), ficha 521.0.

Miguel de Trejo, who obtained his *carta de libertad* in 1623 after paying 50 of the 160 pesos of his purchase price; he agreed to pay his former owner the remaining debt the following year.[52]

Notarial contracts in Jalapa, Puebla, and Mexico City reveal how some enslaved Black people obtained charitable loans from *vecinos* of these towns worth between 250 to 600 *pesos de oro común* to liberate themselves from slavery. In turn, they became indebted to third parties in exchange for their liberty as they pledged their labor to their creditors for specific periods of time or undertook to repay loans over the course of a specified time. For example, an enslaved Black woman named Juana borrowed 300 *pesos de oro común* in Mexico City from a merchant so that she could pay for her liberation from slavery in 1614.[53] Similarly, in 1612, a thirty-year-old Black *criollo* named Gaspar de Fuentes paid 300 *pesos de oro común* for his liberty in Mexico City by borrowing the funds from Dionosio de Merlo, a *vecino* of the city whom he described as a "person who has always helped him in his necessities."[54] Juana de la Cruz obtained a loan after her owner attempted to displace her and her seven-year-old *mulato* son from Mexico City to another region of New Spain in 1624. Cruz requested that her owner allow her to purchase her freedom, reporting that "honorable people intervened" to prevent her forced displacement. Cruz subsequently obtained a gift or a loan in 1624 of 200 *pesos de oro común* from a *vecino* of the city named Martín Saenz. This sum only covered one-third of the cost of her and her daughter's liberty, so she agreed to continue serving her owners until she raised the remaining 300 *pesos de oro común*.[55] Another example of an enslaved person's access to credit is given by the thirty-three-year-old *mulato* named Jusephe de la Cruz, who raised a 200 peso loan in Mexico City in 1634 so that he could purchase his liberty. His

---

[52] "Obligación de pago," in Mijares, *Catálogo de Protocolos del Archivo General de Notarías de la Ciudad de México, Fondo Siglo XVII, En línea* (hereafter *CPAGNXVII*), Protocolos Notariales, Juan Péres de Rivera, Notaría 497, vol. 3362, legajo 2, fols. 5–5^v, ficha 361.

[53] "Autos," [Testament], in Mijares *CPAGNXVII*, Protocoles Notariales, Juan Pérez de Rivera, February 28, 1614, Notaría 497, vol. 3359, fols. 325–338^v (9bis–22^v). "Alhorría," in Mijares *CPAGNXVII*, Protocolos Notariales, Juan Pérez de Rivera, Juan, March 10, 1614, Notaría, 497, vol. 3359, fols. 325–338^v (9bis–22^v), ficha 173.0.

[54] "Alhorría," in Mijares *CPAGNXVII*, Protocolos Notariales, Juan Pérez de Rivera, May 25, 1612, Notaría 497, vol. 3360, fols. 80–82.

[55] "Carta de Pago y declaración," in Mijares *CPAGNXVII*, Protocolos Notariales, Juan Pérez de Rivera, October 5, 1626, Notaría 497, vol. 3362, legajo 2, fols. 125–125^v (340–340^v), ficha 580.0.

creditor was Francisco de Aparicio Arreaga, a royal notary (*receptor*) for the Real Audiencia of the city.[56] Cruz undertook to repay the loan within four months.[57]

These records reveal how local creditors perceived some enslaved Black people as creditworthy, despite their enslaved legal status that prevented them from owning or accumulating property. Such cases explicitly noted the nature of the loan, revealing how they sought to secure their liberty and obtain a coveted *carta de alhorría* by indebting themselves to strangers. Records of enslaved people raising loans from prominent *vecinos* in towns and cities in New Spain represent a series of conversations and negotiations about liberty between enslaved Black people and other residents, often out of sight of slave-owners. These cases reveal how some enslaved people developed relationships beyond the walls of their enslavers' homes and accrued some social capital while enslaved, which permitted them to raise a loan to pay for their liberation from slavery.

Enslaved Black people who obtained these loans could became creditworthy as participants in early modern economic life, but it is worth paying attention to how such credit arrangements were formalized before notaries. Usually, credit agreements between creditor and debtor were drawn up and signed a day or two before the transfer of funds and the owner issuing a *carta de alhorría*. In other words, enslaved people signed agreements with their creditor, undertaking to repay the amount over a specific term, and a day or two later a slave-owner would grant freedom to their slave upon receipt of funds from the creditor. For example, the aforementioned Gaspar de Fuentes signed a contract on May 23, 1612, undertaking to repay 300 pesos to his creditor through his labor or with money (in the event that he managed to raise the sum), his creditor then furnished the funds to his owner, and two days later Fuentes received his *carta de alhorría*.[58] Less commonly, all parties would sign the various agreements simultaneously. For example, the aforementioned Juana borrowed 300 pesos from a merchant to purchase her liberty and all parties were present

---

[56] "Alhorría," in Mijares *CPAGNXVII*, Protocolos Notariales, Juan Pérez de Rivera, February 9, 1634, Notaría 497, vol. 3362, legajo 1, fols. 441ᵛ–442ᵛ, ficha 299.0.

[57] "Obligación de Pago," in Mijares *CPAGNXVII*, Protocolos Notariales, Juan Pérez de Rivera, February 9, 1634, Notaría 497, vol. 3362, legajo 1, fols. 443–443ᵛ, ficha 300.00.

[58] "Alhorría," in Mijares *CPAGNXVII*, Protocolos Notariales, Juan Pérez de Rivera, May 23, 1612, Notaría 497, vol. 3360, fols. 93–93ᵛ, ficha 118; "Recibo," in Mijares *CPAGNXVII*, Protocoles Notariales, Juan Pérez de Rivera, Notaría, 497, vol. 3360, fol. 112, ficha 125.0.

before the same notary to sign notarial contracts between Juana and her creditor, who furnished the price of Juana's liberty, while her owner issued a *carta de alhorría* upon receipt of the funds from Juana.[59]

Occasionally, enslaved Black people obtained loans from *vecinos* who resided in other towns from where they dwelt. Such credit agreements are indicative of how enslaved people who lived in towns along the royal trading routes interacted with regular passersby and sometimes developed social, economic, and communication ties across vast spaces in New Spain. These economic transactions also reflect the surplus of money in the region from the late sixteenth-century silver boom. As a result, some enslaved people developed sufficient social and economic ties to raise credit or capital with passersby to purchase their liberty. For example, in Jalapa, a *morena* named Ana Zavala liberated herself and her six-year-old *mulata* daughter from slavery by obtaining a loan of 500 *pesos de oro común* from a *vecino* of Puebla de los Ángeles named Jerónimo de Vega.[60] Vega paid Zavala's owner directly for her liberation, and two days later signed a contract with Zavala in which she agreed to repay the loan over a four-year period by furnishing her creditor with 125 pesos per year.[61]

Public auctions also became sites where enslaved Black people sometimes negotiated for their freedom with potential creditors, especially when they formed part of the estate of their deceased owners or when owners sought to resell their slaves in a public marketplace. Town criers organized public auctions in marketplaces in towns and cities, but auctions of deceased people's belongings could also take place anywhere where there were willing buyers present, ranging from public squares in metropolitan cities, rural areas, and on ships in the middle of the Atlantic. Black or *mulato* criers, commonly noted for their particularly "loud voices," often administered such auctions in New Spain and in other sites across the Spanish Americas.[62] Black auctioneers'

---

[59] "Alhorría," in Mijares CPAGNXVII, Protocolos Notariales, Juan Pérez de Rivera, October 3, 1614, Notaría 497, vol. 3359, fols. 9bis–22^v (325–338), ficha 173.

[60] "Obligación de pago entre Jerónimo de Vega, y el regidor Luis Pacho Mejía por la libertad de Ana Zavala," USBI Xalapa, Protocolos Notariales de Jalapa, Año del Protocolo, 1617–1631, February 10, 1620, no. 5, clave del acta: 27 1617 2766, fols. 256–256^{vta}.

[61] "Obligación de pago entre Ana de Zavala y Jerónimo de la Vega por 500 pesos de oro común que le prestó para liberarla del cautiverio," USBI Xalapa, Protocolos Notariales Xalapa, February 12, 1620, no. 5, clave del acta: 27 1617 2769, fols. 258^{vta}–259^{vta}.

[62] For examples of Black and *mulato* criers, see "Ana Gómez," AGI, Contratación, 257A, no. 3, ramo 12, fols. 152^v–170^v (a Black *criollo* crier named Francisco); "Juan de Rojas,"

management of these public sales meant that auctions of enslaved Black people sometimes became Black spaces, away from the watchful eyes of the slave-owner who was selling slaves.

Enslaved Black people who were subjected to public auctions sometimes attempted to negotiate their path to freedom with potential buyers who were present at an auction. They engaged in discussions about the terms of slavery and the conditions of their future labor in public spaces with prospective owners or with charitable people who donated funds with the aim of liberating an enslaved person. These ephemeral conversations and bartering about liberty in marketplaces and auction sites became etched in the historical record in fragmentary form through formalized commercial agreements or testimonies about acts of liberation. For example, Hernan Priego bought forty-year-old Juan, an enslaved Black man who had been born in Triana (Sevilla), at an auction in Mexico City for 330 *pesos de oro común* in 1583. The auction likely took place in the Portal de los Mercaderes located on the central square of Mexico City near the cathedral (Figures 3.3 and 3.4, no. 4). As a condition of the purchase that the pair negotiated during the auction, Priego had agreed with Juan that he would be allowed to hire out his labor to raise the sum of his purchase price in return for his freedom.[63] Such a condition suggests that Juan discussed the terms of his purchase with prospective buyers during the live auction and before Priego agreed a purchase price with the crier. Similar conversations and haggling between prospective buyers and enslaved people occurred in 1601 when Alonso de Cerda purchased a *mulato* named Sebastián in a public action in Mexico City, reporting that he wished to "do good for the *mulato*." Apparently, the pair had agreed during the auction that Cerda would liberate Sebastián from slavery if Sebastián served his new owner for three years, or earlier if Sebastián managed to pay the original purchase price of 120 *pesos de oro común*.[64]

AGI, Contratación, 293A, no. 1, ramo 6, fols. 66–68ᵛ (*"por vos de Thomas negro pregonero altos boces,"* *"por voz de Jhoan mulato pregonero,"* and *"por voz de Andrés mulato ladino en lengua castellana y Mexicana"*); "Luis de Pinelo," AGI, Contratación, 296A, no. 2, ramo 3, fol. 8ʳ (a *mulato* crier named Francisco de Cara); "Lucía Tenorio Palma," AGI, Contratación, 526, no. 1, ramo 1, doc. 8, fols. 11ʳ–24ʳ (a *mulato* crier named Juan de Arlete).

[63] "Alhorría," in Mijares *CPAGNXVI*, Protocolos Notariales, Juan Román, April 10, 1583, Notaría 1, vol. 135, fols. 231–233, ficha 81.0.

[64] "Declaración," in Mijares *CPAGNXVI*, Protocolos Notariales, Juan Pérez de Rivera, July 13, 1601, Notaría 497, vol. 3357, fols. 259–259ᵛ, ficha 233.0.

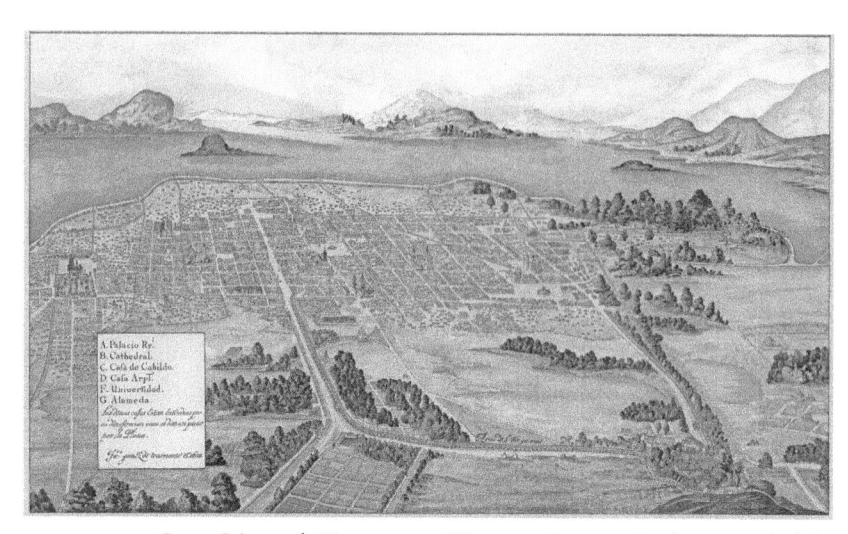

136   *Slavery and Freedom in the Early Spanish Atlantic*

FIGURE 3.3 Juan Gómez de Trasmonte, "Forma y Levantado de La Ciudad de México." A. Ruffoni: Florence, 1628. David Rumsey Map Collection, list no. 13213.000. David Rumsey Map Center, Stanford Libraries.

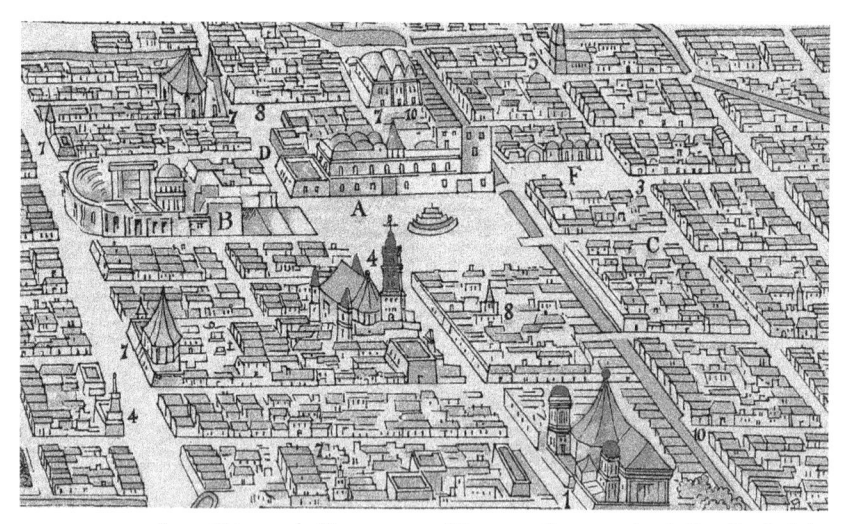

FIGURE 3.4 Juan Gómez de Trasmonte, "Forma y Levantado de La Ciudad de México" (detail). A. Ruffoni: Florence, 1628. David Rumsey Map Collection, list no. 13213.000. David Rumsey Map Center, Stanford Libraries.

Another moment of negotiation about the conditions of slavery during a live auction occurred in Mexico City in 1590. A widow named María del Toral purchased an enslaved Black woman named

María along with her sister, Juana, in an auction for 625 *pesos de oro común*.[65] Within three years, a priest named Pedro de Soto paid 500 *pesos de oro común* to María de Toral on the condition that she liberate her twenty-year-old Black slave named María, whom he described as the daughter of Catalina *Zape*.[66] Although I have not been able to locate further records detailing the nature of Pedro de Soto and María's financial or kinship relationships, there are various possibilities worth exploring. Three years elapsed between María and Juana being sold at an auction in Mexico City in 1590 and Pedro de Soto paying for María's liberation from slavery. It is possible that Soto had been in conversation for some years in Mexico City with María or her mother, Catalina *Zape*, to arrange credit for her liberation. Such conversations or relationships may have commenced during the auction in 1590 or may have dated from an earlier period. Given that María and Juana were both sold following the death of their owner as part of his estate, it is possible that the former owner's death tore apart this enslaved family, and the daughters were sold at auction to pay the debts of the estate.[67] In such a scenario, Catalina *Zape* may have activated her network within Mexico City to find someone to lend her the money or furnish a charitable gift to liberate her daughters. The only record that I have located for this family is the one in which Pedro de Soto paid the price to liberate María. Juana, it seems remained enslaved to María del Toral.

Public auctions also became sites where free Black kin and communities attempted the fraught and time-sensitive enterprise of negotiating the purchase price of their enslaved family member in the hopes of liberating them from slavery. Spouses, kin, and members of religious confraternities often raised the funds to bid on their loved ones at public auctions as acts of charity, solidarity, and kinship. A particularly striking description of this occurred in the town of Portobelo in 1616, when a *criolla morena*

---

[65] "Almoneda," in Mijares CPAGNXVI, Protocolos Notariales, Luis de Basurto (Escribano real), México, January 22, 1590, Notaria, 1, vol. 20, fols. 193/194) (97/97ᵛ) Fols. 2 100/100ᵛ, ficha 107.0.

[66] "Carta de libertad, María, negra," in Mijares *CPAGNXVI*, Protocolos Notariales, "Luis de Basurto" (Escribano real), México, March 18, 1593, Notaría 1, vol. 20, fols. 98r–98v (189–190) (95–95ᵛ), ficha 105.0.

[67] For examples of such auctions of enslaved people to pay estate debts, see "Ana Gómez," AGI, Contratación, 257A, no. 3, ramo 12, fols. 152ᵛ–170ᵛ; "Juan Limón," AGI, Contratación, 5581, no. 72; "Lucía Tenorio Palma," AGI, Contratación, 526, no. 1, ramo 1, doc. 8, fols. 11ʳ–24ʳ.

named Andrea testified that she had been sold at an auction after being left as the property of the previously mentioned Lucía Tenorio Palma.[68] According to Andrea, a *mulato* crier sold her for 400 *pesos de a ocho reales* in an auction in Portobelo to "charitable people of my nation" who wished to liberate her from slavery. Andrea recalled how a free Black woman named Francisca de San Miguel had gifted her enough money to liberate herself, and had not obliged Andrea to repay her.[69]

People heard news from afar about the prospective auctions of their enslaved kin through communication networks along the two trading routes that connected San Juan de Ulúa and Mexico City. As an example, free Black residents of Veracruz sometimes heard about the imminent sales of their kin in nearby towns. Such auctions were a unique opportunity to attempt to liberate kin, and family who heard about such auctions often embarked on lengthy journeys to participate in them. For example, a free Black *vecino* of Veracruz named Cristóbal Sánchez was married to an enslaved Black woman named Elvira Gutiérrez. When Gutiérrez's owner perished in 1610, Sánchez heard that an auction of the deceased's belongings would take place in Jalapa and that his wife was due to be sold. Sánchez traveled from Veracruz to Jalapa to negotiate with the crier and bid on his wife's freedom. During the auction, Sánchez agreed to furnish the auctioneer with a sixteen- to eighteen-year-old healthy enslaved Black man whom he would deliver within four months in return for his wife's liberty.[70] A similar negotiation took place in 1642 when a free Black *vecino* of Veracruz named Juan *Biafara* liberated his Black sister-in-law, Leonor, who was enslaved in a nearby sugar plantation. The agreement for Leonor's liberation involved Juan providing Leonor's owner with a thirty-year-old enslaved Black woman named Magdalena who was "of *Angola* nation," purchased by Juan for 360 *pesos de oro común*. Juan *Biafara* traveled from Veracruz to Jalapa to sign the notarial contract, and within thirteen days Leonor's owner liberated her and furnished her with a *carta de libertad*. Leonor may have gravitated towards Veracruz after her liberation from slavery to join her free Black brother-in-law, or perhaps she attempted to reunite with her own husband, if she knew of his whereabouts.[71]

---

[68] "Lucia Tenorio Palma," AGI, Contratación 526, no. 1, ramo 1, doc. 8, fols. 21^r–21^v.
[69] Ibid.
[70] "Obligación, Cristóbal Sánchez, Elvira Gutiérrez," USBI Xalapa, Protocolos Notariales Xalapa, February 22, 1620, clave del acta: 27 1617 2774, no. 5, fols. 263^{vta}–264.
[71] "Carta de libertad, Leonor," USBI Xalapa, Protocolos Notariales Xalapa, January 23, 1646, Lugar del acta, Ingenio Nuestra Señora De La Concepción La Concha, clave del acta: 85 1632 3818, no. 6, fols. 573–573^{vta}; "Juan Biafara, Magdalena de nación Angola,

Free Black people also acted as lenders to liberate their friends and kin from slavery,[72] these commercial agreements revealing Black solidarity ties. Records of self-purchase transactions in Jalapa, Puebla, and Mexico City reveal instances of charitable lending by Black *vecinos* and Black confraternities to liberate friends and kin from enslavement. In Mexico City in 1573, for example, Juana pleaded with her owner, Pedro Muñoz, to allow her to pay for the price of her liberty as her "godparents (*parientes*) and brothers of the confraternity" were willing to pay 200 *pesos de oro común* for her liberty.[73] After receiving a partial payment of 100 pesos, Muñoz agreed that he would liberate Juana and give her a *carta de alhorría* once he had received the remaining 100 pesos. In 1574, Francisca de Porras, a free Black *vecina* of Mexico City, lent her enslaved Black brother, Antón *Jolofe*, 250 *pesos de oro común* so that he could purchase his liberty, and she also lent him a further 93 pesos for his "other necessities."[74] In 1573, Cosme, an enslaved Black man in Mexico City, raised half of his purchase price after a free *mulato* named Juan Moronta gifted him 300 *pesos de reales*. María de Morales, who owned Cosme, agreed that he could have his *carta de alhorría* once he provided the remaining 300 *pesos de oro común* for his liberation.[75] Within one year, in 1574, Cosme had raised the outstanding 300 pesos through the "help of his godparents (*parientes*)" and from hiring out his labor, and he finally obtained his freedom.[76] In 1600, an enslaved Black woman named Luisa agreed a purchase price of 600 *pesos de oro común* for her liberty with her owner in Mexico City.[77] Luisa managed to obtain a loan or gift from a free Black woman named Luisa de Contresas, who paid 300 *pesos de oro común* towards Luisa's liberty. Luisa's owner agreed that she could have her *carta de alhorria* if she committed to paying the remaining 300 pesos over the

---

Leonor, carta de libertad," USBI Xalapa, Protocolos Notariales Xalapa, October 1, 1646, Lugar, Jalapa, clave del acta: 27 1632 3822, no. 6, fols. 576–576^{vta}.

[72] See, for example, Blumenthal, *Enemies and Familiars*.
[73] "Carta de Pago," in Mijares *CPAGNXVI*, Protocoles Notariales, Pedro Sánches de la Fuente, January 23, 1573, Notaría 1, vol. 151, legajo 11, fols. 182–182^v (326–326^v) ficha 271.
[74] "Obligación de pago," in Mijares *CPAGNXVI*, Protocolos Notariales, Pedro de Trujillo, November 12, 1574, Notaría 1, vol. 169, legajo 3, fols. 118–118^v, ficha 141.0.
[75] "Recibo," in Mijares *CPAGNXVI*, Protocolos Notariales, Pedro Sánchez de la Fuente, January 27, 1573, Notaría 1, vol. 150, fol. 506, ficha 212.
[76] "Alhorría," in Mijares *CPAGNXVI*, Protocolos Notariales, Pedro Sánchez de la Fuente, April 30, 1574, Notaría 1, vol. 150, fols. 1247–1249, ficha 515.
[77] "Declaración," in Mijares *CPAGNXVI*, Protocoles Notariales, Juan Pérez de Rivera, August 19, 1600, Notaría 497, vol. 3357, fols. 223–223^v, ficha 207.

following two years. In addition, the contract stipulated that Luisa could hire her labor back to her owner, who would pay 1 peso per week of work and 2 pesos annually for two years. Presumably, Luisa was to raise the remaining 250 pesos by hiring her labor to others when not attending to her former owner.[78] Also in Mexico City, the aforementioned Ana Hernández developed multiple economic ties with Black people in Mexico City, acting as a moneylender to enslaved people so that they could purchase their own liberty.[79] Although Hernández provided credit to enslaved people, she also owned at least three slaves. In her testament, she freed all of them, although each under different conditions of further labor or capital that they should provide her husband before obtaining their freedom.[80] In Jalapa, an enslaved *moreno* named Luis Coronado and his wife Clara Ruíz de Cabrera obtained a loan of 700 *pesos de oro común* from their godfather (*compadre y padrino*) named Lucas Martín to help them pay for the price of Coronado's liberty in 1620.[81] The couple agreed to repay the loan in four annual instalments of 175 *pesos de oro común*.[82] Finally, in 1583 in the town of Huatusco, north of Orizaba, a free man named Sebastián Hernández [Portilla] negotiated for the freedom of his daughter, María, and her mother, Ana, by pledging to labor on the owner's cow estate for two years in exchange for their liberty.[83]

Other instances of Black kin liberating their family from slavery involved men trying to ensure the freeborn status of their children by paying a slave-owner for the market price of their slave to liberate an enslaved woman who was bearing his progeny. An example of this is when Francisco Carreño, a free *mulato* slave-owner from the Canary

---

[78] Ibid.
[79] "Testamento, Ana Hernández," in Mijares CPAGNXVI, Protocolos Notariales, Escribano Andrés Moreno, July 20, 1593, notaria 374, vol. 2463, libro 2, fols. 38–39^v, ficha 158.0. It is possible that Ana Hernández had also borrowed 90 pesos de oro común from Andrés Sánchez in 1568, twenty-five years earlier, but if so she had repaid that debt by the time she composed her will in 1593: "Obligación de Pago," in Mijares CPAGNXVI, Protocoles Notariales, Pedro Sánchez de la Fuente, August 25, 1568, escribano real Notaria 1, vol. 150, fols. 305–306.
[80] Ibid.
[81] "Luis Coronado, Obligación de Pago," USBI Xalapa, Protocolos Notariales de Xalapa, March 28, 1620, Jalapa, clave del acta: 27 1617 2775, no. 5, fols. 264^{vta}–266.
[82] "Luis Coronado, Obligación de Pago," USBI Xalapa, Protocolos Notariales de Xalapa, March 28, 1620, Jalapa, clave del acta: 27 1617 2775, no. 5, fols. 264^{vta}–266.
[83] "Libertad y ahorría a María, mulata, de 3 años de edad," USBI Xalapa, Protocolos Notariales San Antonio Huatusco, 1583–1584, September 10, 1583, no. 5, clave del acta 220, 1583, 21317, fols. 39–39^v.

Islands who operated as a master of sugar in New Spain, furnished the funds for the price of an enslaved Black woman's freedom to liberate her from slavery before she gave birth to his son.[84] Carreño was seeking to assure the freeborn status of his son, Juan de Carreño. Although he did not name this liberated Black woman in his will, Carreño detailed how he had liberated her from slavery, how her owner had given her a *carta de alhorría*, and how Carreño had also paid to copy the precious *carta de alhorría* of his son's mother with a royal notary in Mexico City, in case his son ever needed to prove his liberty.[85] As it turned out, such precautions were wise as Carreño's *mulato* son was later mistaken for an enslaved person by a royal judge and the paperwork that Carreño senior had safeguarded proved his son's status.[86] White Spanish men also sometimes engaged in these practices to assure the freedom of their progeny.[87]

Enslaved Black people who resided in the towns along the two royal trading routes that connected San Juan de Ulúa and Mexico City sought out friends, kin, associates, and strangers in their quest to purchase their liberty and obtain a coveted *carta de alhorría*. In the process, they engaged in discussions in public and private spheres about their strategies to raise funds and purchase their liberty from their owners. Notarial documents invariably only recorded the contractual details of commercial transactions, rather than the series of discussions, social capital, economic decisions, and relationships that led to the agreements that underpinned these transactions. Nonetheless, these documents show how enslaved Black people were participants in early modern political economies, negotiating the terms of their enslavement and paths to liberation and discussing how to plot a path to freedom through self-purchase. They sometimes became creditworthy in the eyes of their neighbors and passing traders, as they sought to negotiate their liberty by seeking out credit among friends, kin, associates, and strangers when they were unable to raise the funds themselves.

LIFE AFTER LIBERATION FROM SLAVERY

After paying for their liberty, many Black *horros* lived in towns and cities in this region as free or partially liberated people, eking out a living along

---

[84] "Francisco Carreño," AGI, Contratación, 515, no. 1, ramo 5. For a discussion of this case, see Ireton, "The Life and Legacy."
[85] Ibid.
[86] Ibid.
[87] "Alhorría," USBI Xalapa, Protocolos Notariales de San Antonio, Año(s): 1583–1584, clave del acta: 223, 1583, 21289, September 5, 1583, no. 5, fols. 5–6^{vta}.

the royal trading routes; and for the most part their lives disappear from the archival record. Unusually, though, there is a remarkable trail of information about the life of Margarita de Sossa after her liberation from slavery. Testimonies about her life as a free Black woman in Puebla emerged when she petitioned for an ecclesiastical divorce from her husband in 1588 a few years after her liberation from slavery.[88] Six years later, in 1594, further testimonies about her life were also recorded when she was arrested by the Holy Office of the Inquisition in Mexico City.[89] These two sets of documents provide rare insights into the meanings of freedom for a woman who purchased her own liberty, and her life as an economic actor after her liberation from slavery in late sixteenth-century Puebla.

After a lifetime of experiencing violent enslavement and being displaced across the Atlantic world, Sossa found that her freedom as a liberated woman in Puebla remained curtailed. She found herself trapped in a violent marriage with a husband who physically restricted her movements, threatened her life, and failed to fulfil his marital, financial, sexual, and cohabiting duties and obligations. In an attempt to gain a greater degree of freedom, Sossa took the unusual measure in 1588 of petitioning the bishop of Puebla to grant her an ecclesiastical divorce from her husband.[90] She did not request an annulment to the marriage, but rather an ecclesiastical divorce, "a permanent or temporary legal separation that suspended the obligation of marital cohabitation without dissolving the marriage bond."[91] A pronouncement of this kind did not signify the freedom to remarry, but instead permitted the parties the "right to live separately, to settle their estates, and to manage their affairs independently" while retaining "all the other incidents of marriage, including the responsibility of the husband to economically support his wife and the requirement of sexual chastity."[92] As historian Jonathan Bird notes, ecclesiastical divorce was not common in sixteenth- and seventeenth-century New Spain, and was "an absolute last resort" for couples who "had extremely troubled and often violent relationships."[93] Sossa's petition for a divorce fed a

---

[88] "Margarita de Sossa," AGN, Inquisición 208, exp. 3, fols. 92^r–332^r.
[89] Ibid., fols. 16^r–91^v.
[90] "Margarita de Sossa," AGN, Inquisición, vol. 208, exp. 3, fols. 97–97^v. For divorce in New Spain, see Bird, *For Better or Worse*; Gonzalbo Aizpuru, "Afectos e intereses," 200. For ecclesiastical divorce petitions in Lima (Peru), see Wisnoski, "Intimate Knowledge."
[91] Bird, *For Better or Worse*, 2.
[92] Ibid., 8.
[93] Historians have found only 110 petitions for divorce in New Spain, see ibid., 49. For another divorce petition by a Black person, see "Proceso contra Pero Hernández, negro horro," AGN, México, GD61 Inquisición, vol. 102, exp. 3.

whisper network in Puebla that led to accusations she was a practitioner of witchcraft. These accusations eventually led the Holy Office of the Inquisition in Mexico City to arrest her in 1594.

Sossa's petition for divorce and the legal strategies that she and her procurator employed shed light on the importance of interrogating the significance – in terms of lived experience – of a legal pronouncement of freedom. Typical petitions from wives who asked for ecclesiastical divorces cited their husbands' excessive and irrational violence, lack of financial support, and scandalous adultery.[94] Sossa drew on these common themes in her 1588 petition for divorce by describing her husband's multiple failings: He had failed to provide for her while she sustained the pair through her own labor; he had failed to live a married life with her as he ate and slept alone, and was the lover of another a married woman – a matter of public notoriety and scandal across the entire city of Puebla; and he was excessively violent towards her, which endangered her life.[95]

The most egregious of Álvarez's actions, according to Sossa, was his theft of an enslaved Black woman whom Sossa owned. According to Sossa, Álvarez stole her property to furnish his lover with a gift, and a servant of her husband's lover was now acting as Álvarez's personal servant. In other words, Álvarez had stolen one of the public symbols of Sossa's status as a free property-owning woman. Records of dowries among *vecinos* in the region show the importance of slave-ownership as a mark of status.[96] Not only had Sossa lost her own slave because of her husband's theft, but also her husband had benefited from the service of another servant. According to Sossa, this was "a matter of great scandal."[97] While Álvarez had attempted to silence his wife, she described these events as "public and notorious in all of the neighborhoods where I have lived."[98] Sossa's description of the flagrant theft and subsequent regifting of her slave property is indicative of her attempts to mark her status as a free woman through the public symbolism of slave-ownership.

---

[94] Bird, *For Better or Worse*, 9–10.
[95] "Margarita de Sossa," AGN, Inquisición, vol. 208, exp. 3, 78^r–80^r (172^r–174^r).
[96] "Dote, Compromiso," USBI Xalapa, Potocolos Notariales de Jalapa, Año(s): 1578–1594, September 30, 1581, no. 1, clave del acta: 21 1574 182, fols. 55–56^{vta}; "Dote, Compromiso," USBI Xalapa, Potocolos Notariales de México, Año(s): 1617–1631, February 4, 1609, no. 5, clave del acta: 36, 1617, 2996, fols. 477–479^{vta}.
[97] "Margarita de Sossa," AGN, Inquisición, vol. 208, exp. 3, fols. 102–103^v.
[98] Ibid.

Sossa pleaded for a divorce because she foresaw no other remedy for ending the terrible life and dangerous insecurity that she endured under Álvarez's wrath. Her husband physically harmed her on a regular basis.[99] She described a series of violent incidents that left her on the verge of death:

> beating, whipping, caning, and thrashing cruelly left my body injured and mistreated and one time he took out a dagger towards me ... and further, he gave me a very grave injury on my forehead of which I had a risk of death. Another time, he broke three ribs of my body and another time he broke me ... and those times I was on the verge of death.[100]

Sossa described the impossibility of enduring a married life with Álvarez because he physically harmed her so regularly, often locking her in a room to prevent her from seeking justice from the city's *alcalde* or employing a healer to tend to her injuries.[101] Further, Álvarez had also threatened to kill her.[102] Sossa asked the bishop to grant her a divorce and allow her to live alone and separately from her husband, specifying the need for the two to sleep in different rooms.[103] She also requested that the ecclesiastical court should prevent Álvarez from communicating with her and prohibit him from physically abusing her any further.

In the divorce petition, Sossa also made assertions about her husband's inadequacy in fulfilling his financial obligations. She explained that he had failed to provide sustenance for her. She contrasted her husband's financial failures with her own independent economic productivity, both while enslaved and after she obtained her liberty. She had earned everything in her husband's possession and provided the resources for their marriage, noting that "there is no more to consider ... beyond that I am a woman who has earned everything that he has, and he is obligated to give it to me." Sossa told the court that Álvarez had hidden her property – that she had earned through her own "sweat and labor" – with the intention of killing her and escaping with the fruits of her earnings.[104] She described how she had accumulated over 4,000 pesos during her time as a liberated woman and that her husband

---

[99] Ibid., fols. 78ʳ–80ʳ (172ʳ–174ʳ).
[100] Ibid.
[101] Ibid.
[102] Ibid.
[103] Ibid.
[104] Ibid.

had stolen those funds. Sossa's claim to have accumulated 4,000 pesos within a few years of her liberation from slavery represented a significant sum of money at the time: It was the approximate value of purchasing six enslaved adults in New Spain.

The Sossa-Álvarez divorce proceedings became a moment of public reckoning about how to define a legitimate marriage, a husband's responsibilities within such a sacrament, and a wife's freedom and rights within a marriage. A diverse cross-section of Poblano society played a role in assessing the legitimacy of the marriage. Sossa called on twenty-four witnesses to attest to its many injustices and dangers.[105] Those who testified for her included merchants, slave-owners, two enslaved Black people, widows who resided in Puebla, Sossa's former owners, and a young girl who labored as Sossa's and Álvarez's servant, named Inés Pérez. Álvarez also sourced a varied cast of characters to act as witnesses for his defense.

The testimonies for Sossa provide a striking insight into social relations in Puebla. Witnesses described visiting or dining in Sossa and Álvarez's home, sighting Sossa's injuries while in Puebla's public spaces, and discussing the magnitude of Álvarez's violence towards Sossa. They confirmed that Álvarez beat Sossa and caused grave wounds to her body, and that Álvarez would often eat and sleep alone.[106] Two of Sossa's previous owners also testified for her.

Successful divorce petitions were rare in New Spain.[107] Only 13 percent of the known 110 ecclesiastical divorce petitions between 1548 and 1699 resulted in a pronouncement of divorce.[108] Owing to the low success rate for divorce petitions, historian Jonathan Bird has theorized that wives litigated for ecclesiastical divorces not with the hope of obtaining a pronouncement of divorce, but because they knew that if judges granted that their cases be heard, they would be placed in protective custody or deposit (*depósito*), usually in "a private house or institution and out of the control of her husband for the duration of the legal process."[109] Bird notes that 75 percent of ecclesiastical divorce petitions in New Spain remained unresolved, and suggests that wives might have hoped to remain in protective custody in a *depósito* for lengthy periods of time, if not permanently.[110]

---

[105] Ibid., fols. 122–146ᵛ. On witnesses in divorce cases, see Wisnoski, "Intimate Knowledge."
[106] Ibid., fols. 143ᵛ–144.
[107] Bird, *For Better or Worse*, 127–205.
[108] Ibid., 132–133.
[109] Ibid., 55.
[110] Ibid., 132–133.

Perhaps Sossa had not hoped for a pronouncement of divorce, but rather for the freedom to live separately from her husband and to receive maintenance from him while she resided in a temporary or permanent *depósito*. If this was her aim, she emerged victorious, as the ecclesiastical court ordered that her husband sustain her with an advance payment every year of 150 *pesos de oro común* while the case was ongoing and she remain sheltered in another house.[111] Given the high rate of unresolved and pending divorce cases in New Spain in the period under study, Sossa might have judged that her success lay in compelling the bishop to allow for the divorce case to proceed, to place her in a *depósito*, and to order that Álvarez sustain her, rather than any resolution of the case per se.

Perhaps Sossa viewed her placement in a *depósito* and the court-ordered contribution from Álvarez as a way of finally achieving liberty after becoming an *horra*. Her incensed husband certainly suggested that Sossa's *depósito* was a ploy for her to gain greater freedom. Appealing against the court order that he pay maintenance, Álvarez complained that Sossa was roaming the streets of Puebla at night and conducting business as though she were not a married woman. He explained that she had

> maliciously sought a divorce in order for her to have the freedom to walk in her business (*anduras*) and vices because there is no one who can detain her for more than an hour in the house, and she has not adhered to the *depósito*, because every day she is not in the house for more than an hour and she is instead walking the streets from the morning until the night and is accompanied by Juana Limpias, a free Black woman.[112]

In short, Álvarez accused Sossa of litigating for a divorce to enjoy the freedoms of an unmarried free woman while residing in the *depósito*. He was particularly preoccupied that his wife was enjoying the freedom to walk wherever she wanted and at whatever time she desired. It is unclear whether the case reached final resolution, although the undated summary note that arrived at the Holy Office of the Inquisition in Mexico City in 1594 implied that a judgment had decreed that the couple resume cohabitation and married life. However, in 1592, within three years of Sossa litigating for divorce, Álvarez had abandoned Puebla and the viceroyalty of New Spain for the Philippines – perhaps owing to the economic burden

---

[111] Margarita de Sossa," AGN, Inquisición, vol. 208, exp. 3, fols. 214–219^v.
[112] Ibid., fols. 218–219^v.

of high maintenance responsibilities – never to return.[113] Seemingly, the pair did not maintain contact thereafter.

On the one hand, Álvarez's departure and Sossa's depositions in the subsequent Inquisitorial trial implied that the couple became estranged, suggesting that Sossa escaped her husband's violent wrath. Further, in the years since his departure, Sossa testified to working profitably as an innkeeper in Puebla.[114] Inquisitors prosecuting her in 1594 described her as "Margarita de Sossa, Black, native (*natural*) of the city of Porto in the kingdom of Portugal ... *vecina* of Puebla de Los Ángeles where she has as her trade to provide lodgings for guests."[115] Found among her belongings when Inquisitors arrested her in Puebla were five mattresses and a new wooden bed, suggesting that she could provide accommodation for at least half a dozen customers per night.[116] Her former owner, Alonso Hernández de Santiago, explained in his letter to Inquisitors in 1594 that Sossa's "trade and way of living has been and is to provide food and beds in her house to some people and she lives in the small houses."[117] Perhaps this trade also explains how she was able to secure a loan from a *vecino* of Mexico City to pay her bail during her Inquisition trial, allowing her to await the verdict while living freely in Mexico City rather than languishing in the secret jails of the Inquisition.[118] Sossa's ability to do so implied that she possessed social or economic ties that spanned Puebla to Mexico City, and that she found means to send word to one or more of her contacts in the viceregal capital after her arrest and displacement from Puebla to the secret jails of the Inquisition in Mexico City. On the other hand, Sossa continued to be married to Álvarez and would endure public notoriety for her attempt to petition for a divorce. The supposedly false testimonies provided about her witchcraft practices to the Inquisition by her Puebla enemies demonstrate just how dangerous such public notoriety could become.

Sossa's 1588 petition for divorce became the center of her defense strategy six years later in her 1594 Inquisitorial trial. She responded to the accusations levied against her by suggesting that some people in Puebla – who were her enemies and who harbored much hatred against

[113] Ibid., fols. 80–82.
[114] Ibid.
[115] Ibid.
[116] Ibid., fols. 44–45.
[117] Ibid., fol. 40.
[118] Ibid., fol. 90.

her – must have provided false evidence about her life.[119] She explained that her enemies had falsely testified about her practicing witchcraft six years earlier and that they had already been imprisoned in Puebla for their false testimonies. In Inquisitorial proceedings, testimony or accusations based on personal acrimony were dismissed. Sossa knew as much, and accordingly claimed that her enemies must have furnished accusations against her. In the four Inquisitorial hearings for her case between August 8 and 22, 1594, Sossa refused to admit to any crimes that she may have committed or witnessed. Instead, in each hearing, she reaffirmed that people who hated her in Puebla, and who "had threatened her and promised to do all the bad that they could to her," must have provided false testimonies.[120] She demanded that Inquisitors seek the transcript of legal proceedings from six years earlier in Puebla, in which a number of witnesses had falsely accused her of witchcraft and had been imprisoned for their offences; they included a free Black man named Francisco Gallardo.

The commissary of the Inquisition for Puebla and the Archbishopric of Tlaxcala who was responsible for collecting information about any potential crimes against the Catholic faith in the region was Alonso Hernández de Santiago, who had been Margarita de Sossa's first owner in Puebla. Santiago wrote to Inquisitors in 1594 to describe the history of false testimonies against her in Puebla. In that letter, he explained that witnesses in Puebla had testified to him in February 1594 about Sossa's reported witchcraft, but he had dismissed them owing to a long history of false accusations against Sossa:

> in a court case that she [Sossa] had with the ecclesiastical court (*audiencia obispal*) against her husband to petition for a divorce, some people testified that Sossa had put some powders in the food, and that as I had noticed it, and that I punished her [Sossa] for it. It was a false testimony, and that is what I declared in the court case.

Santiago assured Inquisitors that he had sold Sossa because she spoke too much and swore ("*por hablar mucho y no tener buena lengua*"), even though she was a good servant, and not because she practiced witchcraft as some people in Puebla had claimed.[121] Perhaps the arrival of his letter convinced Inquisitors to acknowledge the potential danger of relying on accusations based on hatred or personal acrimony because they

---

[119] Ibid., fols. 81–90.
[120] Ibid., fols. 81–90, 86–97.
[121] Ibid., fol. 40.

subsequently requested from Puebla the documents of the divorce case that Sossa had cited.[122]

Upon receiving the 1588 divorce case from Puebla, an Inquisitor decreed that a free Black man named Francisco Gallardo had provided false testimonies about Sossa stemming from his hatred towards her following the divorce litigation.[123] On September 26, 1594, two months after her initial arrest, Inquisitors granted Sossa license to return to Puebla until any new information arose pointing to her culpability. To fulfill the bureaucratic need for evidence (even in those cases that proved inconclusive), Inquisitors inserted Sossa's litigation for divorce into the file of her Inquisitorial trial. As a result of this bureaucratic precaution, Sossa's petition for divorce in Puebla has been preserved over the centuries.

Sossa therefore continued as an economic actor in Puebla society after her liberation from slavery. She maintained her trade as an innkeeper in Puebla,[124] and also opted to publicly indicate her free status and wealth to the community in Puebla by becoming a slave-owner: She purchased a Black female slave for her personal service.[125] Perhaps, through this, Sossa hoped to assuage any doubts that Poblanos may have harbored about her status as a free woman, doubts that may have been heightened owing to the aforementioned visual branding on her face that signaled to onlookers a history of enslavement.[126] Finally, after experiencing violence in her marriage, Sossa sought to experience a greater degree of lived freedom by petitioning for an ecclesiastical divorce from her husband. All the while, she continued to build her diverse social and economic ties in Puebla and beyond. The details about the life of this woman who purchased her own liberty in late sixteenth-century Puebla and who accumulated significant property is of course unique to her particular set of lived experiences. Yet there is no indication among the various testimonies to suggest that she was exceptional.

CONCLUSION

This history casts important light on how networks and the passing of information operated between Black populations in the early Hispanic

---

[122] Ibid., fol. 90.
[123] Ibid., fol. 91^v.
[124] Ibid., fols. 80–82.
[125] Ibid., fols. 102–103^v.
[126] Ibid., fols. 31–32.

Atlantic. In particular, self-purchase records in the towns along the *caminos reales* between San Juan de Ulúa and Mexico City reveal how the connections among and between free and enslaved Black populations on royal trading routes had a significant impact on the lives and experiences of enslaved Black people who sought to negotiate to purchase their liberty in these places. Inhabitants of these towns lived lives that were marked by the constant flow of passersby and networks of information. Some enslaved people sought out friends, neighbors, and strangers to raise capital to purchase their liberty or attempted to negotiate favorable terms with prospective buyers when they were subjected to a sale by auction. Others, like Sossa, negotiated the price and terms of their own liberty with their owners and raised funds through labor-for-hire arrangements, and went on to build networks and social and economic ties across the towns where they lived. And free and liberated Black people sometimes traveled vast distances to other towns to liberate their kin from slavery by participating as prospective buyers in the public auctions of their loved ones. Collectively, enslaved people's imprints in notarial archives, including the contracts they signed to purchase their own liberty or their kin's freedom, reveal a history of enslaved Black people's participation in early modern political economies as they pursued liberty. Rare documentation of the afterlives of those who were liberated from slavery also provides evidence of how Black *horros* continued to build social and economic ties, while also contending with the diverse and often contradictory meanings of liberty as they embarked on lives as *horros* and how they continued to press for greater degrees of lived freedoms even after liberating themselves from slavery.

4

Defining Freedom

Infrastructures of Black Political Knowledge between Sevilla and Mexico City

Confronted with an archbishop intent on prohibiting their Black confraternity from partaking in public religious life in early seventeenth-century Sevilla, the Black leaders of Our Lady of the Angels in Sevilla built a defense strategy that deployed a powerful rhetoric of Black political belonging in the Spanish empire. The archbishop's attempts to curtail the activities of the Black brotherhood is one example of pervasive Iberian ideas that racialized religious difference in the early modern period and that tended to link Blackness to two key concepts: slavery and exclusion from Catholic society. Yet the Black brothers' response sought to position the Spanish empire and the Catholic Church as resolutely inclusive of Black people. In their carefully crafted defense against the accusations of the archbishop, the Black leaders argued that the archbishop's orders were contrary to Catholic doctrine as Christianity was historically inclusive of Black people. They explained how "Christ put himself on the Cross for everyone, and our Mother of the Church [Mary] does not exclude us, and she adored us, and many other things more than white people, for we descend from gentiles and Old Christians, and Black people are not excluded from priesthood as there are today many Black priests and prebendaries in our Spain."[1] With these lines, the Black brothers sought to reject Iberian ideas that coalesced in the late sixteenth century that regarded Black people's purity of blood as permanently tainted by slavery, thereby preventing their full inclusion into the Iberian community of Old Christians (a term used for people who could claim at least four

---

[1] "Pleito entre la Hdad de Ntra Sra de la Antigua y la de los Ángeles que llaman la de los morenos," AGAS, III.1.6, L.9883, Expte 2. See also Figures 4.2–4.4.

generations of Christianity in their family), while positioning the Church as historically inclusive of Black people. Their inclusive rhetoric of political belonging in the Spanish empire reveals a rich intellectual tradition in which free and enslaved Africans and their descendants reckoned with pervasive anti-Black ideas in the early modern period, and how they proposed alternative political discourses that were inclusive of Black people in the body politic, usually through petitions to the crown for justice.

How did marginalized or subaltern groups, such as liberated or freeborn Black Africans and their descendants, acquire the legal know-how to craft petitions for justice and grace in royal courts? What were the conversations and shared knowledge that created the conditions for freeborn, liberated, and enslaved people to develop the resources and social capital to do this? This chapter traces the development of infrastructures of Black political knowledge in the Spanish empire and explores how people and communities learned about events and political discourses in faraway places, and exchanged ideas and news in their daily lives that they later deployed when they crafted legal arguments. The chapter focuses on these infrastructures of Black political knowledge and ideas about freedom in Sevilla and Mexico City as these are apt sites to explore moments of exchange between Black people across vast distances. These cities were connected by constant flows of people, as colonial officials, religious men, passengers, merchants, soldiers, servants, and other passersby traversed the Atlantic and royal trading routes between them. City dwellers and passersby constantly trafficked information and political know-how. By the turn of the seventeenth century, each city also had a significant Black population, and hundreds of free and liberated Black people embarked on journeys as fee-paying passengers or as wage-earning servants between them.[2]

---

[2] The following list comprises records of 115 free Black people who obtained passenger licenses from Castilla with a destination listed as New Spain in the sixteenth century: AGI, Contaduria, 241, no. 117; AGI, Contratación: 273, no. 22; 303, no. 2; 476, no. 1, ramo 5; 488, no. 3, ramo 2; 938A, no. 10; 5225A, no. 1, ramo 35; 5225B, no. 33; 5227, no. 2, ramo 25; 5328, no. 20; 5229, no. 2, ramo 10; 5232, no. 25; 5235, no. 1, ramo 57; 5237, no. 2, ramo 47; 5241, no. 2, ramo 63; 5248, no. 1, ramo 1; 5261, no. 2, ramo 65; 5282, no. 83; 5324, no. 30; 5338, no. 24; 5340, no. 4; 5343. no. 8; 5352, no. 33; 5355, no. 42; 5357, no. 18; 5360, no. 75; 5361, no. 14; 5370, no. 30; 5375, no. 25; 5406, no. 1; 5420, no. 70; AGI, Contratación, 5536: libro 3, fols. 214$^{(6)}$; libro 5, fols. 73$^{v(3)}$, 80$^{v(6)}$ 84$^{r(3)}$, 113$^{v(2)}$, 169$^{r(1)}$, 215$^{r(1)}$, 360$^{r(2)}$. AGI, Contratación, 5537: libro 2, fols. 151, 173, 177, 180^v, 204^v, 256^v, 279, 287^v; libro 3, fols. 233^r, 405^r, 408^v; AGI, Contratación, 5538: libro 1, fols. 95, 196, 256^v, 427^v, 464^v, 493; libro 3, fols. 127^v, 137, 158^v, 239. AGI, Indiferente: 449, libro A3, fols. 103^v–104^v; 450, libro A4, fols. 44–44^v, 148–148^v; 450, libro A5, fols. 28–28^v, 28^v–29; 1952, libro 2, fols. 208; 1952, libro 3, fols. 195; 1964, libro 10, fols. 88, 354^v; 1968, libro 19, fol. 214^v; 1968, libro 20, fols. 140^v; 1968,

Free and enslaved Black dwellers of each city sometimes became members of Black religious brotherhoods dotted across the respective urban landscapes. In early seventeenth-century Mexico City, there were at least seven Black religious brotherhoods catering to the diverse Black populations of enslaved and free people.[3] In Sevilla, at least three Black and *mulato* religious brotherhoods had been established by the same period, while some Black residents of Sevilla and Mexico City maintained ties with churches and confraternities that were predominantly white.[4] Black religious institutions in both cities suffered parallel repressive policies in the early seventeenth century when local authorities sought to extinguish their activities and suppress their power and prominence across the religious landscapes. In both urban sites, Black confraternities responded to this persecution by maneuvering petitions for justice through royal courts. Until now, there has been no evidence to suggest a connection between Black brotherhoods in these cities that were separated by the vast expanse of the Atlantic. However, this chapter shows that these groups may well have been in communication following the arrival in Sevilla of eight prominent Black leaders from Mexico City in 1612/13 after the Real Audiencia in that city sentenced them to permanent exile from New Spain. Mapping the presence of these eight exiled Black leaders in Sevilla as connected to the powerful patronage ties of a Black brotherhood there and the broader infrastructures of Black political organizing and royal petitioning in the city, spearheaded by Black people who arrived from the Americas to petition the Council of the Indies, allows us to speculate about the possible moments of fellowship and exchange between Black petitioners from different cities in the Spanish empire, and the impact of this on Black political ideas about freedom in this period.

---

libro 21, fols. 131^v, 183^v; 1969, libro 22, fols. 195^v, 130; 1978, fols. 16; 2049, no. 54; 2052, no. 14; 2053, no. 43; 2058, no. 6; 2058, no. 51; 2059, no. 108; 2061, no. 134; 2064, no. 135; 2065, no. 60; 2066, no. 92; 2067, no. 24; 2074, no. 50; 2074, no. 67; 2075, no. 140; 2076, no. 87; "Obligación de Pago, Juana Rodríguez and Elvira Prieta," March 6, 1529, AHPS, signatura P-3276, libro del año 1529, oficio 5, libro 1, Escribanía de Francisco de Castellanos, fol. 604.

[3] Castañeda García, *Esclavitud africana*, "La devoción a Santa Ifigenia," "Modelos de Santidad," "Piedad y participación," and "Santos negros, devotos de color"; Castañeda García and Ruiz Guadalajara, *Africanos y afrodescendientes*; Masferrer León, "Confraternities" and *Muleke*; Valerio, *Sovereign Joy*, "The Spanish," and "'That There Be No Black Brotherhood'"; von Germeten, *Black Blood Brothers*.

[4] Camacho Martínez, *La Hermandad de los Mulatos*; Frachia, "Black but Human." Moreno, *La antigua*; Rowe, *Black Saints*.

BLACK *VECINOS* AND THE CRAFTING OF PETITIONS TO THE CROWN TO DEFEND THE MEANINGS OF LIBERTY

Enslaved people in the Spanish empire who were liberated from slavery through a process of *alhorramiento* experienced a transformation in their legal status within the rule of law from enslaved (*siervos* or *cautivos*) to *horros* and *libertos* (liberated), as specified by the *Siete Partidas*.[5] In theory, liberated people enjoyed the same privileges and access to royal justice as those who were born as free people, as these legal codes specified that "liberty is the power which every man has by nature to do what he wishes, except where the force or right of law or *fuero* [municipal legislation] prevents him."[6] However, liberated and freeborn people who were racialized as Black and *mulato* in the Spanish empire encountered innumerable and often insurmountable challenges to, and attempts to curtail, their freedom. In particular, local royal authorities across the Spanish Americas often perceived the presence of free Black people dwelling in towns and cities as a threat to peace and colonial governance, and attempted to introduce municipal legislation that curtailed their rights, for example, by dictating where they could reside and what they could wear (sumptuary legislation).[7] Local rulers in the port of Nombre de Dios made such an attempt in 1551 by requesting that the crown prohibit free Black men and women from living in the town owing to "inconveniences with the black slaves."[8] This request emerged in the aftermath of fugitive Black people establishing powerful *palenques* (self-governing communities) in the region and engaging in one of the most lengthy slave wars in the Spanish Americas (sometimes referred to as the first and second Bayano Wars of 1549–1556 and 1579–1582). Despite this context, the crown did not respond favorably to the request, and by all accounts the town had a significant population of free Black residents throughout the late sixteenth century.[9] Similarly, in 1562, rulers in Panamá attempted to banish free Black men and women from residing in the city, and in the following decade, *regidores* of the city of Panamá drafted city ordinances for the *cabildo* that sought to banish free Black property owners, noting

---

[5] *Las Siete partidas del Sabio Rey don Alfonso*, "Quarta Partida, Titulo XXI, De los Siervos," 38–39, and "Quarta Partida, Titulo XXII, De la Libertad," 39–40.

[6] Scott, "Freedom"; *Las Siete partidas del Sabio Rey don Alfonso*, "Quarta Partida, Titulo XXII, De la Libertad," 39–40.

[7] For selected scholarship on anti-Black racial thinking in Iberia, see Introduction, note 5. On sumptuary legislation, see Walker, *Exquisite Slaves*.

[8] "Real Cédula," AGI, Panamá, 236, libro 9, fol. 44^v.

[9] Gallup-Díaz, "A Legacy"; Obando Andrade, *De objeto a sujeto*; Schwaller, *African Maroons*, and "Contested"; Tardieu, *Cimarrones*.

that "in this city there is a great quantity of free Black men and women and every day more are being freed and they live in this city and they have their own houses and because there is such a great quantity of free Black men and women in this city and *republica* they cause much harm."[10] The proposed ordinances cited Black *vecinos*' supposed links with Black fugitives, describing how the free Black men and women of Panamá "hide and have in their houses hidden the captive Black men and women who escape from their owners." They ordered free Black dwellers to leave the city within thirty days to "populate an island," where they could work the land and later sell their agricultural wares in Panamá.[11] These ordinances never came into effect, probably owing to collective legal action of free Black *vecinos*, who may have crafted petitions to royal courts in order to protect their rights and privileges as free people.

Freeborn and liberated Black people in the Spanish Americas invested significant resources to defend and expand the meanings of political freedom in the Spanish empire by crafting petitions to the crown. In particular, they often deftly expended social and political capital when facing repressive policies introduced by local or municipal authorities or disturbances of their freedom enacted by private individuals. Free Black people's petitions for justice to the crown broadly sought to protect their rights as free people, while petitions for grace tended to request additional privileges that would expand the meanings of freedom, most notably the right to carry arms.

Free Black individuals and communities across the Spanish Americas petitioned the crown before royally appointed local authorities such as *alcaldes*, *asistentes*, *corregidores*, or *governadores* of towns and cities, as well as in the appellate royal courts of the American viceroyalties, namely the Real Audiencias. Others pooled resources to appoint procurators to submit petitions to the Council of the Indies in Castilla. For example, two free Black *vecinos* of Panamá named Luis Hernández and Pedro Hortiz de Espinosa submitted a petition between 1560 and 1562 through a procurator named Sebastián Rodríguez to request that the monarch intervene because the governors of the province had tried to expel them from the region, even though they were free property-owning *vecinos* who had defended the crown in the Bayano Wars. In response, Phillip II issued a royal decree in 1562 ordering the governor and local authorities in Tierra

---

[10] "Ordenanzas de la ciudad de Panamá," AGI, Panamá, 236, libro 10, fols. 210ᵛ–214ʳ. For discussion of these proposals and further context, see Tardieu, *Cimarrones*.
[11] Ibid.

Firme to protect and safeguard the privileges of all free Black *vecinos* and to ensure their right to live in the region, explaining that these "Black people are free people who have always been loyal vassals of mine."[12] Free Black people who could not access a procurator or who did not trust the services of these specialized legal go-betweens sometimes embarked on lengthy, expensive, and risky journeys, crossing the Atlantic to submit their petitions to the Council of the Indies in person. In doing so, these petitioners joined a rich political tradition of representatives from a broad spectrum of colonial society who traveled to Castilla from the Spanish Americas for this reason.[13] Such petitioners included representatives of elite lettered Indigenous communities, rural Indigenous groups, free Black communities, women, landowners, and many other interest groups. Free Black people who petitioned for justice across local, viceregal, and metropolitan royal courts often deployed discourses of political belonging that sought to position the Spanish crown and Catholicism as inclusive of Black people, and in so doing they sought to protect and expand the meanings and privileges of the legal status of freedom in the Spanish empire.

THE CROWN'S INTRODUCTION OF A TRIBUTE TAX FOR FREE BLACK MEN AND WOMEN, AND PETITIONS FOR EXEMPTIONS

A petition to the Council of the Indies penned in Mexico City in 1583 by a free *mulato* named Juan Bautista de Cárdenas reveals a history of collective knowledge, memory, and word-of-mouth about Black political discourses across the early Spanish Atlantic and the importance of the cities of Sevilla and Mexico City and other port towns as key nodes in relays of news about distant people and events.[14] Juan Bautista de Cárdenas was born as a free *mulato* to a white father and a Black mother in Valencia (in present-day Spain). He crossed the Atlantic to New Spain in 1576 and settled in Mexico City, where he developed a trade as a tailor (*sastre*).

---

[12] "Real Cédula, Justicia a los negros libres de Panamá," AGI, Panamá, 236, libro 9, fols. 369ʳ–369ᵛ.

[13] de la Puente Luna, *Andean Cosmopolitans*; Masters, *We, The King*; Restall, *The Black Middle*.

[14] "Juan Baptista de Cárdenas, vecino de México. Información sobre Tributo, 1583," AGI, Indiferente, 1233. My interpretation of Juan Baptista de Cárdenas' biography and date of arrival in Mexico City differs from that of Miguel Valerio, who concludes that Baptista de Cárdenas was already in Mexico City by 1568. See Valerio, "The Spanish Petition."

Defining Freedom

Within seven years of arriving there, Bautista de Cárdenas sent a petition to the Council of the Indies in Madrid to request that he be exempt from paying the punishing tribute tax that the Castilian crown had recently required of all free Black and *mulato* men and women who resided in the Spanish Americas. Bautista de Cárdenas requested this based on his previous loyal service to the crown as a soldier in Castilla.

The tax to which Bautista de Cárdenas was referring had been introduced two years before his arrival in the Spanish Americas. A royal decree issued in 1574 required that all Black and *mulato* men and women in the Spanish Americas pay a tax, known as tribute.[15] The decree explained that the vast riches accumulated by liberated Black and *mulato* men and women justified this. Such a tax would allow free Black and *mulato* men and women to live in peace and enjoy access to justice in the Spanish crown's realms. In other words, the crown positioned the tribute as an important element of Black subjecthood. To this extent, the logic mirrored the crown's reasoning for imposing similar taxes on Indigenous subjects in the Americas. Further, the royal decree reasoned that the tax was justified because West African kingdoms had a custom of charging tribute to their subjects:

> we have been informed that many of the Black and *mulato* female and male slaves who have passed to the Indies … who in those parts have come and have been liberated and now are free, and that these [people] have a lot of work and riches and therefore for many just causes and particularly for living in my realms and to be maintained in peace and justice, and having been slaves and at present are free, and in the same way because they had the custom of paying tribute to their kings and leaders and in great quantities, it is just and legal to ask them to pay.[16]

Various Black communities across the Spanish Americas petitioned the crown to be excluded from this tax. These included a group of Black *horros* and *vecinos* in Panamá.[17] They sent a petition to the Council of the Indies in 1575, only a year after the royal decree had been issued.[18] Historian Karen Graubart traces how Black and *mulata* women of

---

[15] On the introduction of tribute tax for Black people and responses, see Gharala, "Black Tribute," *Taxing Blackness*, and "This Woman's Resistance."
[16] "Real Cédula," AGI, Indiferente, 427, libro 30, fols. 248ʳ–249ʳ.
[17] Karen Graubart's current research projects, tentatively titled "Depositional Dialogues" and "Making Malambo: The Free Black Population of Panama in the Sixteenth Century," explore these petitions from Panamá in greater detail. I thank Karen Graubart for sharing some of this work with me in private correspondence. See also Gharala, *Taxing Blackness*, "Black Tribute," and "'This Woman's Resistance.'"
[18] "Real Cédula," AGI, Panamá, 237, libro 11, fols. 38ᵛ–39ᵛ.

Panamá organized to ensure that their voices and requests for an exemption from the tax were also represented in this 1575 petition. The Black men and women of Panamá were successful in their request. A royal decree dated October 21, 1578, exempted Black men and women residing in Panamá from the obligation to pay tribute because of the poverty that they were experiencing.[19] In Mexico City, Bautista de Cárdenas kept abreast with key political developments relating to Black communities across the Spanish Americas. In particular, he heard about this successful petition, and also obtained a copy of the 1578 royal decree that exempted the Black residents of Panamá from paying tribute. Bautista de Cárdenas' possession of this physical document six years after the decree had been issued reveals how knowledge about – and paperwork pertaining to – petitions to the crown spread across the Spanish Americas, especially between key towns and cities, likely being propagated by procurators who specialized in petitions to the Council of the Indies.

This example indicates that Black individuals' and communities' petitions to the crown often became common knowledge among Black people residing in other regions, even among those living a great distance away. Bautista de Cárdenas also possessed the resources, social capital, and know-how to send a petition to the Council of the Indies from Mexico City. In particular, his previous experience of working for noble men at the royal court in Madrid likely imbued him with the know-how to gather the requisite resources to organize this. Bautista de Cárdenas sent his petition via a procurator to the Council of the Indies in Madrid in 1584.[20] In it, he included a copy of the royal decree issued in 1578 that exempted the Black residents of Panamá from paying tribute. However, Bautista de Cárdenas' knowledge of the Panamá case was perhaps limited and fragmentary, as he used the existence of the 1578 decree to argue that the crown had never meant to include *mulato* people in tribute obligations. Perhaps he had not yet heard that a group of *mulatos* from Panamá had followed in the footsteps of the Black *horros*, and had petitioned the crown in 1579 to request that they should also be excluded from the obligation to pay tribute.[21] Nonetheless Bautista de Cárdenas' petition – and his inclusion of the 1578 decree – reveals how Black and *mulato* individuals and communities often formed broad webs of knowledge, information, and communication that sometimes stretched across

---

[19] Ibid.
[20] On the introduction of tribute tax for Black people, see Gharala, "Black Tribute."
[21] "Informe," AGI, Panamá, 237, libro 11, fols. 47^r–47^v.

the Atlantic world. Although it is unclear whether Bautista de Cárdenas' petition to the Council of the Indies was successful, he was still active as a tailor in Mexico City a decade later when he lent 549 *pesos de oro común* to the *alcalde* of the city in 1597.[22]

Other Black and *mulato* people sought to solve the question of their tribute obligations locally. For example, Francisco Carreño, a freeborn *mulato* from the Canary Islands who settled in New Spain (see Chapter 3), engaged in disputes locally about his tribute obligations.[23] He described the details of an ongoing legal battle with the *alcalde mayor* of the village of Metepec (west of Mexico City, near Toluca) about payment of royal tribute in his 1603 testament. As a result of Carreño's refusal to pay tribute, the *alcalde* of Metepec had reportedly embargoed fine Castile-made clothes that Carreño had sold on credit to the *alcalde*'s wife. The case was ongoing at the time of Carreño's death in Mexico City in 1603; he asked that an executor continue to represent his interests in the ongoing case.

Other people liable for the tribute tax sometimes requested exemptions in Real Audiencias in the American viceroyalties.[24] For example, an eighty-year-old Black *horro* named Melchor Alaves, who resided in the town of León in New Spain, submitted a petition to the Real Audiencia of Mexico City on March 7, 1616.[25] In his petition, he described how he had served the king loyally and bravely for sixty years as a soldier, including in the Chichimeca War (1550–1590). Further, once the war ended, Alaves claimed to have captured and arrested many "Black waylayers" (*salteadores*, fugitives and criminals) and delivered them to the *alcalde mayor* of León. In León, local authorities reportedly recognized Alaves's status and loyalty, and had exempted him from paying tribute and permitted him to bear arms. Alaves detailed how, since the end of the war, he had administered plantations in León and that he regularly journeyed to the viceregal capital to provide accounts of them. However, in Mexico City, officers at the Real Audiencia interrogated him about his tribute payments and questioned his right to bear arms. Alaves likely

---

[22] "Obligación de pago" in Mijares *CPAGNXVI*, Protocolos Notariales, Cristóbal de Tejadillo, May 16, 1597, Notaría 1, vol. 168, legajo 2, fol. 810, ficha 469.
[23] "Francisco Carreño," AGI, Contratación, 515, no. 1, ramo 5. See also Ireton, "The Life and Legacy."
[24] This follows common practices among Indigenous communities: Cunill, "El uso indígena" and "Pobres, esclavos, indígenas"; Pollack, "Hacia una historia social."
[25] "Petición de Melchor Alaves, negro libre," AGN Mexico, Indiferente Virreinal, Real Audiencia. caja-exp.: 6455-053.

tapped into networks of procurators with knowledge of tribute, akin to those used by prospective Indigenous petitioners who traveled to Mexico City to submit petitions for royal justice to the Real Audiencia.[26] In preparation for his petition, Alaves compiled a cache of evidence signed by a "justice of the city of León," and presented this physical evidence to the Real Audiencia. Within four months, there was a ruling in favor of Alaves' request for a royal license to bear arms and an exemption from paying tribute, with the reason that this "genre of people, of which there is such a great quantity in the kingdom, should always be prized when they serve the king."[27]

Other prospective petitioners embarked on lengthy and expensive journeys to Castilla to present their cases for exemption from tribute taxes in person to the Council of the Indies. They would inevitably have conversed with a diverse array of people in one or more of the Spanish Atlantic's main ports of embarkation, such as Veracruz, Nombre de Dios, Cartagena, and Havana. Petitioners' testimonies about relationships forged on ships and in ports reveal how conversations in such spaces armed petitioners with knowledge about how to present their cases.

Sevilla's position as port of disembarkation from the Americas in the late sixteenth century meant the city became a site where prospective petitioners exchanged ideas and legal know-how in anticipation of their journeys to the Council of the Indies in Madrid. Prospective petitioners would invariably sojourn in Sevilla while organizing their onward journey. For example, Sebastián de Toral (see Chapter 1) undertook a lengthy journey from New Spain to Madrid in 1575 to request an exemption from tribute tax at the Council of the Indies.[28] In New Spain, Toral had been a soldier in royal armies and had played a key role in the wars of Spanish conquest in Yucatán. Prior to his life as a soldier, he had been born enslaved in Mora (Portugal), and had later gained his freedom owing to his bravery in the wars of conquest of New Spain.[29] As a liberated man, Toral resided in Mérida, where he was married and owned property. Within one year of learning about the introduction of the tribute for all Black men and women in 1574, he obtained a license from the *alcalde* of Mérida to travel to Madrid to submit a petition to the

---

[26] Cunill, "Pobres, esclavos, indígenas"; Owensby, *Empire of Law*.
[27] "Petición de Melchor Alaves, negro libre," AGN Mexico, Indiferente Virreinal, Real Audiencia. caja-exp.: 6455-053.
[28] "Sebastián de Toral," AGI, Indiferente, 2059, no. 108; "Jerónimo González," 1592, AGI, Contratación, 5238, no. 1, ramo 38.
[29] Restall, *The Black Middle*; "Sebastián de Toral," AGI, Indiferente, 2059, no. 108.

Council of the Indies. Toral spent less than one year in Castilla, attending to this business. In Madrid, he beseeched the crown to recognize his loyal service and to exempt him and his descendants from tribute. He also requested that the crown issue him a license to carry arms so he could continue defending himself and the crown.[30]

Black petitioners such as Sebastián de Toral often spent time in Sevilla, where they met others and discussed their intention to petition the Council of the Indies. For his petition for an embarkation license, Toral presented three witnesses in Sevilla who claimed to have either seen him arriving there on the fleet that arrived from New Spain in 1575 or who had crossed the Atlantic on the same ship as him.[31] In Sevilla, he spoke with other people about his onward journey to Madrid, and one witness described seeing how "Sebastián de Toral went to the royal court where he was given a license to return to the province of Yucatán."[32] After obtaining a favorable royal decree in 1578 that permitted him to carry four swords and four daggers across the Atlantic, as well as exempting him and his descendants from paying tribute, Toral appeared at the House of Trade in Sevilla in 1579 to request an embarkation license to return to the Indies.[33] Presumably, Toral would have discussed the content of his petition with those he encountered on his journey, but if he did not, people in Sevilla would have witnessed this elderly Black *horro* soldier carrying swords and daggers on the streets of Sevilla with a royal license.

Another indication of the importance of the city of Sevilla for the emergence of Black knowledge networks in connection with royal petitioning to the Council of the Indies emerges in the testimonies about Jerónimo González's journey from Quito to Madrid in the early 1590s.[34] We do not know what business spurred González to embark on a lengthy, dangerous, and costly journey from Quito to Madrid to attend the royal court and then return within a few months, but the fact that he was literate and signed his name on his petition may mean that a particular

---

[30] Ibid.
[31] "Sebastián de Toral," AGI, Contratación, 5227, no. 2, ramo 25, fols. 2^r–2^v.
[32] Ibid.
[33] Toral's 1578 petition for passenger license in Madrid: "Sebastián de Toral," AGI, Indiferente, 2059, no. 108. Toral's 1579 petition for embarkation license in Seville: "Sebastián de Toral," AGI, Contratación, 5227, no. 2, ramo 25. Toral's passenger record: "Sebastián de Toral," AGI, Contratación, 5538, libro 1, fol. 196 (Galbis Díez, *Catálogo de Pasajeros*, vol. VI, catalogo 2053).
[34] "Jerónimo González," 1592, AGI, Contratación, 5238, no. 1, ramo 38.

community appointed him to represent their political interests.[35] The witness statements that González secured in Sevilla for his petition for an embarkation license attest to discussions between residents and passersby in Sevilla and free Black people. These testimonies provide tantalizing details about the probable role that people in Sevilla played in helping Black petitioners gather requisite information and advice about how to present their petitions at court.

Word of mouth preceded González's arrival in Cartagena and Sevilla, as people journeying along the same route exchanged the news that a free Black man was traveling to the court in Madrid. A *vecino* of Sevilla recounted how he had been in Cartagena some years earlier and had heard from other travelers that Jerónimo González was journeying from Quito towards Madrid, hearing the news of González's imminent arrival from people who had already arrived in Cartagena from Quito. The two later met on a *fragata* (small vessel) that sailed from Cartagena to Havana. Thereafter, the witness saw González embark on the fleet of ships that sailed from Havana to Sevilla, and the pair reportedly met some time later in Sevilla, when González gave the witness "an account of his journey" from Havana to Sevilla.[36] Another witness in Sevilla who had known González for about seven months explained that he had been expecting González's arrival in Sevilla as he had heard from many other people who had previously arrived from Quito that González was journeying there with a royal license. He also subsequently witnessed that González "went to the town of Madrid to obtain the royal decree that he has presented."[37] These testimonies indicate that acquaintances and passersby became aware of Black petitioners traveling from the Indies to the royal court in Madrid and also any royal decrees in their favor.

Black women were also adept at moving between Sevilla and Madrid to deliver royal petitions, especially those who regularly crossed the Atlantic to Castilla as wage-earning servants. Their maneuverings between the House of Trade and Council of the Indies reveal their knowledge about how to obtain coveted passenger licenses after their Atlantic crossings. For example, after arriving in Sevilla in 1595, and aware that she must obtain a passenger license to return to Panamá, Angelina Díaz (see Chapter 1) departed from Sevilla for Madrid to present a petition to

---

[35] This might reflect some of the practices traced by de la Puente Luna in *Andean Cosmopolitans* for Indigenous communities in the Andes.
[36] "Jerónimo González," 1592, AGI, Contratación, 5238, no. 1, ramo 38.
[37] Ibid.

Defining Freedom

the Council of the Indies.[38] In Madrid, Díaz explained to judges that she owned a house and other property in Panamá and that her many children and grandchildren resided there too. Over the next two months, between November 9, 1595, and January 11, 1596, Díaz presented three witnesses to support her petition. This two-month delay to gather sufficient witnesses implies that she remained in Madrid for at least two months, waiting for people whom she might know to pass through the royal courts, while conversing with others about her petition.[39] After she had secured three witnesses in Madrid, the court granted Díaz a passenger license that permitted her to return to Panamá. Within a few weeks, she traveled from Madrid to Sevilla, where she also secured employment for her return journey to Panamá with Licenciado Clemente Peres de Tudela, who had a passenger license that allowed him to take a *criada*, the position that Díaz would occupy. On January 31, 1596, Díaz appeared at the House of Trade with her new employer to request an embarkation license.[40] Even though she had spent the last few months in Madrid, she was able to secure a further two witnesses in Sevilla who claimed to know her, one of whom described how he had met Díaz in previous years in the cities of Panamá, Havana, and Sevilla. Judges at the House of Trade granted Díaz an embarkation license, and she returned to Panamá laboring as a wage-earning servant on the crossing.[41] Free Black women who specialized as wage-earning servants for different passengers on Atlantic crossings often knew how to maneuver through royal courts and institutions in the Spanish empire, and how to present a petition for a passenger license to the Council of the Indies.[42]

---

[38] "Angelina Díaz," AGI, Indiferente, 2102, no. 166; "Angelina Díaz," AGI, Contratación, 5251B, no. 2, ramo 42, fols. 2^r–2^v. See also Garofalo, "The Shape of a Diaspora"; Ireton, "They Are."

[39] "Angelina Díaz," AGI, Indiferente, 2102, no. 166, fols. 2^v–3^v.

[40] "Angelina Díaz," AGI, Contratación, 5251B, no. 2, ramo 42.

[41] Ibid.

[42] Selected examples of Black and *mulata* women who were *naturales* of the Spanish Americas and who labored on Atlantic crossings as wage-earning servants: "Agustina de Lumbreras, mulata," AGI, Contratación, 5258, no. 1, ramo 45; "Angelina Corza, mulata," AGI, Contratación, 5266, no. 2, ramo 72; "Antonia, negra, con sus hijos mulatos," AGI, Contratación, 5326, no. 49; "Beatriz Velázquez," AGI, Contratación 5538, libro 3, fol. 212^v; Galbis Díez, *Catálogo de Pasajeros*, Vol. VII, 3361; "Dominga Díaz," AGI, Indiferente, 2100, no. 3; "Dominga Díaz de Cea," AGI, Contratación, 5245, no. 1, ramo 41; "Dominga Díaz de Sea," AGI, Contratación, 5538, libro 3, fols. 207^v; Galbis Díez, *Catálogo de Pasajeros*, Vol. VII, 3254; "Felipa Pérez," AGI, Indiferente, 2105, no. 32; "Felipa Pérez," AGI, Contratación, 5266, no. 1, ramo 59; "Isabel de Bustos," AGI, Contratación, 5327, no. 83; "Isabel Ortiz, negra, y su hijo Diego, mulato," AGI, Contratación, 5324, no. 30; "Hipólita de los Angeles," AGI, Indiferente, 2074, no. 67;

They were also well known among itinerant communities of merchants, religious men, mariners, and colonial officials, and knew how to locate potential witnesses who would agree to testify as to having known them in the cities where they resided.

Late sixteenth-century Sevilla was therefore a city with infrastructure and networks of legal knowledge that supported Black petitioners from the Americas who had embarked on lengthy journeys to seek the ear of the monarch. Jerónimo González's journey spells a history of word of mouth that anticipated his arrival in every port of departure, and especially in Sevilla. Enslaved Black people who never left Sevilla, such as Felipa de la Cruz (see Chapter 2), also knew how to employ a procurator and send a petition to the Council of the Indies: She sent a petition in 1612 urging the crown to investigate the whereabouts of her deceased husband's estate.[43]

Finally, much as Mexico City was a key site for the circulation of news about royal decrees and petitions in distant lands, evidenced by Bautista de Cárdenas' possession of the royal decree exempting Black people in Panamá from paying tribute tax, Sevilla was also an important site for gossip and Black political knowledge. The witness testimonies that Bautista de Cárdenas gathered before a notary in Mexico City in 1582 reveal a history of word of mouth in Sevilla. The city served as a site for gathering information and knowledge about distant people and places, as passersby gossiped and exchanged news about distinguished and noteworthy people across Castilla, including free Black and *mulato* people who resided in other regions. Three witnesses claimed to have never interacted with Bautista de Cárdenas prior to meeting him in Mexico City in the late 1570s, while describing how they had heard about him through hearsay in Sevilla. Their testimonies reveal that Bautista de Cárdenas became a soldier in royal armies in Castilla in the 1560s and 1570s and was well known in Sevilla as a distinguished soldier and later as a servant to knights and other honorable people in the royal court in Madrid. The witnesses explained that they had heard merchants from Valencia talking in Sevilla and Málaga about a distinguished *mulato* soldier named Juan

---

"Hipólita de los Angeles," AGI, Contratación, 5340, no. 4; "Magdalena de Coronado," AGI, Indiferente, 2061, no. 134, fols. 3^r–5^v; "María, negra, natural de Guinea," AGI, Contratación 5538, libro 1, fol. 207; Galbis Díez, *Catálogo de Pasajeros*, Vol. VI, 2205; "Melchora de los Reyes," AGI, Indiferente, 2065, no. 60; "Melchora de los Reyes," AGI, Contratación, 5232, no. 25.

[43] "Real Cédula," AGI, México 1094, legajo 18, fols. 102^r–103^r. See Chapter 2, notes 157–160.

Bautista de Cárdenas and had seen him embarking on ships in military expeditions; they had later heard news that Bautista de Cárdenas had moved to Madrid to serve honorable people in the royal court. When Bautista de Cárdenas arrived in Mexico City, he encountered these three Castilian tailors who already knew about him through hearsay and word of mouth in Sevilla.[44]

INFRASTRUCTURES OF BLACK POLITICAL KNOWLEDGE IN SEVILLA

Black political knowledge in Sevilla likely stemmed in part from the experiences of Black religious associations in the city. There were at least three Catholic confraternities that identified as Black or *mulato* in late sixteenth-century Sevilla (Figure 4.1).[45] The most prominent of these brotherhoods was Our Lady of the Angels, whose church was located on Calle Conde Negro in the parish of San Roque outside the city wall. The confraternity had reportedly been founded in the late fifteenth century as a hospital for Black people.[46] Within the city walls, the Brotherhood of Mulatos of Ildelfonso was established in the San Ildefonso parish in the mid sixteenth century on a street known as Calle de los Mulatos (present-day Calle Rodríguez Marín) and near the Plaza de los Mulatos (present-day Calle Lirio).[47] The nearby parish of Santa María la Blanca had a significant population of free and enslaved Black people.[48] A character in *Los Mirones*, an early seventeenth-century play attributed to Alonso Jerónimo de Salas Barbadillo (1581–1635), explained how in the "neighborhood of Santa María la Blanca, there is a small square where an infinite number of Black men and women tend to meet each other," and reported how he surreptitiously eavesdropped on a conversation between a group of Black men discussing whether their owners had sold them and

---

[44] Although it is unclear whether his petition to the Council of the Indies was successful, Juan Bautista was still active as a *sastre* in México in 1597 when he acted as a lender to the alcalde de México for 549 pesos de oro común: "Obligación de pago" in Mijares CPAGNXVI, Protocoles Notariales, Cristóbal de Tejadillo, May 16, 1597, Notaría 1, vol. 168, legajo 2, fol. 810, ficha 469.
[45] Camacho Martínez, *La Hermandad de los Mulatos*; Moreno, *La antigua*.
[46] Moreno, *La antigua*.
[47] Camacho Martínez, *La Hermandad de los Mulatos*. Collantes de Terán Sánchez et al., *Diccionario Histórico*, see entry for "Rodríguez Marin."
[48] Franco Silva, *La Esclavitud*, "La Esclavitud en Sevilla entre 1526 y 1550"; Corona Perez, *Trata Atlántica*, 106, 427–435.

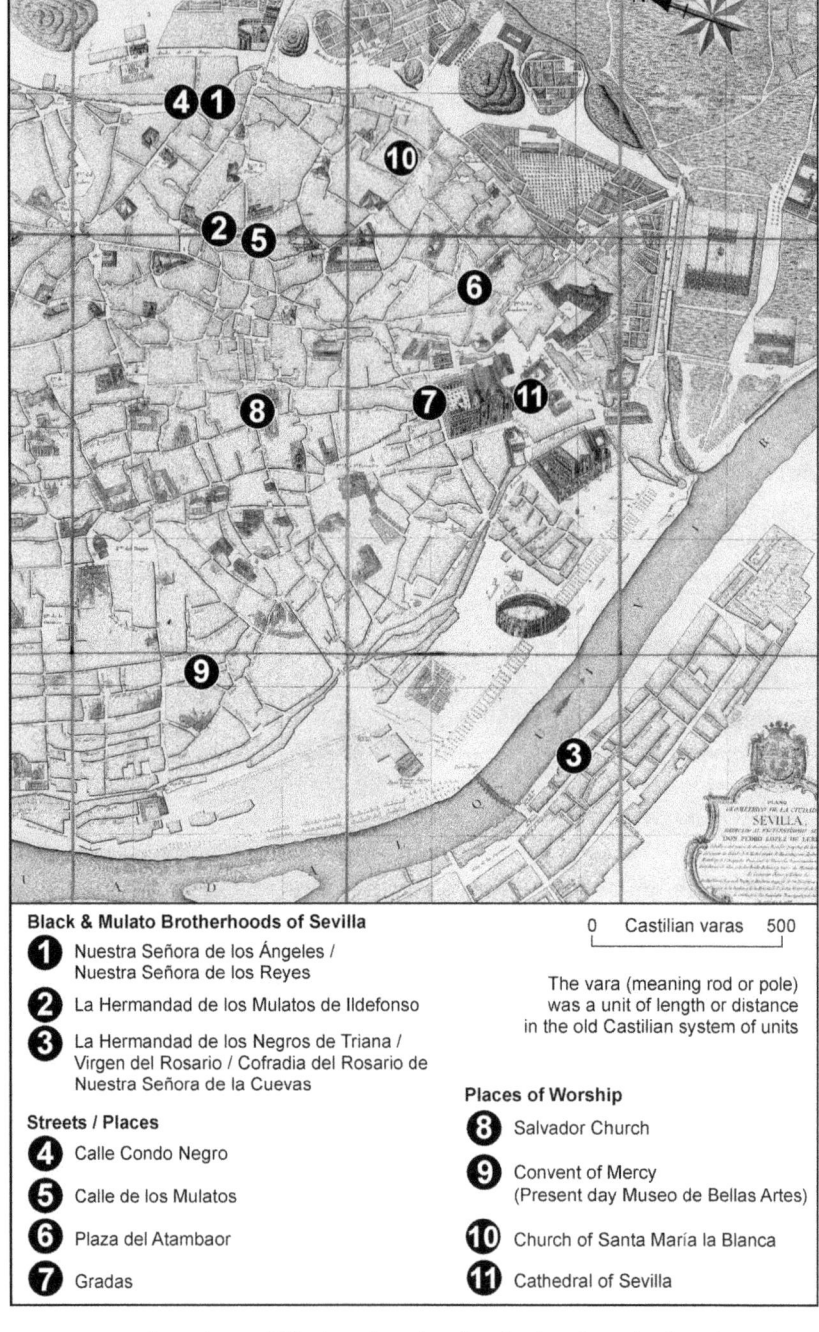

FIGURE 4.1 Locations of Black and *mulato* brotherhoods and other sites where Black people gathered and worshiped in late sixteenth-century Sevilla, overlaid onto Tomás López de Vargas Machuca, "Plano geométrico de la ciudad de Sevilla…" (detail). Tomás López: Madrid, 1788. David Rumsey Map Collection, List no. 10717.000, David Rumsey Map Center, Stanford Libraries. Adaptation of the map by Cath D'Alton, Drawing Office, University College London.

at what price.[49] Sixteenth-century chroniclers of Sevilla also described how free and enslaved Black people gathered on Sundays in the nearby Plazuela del Atambaor (present-day Calle Rodrigo Caro) to play drums and dance.[50] West of the Guadalquivir river, Black residents established a confraternity in Triana that was devoted to Our Lady of the Rosary.[51]

These three Black and *mulato* religious associations were highly visible in the late sixteenth-century urban landscape. In particular, the Black brotherhood in San Roque featured prominently in the highly competitive public displays of piety between religious associations after changing its name from Our Lady of the Kings to Our Lady of the Angels when it introduced formal ordinances in 1554. The brotherhood adopted twenty-seven chapters that established the association as a penitent confraternity, and stipulated the devout Catholic behavior expected of its brothers and strict practices for discipline and penitence rituals.[52] Claims to antiquity were important among Sevilla's confraternities because the age of an association, rather than the social status of its members, determined its place and order during Holy Week processions.[53] The Black brothers likely used their 1554 ordinances to justify their organization's antiquity, as these claimed the founding of Our Lady of the Angels as a hospital in the fifteenth century.

These Black religious organizations had spent years developing influential patronage ties in Sevilla and the juridical knowledge to defend their interests across various legal jurisdictions. For example, Our Lady of the Angels faced an existential crisis in the early seventeenth century after the Archbishop of Sevilla, Fernando Niño de Guevara (b. 1541–1609), attempted to prohibit it from participating in religious processions within the city walls. This ruling stemmed from a night of violence during Holy Week festivities in 1604 (as discussed in Chapter 2), when a white confraternity named Our Lady of Antiquity – whose members tended to belong to professions related to carpentry – claimed that the Black brothers had attacked them in Salvador Square on Maundy Thursday and tried to harm

---

[49] De Salas Barbadillo, *The Gawkers/Los Mirones*. Previously, this play was attributed to Miguel de Cervantes Saavedra (1547–1616): Cervantes Saavedra, *Cuatro Entremeses*, "Entremes de los Mirones," 25–26. I thank John Beusterein for introducing me to this text.
[50] Padrón, "La Historia," 140: "*El Varrio del Alambor a Santa Cruz, se llama por quee allí ivan a tañer los negros con su atambor los domingos*"; 134: "*Hay infinita multitud de negros y negras de todas las partes de Etiopía y Guinea, de los quales nos servimos en Sevilla, y son traídos por la vía de Portugal.*"
[51] Moreno, *La Antigua*, 73–77.
[52] "Pleito, Nuestra Señora de los Angeles," AGAS, 1.III.1.6, L.9885, no. 1, Reglas de Nuestra Señora de los Ángeles, unnumbered folios.
[53] This point is also made by Moreno, *La Antigua*.

and kill them. They petitioned that the archbishop suspend Our Lady of the Angels' license and order that the Black brothers conduct their processions in the Cruz del Campo outside the city walls. Such a ruling would have resulted in the exclusion of the Black brotherhood from public religious life in Sevilla.[54] After being hauled into a trial in the archbishopric court in 1604 that sought to terminate Our Lady of the Angels' right to participate in religious processions, the Black brothers defended themselves by employing a skilled procurator who maneuvered their case away from ecclesiastical jurisdiction and into the royal courts. The Black brothers also activated their social capital and patronage ties with influential churches in the city to seek the intervention of the papal court in the Vatican. This reveals how the Black brotherhood was well versed in legal arguments concerning their right to exist, the meanings of Black freedom, the protections that they expected as subjects of the crown and as Catholics.

The Black brothers' response to this crisis reveals their extensive legal knowledge and patronage ties within Sevilla. On June 9, 1604, thirteen Black brothers and governing members of Our Lady of the Angels gathered in the church that housed the brotherhood in the San Roque parish to sign a power of attorney (*poder*) for a procurator named Bartolomé de Celada before a public notary of the city.[55] By appointing Celada, the Black brothers had chosen a procurator experienced in defending legal disputes between confraternities and the archbishop, and in negotiating delicate cases between different legal jurisdictions, namely between the archbishopric and the royal court in Sevilla, to obtain favorable results.[56] A Black brother named Antonio de Villalobos, who was listed as the appointed *escribano* (notary/writer) for the brotherhood, signed this legal power of attorney on behalf of the other twelve Black brothers who were present that evening.

The Black brothers had already deliberated on the strategy for their defense before appointing Bartolomé de Celada. This becomes evident when Celada returned to the Black confraternity's church in San Roque to prepare their defense two weeks after his initial appointment. The document that he composed, dated June 22, 1604 and signed by those listed in Table 4.1, is an example of collective Black authorship and legal know-how. Although Celada signed the document as though he was the author of the legal strategy, the text contains various instances where

---

[54] Other scholars have also explored this incident and the subsequent ecclesiastical trial, see Chapter 2, note 30.
[55] "Pleito entre la Hdad de Ntra Sra de la Antigua y la de los Ángeles que llaman la de los morenos," AGAS, III.1.6, L.9885, no. 1, fol. 15ʳ.
[56] Cerquera Hurtado, "El Pleito"; Ostos-Salcedo, "Un pleito"; Pineda Alfonso, "El delito."

TABLE 4.1 *Membership and leadership roles within the Black Brotherhood, Our Lady of the Angels, 1604–1606*

List of Black brothers who gathered in the Church in San Roque to appoint Bartolomé Celada as their *procurador* on June 9, 1604	List of Black brothers and their roles in the confraternity in 1606
Antonio Luis (*alcalde*)	Luis de Mendoza (*alcalde*)
Francisco de Gongora (*mayordomo*)	Amar O Gasco
Sebastián de Mendoza (*prioste*)	(*mayordomo*)
Antonio de Villalobos (*escribano*)	Antonio Luis (*prioste*)
Amar O Gasco	Pedro Ramírez (*moreno*)
Francisco Lorenzo (*diputado*)	
Mateo Romero (procurator of assets)	
Juan Bautista (*fiscal*)	
Gabriel Hernández (*cofrade*)	
Antón de la Torre (*cofrade*)	
Josefe Hernández (*cofrade*)	
Beltrán Pisana (*cofrade*)	
Lacayo de Arriaga (*cofrade*)	

Source: "Pleito entre la Hdad de Ntra Sra de la Antigua y la de los Ángeles que llaman la de los morenos," AGAS, III.1.6, L.9883, Expte 2. "Pleito, Nuestra Señora de los Angeles," AGAS, 1.III.1.6, L.9885, no. 1.

he used first-person pronouns, revealing how the Black brothers were likely collectively orally dictating their defense strategy during this meeting. A scribe later struck through some of the "we" pronouns to replace them with "they," an example being "y fueron tan demassiados que fue forcoso ussar de nuestra (su) defenssa (and they were so many that it was necessary to use our (their) defense)." Later in the same document, the scribe made the following amendment: "Y menos obstara [bastara] decir que somos (son) negros" (and it is enough to say that we are (they are) Black). In this second instance the scribe did not strike through the text and insert a new word; instead he scribbled out the final two letters "os" and converted the letter "m" into an "n." The scribe made the same amendments to the following lines, converting a letter "m" into an "n" in order to change the pronoun from "us" to "them": "pues procedemos (proceden) de gentiles y xpianos viejos" (as we descend (they descend) from gentiles and old Christians)."[57] A representative sample of these additions to the declaration are printed in Figures 4.2–4.4. It is also possible that the editing of the text was not the work of Celada, but rather

[57] "Pleito, Nuestra Señora de los Angeles," AGAS, 1.III.1.6, L.9885, no. 1, fols. 14^r–14^v.

FIGURE 4.2 "Pleito entre la Hdad de Ntra Sra de la Antigua y la de los Ángeles que llaman la de los morenos con sede en San Roque extramuros" (detail of in-text edits to the declaration that the Black confraternity members made before their procurator, Bartolomé de Celada, on June 22, 1604), in Archivo General del Arzobispado de Sevilla (AGAS), Fondo Arzobispal, Sección III, Hermandades, sign. 09885, expte 1, fols. 14^{r-v}. © Cabildo Catedral de Sevilla.

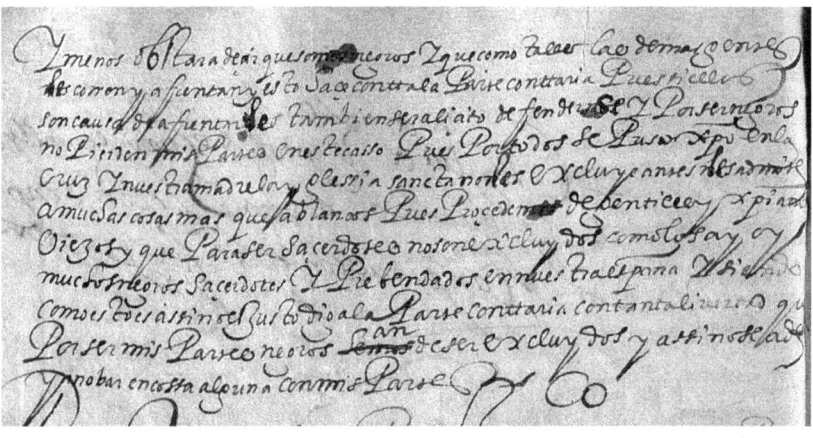

FIGURE 4.3 "Pleito entre la Hdad de Ntra Sra de la Antigua y la de los Ángeles que llaman la de los morenos con sede en San Roque extramuros" (detail of in-text edits to the declaration that the Black confraternity members made before their procurator, Bartolomé de Celada, on June 22, 1604), in AGAS, Fondo Arzobispal, Sección III, Hermandades, sign. 09885, expte 1, fols. 14^{r-v}. © Cabildo Catedral de Sevilla.

the interventions of the appointed *escribano* of Our Lady of the Angels, which in that era was the Black brother named Antonio de Villalobos.[58]

The legal argument that the Black brothers dictated to Celada was twofold. In the first instance, they argued that the conflict was a matter of "good governance which is the crown's jurisdiction," and that therefore

---

[58] Ibid., fol. 15^r.

Defining Freedom

Transcription of Figure 4.2 (lines 2-4):

² dice en su petición que por ser negros podían hacer semejante attrevimiento
³ y fueron tan demassiados que ~~nos~~ ˡᵉs fue forzosso ussar de ~~nuestra~~ ˢᵘ defenssa
⁴ que es lo que el derecho natural permite de una parte y otra hubo....

Transcription of Figure 4.3:

¹ Y menos obstara decir que so ⁿ ~~mos~~ negros y que como tales las demás gentes
² ~~nos~~ ˡᵉˢ corren y afrontan y esto hace contra la parte conttraria. Pues si ellos
³ son causa de afrentar ~~nos~~ ˡᵉˢ también será licito de defender ~~nos~~ ˢᵉ y por ser negros
⁴ no pierden mis partes en este caso. Pues por todos se puso Cristo en la
⁵ Cruz, y Nuestra Madre la Yglesia Santa no ~~nos~~ ˡᵉˢ excluye y ansi ~~nos~~ ˡᵉˢ adoró
⁶ a muchas cosas más que a blancos. Pues procede ⁿ ~~mos~~ de gentiles y cristianos
⁷ viejos y que para ser sacerdotes no son excluidos como los [h]ay hoy
⁸ muchos negros sacerdotes y prebendados en nuestra España y siendo como esto es
⁹ assi, no es justo [que] diga a la parte contraria con tanta libertad que
¹⁰ por ser mis partes negros h ~~emos~~ ᵃⁿ de ser excluidos y asi no se [h]a dicho
¹¹ y no van en cossa alguna con mis partes

Notes: Author has added strikethroughs to the transcription to convey where a scribe has struck through words and added letters to change the meaning of the word, most commonly to change verbs from first-person plural (us/we/our) to third person plural (them/they/their). In the instances where a scribe inserted new letters to change the meaning of the word, these have been added in superscript font. Author has added bold emphasis and a backgournd highlight shade on the letters that form the new word to visually convey the transformed meaning of the word.

FIGURE 4.4 Spanish transcription of Figures 4.2 and 4.3. Author's illustration.

neither archbishop nor any ecclesiastical court should intervene.[59] In the second instance, they questioned whether the archbishop had the authority to prohibit them from partaking in religious life. They argued that he had no standing in the case because the Church was inclusive of Black people. As discussed in the introduction to this chapter, they explained that "Christ put himself on the Cross for everyone, and our Mother of the Church does not exclude us, and adored us, and many other things more than white people for we proceed from gentiles and Old Christians, and Black people are not excluded from priesthood as there are today many Black priests and prebendaries in our Spain."[60] The Church, the Black brothers argued, did not ostracize Black people any more than it did white people – a point that echoed Black poet Juan Latino's cautionary words to King Phillip II three decades earlier, in which Latino stated "If Christ, giver of life, did not disdain Black people / as a Catholic, justly turn your eyes to your bard (45–46)."[61] The Black brothers argued that because Black people were descended from gentiles and Christians, the Church did not prohibit them from priesthood.[62] They underscored that there were many Black priests and prebendaries across "our Spain."[63] They therefore envisioned themselves as descendants of Black Christians who played an integral role within the Castilian community of Christians, noting that they were "old Christians," while also presenting a view of Catholicism that wholly included Black people. The Black brothers reasoned that since the Church did not exclude Black people and nor did Christ, it was unjust for a white confraternity to prevent them from participating in Sevilla's public celebrations of piety: Their exclusion from religious life would be a gross contravention of ecclesiastical policies. They added that their confraternity was one of the oldest

---

[59] "Pleito entre la Hdad de Ntra Sra de la Antigua y la de los Ángeles que llaman la de los morenos," AGAS, III.1.6, L.9883, Expte 2.

[60] "Pleito, Nuestra Señora de los Angeles," AGAS, 1.III.1.6, L.9885, no. 1, fols. 14–17 (Bartolomé de Celada, in the name of the confraternity Nuestra Señora de los Ángeles, June 22, 1604). For select studies on how Black people shaped Catholicism in Spanish empire, see Brewer-García, *Beyond Babel*, Fisk, "Transimperial mobilities," Rowe, *Black Saints*, and Valerio, *Sovereign Joy*.

[61] Juan Latino, "Elegy for Phillip II" and "On the Birth of Untroubled Times," in Wright, *The Epic*, Appendix 1, 188. For knowledge about Juan Latino among Black brotherhoods in Cádiz, see Sancho de Sopranis, *Las cofradías de morenos*.

[62] "Pleito entre la Hdad de Ntra Sra de la Antigua y la de los Ángeles que llaman la de los morenos," AGAS, III.1.6, L.9883, Expte 2., Testimony, unnumbered folios.

[63] "Pleito, Nuestra Señora de los Angeles," AGAS, 1.III.1.6, L.9885, no. 1, fols. 14–17. For presence of Black priests in early modern Europe, see Peraza, *La historia de Sevilla*, 134; Salvadore, "African Cosmopolitanism" and *The African Prester*.

in the city, and that is was unfair "that the modern ones want to exclude those that are so old and which has always done so [the confraternity's processions (*pasos*)] with such devotion."[64] They therefore defined their old Christian lineage by their skin color (the Church did not exclude or prohibit Black people) and the antiquity of their brotherhood (its foundations as a hospital in the late fifteenth century meant that it was one of the oldest in the city).

In addition to appointing Celada, who would shepherd the Black brotherhood's defense in the archbishop's court, the Black brothers instigated a second line of defense. They tapped their powerful patronage ties with an influential convent in Sevilla to submit a petition for a hearing in the papal courts in the Vatican. They presented their case to the Vatican through a network of powerful churches in Sevilla who allied themselves with the Black brotherhood against the archbishop. Principally, Friar Francisco del Prado of the "monastery Nuestra Señora de las Mercedes" (this is likely to be the Convento Nuestra Señora de la Merced, or Convent of Mercy, Figure 4.1 no. 9) in Sevilla intervened in the case.[65] Friar Prado explained in a letter to the archbishop's court on April 28, 1605 that the monastery had intervened in the case by appealing on behalf of the Black brothers to the pope's ambassador (*nuncio*) in Sevilla.[66] The friar wrote that the monastery had delivered a copy of the Black brotherhood's 1554 ordinances with its twenty seven rules of association to the ambassador, and had also presented him with transcripts of the archbishopric trial so that the case could be presented to the pope.[67] This communication between a Black Brotherhood and the Vatican via a *nuncio* took place eighty years earlier than the first such recorded case, when Lourenço da Silva de Mendonça, likely from the Kingdom of Kongo, obtained the ear of the papal *nuncio* in Lisbon in 1681 with whose support he later arrived in Rome in 1684 to present a petition against slavery.[68] Prado explained that the papal ambassador had asked for the archbishop's ruling to be suspended while the Vatican considered the matter. A generation after the archbishopric trial, the Black brothers of Our Lady of the Angels obtained a highly unusual papal bull that confirmed the confraternity's

---

[64] "Pleito, Nuestra Señora de los Angeles," AGAS, 1.III.1.6, L.9885, no. 1, fols. 14–17.
[65] Ibid., unnumbered folios (Letter dated April 28, 1605, written by Friar Francisco del Prado of the monastery Nuestra Señora de las Mercedes).
[66] Ibid.
[67] Ibid.
[68] Lingna Nafafé, *Lourenço da Silva*, 384–430.

1554 founding Ordinances, presumably in response to this petition.[69] For many generations, Our Lady of the Angels remained unique among Sevilla's highly jealous and competitive confraternities for possessing a papal bull that confirmed its right to exist.[70]

Between 1604 and 1607, the Black brothers continued to press their case for justice across three jurisdictions (archbishop's court, royal court, and the Vatican court). For example, in 1606, after learning that the archbishop had suspended the Black confraternity's license and had prohibited them once again from participating in the processions of Holy Week under penalty of excommunication and one hundred lashes, three of the governing members of the confraternity, Luis de Mendoza (the *alcalde*), Amar O Gasco (*mayordomo*), and Antonio Luis (*prioste*) protested in the court that the archbishop had no standing in such matters.[71] Mendoza appealed that the ruling was null and unjust, and requested that the archbishop's court provide him with copies of the rulings so that he could contest the court's decisions. The archbishop finally responded to this in March 1606.[72] The Black brotherhood's procurator, Celada, had already taken their plight to a different legal jurisdiction by presenting an appeal in the Real Audiencia of Sevilla, which ruled on April 17, 1606, in favor of the brotherhood.[73] The royal court stated that the Black brothers should be free to participate in the processions of Holy Week and ordered absolution from the archbishop's court's rulings. A month later, after complaints from the Black brothers that the archbishop had not yet done this, the Real Audiencia of Sevilla ordered the archbishop to absolve the brotherhood from his ruling within two months or suffer greater penalties.[74]

The Black brotherhood therefore navigated various overlapping structures of justice to defend their right to participate in Holy Week

---

[69] Papal Bull quoted in Moreno, *La Antigua*, 89–90. At the time *Nuestra Señora de los Ángeles* was the only confraternity in Sevilla to possess papal confirmation and remains so to this day. "*Real Provision firmada por el Rey Felipe III* (March 1614)," quoted in ibid., 76–78. Actions of members: See ibid., 73–90.

[70] Moreno, *La Antigua*.

[71] "Pleito, Nuestra Señora de los Angeles," AGAS, 1.III.1.6, L.9885, no. 1, fols. 14–17; "Pleito entre la Hdad de Ntra Sra de la Antigua y la de los Ángeles que llaman la de los morenos," AGAS, III.1.6, L.9883, Expte 2., unnumbered folios (Testimony of Pedro Ramírez, moreno, en el nombre del priost y cofrades de nuestra señora de los Ángeles (April 3, 1606).

[72] "Pleito, Nuestra Señora de los Angeles," AGAS, 1.III.1.6, L.9885, no. 1, fol. 24ʳ (approx.: unnumbered folios).

[73] Ibid., unnumbered folios (Ruling by the Real Audiencia de Sevilla in favor of the Black brothers).

[74] Ibid.

processions in Sevilla, namely as defendants in the archbishop's court, as petitioners for justice at the Real Audiencia in Sevilla, and as appellants in the Vatican courts. In the first instance, they employed a well-known procurator to help them maneuver the case through the archbishop's court between 1604 and 1606 and the Real Audiencia of Sevilla in 1606, the latter eventually ruling in their favor. Celada's choice to move the case between religious and royal jurisdictions reflected his experience as an expert procurator for Sevilla's litigious confraternities, but also the Black brothers' reasoning that neither the archbishop nor any other confraternity had any right to prohibit the confraternity from participating in public religious life because the issue concerned "good governance" which pertained to the monarch (rather than the Church), and their rejection of the ecclesiastical court's authority over them was based on their reasoning that the Church and Christ were historically inclusive of Black people. The Black brothers also sought the help of a powerful and influential convent that had the ear of – or the knowledge to seek the council of – the papal ambassador in Sevilla. The Covent of Our Lady of Mercy delivered the Black brothers' petition to the ambassador to circumvent the archbishop's authority and agreed to provide evidence in support of the Black brotherhood in their defense in the archbishop's court. The Black brothers continued to defend their case across all legal jurisdictions available to them; as late as April 1606, knowing that their case was winding through the Vatican courts, they were continuing to petition the Real Audiencia in Sevilla to rule against the archbishop's latest prohibitions. The Black brothers of Our Lady of the Angels perceived Black freedom and political belonging in expansive terms and made very specific decisions about how to settle conflicts through different legal jurisdictions. They also built political ties with other religious associations and places of worship in Sevilla that they activated in order to drive their case through various branches of justice, in particular to the papal courts at the Vatican.

BLACK CONFRATERNITY LEADERS FROM MEXICO CITY IN SEVILLA

Given this backdrop, it is not surprising that Sevilla was an important site for gathering knowledge and information about how to petition the Council of the Indies, especially among Black petitioners from the Spanish Americas. Sometimes, prospective petitioners might spend a few years in Sevilla gathering information, strategizing, and building their cases. This was the case of eight Black *vecinos* of Mexico City who arrived in Sevilla after receiving sentences of permanent exile by the Real Audiencia of Mexico City in 1612. They each spent at least three to four years in the city, and their sojourn there provides tentative evidence of ties between Black leaders of Black confraternities in Sevilla and Mexico City in the early seventeenth century.

The episode that led to eight Black exiles arriving in Sevilla commenced on the other side of the Atlantic in the viceregal capital of New Spain in 1612, when authorities in Mexico City believed that they had foiled a large-scale plan by enslaved and free Black dwellers of the capital to rebel against slave-owners and royal authorities.[75] These fears were sparked by a mass protest led by free and enslaved Black people on the streets of Mexico City in 1612, following the death of an enslaved Black woman there. Suspecting that her owner had killed her, over 1,500 free and enslaved Black residents marched with her body across the city demanding justice. This commotion followed various years of tensions between colonial authorities and Black communities in Mexico City, especially Black brotherhoods.[76] In particular, on Christmas Eve of 1608, Black confraternity members had gathered in the house of a Black woman to partake in festivities for the election and coronation of a Black king and queen. As scholar Miguel Valerio has explored, such festivities caused panic among officials at the Real Audiencia, who feared a Black conspiracy and ordered the arrest of almost fifty free and enslaved Black people in February 1609.[77] This followed increased concern and consternation among the viceroy and Real Audiencia of Black conspiracies, following the establishment of a powerful Black *palenque* community in Córdoba (New Spain), led by a Black fugitive named Yanga, that consistently attacked caravans and wagons along the *caminos reales* between San Juan de Ulúa and Mexico City and had gained significant power and influence by 1609.[78] Finally, the state-sponsored violence of 1612 that led to the exile sentences occurred in a period when the viceroyalty of New Spain was experiencing a power vacuum: Luis de Velasco y Castilla (viceroy, 1590–1595, 1607–1611) had departed New Spain in 1611 when

---

[75] Various scholars have analyzed accounts of the 1612 conspiracy: Apodaca Valdez, *Cofradías Afrohispánicas*; Martínez, *Genealogical Fictions* and "The Black Blood"; Nemser, *Infrastructures of Race* and "Triangulating Blackness"; Valerio, *Sovereign Joy*; Velázquez Gutiérrez, *Mujeres de orígen africano*.

[76] Ibid.

[77] Valerio, *Sovereign Joy*.

[78] Landers, "Cimarrón and Citizen"; Naveda Chávez-Hita, "De San Lorenzo"; Proctor III. "Slave Rebellion."

he was appointed President of the Council of the Indies in Madrid. This departure left the power of the Real Audiencia in Mexico City unchecked from June 19, 1611 to October 18, 1612, when Diego Fernández de Córdoba y López de las Roelas (viceroy, 1612–1621) was appointed the next viceroy of New Spain.[79]

The Real Audiencia responded to the protests by free and enslaved Black people on the streets of Mexico City in 1612 with violent reprisals against Black confraternities in the city. Claiming that the events represented a Black conspiracy in which free and enslaved Black residents of the city were plotting an uprising, the Real Audiencia arrested the supposed perpetrators and sentenced thirty-five Black men and women to brutal public hangings in the Plaza Mayor, causing widespread terror among the Black population.[80] An anonymous account of the event detailed the gruesome capital punishments.[81] In addition to these executions, the Real Audiencia ordered that the mutilated bodies be left in public for an entire day, and that six of the corpses be quartered and their heads displayed on spikes. The anonymous author noted that they would have quartered more bodies, but doctors had advised that doing so might cause infections and diseases.

The Real Audiencia sentenced the remaining people in custody to perpetual exile from New Spain, exiling those whom they perceived as less of a threat because their "culpability was not of such great consideration."[82] Among those sentenced to exile were some of those who "had been arrested in earlier processes," such as two free *mulato* men named Francisco de Loya and Domingo Pérez.[83] Both had previously been arrested in 1609 for their prominent roles in the coronations of Black monarchs held over Christmas 1608 in the house of a Black woman named Melchiora de Monterrey.[84] Pérez had been a key figure in the events of 1608, being described as the brother of Melchiora de Monterrey, while Loya was described as the person who had crowned

---

[79] Valerio, *Sovereign Joy*.
[80] "Relacion del alçamiento que negros y mulatos libres," Biblioteca Nacional de España (henceforth BNE), MSS 2010, fols. 158–164 (*"grande concurso de gente"*). Also discussed in Valerio, *Sovereign Joy*.
[81] Ibid.
[82] Ibid.
[83] Ibid., and "Antonio de Loya," AGI, Contratación, 5338, no. 24.
[84] Apodaca Valdez, *Cofradías Afrohispánicas*, Appendix, Doc. 2, "Memoria de los culpados en la junta y coronación de reyes y nombramientos de duques, condes y marqueses con los ditados que a cada uno les dieron y los presos que ay por esta causa. Ciudad de México, 1609"; Valerio, *Sovereign Joy*, Appendix, "Persons Charged in 1609."

the king and queen during the same event.[85] In other words, the 1612 exiles who arrived in Sevilla were key members of Black confraternal life and leadership in Mexico City. Perhaps Loya's employment as the pastry chef to the then Viceroy Luis de Velasco y Castilla had saved him from further punishment in 1609.[86] Or perhaps the close relationship that Francisco de Loya's father, a Black man named Antón de Loya, had forged with Viceroy Luis de Velasco y Castilla had protected his son from further prosecution in 1609.[87] In any case, the Real Audiencia rearrested both Domingo Pérez and Francisco de Loya in 1612 and sentenced them to perpetual exile, along with Loya's father and at least five other free Black and *mulato vecinos* of Mexico City.

The 1612 events in the viceregal capital affected Black communities in other regions of New Spain too, as Black people residing outside the city became aware of the supposed conspiracy and its political aftermath over the next few months. Some Black communities across New Spain learned of the events in Mexico City in 1612 when the Real Audiencia ordered the prohibition of free Black people from living in certain cities and towns, and town criers proclaimed these new policies in particular sites across New Spain in the winter of 1612.[88] The rules were also described in the anonymous account of 1612 that detailed the prohibition of "gatherings, dances, burials of Black people, contests between them [coronations]."[89] In addition the author stated that "the free [free Black people] will not live on their own, and they should enter as servants, or occupy themselves in trades," while Black and *mulata* women were prohibited from wearing cloaks, jewels, silk dresses, and other expensive items.[90]

A petition by the Black and *mulato vecinos* of San Miguel de Allende, a town north of Mexico City, shows how information about the 1612 events spread across New Spain. In January 1613, one Black and three *mulato vecinos* of the town sent a petition to the Real Audiencia requesting to be excluded from a ruling that prohibited free Black and *mulato* people from owning their own homes or renting land or any other types of property in the town.[91] The petitioners explained that they had heard

---

[85] Ibid.
[86] Ibid.
[87] "Antonio de Loya," AGI, Contratación, 5338, no. 24.
[88] "Diego Ramírez y Juan María y Pedro Villegas," AGN, México, Indiferente Virreinal, caja-exp.: 4156-039, Real Audiencia, 1612–1613, fols. 1–12.
[89] "Relacion del alçamiento que negros y mulatos libres," BNE, MSS 2010, fols. 158–164.
[90] Ibid.
[91] "Diego Ramírez y Juan María y Pedro Villegas," AGN, México, Indiferente Virreinal, caja-exp.: 4156-039, Real Audiencia, 1612–1613, fols. 1–12.

about the prohibitions – and the 1612 Mexico City rebellion (if they had not already) – from a town crier who sang the new policy directive in San Miguel de Allende in the winter of 1612. They noted that the ruling in question that prohibited free Black people from dwelling in the town was "the same that was announced in this city [Mexico City] when the disturbances of the Black people [took place]," highlighting their awareness not only of the events of the supposed conspiracy of 1612 in the capital, but also of the political aftermath – new prohibitions for Black people in Mexico City and across New Spain.[92]

The petitioners were Black soldiers, some of whom were formerly enslaved, who had fought for the crown in the Chichimeca Wars.[93] They were also property owners and *vecinos* in San Miguel de Allende. They sought assurances of their rights to live as free Black *vecinos* in that town. They argued that the 1612 prohibitions should not apply to them for they were peaceful, quiet, and hard working. All four rented agricultural land or plantations, which they productively cultivated to support themselves.[94] For example, the free *mulato* Pedro de Silva had collected more than 1,500 *fanegas* of corn that year alone. A Black *horro* named Pedro de Villegas lived in houses that his former owner had gifted to him upon liberating himself and his four children from slavery. Villegas also rented separate land to sustain himself. Another free *mulato* named Diego Ramírez explained that he had been a *vecino* in San Miguel for thirty years and that he had served the king – with his weapons and horses – to defend that town during the Chichimeca War.[95]

To support their petition, these Black and *mulato vecinos* of San Miguel de Allende collected witness statements of well-respected *vecinos* and military officials and the town's *alcalde* who described their loyalty to the crown and freedom.[96] Captain Diego de Barbas, the *alcalde ordinario* of the town, credited Ramírez's efforts in ending the war, explaining that Ramírez "was part of why the said *indios* came to peace and was an important cause and of the service of his majesty."[97] The witnesses

---

[92] Ibid.
[93] For another liberated Black man who made similar claims about his bravery in the Chichimeco war, see "Petición de Melchor Alaves," AGN Mexico, Indiferente Virreinal, Real Audiencia. Caja-exp.: 6455-053; and see notes 24–27.
[94] "Diego Ramírez y Juan María y Pedro Villegas," AGN, México, Indiferente Virreinal, caja-exp.: 4156-039, Real Audiencia, 1612–1613, fols. 1–12.
[95] Ibid.
[96] Ibid.
[97] Ibid.

also noted that no one had ever questioned Ramírez's right to bear arms. Tomás de Espinosa had "seen Ramírez live as an armed man with much approval by the justices and principal people" of the town, and had also witnessed Ramírez risk his life many times for the monarch.[98] In addition to Ramírez's bravery and service to the monarch, witnesses noted that he had previously administered many *haciendas* in the town. After the war, he had been an economically productive *vecino* of the town, as he rented a *recua* where he kept mules, working to support himself and his children. Ramírez also recounted how he had invited many friars and clerics, justices, gentlemen, and other honorable people to lodge in his home, entertaining them with food and accommodation at his own cost.[99] A *vecino* named Francisco de Jaen posited that Ramírez "is in reputation of a good Christian and man of good, and obedient in the matters of service to his majesty."[100] He argued that Ramírez deserved the king's mercy even though he was "of *mulato* color," adding that "the rigors against others of his color should not apply." Another *vecino*, Tomás de Espinosa, stated that although Ramírez was "of *mulato* color, he is a man of much good and a good Christian."[101]

The Black petitioners of San Miguel who sought to be excluded from the 1612 prohibitions succeeded. On March 1, 1613, the Real Audiencia ruled that they were exempt from the order that prohibited free Black and *mulato* men and women from owning or inhabiting their own separate houses.[102] The ruling underlined that that there was no just cause to prohibit these petitioners from owning or renting their own *haciendas* because the 1612 order had been intended solely for the "idle people of this *caste*," those who lacked an *oficio* (profession), or were transient.[103] This 1613 judgment was issued by the same Real Audiencia that had so feared the threat of a conspiracy among Black dwellers of Mexico City one year earlier that its deputies preemptively investigated possible conspiracies and ordered brutal capital punishments and permanent exile sentences.[104] By March 1613, however, the new viceroy Diego Fernández de Córdoba y López de las Roelas (viceroy, 1612–1621) had arrived in the capital, which may explain the change in the Real Audiencia's attitude.

---

[98] Ibid.
[99] Ibid.
[100] Ibid.
[101] Ibid.
[102] Ibid.
[103] Ibid. The word used in the ruling is "*genero*," which I have translated here as "caste."
[104] Martínez, "The Black Blood."

News about the events of 1612 in Mexico City spread across New Spain when at least eight free Black and *mulato* men were sentenced to perpetual exile and journeyed overland along one of the royal trading routes from Mexico City to San Juan de Ulúa. These exiles were uprooted from their lives as free Black *vecinos* in Mexico City and from their wives, family, and property. At least three of these men knew each other already: Antón de Loya and Francisco de Loya were father and son, while Francisco de Loya and Domingo Pérez had both been arrested together in Mexico City in 1609 owing to their roles in the coronation of Black kings and queens that took place in December 1608. The others may or may not have known each other previously in the city. It is also unclear whether the Real Audiencia of Mexico City ordered their removal from New Spain to Castilla, or whether these individuals chose to embark on journeys to Castilla with the intention of petitioning the crown for a reprieve or a pardon.[105] Testimonies about these men's journeys do not indicate whether they traveled as convicts, except in one case, when a witness described how Bartolomé, a Black *criollo* from Mexico City, had been brought to Castilla, "imprisoned on the order of the crown," and spent some time in the jails of the House of Trade.[106] Regardless of whether these eight exiles traveled as convicts or freely, such an overland convoy of exiled Black and *mulato* confraternity leaders from Mexico City would have alerted Black people in urban and rural settings as well as those in *palenque* communities across those regions to the events in Mexico City, in the unlikely event that they had not already heard about them.

These eight free Black and *mulato* men, who were sentenced to perpetual exile, arrived in Sevilla in the summer of 1613. By the time they crossed the Atlantic, they may have heard about the successful petition against the prohibitions by the Black *vecinos* of San Miguel de Allende. Each of these exiles spent between three to five years dwelling in Sevilla; they communicated with each other and others about strategies to request a royal pardon for their exile sentences so that they could return to Mexico City. Each Black exile met at least two people in Sevilla whom they already knew from Mexico City. Sixty-six-year-old Antón de Loya knew two Sevilla *vecinos*, one of whom traveled to Castilla on the same ship from San Juan de Ulúa to Castilla in 1612 or 1613.[107] Sebastián

---

[105] "Relacion del alçamiento que negros y mulatos libres," BNE, MSS 2010, fols. 158–164.
[106] "Bartolome," AGI, Contratación, 5343. no. 8.
[107] "Antonio de Loya," AGI, Contratación, 5338, no. 24.

de Robles, a fifty-year-old Black man, who was married and had children and owned property in Mexico City, met an enslaved Black man named Juan Miguel in Sevilla whom he had known for fourteen years because Miguel had previously lived in Mexico City before being brought to Sevilla by his owner some years earlier.[108] Robles also made contact with Pedro de Herrera, a *vecino* of Sevilla who had spent ten years living in Mexico City and had known Robles as a free Black *vecino* there. During their three- to five-year residencies in Sevilla, these men would have developed day-to-day relationships with other residents in the city as they endeavored to survive in an unknown urban space, while experiencing inevitable precarity and poverty resulting from their forced displacement from their livelihoods, families, and property in Mexico City.

Seeking a pardon for a ruling of permanent exile ordered by a Real Audiencia in the Spanish viceroyalties was no easy feat. The years that elapsed between their forced exiles and their petitions for a royal pardon in the Council of the Indies in Madrid likely represent the time and effort they took, and the conversations they had among themselves and with other Black *vecinos* of Sevilla and sympathetic residents to develop a convincing legal strategy. In Castilla, they joined a community of *vecinos* who were accustomed to petitioning the crown via the *consulta de gracia* to pardon exile sentences that overzealous city authorities had ordered. In Madrid, those exiled from the city by local authorities would regularly petition the Camara de Castilla for a *consulta de gracia* to obtain royal pardon.[109] Other residents of the Americas who had been subjected to varying lengths of exile sentences sometimes also petitioned for pardons via the *consulta de gracia*, but most submitted petitions of this type to the Council of the Indies as this served as an appellate court to the Real Audiencias in the Indies.[110] It is likely that these eight Black exiles built their cases for a petition to overturn their convictions by gathering witnesses in Sevilla and compiling their testimonies before public notaries there. Each of these individuals later presented their own *relación* (paperwork with relevant information) to the court, relaying their innocence during the events of 1612 and noting their status as respected *vecinos* of Mexico City. It is unlikely that they had

---

[108] "Sebastián Robles," AGI, Contratación, 5352, no. 33.
[109] Mierau, "El discurso" and "Transient."
[110] "Inventario de consultas de Gracia, 1571–1621," AHN España, Consejos, libro 2754; "Inventario de decretos de Gracia, 1571–1621," AHN España, Consejos, libro 2752. Select examples of petitions for gracia by other American-residents who had been sentenced to exile from the Indies include AGI, Indiferente: 449, libro A2, fols. 101–101^v; 450, libro A5, fols. 1–1^v, 202^v–203, 253^v–254^v; 1969, libro 22, fol. 248^v.

sufficient time to gather relevant witnesses and generate such paperwork before they were exiled, so these men probably gathered and notarized such testimony in Sevilla, relying on travelers passing through who could attest to their innocence during the events in Mexico City.

The first three of the exiles to petition the royal court in Madrid (likely to be the Council of the Indies) were Antón de Loya, his son Francisco de Loya, and Domingo Pérez.[111] They left Sevilla sometime before March 1, 1614. It is not surprising that these three were the first to present a petition as their evidence of their loyalty to the Spanish crown was the most persuasive. Loya senior and junior had also enjoyed the protection of the former viceroy Luis de Velasco y Castilla, who was by then the president of the Council of the Indies. In his petition, Loya senior depicted himself as innocent of the charges and as being an outstanding Black *vecino* of Mexico City who had been a loyal vassal to the crown and was married to a Spanish woman there. Antón Loya explained that he had been granted many royal privileges for his service to the crown, notably being granted favor and privileges from three separate viceroys in New Spain over his sixty-six-year life. Loya reported that the viceroy Lorenzo Suárez de Mendoza Jiménez (viceroy, 1580–1583) had granted him permission to carry arms in 1582, while the subsequent viceroy, Luis de Velasco y Castilla, had commissioned him to collect tribute payments from free Black and *mulato* men, an appointment that was confirmed by the following viceroy Juan de Mendoza y Luna (viceroy, 1603–1607), who had also exempted Loya and his descendants from paying tribute owing to his work protecting the crown's coffers. In short, Loya appeared at the royal court in Madrid with paperwork that proved he had received grace and privileges from three viceroys of New Spain over his lifetime. While it is unclear whether Loya brought original certificates that had been signed in Mexico City by viceroys or their deputies, or whether he presented witness testimony collected in Sevilla to attest to these facts, we can be certain that he produced some form of paperwork to the court because the resulting royal decree explicitly mentioned the existence of this documentation.

There is also a possibility that Loya was able to seek the ear of the most recent viceroy, Luis de Velasco y Castilla, or his deputies or members of his household in Madrid. In particular, Antón de Loya's son, Francisco, had formerly worked as the viceroy's pastry chef. As a result, Loya senior and junior may have also been acquainted with other Black servants in

---

[111] "Antonio de Loya," AGI, Contratación, 5338, no. 24.

the former viceroy's retinue in Castilla.[112] For example, a freeborn *mulato* named Baltasar de los Reyes had come to Castilla from Mexico City in 1610 as the servant of don Lope de Velasco, who was the *criado* of don Luis de Velasco y Castilla (president of the Council of the Indies, and former viceroy of New Spain), and Baltasar de los Reyes remained in Castilla until 1618.[113] It is possible that Loya father and son knew Baltasar de los Reyes and may have communicated with him in Sevilla and/or Madrid about the events of 1608 and 1612 in Mexico City, and about their exile sentences.

Loya's petition to the royal court in Madrid for a pardon was successful. The resulting royal decree granted these three Black and *mulato* men – Antón de Loya, Francisco de Loya, and Domingo Pérez –permission to return to Mexico City.[114] They returned to Sevilla from Madrid with the royal decree in their name and requested an embarkation license at the House of Trade.[115] It is unclear where they stayed or who they conversed with during the four months they remained in Sevilla prior to their departure. They may have spoken about their successful petition in Madrid with a procurator or with the other five Black exiles with whom they had traveled to Castilla.

The remaining Black exiles followed Antonio de Loya's strategy to petition for a royal pardon. The next to travel from Sevilla to Madrid was thirty-year-old Bartolomé, a Black *criollo* from Mexico City, who delivered a petition to the royal court in Madrid in the spring of 1615 and received a royal decree with a pardon on May 21, 1615.[116] It is possible that Bartolomé traveled from Sevilla to Madrid with one or two other free Black men who had also been exiled from New Spain, as they presented their petitions in quick succession between May and June 1615. A witness at the House of Trade, who later attested to Bartolomé's royal decree, stated that he knew that "many others [Black people] were requesting such decrees in Madrid" at the same time.[117] Another exile who traveled to Madrid from Sevilla in 1615 to request a pardon was a *mulato* named Pedro de Luna.[118] The king granted Luna a pardon, explaining in the royal decree that other Black people who came to Castilla with Luna had already arrived at the court to plead for pardons for the sentences of exile decreed by the Real Audiencia in Mexico City.

[112] Valerio, *Sovereign Joy*, Appendix, "Persons Charged in 1609."
[113] "Baltasar de los Reyes," AGI, Indiferente, 2076, no. 87.
[114] "Real Cédula, Antón de Loya," AGI, Indiferente, 449, libro A3, fols. 103ᵛ–104ᵛ.
[115] "Antonio de Loya," AGI, Contratación, 5338, no. 24.
[116] "Bartolome," AGI, Contratación, 5343. no. 8.
[117] Ibid.
[118] "Real Cédula, Pedro de Luna," AGI, Indiferente, 450, libro A4, fols. 148–148ᵛ.

Defining Freedom 185

A free Black man named Sebastián Robles obtained a similar decree one month later, on June 19, 1615.[119] People in Sevilla were aware that Robles was traveling to Madrid to seek an audience with the royal court. The aforementioned Juan Miguel, who lived in Sevilla and would later serve as Robles' witness for an embarkation license at the House of Trade, explained that he had known Robles in Mexico City and that he had also been in the royal court in Madrid at the same time that Robles was petitioning for a royal decree. Another witness named Pedro de Herrera explained that he had witnessed Robles depart from Sevilla to journey to the royal court in Madrid in order "to resolve his issues with the Audiencia in México."[120] In Madrid, Robles presented his *relación* and pleaded that the judges should pardon his exile sentence as he was innocent of the events in Mexico City of 1612 and was a free and honorable Black *vecino* who was married and had children and property in Mexico City.[121] In response, the crown pardoned Robles, thus allowing him to travel freely to Mexico City or wherever else in the Indies that Robles wished to live.[122]

Like Antón de Loya before them, these three Black individuals sparked discussions in Sevilla and Madrid about their petitions and pleas for justice in the period between 1612 and 1617. Armed with their respective royal decrees, Bartolomé, Pedro de Luna, and Sebastián de Robles journeyed from Madrid to Sevilla. They each petitioned for embarkation licenses at the House of Trade in June 1616.[123] Upon returning to Sevilla between March and June 1616, these three likely communicated news of their successful petitions to the final two exiles, Francisco de Tamayo and Juan de Arellano, both of whom followed closely in their footsteps, traveling to Madrid to present their respective petitions for pardons the

---

[119] "Real Cédula, Sebastián de Robles," AGI, Indiferente, 450, libro A4, fols. 44–44ᵛ.
[120] "Sebastián Robles," AGI, Contratación, 5352, no. 33, fols. 1ᵛ–2ʳ.
[121] The royal decrees explicitly mention the *relaciones* presented by the Black petitioners to the court. However, I have not located the copies of their petitions. For reference, so far, I have searched in the following: AGI, Indiferente: 1258, 1259, 1260, 1438, 1439, 1440; "Inventario de consultas de Gracia, 1571–1621," AHN, España, Consejos, libro 2754; "Inventario de decretos de Gracia, 1571–1621," AHN, España, Consejos, libro 2752. I have also searched in the electronic database of El Archivo Histórico de Protocolos de Madrid, and in Matilla Tascón, *Americanos*.
[122] "Sebastián de Robles," AGI, Indiferente, 450, libro A4, fols. 44–44ᵛ.
[123] "Sebastián Robles," AGI, Contratación, 5352, no. 33; "Bartolome, negro," AGI, Contratación, 5343, no. 8. I have not been able to locate Pedro de Luna's embarkation license application, but I have no reason to believe that he did not return to Mexico: "Real Cédula, Pedro de Luna," AGI, Indiferente, 450, libro A4, fols. 148–148ᵛ.

following year, 1617.[124] They presented identical legal strategies to those who had already sought the ear of the crown. They positioned themselves as honorable Black or *mulato vecinos* of Mexico City who were married with children and who owned property. They also obtained royal decrees that pardoned their sentences of exile on June 22, 1617, and within a week they each journeyed to the House of Trade in Sevilla to request embarkation licenses to return to Mexico City.[125]

These eight men therefore lived in the viceregal capital of New Spain during the supposed conspiracy – which they may or may not have played a key role in sparking, but they most likely witnessed the fatal punishments of other Black men and women in the streets of Mexico City – and once exiled, they organized and strategized with each other in Sevilla to petition the monarch to pardon their punishment, and succeeded. These Black and *mulato vecinos* of Mexico City thus sought to appeal the judgments of the Real Audiencia in New Spain by seeking a direct audience with the royal court in Madrid, where the crown recognized them as loyal and free Black and *mulato* vassals and *vecinos* of Mexico City. In Sevilla, they mobilized transatlantic networks when gathering information for their respective petitions. They spoke to others about their convictions and gathered knowledge about how to petition the royal court in Madrid. In at least one case, an exile also spoke to an enslaved Black person in Sevilla who had previously lived in Mexico City.[126] It is also possible that they communicated with their kin and associates in Mexico City via word of mouth, letter writing, and the use of *poderes*, modes of communication discussed in Chapter 2. In addition to discussions between themselves and possibly also with procurators in Sevilla, these eight Black individuals discussed their fate and political strategies with others they met and interacted with during their overland and transatlantic displacement from Mexico City to Sevilla, and possibly also on their return journeys to Mexico City between 1614 and 1617.

CONCLUSION

Free Black individuals and communities in the late sixteenth and early seventeenth centuries deftly negotiated various, and often overlapping,

---

[124] "Real Cédula, Juan de Arellano," AGI, Indiferente, 450, libro A5, fols. 28ᵛ–29; "Real Cédula, Francisco Tamayo," AGI, Indiferente, 450, libro A5, fols. 28–28ᵛ.
[125] "Juan de Arellano," AGI, Contratación, 5357, no. 18; "Francisco Tamayo," AGI, Contratación, 5355, no. 42.
[126] "Sebastián Robles," AGI, Contratación, 5352, no. 33.

legal jurisdictions, and deployed political discourses of belonging in the Spanish empire to broaden the meanings of Black freedom. Black petitioners engaged in conversations with the crown about how to define freedom, in particular the privileges, responsibilities, and rights for those who enjoyed the natural state of liberty, whether their petitions concerned exemptions from tribute taxes, the right to live in a particular locale as a *vecino*, the right to bear arms, a pardon for an exile sentence, or a request for a passenger license. Throughout, Black petitioners sought to define liberty in expansive terms and positioned the Spanish crown and Catholicism as inclusive of Black people. These discourses of belonging and the meanings of freedom flowed across the Spanish Atlantic world and seeped into petitions to the crown from distant corners of the Spanish empire. While procurators who specialized in maneuvering petitions through certain courts inevitably played a significant role in providing legal advice on legal codes and legal custom, Black people also invested significant resources and social and political capital to accrue this knowledge and present their cases for justice and grace to the crown. In doing so, Black petitioners sought to combat increasingly intolerant views of Blackness in Iberian society that tended to regard Black people as possessing irredeemably stained blood, as outsiders in society, and as slaves and "enslavable." Free Black petitioners fought against such narratives and presented alternative visions of Blackness and freedom in their petitions for justice and grace to the crown in local, viceregal, and metropolitan courts.

The chapter has tentatively traced how Black people acquired legal knowledge, shared political discourses of inclusion, and defined expansive meanings of freedom by exploring a history of knowledge about royal petitioning among Black people in and between the cities of Sevilla and Mexico City. Disparate cases of free Black people arriving in Sevilla – either through forced exile or as passengers – and their subsequent petitions to the Council of the Indies in Madrid point to the existence of patronage ties and knowledge among Black people who resided in – and passed through – Sevilla. Evidence of such ties remains difficult to trace, often being fragmented across diverse witness testimonies. Nonetheless, witnesses' assertions about seeing or hearing about Black petitioners departing Sevilla for Madrid, and their discussions with petitioners about the nature of their cases at the Council of the Indies, reveal the existence of a loose infrastructure of knowledge in the city of Sevilla that facilitated Black people's petitions to the crown, even if it remains difficult to trace the exact contours of this infrastructure. Part of the knowledge among

Black petitioners in Sevilla must have stemmed from the politically astute Black brotherhood, Our Lady of the Angels, whose political know-how and patronage ties within Sevilla allowed them to enact a three-pronged defense against the attacks of a powerful archbishop who was intent on extinguishing their brotherhood. In addition, the years between 1612 and 1617 in Sevilla represent a unique era when leaders of Black religious confraternities both there and in Mexico City may have met and communicated when at least eight Black leaders from Mexico City were exiled from New Spain and arrived in Sevilla. These eight Black exiles spent three to five years in Sevilla organizing to overturn their sentences by petitioning the crown in Madrid for a royal pardon. The succession of their petitions over four years highlights the ways in which the first and second group of petitioners reported back to the exiles in Sevilla to share their strategies, while fragmentary accounts within the royal decrees and the witness statements at the House of Trade also reveal how various pairs traveled to the Council of the Indies to present their petitions for pardons together and note those people whom they communicated with in preparation for their journeys. Tracing the history of petitioning and political knowledge among Black confraternity leaders in Sevilla in the early seventeenth century and reading this history alongside the arrival in Sevilla of exiled Black confraternity leaders from Mexico City reveals for the first time the possibility that representatives of these two groups met and exchanged news and strategies in Sevilla. This view of Black royal petitioning through records of Black petitioners' arrivals and departures in Sevilla, the infrastructures of powerful Black patronage ties that Black brotherhoods built in Sevilla, and the possible ties between Black confraternity leaders in Sevilla and México City in the early seventeenth century suggests that Black political and legal know-how was created and exchanged between disparate communities often separated by vast distances across the Spanish empire.

5

Reclaiming Freedom

The Illegitimacy of Slavery in Black Thought

West Africans and West-Central Africans and their descendants in the Spanish empire were forced to grapple with laws and theological discourses in European empires that sought to legitimize the enslavement of Black people. Enslaved people who disembarked in chains in the port towns of the Atlantic world after surviving the horrors of the Middle Passage often learned about the laws that governed slavery and freedom in European imperial realms and their American colonies through their discussions with other enslaved people in West Africa and West-Central Africa, on slave ships crossing the Middle Passage, and during punishing labor regimes in nascent American slave societies. These ephemeral conversations between enslaved people about the laws of slavery and freedom constituted an exchange of precious knowledge and legal know-how that shaped Black life and thought in the early Atlantic world. In the Spanish empire in particular, enslaved people soon learned that their status was governed by Castilian legal codes of slavery and freedom that outlined limited rights for enslaved people, namely to participate in Christian sacraments of baptism and marriage, and the obligations of a slave-owner to provide sustenance and to refrain from exerting excessive violence and cruelty or abandoning their slaves.[1] Despite enslaved people's acute awareness that plotting for their liberty or for elements of freedom through litigation could have violent and fatal consequences

---

[1] *Las Siete partidas del Sabio Rey don Alfonso*, "Quarta Partida, Titulo XXI, De los Siervos," 38–39, "Quarta Partida, Titulo XXII, De la Libertad," 39–40. For an overview of slavery and freedom in Christian theology, see Pérez García, "Christian." For theological debates about the legitimacy of the enslavement of Black Africans in Catholic thought, see Ireton, "L'imaginare Ethiopienne" and "Black African's," and Pérez García, "Christian."

for them at the hands of irate enslavers, such conversations sometimes spurred calculated decisions to take the risk and press for their liberty in courts. Historians have documented how enslaved litigants across the Spanish Americas deployed diverse legal strategies to argue for their liberty in royal and ecclesiastical courts.[2] Some sought to reclaim the liberty that enslavers had illegitimately stolen from them. They drew on Castilian laws of slavery to argue that their enslavement was illegitimate because legal customs prohibited Christians from enslaving other Christians, or that they had been born as free people and therefore could not be enslaved without a just cause that was dictated by the rule of law in their regions of origin, or that they had already been liberated from slavery under Castilian laws and could not be reenslaved.[3]

Ephemeral conversations among enslaved people about the laws of freedom and slavery shaped Black legal consciousness, and also propelled some people to petition royal courts for their liberty on the basis of their illegitimate enslavement. This chapter charts a history of conversations among enslaved Black people about Castilian laws of slavery and freedom, analyzing the discourses of illegitimate enslavement that were deployed by enslaved litigants and their witnesses across three freedom suits in Castilian royal courts in 1536, 1547, and 1614 (Figure 5.1).[4] These litigants argued for their freedom on the basis that they had been illegitimately enslaved and that their freedom had been stolen from them. Pedro de Carmona, for example, protested in his petition in 1547 about the "great injury and disturbances (*agravios y turbación*) that have been done to my liberty."[5] These rare instances when enslaved people managed to plead their cases in royal courts for freedom from illegitimate enslavement reveal hushed whispers among enslaved and free people about the laws of slavery and freedom and the illegitimacy of certain types of enslavement. Each of the litigators participated in conversations with others about their illegitimate enslavement and shared strategies and experiences with other enslaved, liberated, and freeborn Black people whom they encountered in different sites across the Atlantic world. Discussions about the illegitimacy of certain types of enslavements moved from place to place through diverse exchanges of information, fractured

---

[2] See Introduction, note 8.
[3] For a history of the theological debate about the legitimacy of enslaving between Christians, see Pérez García, "Christian."
[4] For an analysis of the significance of discussions about slavery among captives in this period in the Mediterranean context, see Hershenzon, *The Captive Sea*.
[5] "Pedro de Carmona," AGI, Justicia, 978, no. 2, ramo 1.

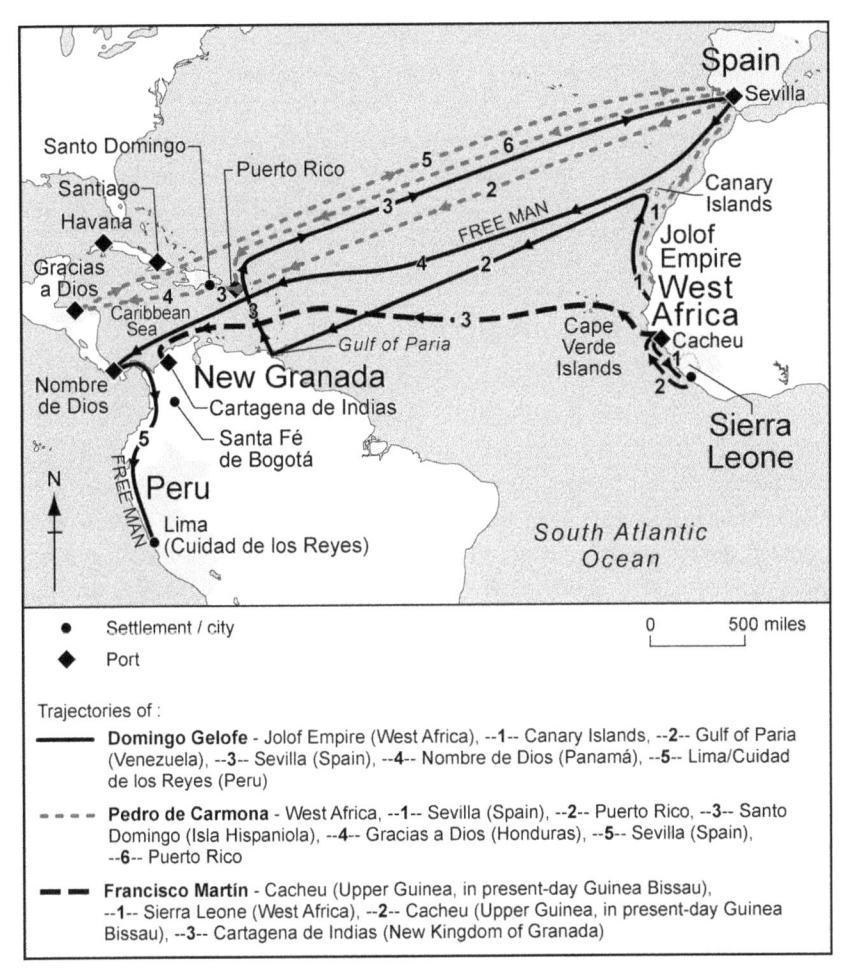

FIGURE 5.1 Map of the Southern Atlantic, with lines showing the enslavement and forcible displacements across the Atlantic of Domingo de *Gelofe*, Pedro de Carmona, and Francisco Martín. Map drawn by Cath D'Alton, Drawing Office, University College London.

memories, and knowledge, often being spearheaded by enslaved people seeking to reclaim their stolen freedom. Black litigants often accrued their knowledge through discussions with other enslaved and free Black people during desperate attempts to reclaim the freedom that had been stolen from them. This is most evident in my assessment of the role of the famed Dominican friar Bartolomé de Las Casas in Pedro de Carmona's litigation for freedom in the Council of Indies in 1547. While Carmona enlisted the help of the friar in his desperate pursuit of his looted liberty, the chapter concludes that Casas' shaping of Carmona's legal knowledge was likely minimal, as Carmona had already spent years pursuing his case for freedom from illegitimate enslavement in local royal courts before meeting the friar. Instead, perhaps Carmona influenced Casas' shifting views; the friar began to regard the enslavement of Black Africans as illegitimate soon after meeting Carmona, an idea that he elaborated in *Brevísima relación de la destrucción de África* in the mid sixteenth century.[6]

DOMINGO *GELOFE*

In 1536, Domingo *Gelofe* submitted a petition for his liberty to a *fiscal* (official) of the Council of the Indies who was stationed in Sevilla.[7] In his petition, Domingo pleaded that judges should liberate him from slavery and declare him a free man because he had been born as a free person in West Africa, and had been illegitimately enslaved by a Portuguese ship captain, being forcibly displaced to the Americas and then to Castilla.[8] According to Domingo's petition, he was born a free Christian and his father was an "honorable man" (*hombre principal*) in West Africa, likely in the Jolof empire, where he had learned how to speak Portuguese.[9] Domingo positioned his initial departure from his native land as a voluntary act,[10] relaying that he had developed relationships through trade and friendship with Portuguese traders in Gelofe and had decided to leave with a Portuguese trader in order to learn more about Christianity and to become fluent in the language of the Christians. Domingo and his Portuguese party reportedly departed Gelofe and arrived at the island of Tenerife in approximately 1529/30.

Domingo explained that a captain in a Spanish armada had illegitimately enslaved him in Tenerife. He soon found himself aboard a ship in the fleet of an early sixteenth-century conquistador named Diego de Ordás, who was crossing the Atlantic in search of El Dorado.[11] Ordás had left the town of San Lucar de Barrameda, located at the mouth of the Guadalquivir River in southern Castilla, on October 20, 1530 with 500 men and thirty horses, and at least one Indigenous American interpreter.[12]

---

[6] Casas, *Brevísima relación de la destrucción de África*.
[7] "Domingo Gelofe," 1537, AGI, Indiferente, 1205, no. 21, fols., 1ʳ⁻ᵛ.
[8] For discussion of *naturaleza*, see Herzog, *Defining Nations*; Ireton, "They Are."
[9] "Domingo Gelofe," AGI, Indiferente, 1205, no. 21.
[10] Ibid., fols. 1ʳ⁻ᵛ.
[11] Ibid., fols. 1ʳ⁻ᵛ.
[12] "Ordas," AGI, Indiferente, 416, libro 3, fol. 19ᵛ.

The fleets docked in Tenerife, where Ordás possessed a royal license to source an extra 100 men and horses for his armada, and where the fleet would also collect provisions for the journey.[13] Domingo's forced Atlantic journey from Tenerife to the Americas lasted two years, with the armada reaching the Gulf of Paría (present-day coastal Venezuela) and returning to Castilla in 1532; Ordás perished at sea.[14] During the two-year Atlantic odyssey, ownership of Domingo transferred from the captain who had reportedly snatched him in Tenerife to Diego de Ordás, suggesting that perhaps Domingo became the personal slave to the conquistador who was at the helm of the armada.[15] After the surviving members of the armada returned to Castilla in 1532, judges at the House of Trade in Sevilla considered Domingo as part of the late Ordás' estate when adjudicating between competing heirs in the probate case.[16]

Domingo's petition to the Castilian monarch for his liberty reflects a history of ideas and legal customs about slavery and freedom in his native tierra Gelofe. Domingo engaged in a conversation, through his 1536 petition, with Castilian rulers who were well acquainted with his place of origin. Since at least the early fifteenth century, Portuguese and Castilian monarchs had been aware of the kingdoms and polities that constituted Western Africa, in particular of the Jolof "expansionist kingdoms" and the subsequent political fragmentation of the Jolof empire in the fifteenth century.[17] These political pressures had led to Jolofs being the majority of enslaved Black people who were exported to the Atlantic world in the first two decades of the sixteenth century.[18] An uprising led by enslaved Jolof people in 1522 in Isla Hispaniola led to a decade-long attempt by the Spanish crown to prohibit slave traders from exporting enslaved *Gelofes* to the Spanish Indies.[19]

Domingo's argument that the illegitimacy of his enslavement rested on his voluntary departure from tierra Gelofe may relate to ideas about just war in the Jolof empire. The custom in Jolof kingdoms (and Senegambia more broadly) was that war between major political foes was a legitimate reason for enslavement, but intralineage and village raids were not; these reasons were common in Upper Guinea, for example.[20] Consequently, as

---

[13] "Ordas," AGI, Indiferente, 416, libro 3, fols. 23ᵛ, 34ᵛ–35ʳ.
[14] "Ordas," AGI, Justicia, 712, no. 1.
[15] "Domingo Gelofe," AGI, Indiferente, 1205, no. 21. fol. 2ʳ.
[16] "Ordas," AGI, Justicia, 712, no. 1. For studies on *bienes de difuntos*, see Chapter 2, note 87.
[17] Green, *The Rise*, 69–94; Bennett, *African Kings*, 1–15.
[18] Green, *The Rise*; Gómez, *Black Crescent*; Wheat, "The First Great Waves."
[19] Lucena Salmoral, *Regulación de la esclavitud*, 45.
[20] Green, *The Rise*, 91; Lofkrantz and Ojo, "Slavery, Freedom."

Toby Green has argued, most of those taken from Jolof were "war captives procured through attacks from Cajor and the Sereer."[21] Domingo's legal strategy of identifying as a Christian in order to argue for the illegitimacy of his enslavement may also have been the result of his exposure to ongoing inter-African creolization processes in the Jolof kingdoms or syncretic New Christian–Sephardic–Senegambian communities that emerged in the late fifteenth and early sixteenth centuries on the Petite Côte in Senegambia, following the settlement of exiled New Christian communities from Iberia and Amsterdam.[22] Descendants of New Christian–Sephardic–Senegambian communities formed part of extensive trading networks and possessed a deep knowledge of Iberian laws and Catholicism.

Displaced into early sixteenth-century Sevilla, Domingo navigated various avenues of royal justice to pursue his case for freedom, culminating in his petition to the Council of the Indies in 1536. This appeal to the crown also suggests an engagement with broader discussions about just war and the illegitimacy of enslaving non-Christians that were ongoing in Sevilla, the city where he languished for four years as a slave owned by Ordás heirs prior to submitting his petition for freedom. As Nancy Van Deusen has noted, intense debates about the legitimacy of the enslavement of Indigenous Americans took place in early sixteenth-century Sevilla, following the enslavement and forcible displacement of more than 650,000 Indigenous Americans across the Indies. Over 2,000 Indigenous Americans were displaced to Castilla, mostly to Sevilla, as slaves.[23] During this period, Dominican friar Bartolomé de Las Casas was involved in a protracted effort to outlaw the enslavement of Indigenous Americans in the New World on the basis that such enslavements occurred as a result of just wars.[24] The debates resulted in what Van Deusen describes as the passing and rescinding of "contradictory and piecemeal" legislation in Castilla that "excluded slavery only in some areas, temporarily prohibited slavery (1530), and later reestablished slavery under conditions of just war and ransom (1534, 1550), and granted exceptions to individual merchants and families making transatlantic journeys to Castilla by ignoring laws that prohibited the transportation of slaves away from

[21] Green, *The Rise*, 69–94.
[22] de Ataíde Vilhena Cabral, *A primeira elite*; Green, *The Rise*, 69–148; Mark and da Silva Horta, *The Forgotten Diaspora*.
[23] Van Deusen, *Global Indios*.
[24] Brunstetter, "Bartolomé de Las Casas"; Castro, *Another Face of Empire*; Clayton, *Bartolomé de Las Casas*, 82–120; Hanke, *All Mankind*; Orique, "A Comparison"; Orique and Roldán-Figueroa, *Bartolomé*.

their places of origin."[25] Finally, the crown introduced the New Laws in 1542, prohibiting Indigenous slavery. As Van Deusen has explored, the New Laws were followed by two royal inspections in Sevilla in 1543 and 1549, to investigate whether any Indigenous Americans continued to be illegitimately enslaved in that city and its environs; this resulted in the liberation from slavery of 100 Indigenous people.

A thriving discourse therefore existed in Castilla, and particularly in Sevilla, in the 1530s regarding the legitimacy of enslaving Indigenous Americans. This discourse was not limited to theological and royal spheres, as neighbors and friends on street corners in Sevilla and neighboring towns also discussed and debated the laws with regard to just war and Indigenous slavery. As Van Deusen shows, hundreds of enslaved Indigenous Americans who litigated to secure their freedom between 1530 and 1585 shaped discourses of slavery in Sevilla by seeking witness testimonies from their friends and neighbors.[26] City dwellers also heard about broader discussions concerning the illegitimate enslavement of Indigenous Americans through town criers at Gradas and other prominent sites in Sevilla, who sung royal decrees that announced the prohibition of Indigenous slavery.[27]

Domingo's petition is indicative of how debates about illegitimate slavery in Sevilla also extended to the enslavement of Black Africans. Such a development is not surprising given that free Black individuals from Sevilla and the nearby town of Carmona often served as witnesses in cases involving Indigenous litigators' American *naturaleza*.[28] In so doing, they played a role in shaping discourses of just war and the illegitimacy of Indigenous Americans' enslavement in the city's courts. One might surmise that Black dwellers of Sevilla who provided witness testimonies in this way might also have questioned the legitimacy of their own enslavement. Familial and commercial ties between Black witnesses living in Carmona and Sevilla, as documented by Van Deusen, also highlight that ideas and knowledge about Indigenous people's freedom trials were exchanged between Black residents in neighboring towns in southern Castilla. However, ties between free and enslaved Black people living in Sevilla and Carmona were only a fraction of the webs that connected Black communities in Sevilla and towns dotted across southern Castilla

---

[25] Van Deusen, *Global Indios*, 5.
[26] Ibid., 19.
[27] Ibid.
[28] Ibid., 46, 55.

and the Spanish Atlantic more broadly. Early sixteenth-century Sevilla had a significant Black population of free and enslaved people who had ties with the broader Atlantic world.[29] In the city, Domingo would have encountered Black individuals from the Jolof empire, in addition to enslaved Black people from Cabo Verde, Upper Guinea, as well as those born in Spain, Portugal, and the Americas.

Domingo's argument for freedom differed in important ways from the arguments put forward by Indigenous litigants in the same period. Indigenous people argued that their illegitimate enslavement stemmed from the fact that they were not Christians at the time of their capture.[30] This was the opposite to enslaved Black litigants, such as Domingo, who argued that he was a freeborn Christian and that his Christianity predated contact with the Portuguese. Domingo's argument for the illegitimacy of his enslavement rested on two key ideas: (1) the illegitimacy of enslaving someone who was born free and who had not been subject to enslavement as a result of a just war, and (2) the Castilian rule of law, derived from the *Siete Partidas*, that Christians could not legitimately enslave other Christians, regardless of their skin color. In other words, Domingo did not propose that the enslavement of Black people per se was illegitimate. Instead, he implicitly argued that it was the enslavement of freeborn Black Christians that was illegitimate. Domingo played on four issues in his petition: (1) his father being a man of honor; (2) his being a freeborn Christian prior to meeting the Portuguese; (3) his desire to voluntarily travel with Portuguese traders in order to learn more about the Christian faith and Christian languages; and (4) the conquistador, Diego Ordás, recognizing that Domingo was a free man who had been illegitimately enslaved, and subsequently freeing him. Domingo's legal argument of illegitimate enslavement thus relied on the notion that he was already in possession of his liberty and that he was a Christian in Gelofe, which rendered any enslavement illegitimate.

Strikingly, the monarch's response to Domingo's petition highlights an element of doubt in the official mind of the Spanish empire (in this case, the Council of the Indies) regarding the legitimacy of enslaving free Black Christians. In March 1537, four months after launching his petition, Domingo obtained a royal decree that guaranteed his status as a free man.[31] The royal decree stated unequivocally that Domingo, "of Black

---

[29] Chapter 1, note 33.
[30] Van Deusen, *Global Indios*, 150–159.
[31] "Real Cedula, Domingo Gelofe," AGI, Indiferente, 422, libro 17, fols. 114^r–115^r, and all further quotations in this paragraph.

Reclaiming Freedom

color," was – and always had been – free and should be treated as a free man in all the kingdoms of Castilla, the Indies, and Tierra Firme. The decree reasoned that not only had the conquistador Diego de Ordás freed Domingo in his testament, but also that Domingo's freedom was guaranteed because he "came with them [the Portuguese] to be a Christian, as he is," suggesting that the crown agreed with Domingo as to the illegitimacy of his entire ordeal in captivity because of his status as a freeborn Christian in tierra Gelofe. The existence of the royal decree suggests that the crown's view on the legitimacy of the enslavement of Black people in West Africa – especially Christians – was sometimes piecemeal and reactive to individual petitions.[32] Domingo's petition of 1536, and the royal response in 1537, demonstrate the existence of a discussion between rulers and enslaved subjects about the conditions that rendered slavery legitimate in the early decades of the sixteenth century, especially in relation to free Black Christians.

The available evidence suggests that the royal decree stipulating Domingo's freedom in 1537 resulted in his obtaining the status of a free man in the Castilian realms, as he was recorded as a passenger on a ship in Sevilla the following year, poised to travel to Peru using the 1537 royal decree as evidence of his freedom.[33] House of Trade officials recorded Domingo as a free Black man and noted the 1537 royal decree that established his freedom.[34] Domingo's travel record specified that he left Sevilla for Peru employed as a wage-earning servant (*criado*); he may well have taken this job for a specified time period in order to pay for his Atlantic crossing, or he may have found himself in a state of forced servitude even though he was legally free.[35] Over the course of his life, Domingo likely discussed his litigation for freedom with others he encountered in Castilla, on the ship that sailed across the Atlantic, and in Peru.

Judges at the Council of the Indies continued to receive other information about the illegitimate enslavement of Black people in the crown's realms during this period, and issued royal decrees that attempted

---

[32] This reflects some of the arguments made by Masters, "A Thousand."
[33] "Domingo Gelofe," AGI, Indiferente, 1205, no. 21; "Real Cedula, Domingo Gelofe," AGI, Indiferente, 422, libro 17, fols. 114ʳ–115ʳ; "Domingo Gelofe," AGI, Contratación, 5536, libro 5, fol. 156ʳ⁽¹⁾.
[34] "Domingo Gelofe," AGI, Contratación, 5536, libro 5, fol. 156ʳ⁽¹⁾.
[35] For discussion of *criados* in Atlantic crossings, see Chapter 1; Garofalo, "Afro-Iberian Subjects"; Green, "Beyond an Imperial Atlantic"; Ireton, "They Are"; Wheat, "'Otros pasajes."

to ensure that structures of royal justice were available to those who claimed that they had been illegitimately enslaved. For example, in 1537, the Council of the Indies adjudicated on a case of appeal pertaining to the freedom from illegitimate enslavement of a Black *horro* named Rodrigo López who had been snatched from Cabo Verde and displaced to the Caribbean as a slave.[36] After many frustrated attempts to access royal justice, López managed to prove his freedom in the Real Audiencia of Santo Domingo after his liberated Black sister heard news of his whereabouts and sent copies of his freedom papers from Cabo Verde to Santo Domingo via a relay of merchants and messengers.[37] Such complaints of illegitimate enslavement continued to reach judges at the Council of the Indies. In 1540, the monarch issued a royal decree noting that the royal court had received complaints from enslaved Black people in the Spanish Caribbean, who described how slave owners in the Tierra Firme region routinely enslaved many free Black Africans and prevented them from accessing the courts to prove their freedom.[38] The decree ordered officials in Tierra Firme to ensure that any Black people who sought to reclaim their freedom after being illegitimately enslaved could access local courts to prove their cases for liberty.

PEDRO DE CARMONA

In August 1547, an enslaved Black man named Pedro de Carmona appeared in person at the Council of the Indies and presented a petition that described his history of violent enslavement, dispossession, and displacement across various sites in the Atlantic world.[39] In his 1547 petition, Carmona described that he was a Black man born in West Africa, who had been "stolen and brought from my land [West Africa] from the breasts of my mother," and forcibly displaced to Castilla as a child.[40] By the age of thirteen or fourteen, Pedro de Carmona's owner, Juan de Almodóvar, had taken him from Castilla to Puerto Rico.[41] Carmona

---

[36] "Rodrigo López," AGI, Justicia, 11, no. 4. See also Cortés Alonso, "La Liberacion," 533–568; Liddell, "Social Networks"; Turits, "Slavery."
[37] "Rodrigo López," AGI, Justicia, 11, no. 4.
[38] "Real Cedula," 1540, AGI, Panama, 235, libro 7, fols. 121^v–122^r.
[39] "Pedro de Carmona," AGI, Justicia, 978, no. 2, ramo 1. Scholarship on this case includes Sued Badillo, "El pleito"; Pérez Fernández, "Bartolomé de las Casas y los esclavos negros," 57, and *Fray Bartolomé*, 118–123; Dussel, *Política de la liberación*; Wheeler,"(Re)Framing *Raza*," 61–66.
[40] "Pedro de Carmona," AGI, Justicia, 978, no. 2, ramo 1. fols. 1^r–11^v.
[41] "Pérez Fernández," *Fray Bartolomé*, 118–123.

relayed that he enjoyed a close relationship with his owner, describing how Almodóvar had entrusted him to look after his mines on a nearby island in the Spanish Caribbean. He also reported that Almodóvar had permitted him to save some money to purchase an enslaved Black woman named Isabel Hernández, whom Carmona had subsequently married in 1533; the pair had lived as husband and wife while enslaved to Almodóvar.[42] Carmona reported that his owner had promised to liberate himself and his wife upon his death in gratitude for his service, and had written a liberation clause in his testament. He explained that "to discharge his conscience and for the good services that I gave him and the profit that my labor brought to his estate, in the testament that he made before he died, he left me in absolute freedom and without imposing any condition or limitation on my freedom."[43]

Carmona's 1547 petition for freedom owing to his illegitimate enslavement rested on the fact that he had been illegitimately sold into slavery after his liberation on Almodóvar's death. Despite the liberation clause, Carmona reported that he did not receive his liberty after his owner's death.[44] He described how he had heard news of Almodóvar's death while overseeing his owner's mines and estate on a nearby island. Carmona reported that after this he had returned to San Juan in Puerto Rico to retrieve Almodóvar's testament, with the intention of obtaining his freedom.[45] In San Juan, the notary refused to show Carmona the testament, thereby denying him the opportunity to claim his liberty. Instead, the notary secretly sold Carmona's wife, Isabel Hernández, to religious clerics, and then sold Carmona to a merchant named Hernando Alegre. Carmona described how he had fled from the city of San Juan to his late owner's estate after learning that his wife had been sold into slavery and that his new owner had sought to imprison him in chains. Having approached the archbishop of Puerto Rico to seek justice for his case within a few days of fleeing, Carmona reported that the archbishop had been unwilling to intervene. Thereafter, he learned that his wife had been displaced to the city of Santo Domingo in Isla Hispaniola. He subsequently obtained permission from his new owner, Alegre, to travel there to search for her. Alegre, however, had surreptitiously instructed his son, Francisco, who was living in Santo Domingo, to sell Carmona – who

---

[42] "Pedro de Carmona," AGI, Justicia, 978, no. 2, ramo 1. fols. 1^r–11^v.
[43] Ibid.
[44] Ibid.
[45] Ibid.

detailed how Alegre junior sold him secretly when he arrived in Santo Domingo to a merchant named Melchor de Torres, who resided there.

Although Carmona had been reenslaved twice since his owner's death, the city of Santo Domingo proved to be a place where he had a greater chance of accessing the ear of the king through royal courts than he had in Puerto Rico: Santo Domingo was the seat of the Real Audiencia for the region. While enslaved there, Carmona pursued a litigation-for-freedom suit in the Real Audiencia.[46] However, the centrality of paperwork for evidentiary thresholds in royal courts of justice thwarted his initial efforts. Carmona did not have a copy of Almodóvar's testament, as the notary in Puerto Rico had refused to share a copy with him. As he lacked any proof of his liberation from slavery, the judges in the Real Audiencia declared that he had not proved that he was free and pronounced in favor of his owner, Melchor de Torres.[47] In his later petition to the Council of the Indies, Carmona described how the judicial process in Santo Domingo's Real Audiencia was beset with corruption, the courts acting in favor of the powerful mercantile interests of his new owner rather than himself. He complained that those who had promised to defend his interests had done so insincerely, likely referring to his court-appointed procurator.[48]

Despite the ruling, Carmona managed to launch an appeal at the Real Audiencia. The judges ruled in his favor, granting the litigant a two-year period to travel to Puerto Rico, gather the necessary paperwork, namely his previous owner's testament, then return to the court and prove his freedom.[49] As far as Carmona was concerned, this judgment granted him temporary reprieve from his illegitimate enslavement, and the freedom and protection to travel to Puerto Rico to seek proof of his liberty before returning to the court. Melchor de Torres took a different view, and sold Carmona within four or five days of the judgment to an unsuspecting new owner. According to Carmona, Melchor de Torres imprisoned both him and his wife in chains and forced them to board a ship that departed from Santo Domingo to Honduras.[50] Carmona's efforts to seek royal justice through the local royal courts and religious authorities in Puerto Rico and Santo Domingo were therefore frustrated by corruption in the local courts, uninterested judges, and unscrupulous and powerful

---

[46] Ibid.
[47] Ibid.
[48] Ibid.
[49] Ibid.
[50] Ibid.

slave-owners who disregarded the rule of law and rulings issued by the Real Audiencia.

The series of events that led Carmona to cross the Atlantic to the Council of the Indies in Castilla highlights his indefatigable quest for royal justice, and how he shared and exchanged information about his legal strategies to recover his stolen freedom across various sites in the Spanish Caribbean. Although Melchor de Torres displaced Carmona from Santo Domingo, the city where the royal court had finally ruled in his favor, Carmona did not abandon his quest for justice. Reportedly, he voiced concerns about his illegitimate enslavement with those he met along the way, and also after arriving in San Juan de Puerto de Caballos (present-day Puerto Cortés), where he and his wife were resold by one of Torres' agents. In San Juan de Puerto de Caballos, Carmona may have been advised by passers-by to travel to the city of Gracias a Dios, where the Real Audiencia for Guatemala had recently been established, in 1544, or he may have been sent by Torres to be sold in that city, which was 225 km from the port.[51] Carmona later reported that the power and influence of his previous owner, Torres, had thwarted his attempt to have his case for justice heard in that court.[52]

In Gracias a Dios, Carmona continued to discuss his litigation to reclaim his liberty. These conversations resulted in his receiving advice to seek the counsel of some priests who had arrived in Cabo de Gracias a Dios and were also petitioning the Real Audiencia.[53] This was when Carmona first encountered Bartolomé de Las Casas, the famed bishop of Chiapas and Dominican friar who had been engaged in a protracted political effort to outlaw the enslavement of Indigenous Americans and was stationed at the Real Audiencia between July 21 and November 10, 1545, to submit petitions to ensure the proper implementation of the New Laws in the region.[54] Among Casas' entourage was a Black man named Juanillo, who may have been the person who Carmona first spoke with about his case.[55] After Carmona had established contact with the priests, Casas took an interest in his plight and convinced him to cross the Atlantic to Castilla to present his case for freedom from illegitimate

---

[51] Chamberlain, "The Founding."
[52] "Pérez Fernández," *Fray Bartolomé*, 118–123; "Pedro de Carmona," AGI, Justicia, 978, no. 2, ramo 1, fols. 1^r–11^v.
[53] "Pedro de Carmona," AGI, Justicia, 978, no. 2, ramo 1, fols. 1^r–11^v.
[54] "Pérez Fernández," *Fray Bartolomé*, 118–123.
[55] Ibid.

enslavement to the highest royal court for issues pertaining to the Spanish Americas, the Council of the Indies.[56]

This transatlantic history of a Black man's quest for justice and freedom from illegitimate enslavement in the mid sixteenth century reflects the importance of paying attention to how ideas moved across different sites. Carmona spoke about his litigation to recover his stolen freedom after his illegitimate enslavement with people he encountered in the four sites of the Caribbean to which he was displaced (Puerto Rico, Santo Domingo, San Juan de Puerto de Caballos, and Gracias a Dios), while also instigating litigation and appeal suits in the highest royal court in the Spanish Caribbean, namely the Real Audiencia in Santo Domingo. His petition for freedom there forced judges, procurators, and owners to deliberate on his case; but he also discussed his case informally with passersby, other enslaved people, and free people as he desperately sought anyone who might be able to help him to find justice. For example, when Carmona and his wife arrived in San Juan de Puerto de Caballos, in chains on board a ship, he spoke with enough people about the injuries to his liberty and his illegitimate enslavement to eventually receive the advice to go to the Real Audiencia of Guatemala in Gracias a Dios and to seek the counsel of some priests stationed there who might help him. Through those conversations, Carmona spearheaded the exchange of knowledge and ideas about litigation for freedom in royal courts, legal strategies, and questions about the Castilian laws of legitimate enslavement and how to reclaim stolen freedom, while also informing other enslaved and free Black people about his fight for freedom and the arguments that he deployed in the courts.

Although it might be tempting to attribute Carmona's crossing of the Atlantic to the Council of the Indies in 1547 to Bartolomé de Las Casas' support and patronage, this would be paying a disservice to Carmona and his bid for freedom using the royal courts prior to encountering the friar. Carmona was a knowledgeable imperial subject who understood Castilian laws of slavery and freedom, and how to present his arguments forcefully and convincingly. Before meeting Casas, Carmona had already appealed to ecclesiastical justices in Puerto Rico, then fled, taken his case to be heard at the Real Audiencia in Santo Domingo, and mounted his own appeal, which he partially won. And when his owner did not respect the judgment, Carmona once again sought the ear of another court of

---

[56] "Pedro de Carmona," AGI, Justicia, 978, no. 2, ramo 1. fols. 1^r–11^v.

justice, the Real Audiencia in Guatemala, and only then finding his way into the path of Casas. When Casas suggested that he submit a petition to the Council of the Indies regarding the theft of his liberty, it is likely that Carmona was already aware that this court existed.[57] The historian Pérez Fernández has suggested that Casas provided Carmona with a *vale* (certificate) to travel from Gracias a Dios to Havana, where the pair met again, traveling together to Castilla via Lisbon.[58] While this is plausible, Carmona's multiple litigations and conversations across different sites also reveal his acute awareness of the law, structures of justice, and how to move across vast spaces in the Spanish Atlantic. Lacking a freedom certificate, however, would have made any Atlantic journey more difficult and dangerous without the help of Casas.

Through a series of well-presented written petitions dated between August and September 1547, most likely guided by Casas, Carmona described how he had crossed the Atlantic in pursuit of his liberty: "Pedro de Carmona, of *moreno* color, I say that having come from the Indies to your Royal Council of the Indies to ask for justice for the great injury and disturbances (*agravios y turbación*) that have been done to my liberty."[59] He described this transatlantic journey to pursue his liberty as his final chance for justice after his owner had imprisoned him and his wife in chains on a ship to be sold in Honduras. Carmona described the injustice that he and his wife faced with the following lines:

as disfavored and scorned and despised people, we could not find justice for these mistreatments and injustices. And seeing that I had no other remedy but to request that your majesty order that justice be served. Of which, I humbly supplicate that your majesty order in such a way that I obtain my rightful/owed liberty and that of my wife too.[60]

Carmona was well aware of the Castilian laws of slavery that prevented the reenslavement of liberated people. He presented himself as a Christian who deserved access to justice, while describing how his former owners, the notary in Puerto Rico, and royal judges in Santo Domingo had behaved in an un-Christian manner as they had looted his liberty.[61] This notion of the illegitimacy of a third party disturbing or looting someone's liberty in Castilian law is summed up by a procurator in another

---

[57] Ibid.; "Pérez Fernández," *Fray Bartolomé*, 118–123.
[58] Pérez Fernández, *Fray Bartolomé*, 118–123.
[59] "Pedro de Carmona," AGI, Justicia, 978, no. 2, ramo 1. fols. 1^v–2^r.
[60] Ibid.
[61] Ibid.

petition for freedom half a century later, this time in royal jurisdiction of the property court (*camara y fisco real*) within the Holy Office of the Inquisition of Sevilla in 1594. The litigant, a Black man named Juan Rodríguez, who resided in Cádiz and found himself listed as the property within his previous owner's estate, argued that Castilian laws spelled that his enslavement was illegitimate because he was a Catholic owned by an enslaver who the Inquisition had condemned as a "Judaisizer." In doing so, he drew on the Castilian laws of slavery as outlined in the *Siete Partidas* that specified that people of Jewish and Muslim faith could not own Christian slaves.[62] Juan Rodríguez's procurator explained that once someone obtained liberty – as Juan Rodríguez had – such a person could not be "returned to captivity," arguing that "Juan Rodrigues obtained his liberty ... and having obtained liberty one time, he who obtained liberty cannot be returned to slavery except if there is a new cause and there has not been a new cause."[63] Here, the procurator was referring to another stipulation within the *Las Siete Partidas* that detailed how a liberated person could not be returned to slavery unless a new legitimate cause for enslavement emerged, such as becoming a captive in a just war. In his petition half a century earlier, Carmona was drawing on similar knowledge of these legal codes that prohibited the reenslavement of someone who had been liberated from slavery without a just cause. In particular, he also positioned his latest owner, Melchor de Torres, as a corrupt figure who had disregarded the rule of law by selling him after the Real Audiencia in Santo Domingo had issued a judgment that permitted Carmona to travel to Puerto Rico to search for his freedom papers.

Casas accompanied Carmona to the Council of the Indies, which prior to 1561 was an itinerant court and was at this time located in the town of Aranda. He offered Carmona unwavering support and patronage throughout his petition to the Council of the Indies in 1547. In the first instance, various witnesses in Casas' retinue testified on Carmona's behalf, explaining that he had met Casas in Cabo de Gracias a Dios near Honduras and describing how he had become Casas' *criado* after that interaction.[64] In the second instance, Casas offered to pay a bond to the court of the Council of the Indies as an assurance of Carmona's

---

[62] *Las Siete partidas del Sabio Rey don Alfonso*, "Quarta Partida, Titulo XXII, De la Libertad," 39–40.
[63] "Juan Rodríguez," AHN, España, Inquisición, 4672, exp. 8, fol. 4ᵛ. For similar, see also Owensby, "How Juan and Leonor," and "Juan Negro," AHN, España, Inquisición, 4673, exp. 6.
[64] "Pedro de Carmona," AGI, Justicia, 978, no. 2, ramo 1. fols. 12ʳ–22ʳ.

integrity.⁶⁵ This is because de Torres had alerted officials across the Atlantic that Carmona was a fugitive slave after he left Honduras, and requested that they detain him. As a result, upon arriving in Aranda, Carmona was arrested and imprisoned. During the judges' deliberations, Casas agreed to pay a bond to the court – staking his worldly possessions – for Carmona to be freed from jail.⁶⁶ This document bears Casas' signature and those of others in his retinue who witnessed the agreement.

It is possible that Carmona's story of illegitimate enslavement contributed to Casas' shift in perspective about the illegitimacy of the enslavement of Black Africans, as Casas came to view African slavery as similarly illegitimate to indigenous slavery by the mid sixteenth century.⁶⁷ In 1552, Casas wrote a scathing attack of the enslavement of Africans in *Brevísima Relacion de la Destruccion de Africa*, describing how "of more than 100,000 [Black slaves], it is not believed that more than ten had legitimately been enslaved."⁶⁸ Casas argued that only three acceptable causes existed for a just war against infidels and their enslavement, and that no such conditions existed for the legitimate enslavement of Black Africans anywhere in Atlantic Africa between the Canary Islands and the Cape of Good Hope.⁶⁹ The first cause related to contexts where infidels waged war against Christians and attempted to destroy Christianity. Only the Turks of Barbary and the Orient counted in this claim, he argued, because they waged war against Christians every day and had a long history of showing intent to harm them. There was thus no doubt that the Christians were engaged in a just war against Turks. In fact, to Casas, Christians should not describe such a situation as a just war, but rather as legitimate and natural defense. The second cause related to infidels persecuting or maliciously impeding the Christian faith, for example by killing its devotees and preachers without any legitimate cause, or by forcing Christians to renege on their faith. Such acts hindered the practice of the Christian faith and were grounds for just war and enslavement. The third and final reason that would allow for a just war in Africa applied when infidels attempted to destroy or conquer Christian kingdoms. Casas added

---

⁶⁵ Ibid.; "Pérez Fernández," *Fray Bartolomé*, 118–123.
⁶⁶ "Pedro de Carmona," AGI, Justicia, 978, no. 2, ramo 1. fols. 12ʳ–22ʳ.
⁶⁷ Las Casas, *Brevísima relación de la destrucción de África*, 253–256, 267. See also Camplani, "La defensa"; Ireton, "Black African's"; Pérez Fernández, *Fray Bartolomé*; Sánchez-Godoy, "Bartolomé de Las Casas" and *El peor de los remedios*. For another sixteenth-century theologian who posited the illegitimacy of the enslavement of Africans, see Fray Alonso de Montúfar's (1489–1572) letter to the king, quoted in Lucena Salmoral, *Regulación de la esclavitud*, 88–89; Sierra Silva, *Urban Slavery*, 40–42.
⁶⁸ Casas, *Brevísima*, 267.
⁶⁹ Ibid., 253–256.

that under no circumstances could an individual's infidel status alone serve as a just cause for his or her enslavement. In short, by the mid sixteenth century, Casas had rejected the enslavement of Black Africans as illegitimate; the practice was as abhorrent and illegal as the enslavement of Indigenous people in the Americas. He posited that King João III of Portugal (King of Portugal and the Algarves 1521–1557) had realized the legal error of trading slaves with Muslims and had prohibited the practice, but noted that the monarch had failed to realize the widespread sin of stealing Black individuals from their lands. Casas wrote, "but he [João III] did not prevent the *rescate* [purchase of enslaved people] and the one thousand mortal sins that are committed in it, swelling the world of Black slaves, at least in Spain, and even making our Indies overflow with them."[70] While such critiques did not spark a ferocious debate, such as those about the legitimacy of the enslavement of Indigenous Americans that had taken place mere decades earlier in Castilla and had led to legislation outlawing their enslavement, Casas' refutation of the legality of the enslavement of Black Africans demonstrates that these debates were taking place in the sixteenth century.[71]

Judges at the Council of the Indies ruled in 1547 that Carmona should be given a two-year license to travel to Puerto Rico in order to retrieve the documentation that would prove his freedom and then to pursue his case for freedom from illegitimate enslavement in the courts in the Spanish Caribbean.[72] They then issued three royal decrees in the year following their initial pronouncement, these serving as temporary freedom papers for Carmona.[73] The decrees sought to compel royal officials to ensure Carmona's safe passage to Puerto Rico and access to royal justice for his case. In the first instance, Carmona's initial departure from Castilla was delayed because judges at Sevilla's House of Trade refused to grant him an embarkation license. On April 17, 1548, one year after the courts' initial pronouncements, the crown sent a royal decree to the House of Trade in Sevilla instructing judges to allow Carmona to travel to Puerto Rico, noting that the Council of the Indies had received information that judges had refused to grant him a license.[74] Another royal decree, dated February 21, 1548, instructed judges at the House of Trade and other ports to allow Carmona to travel freely to Puerto Rico and to

---

[70] Ibid., 267.
[71] See note 65.
[72] "Pedro de Carmona," AGI, Justicia, 978, no. 2, ramo 1. fols. 12^r–22^r.
[73] "Pedro de Carmona," AGI, Indiferente, 1964, libro 10, fols. 351^v–352; "Real cédula, Pedro de Carmona," AGI, Indiferente, 424, libro 21, fols. 124^v–125^v.
[74] "Pedro de Carmona," AGI, Indiferente, 1964, libro 10, fols. 351^v–352.

present his case for freedom at the Real Audiencia in Santo Domingo.[75] The decree instructed royal officials not to harm or imprison him because he had paid a bond. This had been insured by Casas, who had staked his worldly possessions. A third royal decree compelled the public notary who had certified Carmona's owner's testament in Puerto Rico to make the document available to Carmona for his case.[76] The existence of these decrees suggest that Casas followed the case after the initial judgment and continued to lobby for Carmona over the following months. Perhaps he foresaw possible problems, such as Carmona's ability to obtain an embarkation license at the House of the Trade in Sevilla, in compelling an unwilling notary in Puerto Rico to produce the testament, or that one of the slave-owners who claimed Carmona as their slave might attempt to recapture him. These royal decrees would have provided Carmona with some added security and protection during his quest for freedom.

These royal decrees reveal some of the conversations about slavery and freedom that Carmona participated in across the Atlantic world while he pursued his case for freedom, most notably during his residence in the city of Sevilla in 1547/8 while he awaited royal permission to cross the Atlantic to Puerto Rico. It is likely that he continued to discuss his ongoing legal fight for freedom with free and enslaved Black people in the city of Sevilla and on the ship destined to the Americas, if he did eventually embark on the voyage. Unfortunately, I have not been able to locate any further records to determine whether Pedro de Carmona crossed the ocean to Puerto Rico and whether he was able to retrieve his owner's testament and prove his freedom in the courts in the Spanish Caribbean. Nor do I know whether he was ever reunited with his beloved wife, Isabel Hernández, whom he had last seen in chains in Honduras about to be sold and reenslaved.

FRANCISCO MARTÍN

Early seventeenth-century Cartagena de Indias became the highest-volume slave-trading port of the Hispanic Atlantic with at least 487 slave ships disembarking over 78,453 enslaved Africans between 1573 and 1640.[77] According to a procurator in early seventeenth-century Cartagena, it was widespread knowledge in the port town of Cartagena de Indias that slave traders often brought enslaved Africans to the port in "bad faith"

---

[75] "Real cédula, Pedro de Carmona," AGI, Indiferente, 424, libro 21, fols. 124ʳ–125ᵛ.
[76] Ibid.
[77] On number of slave ships, see Borucki et al. "Atlantic History," and Wheat, *Atlantic Africa*, and The First.

as "[slave traders] trick free black people and take them from their lands and bring them here to be sold as slaves."[78] So endemic was the problem of illegitimate enslavement in West Africa that illegitimately enslaved free Black Africans who had endured forced displacements on slave ships through the Middle Passage would arrive in Cartagena proclaiming their liberty "with loud voices (*a voces*)" when they were coming ashore. These proclamations are those made by a procurator named Francisco Gómez who defended an enslaved litigant seeking his freedom in the Cartagena court in 1614. Gómez explained how such Africans "arrive here shouting that they had been born free and that they are children of free parents and had come to a state of servitude." That act of shouting and using their voices to proclaim their liberty, Gómez clarified, allowed Cartageneros to "know they are free" and that they had been illegitimately enslaved, for such Africans "know how to proclaim their liberty." Noting legal precedent, Gómez referred to former legal cases in Cartagena courts in which illegitimately enslaved Black Africans had pursued justice, of which he noted, "there are a great number in which they have been liberated as free." Gómez's argument is revealing, suggesting that in Cartagena the illegitimate enslavement of free Africans might have been notorious, that some Africans may have disembarked in Cartagena loudly proclaiming their freedom in Spanish or Portuguese, and, more importantly, that similar litigations for illegitimate slavery had been heard and won in the past.

The Jesuit priest, Alonso de Sandoval, who was based in Cartagena and dedicated his missionary life to tending to enslaved Black Africans' souls, also described the existence of these lawsuits. In his treatise titled *Naturaleza, policia sagrada i profana, costumbres i ritos, disciplina i catechismo evangelico de todos Etiopes* (The nature, sacred and profane government, customs and rites, and discipline and evangelical catechism of all Ethiopians), dated 1627, Sandoval dedicated an entire chapter to the question of the legitimacy of the enslavement of Black Africans and pointed to such litigations in Cartagena.[79] As he explained, "the debate among scholars on how to justify the arduous and difficult business of slavery has perplexed me for a long time."[80] Sandoval described how different slave traders had approached

---

[78] "Francisco Martín," AGN, SC, NE 43, legajo 13, doc. 9, fols. 9ᵛ–10ᵛ. This is the source of all further quotes in this paragraph.

[79] Sandoval, *Naturaleza*, Bibliothèque Nacionale de France (cited as BnF), Livres Raires (cited as LR), 4-O3C-6, fols. 65ʳ–70ᵛ. See also Cárdenas, "La ética cristiana"; Sandoval, *Treatise on Slavery*, 50–55.

[80] Sandoval, *Naturaleza*, BnF, LR, 4-O3C-6, fols. 65ʳ–70ᵛ, and all further quotations in this paragraph. All translations of Sandoval are my own.

him in Cartagena to seek his counsel on whether their slave trading was legitimate and moral, as they doubted whether the Africans that they had brought to the Indies had been legitimately enslaved. He recounted how "a captain who owned slave ships that made many voyages to those places [São Tomé]," and who had enriched himself, found that "his conscience was burdened with concern over how these slaves had fallen into his hands." The captain reported to Sandoval his discomfort with how "one of their kings imprisoned anyone who angered the king in order to sell them as slaves to the Spaniards." Another slave-ship captain confided in Sandoval:

Father, I go to buy Black people (as an example) to Angola, and along the way I endure a great amount of effort, costs, and many dangers. In the end, I leave with my cargo, some of the Black people legitimately enslaved and others not. I ask, do I satisfy the justification of this captivity with the efforts, costs, and dangers that I had to endure in going and coming until selling them in Christian lands, where they might continue to live as gentiles?

Sandoval's concern for the legitimacy of the enslavement of Black Africans led him to conduct interviews with slave traders, captains, free and enslaved Africans, priests, and officials in Cartagena de Indias, while he also engaged in correspondence with Jesuits in Luanda and São Tomé to inquire about their views on the legitimacy of enslaving Africans. Importantly, he also reviewed legal cases from Cartagena courts in which Black people argued that they had been illegitimately enslaved in West Africa. Sandoval summarized the transcript of a legal case that he had consulted in which a Black man from Guinea was trying to prove that he was legally free in Cartagena courts. The enslaved man reported that he had been illegitimately enslaved and forcibly displaced to Cartagena, being considered and treated as a free man in Guinea, but Sandoval reported that the court ruled that "although it could be proved that he was legally a slave, he could not prove his freedom."[81]

Discussions about the legitimacy of enslavement in Cartagena among enslaved people are also evident in the litigation for freedom suit that was brought by a young enslaved Black man named Francisco Martín who hailed from the port of Cacheu in Upper Guinea. Martín disembarked from a slave ship in Cartagena on June 5, 1614.[82] According to the ship's register, the captain named Antonio Rodríguez de Acosta had set sail with 359 enslaved people onboard, but only were 287

---

[81] Sandoval, *Naturaleza*, BnF, LR, 4-O3C-6, fols. 65ʳ–70ᵛ. For discussion of this debate, see also Ireton, "Black African's" and "L'imaginaire éthiopien."
[82] "Francisco Martín," AGN, SC, NE 43, legajo 13, doc. 9.

disembarked in Cartagena, meaning that 72 people likely perished during this treacherous journey through the Middle Passage.[83] Upon arrival, Martín litigated for his freedom on the basis that his enslavement had been illegitimate.[84] In Cartagena he was able to locate enslaved and free Black people who knew him from the port town of Cacheu and who agreed to testify, and their testimonies reveal extended discussions among enslaved people about the meanings and legitimacy of slavery across legal jurisdictions.

Martín's first encounter in Cartagena de Indias – or, more likely, in a bay where the ship would have docked prior to arriving at the port – may have been with Alonso de Sandoval and his coterie of free and enslaved African interpreters. This is because Martín arrived into a spiritual world that was concerned with the ubiquitous practice by religious clerics in West and West-Central Africa and on slave ships of administering the sacrament of baptism without ensuring that those receiving the baptism understood or agreed to it, thereby rendering the sacrament null or false.[85] Sandoval, and later his disciple Pedro de Claver (1580–1654), who joined the Cartagena Jesuits in 1615, dedicated their missionary energies to tending to enslaved Africans' souls.[86] Sandoval, in particular, became concerned, through his contact with enslaved Africans, that many baptisms that took place in "those lands [Africa], and ships" were "commonly null and at least doubtful."[87] This concern strengthened his sense of the importance played by priests in the principal ports of disembarkation of African slaves – "Lisbon, Sevilla, the Baya, Pernambuco, Rio Geneyro, Buenosayres, San Iuan de Lua, Puertorico, Cartagena, Panama, and Lima, and wherever else boats arrived to sell captives" – who had the obligation to examine whether null baptisms had taken place, and to "examine, catechize, and baptize those Black people that bring Christian names, and ordinarily are not Christians." Sandoval urged priests to meet ships as they arrived, before "[slave traders] commence to sell and distribute them [enslaved Africans] to different places." This was

[83] Slave Voyages, Trans-Atlantic Slave Trade Database, voyage id 28143, (accessed May 2024), www.slavevoyages.org/voyages/lY8zh35r.
[84] Ibid.
[85] Queija, "La cuestión del bautismo"; Brewer-García, *Beyond Babel*; Cárdenas, "La ética cristiana"; Guerrero Mosquera, "African diaspora protection," "Alonso de Sandoval," "Bolsas mandingas," "De esclavizados a traductores," "Los jesuitas," and "Misiones, misioneros"; Ireton, "L'imaginaire éthiopien"; Vignaux, *L'Église et les Noirs*, 33–83.
[86] For a discussion of the Jesuits' reports on these activities, see Navarrete Peláez, "Las cartas."
[87] Sandoval, *Naturaleza*, BnF, LR, 4-O3C-6, book 3, chapter 1, fols. 286^v–287^r.

necessary, he argued, because slave owners and priests in other regions of the Indies tended not to doubt the baptism of enslaved Black Africans, as they were persuaded that "having passed through the port they [enslaved people] will already have been baptized." Sandoval stated that priests in ports should determine, as soon as ships arrived, whether enslaved Black Africans were "of Jesus Christ, and his church, and upon discovery that they are not, to ensure that they become so." For such purposes, the Cartagena Jesuits trained a cadre of free and enslaved skilled African interpreters who aided in communicating with enslaved individuals of varied African linguistic backgrounds, noting that "if speaking to them through their languages and interpreters, we will judge by the responses that they give to the questions that we ask them."[88]

After experiencing the constant specter of death and brutality over the course of a forcible displacement through the Middle Passage, enslaved people on ships destined to Cartagena would then be forced to endure further torturous detentions when captains anchored their vessels for days or weeks in bays surrounding the port in an attempt to contain any infectious diseases onboard. That is when Sandoval and Claver or their African interpreters would row from Cartagena to the anchored ships to meet the captives and conduct extensive investigations into their religious knowledge that would determine their spiritual needs, principally whether or not they had been correctly baptized in African ports.[89] Upon reaching land, Claver would reportedly perform elaborate baptisms during which he was assured, through interpreters, that his enslaved flock understood the meaning of the baptism and wished to become Christians.[90] Had Francisco Martín encountered Sandoval and his African interpreters upon arriving in Cartagena – either while still on the ship or upon disembarking – Sandoval would have soon discovered that there was no need for an interpreter, for Martín spoke Spanish (and perhaps Portuguese too), and nor was there need for a baptism as Martín was well versed in the Christian faith. Martín may also have informed his Jesuit interlocutors that he was free and that his enslavement was illegitimate, because three months earlier, a Portuguese *converso* named Manuel Bautista Pérez had illegitimately purchased him from another

---

[88] On Black interpreters in Cartagena, see Brewer-García, *Beyond Babel*; Guerrero Mosquera, "De esclavizados a traductores" and "Los jesuitas"; Vignaux, *L'Église et les Noirs*, 327–504.
[89] Splendiani and Aristizábal Giraldo, *Proceso de beatificación*, 84–124.
[90] Brewer-García, *Beyond Babel*; Splendiani and Aristizábal Giraldo, *Proceso de beatificación*, 84–124.

Portuguese trader in the port of Cacheu in West Africa.[91] It is likely that Martín was listed as a Black *ladino* in an inventory compiled by Bautista Pérez that listed his trading activities in Cacheu in 1614.[92] However, he may well have been justifiably suspicious of priests in and around slave-trading ports, as he later recounted that his illegitimate enslavement had taken place at the hands of a priest named Manuel de Sossa on a beach in Sierra Leone.[93]

Martín disembarked from the ship in June 1614 into what might ostensibly have been regarded as a Black city. Early seventeenth-century Cartagena de Indias served as the epicenter of the Atlantic trade in enslaved Black people who hailed from various regions of Upper Guinea and West-Central Africa. From there, merchants sold slaves for onward journeys to Lima, Panama, and New Spain, while other enslaved Africans remained in Cartagena or were displaced inland to New Granada.[94] The port city thus comprised a large, transient population of enslaved Black people. In addition, Cartagena's urban landscape was composed of enslaved Black people laboring in private households, free Black *vecinos*, and increasingly large communities of Black fugitives in the hinterlands, who established *palenques* and maintained ties with enslaved and free Black populations in urban centers.[95] The large Black population of the port – especially the free individuals – also caused concern among royal officials and Spanish *vecinos*. A tribunal of the Holy Office of the Inquisition was established in Cartagena in 1610, mainly to police Black ritual healing practitioners, especially women.[96] The port also served as a major crossroads for travelers between Castilla and the Spanish Americas, who included free Black individuals who sojourned in Cartagena while organizing their onward journeys.[97]

---

[91] "Francisco Martín," AGN, SC, NE 43, legajo 13, doc. 9, fols. 3^r–4^r.

[92] I thank Linda Newson for sharing her transcription of the following source with me. "Concurso de Acreedores de Manuel Bautista Pérez," AGN, Peru, Tribunal de la Inquisición, legajo 35, fols. 153–154, 165–166, 173–174, 179–182.

[93] "Francisco Martín," AGN, SC, NE 43, legajo 13, doc. 9, fols. 3^r–4^r.

[94] O'Toole, *Bound Lives*, 1–16, 35–63.

[95] On free Black *vecinos* in Cartagena, see Gómez, *The Experiential*; Navarrete Peláez, "Consideraciones en Torno," 1–23, "Consideraciones en Torno," *Esclavitud negra e Inquisición*, *Génesis y desarrollo*, and "Los artesanos"; Silva Campo, "Fragile Fortunes"; Vidal Ortega, *Cartagena*; von Germeten, *Violent Delights*; Wheat, *Atlantic Africa*. On Black *palenques*, see Brewer-García, *Beyond Babel*, 116–163; Landers, "The African" and "Cimarrón"; McKnight, "Confronted Rituals"; Navarrete Peláez, "De reyes," "Por haber," and *Cimarrones*; Silva Campo, "Through the Gate."

[96] Splendiani et al., *Cincuenta años*, 2:35–459; Gómez, *The Experiential*.

[97] Ireton, "They Are."

The world of commerce, slave trading, and policing of Catholic religiosity in Cartagena de Indias was not unfamiliar to Martín. Cartagena as a key port city in the transatlantic slave trade occupied a similar position to that of his native Cacheu during the previous half-century. As Sandoval described in 1627, following interviews with enslaved Africans, slave traders, and priests, "[Cacheu] is the most important port of all of Guinea. Ships from Sevilla, Portugal, the island of Santiago and many other places come here to trade in Black slaves and many other things"; he also noted that Cacheu had "a trading port, market, and church, which has a priest appointed by the king."[98] Martín had been born in the Cacheu household of a Portuguese captain to free Black parents who hailed from the *Zape* nation and Cabo Verde, and would later testify to knowing most of the Portuguese *converso* merchants who resided in that port and those who passed through on slave-trading ventures.[99] It is possible that Martín formed part of the Kriston community in Cacheu – otherwise known by the Portuguese as Christianized Africans – who came to play a prominent role in facilitating trade and commerce between European traders and different African rulers; Martín and his African witnesses argued that his parents were well known as free Black Christians in Cacheu.[100]

Martín also testified that he labored as a wage-earning *grumete* on Portuguese ships along the coasts of Guinea, Sierra Leone, and Gambia.[101] Historian Philip Havik defined the *grumetes* of Cacheu as "Kristo rowers, pilots, interpreters, and petty traders, who acted simultaneously as traders and brokers, negotiating with African and Atlantic actors, whose existence therefore depended and thrived on making themselves indispensable."[102] Havik pointed out that Kriston actors such as *grumetes* and *tungumás* (free Christian women from coastal ethnic groups) "formed an internal African trading diaspora that scouted the coast for commodities, while building and mediating extensive patron–client relations with local African elders and chiefs along its shores."[103] Indeed, as a wage-earning

---

[98] Sandoval, *Naturaleza*, BnF, LR, 4-O3C-6, book 1, chapter 12, fols. 38ʳ–41ʳ.
[99] "Francisco Martín," AGN, SC, NE 43, legajo 13, doc. 9, fols. 3ʳ–4ʳ.
[100] Havik, "Gendering" and "Walking the Tightrope."
[101] "Francisco Martín," AGN, SC, NE 43, legajo 13, doc. 9. For discussion of Africans employed on trading expeditions from Guinea to Sierra Leone, see Newson, "Africans and Luso-Africans," 13–14.
[102] Havik, "Gendering."
[103] Havik, "Gendering," 321–322. For further definitions of Kriston and *tungumás*, see Green, *The Rise*, 260–277, and "Baculamento or Encomienda."

grumete on Portuguese slave-trading fleets in Guinea and in Sierra Leone, Martín came into contact with a wide array of Europeans and Africans who traveled to and traded in Castilla, Portugal, the Indies, and Africa, in addition to enslaved Africans who were forcibly displaced from African shores to the Americas.[104] Exemplary of such relationships, Martín testified that Antonio Rodríguez, the captain of the ship in which Martín had been forcibly displaced from Cacheu to Cartagena, had known him for many years as a free man in Cacheu, while he claimed to know three other Spanish merchants or captains who arrived in Cartagena between June 1614 and March 1615 from his time in Cacheu and Sierra Leone.[105]

Finally, Martín would not have been surprised by the presence of priests in Cartagena de Indias, nor by the reach of the Holy Office of the Inquisition that had recently been established in the port. He was intimately acquainted with Iberian Catholicism. In Cacheu and the surrounding locales, inquisitorial investigations into residents – both Black Christians and Portuguese *conversos* – had been active since 1540 (just four years after the establishment of the Holy Office of the Inquisition in Lisbon).[106] Inquisitorial authorities persecuted Black Christian women for ritual healing practices there, much as Inquisitors would do in Cartagena after 1610.[107]

Martín thus arrived in Cartagena in 1614 with significant knowledge of the Atlantic world, Iberian laws, and Atlantic commercial systems, and well versed in the meaning and significance of a Christian profession of faith in the early Iberian Atlantic. But he also arrived in a port city where residents possessed intimate knowledge and awareness of well-established Christian pockets in Africa.[108] Sandoval, the Cartagena-based Jesuit who had spent his career investigating enslaved Africans' places of origin, recognized that some Black Christians lived in Cacheu, as he noted that "many people have been successfully baptized here," but he offered a word of warning that "these Black Christians have little knowledge of Christianity and interact with gentiles. This means they easily return to rites that are not part of our faith."[109] However, as I

---

[104] "Francisco Martín," AGN, SC, NE 43, legajo 13, doc. 9.
[105] "Francisco Martín," AGN, SC, NE 43, legajo 13, doc. 9. fols. 3ʳ, 38ʳ–38ᵛ.
[106] Havik, "Gendering" and "Walking the Tightrope."
[107] Ibid., Splendiani et al., *Cincuenta años*, 2:35–459.
[108] Most prominently, the conversion of the Kingdom of Kongo to Catholicism: see Fromont, *The Art*; Heywood and Thornton, *Central Africans*; Thornton, "The Development." Sandoval discussed this conversion in his treatise: see Ireton, "*L'imaginaire*."
[109] Sandoval, *Naturaleza*, BnF, LR, 4-O3C-6, fols. 38ʳ–41ʳ.

argue elsewhere, Sandoval weaponized the history of Catholic conversion by kingdoms in West Africa and West-Central Africa, and legends about the establishment of a glorious ancient Ethiopian Church, which he argued that God had chosen as the first Christian church, in order to justify the mass enslavement of all Africans and their removal from Africa to the New World in the name of the establishment of a Black elected church.[110]

Martín's arrival in Cartagena also tells a story of connections between enslaved and free Black people dwelling in the city who maintained knowledge and memories of Cacheu and Upper Guinea. As his captors disembarked him from the ship, Martín reportedly encountered Pedro de Tierra Bran.[111] Pedro, a forty-five-year-old free Black Christian who resided in Cartagena, testified to recognizing Martín, for he had previously dwelt in the same house in which Martín had grown up in Cacheu. In their conversation, Martín informed Pedro that he was to be sold as a slave in the port. Pedro reportedly expressed disbelief, saying that Martín could not be sold, for he was a free man. Another figure who is reported to have recognized Martín as he disembarked from the ship was Sebastián Barroso, a thirty-year-old free *mulato* and merchant (*tratante*) who resided in Cartagena. He later explained that he had known Martín for sixteen years, and claimed to have sojourned in the captain's house in Cacheu for six years a decade earlier, before Barroso traveled to Cartagena. Barroso and Pedro were two of seven free and enslaved Black individuals in Cartagena who testified – in 1614, within three months of Martín's arrival – to knowing Martín as a freeborn person in Cacheu or on fleets across West African coasts prior to their arrival in Cartagena some years earlier. Some of the witnesses had been brought as slaves from Cacheu, while others reported that they traveled to the New World as free men or women.[112]

On July 4, 1614, one month after arriving in Cartagena, Martín presented a petition to the justice of the city for freedom on the basis that his enslavement was illegitimate. Presiding over the case was Luis de Coronado, the *teniente general* (chief legal counsel) of the governor of

---

[110] Ireton, "L'imaginaire éthiopien." Pérez García draws similar conclusions on Sandoval's rhetorical use of Ethiopia and his arguments to justify the enslavement of all Black people, in Pérez García "Christian Freedom."

[111] "Francisco Martín," AGN, SC, NE 43, legajo 13, doc. 9, fols. 17^r–26^v.

[112] Ibid., fols. 17^r–26^v. On free Black Africans who traveled (or labored) between Upper Guinea and West-Central Africa and the Americas, see Green, "Beyond an Imperial Atlantic"; Ferreira, *Cross-Cultural*, 203–248; Wheat, "Otros pasajes."

Cartagena.[113] Martín explained that he was from Cacheu in Guinea and the son of Antón Martín, born in Cabo Verde, and his wife named Elena, of the *Zape* nation. He described how he and his parents were "free people and Christians" who had lived in Cacheu in the house of a Portuguese captain.[114] According to Martín's testimony, about eight and a half years earlier, in 1606, he had left Cacheu for Sierra Leone to labor on a ship as a wage-earning *grumete* for a Cacheu-based captain named Ambrosio Dias. Martín recalled that after about four years Dias sent him to the "beach of the sea" with a letter for a cleric named Manuel de Sossa. There, on the shore, they "tied my hands and put me on a ship and took me to Cacheu to the house of Juan Méndez."[115] Martín recalled that Méndez had attempted to sell him to Antonio Rodriguez, the captain who eventually brought Martín to Cartagena. According to Martín, Rodríguez had refused to purchase him since the captain knew he was a free man. Thereafter, Méndez sold Martín to a Portuguese *converso* named Manuel Bautista Pérez, who took Martín to Cartagena on Rodríguez's ship along with his other enslaved cargo. It was only after arriving in Cartagena, Martín noted, that Bautista Pérez branded his body with a hot iron to mark his status as a slave. He pleaded that the Cartagena court would recognize that "being free of free parents, and there not having been cause or title nor reason why for having been free and having been born free that I have come to this servitude," and asked that the court grant him freedom on the basis that his enslavement was illegitimate.[116]

In his litigation, Martín and his aforementioned procurator, Francisco Gómez, presented an argument for the illegality of enslaving "between Christians."[117] Gómez argued that even "in the case that [Martín] had been sold one hundred times," such an occurrence "could not harm his natural right" to freedom because Martín was the:

son of free parents and he has been brought up and lived as a free man, and it is not legal (*no consta, ni puede constar*) that he [Francisco Martín] has become enslaved (*cautivo*) in a just war, or even an unjust war, nor that he has been sold by his parents, nor [enslaved as punishment] for a crime that he might have committed because there is no right [law] (*no hay derecho*) to enslave between Christians for any of these reasons.

---

[113] "Francisco Martín," AGN, SC, NE 43, legajo 13, doc. 9, fols. 3r–4r.
[114] Ibid.
[115] Ibid.
[116] Ibid.
[117] Ibid., fol. 10r, and all further quotations in this paragraph.

Martín's argument therefore relied on the fact he was already a Christian in Cacheu, and that it was illegal for a Christian to enslave a fellow Christian for any reason.

A number of possibilities explain why the case was heard and eventually won, not just in Cartagena, but also on appeal in the higher court of the Real Audiencia in Santa Fé (in present-day Bogotá) the following year. The first possibility is a general concern in Cartagena that free Black people were being illegitimately enslaved in West Africa. As noted earlier in the chapter, Gómez, Martín's legal defender, proposed such a possibility.[118] Hushed discourses also existed among Black residents of Cartagena about the legality of slavery and the possibilities for legal and extralegal routes to obtain freedom among Black city dwellers. In this period, a number of enslaved Black people litigated for their freedom in Cartagena, not because of illegitimate enslavement, but because of unduly harsh physical violence by their enslavers.[119] In addition, there was the presence of *palenques* in the hinterlands and the seemingly fairly common aspiration – as documented by Larissa Brewer-García, Jane Landers, Kathryn J. McKnight, María Cristina Navarrete Peláez, and Ana María Silva Campo – among enslaved Black city dwellers to flee to them in search of freedom.[120] These scholars have explored how royal officials' interviews with former residents of the Palenque del Limón and the Matudere Palenque – two maroon communities that Cartagena officials destroyed in 1634 and 1693, respectively – shed light on the emergence and circulation of alternative ideas about governance and freedom among enslaved and free Black individuals in seventeenth-century Cartagena. Such ideas often disregarded Castilian legal codes and involved collective acts of resistance. In particular, these scholars have traced the ties that residents of *palenques* in the hinterlands often maintained with Black port dwellers in Cartagena, suggesting a constant circulation of information and ideas about alternative and illicit forms of governance and the means by which they could experience different forms of freedom from slavery.

---

[118] Ibid. fols. 9^v–10^v. See note 69.
[119] For example, "Juana negra, sobre su libertad," AGN, SC, NE 43, legajo 9, doc. 1. See also Navarrete Peláez, "Consideraciones," 16–19; Salazar Rey, *Mastering the Law*.
[120] Brewer-García, *Beyond Babel*; Landers, "The African Landscape," 147–162; McKnight, "Confronted Rituals," 1–19; Navarrete Peláez, *Cimarrones y Palenques*, "De reyes, reinas y capitanes," 44–63, and "Por haber todos," 7–44; Silva Campo, "Through the Gate," 197–213.

Martín's ability to command free and enslaved Black witnesses who claimed to know him from Cacheu also attests to the existence of discourses about legal and extralegal means of evading slavery in Cartagena. Certainly, Martín's owner, Manuel Bautista Pérez, posited exactly this theory in the trial: He claimed that it was well known in the city that "the Black people conspire to free one another by providing false testimonies."[121] Further, upon arriving in Cartagena de Indias, Martín dwelt in a townhouse with his owner and with at least two other enslaved Black people, who may or may not have arrived on the same slave ship as Martín. As criminal trials and other Black Cartageneros' freedom suits of the period demonstrate, city dwellers were often intimately connected to the business and affairs of their neighbors.[122] Word of Martín's litigation might have spread rapidly among Black residents in the port. Certainly, in the house where Bautista Pérez resided, Martín would have had daily relationships with other servants and slaves and with other neighborhood residents, apart from when his owner restricted his movements by incarcerating him in chains and giving him life-threatening physical injuries.[123] Perhaps such daily interactions – even if infrequent owing to Bautista Pérez's harsh violence and imprisonment – were how Martín gathered his witnesses.

A coterie of Black and *mulato* witnesses from West Africa (and one from Portugal) who resided in Cartagena either in captivity or as free individuals testified to knowing Martín in Guinea and communicating with him in Cartagena in the three months since his arrival (witness testimonies were presented in late August 1614). These statements demonstrate the existence of a discourse among Black port dwellers about the illegitimacy of enslaving free Black Christians: The witnesses argued that Martín's enslavement was illegitimate because he was a free Christian in Guinea.[124]

The previously mentioned forty-five-year-old Pedro *de Tierra Bran*, for example, who described himself as a free Black Christian, explained that he knew Martín from Guinea. Before Pedro had traveled to Cartagena seven years earlier, he had spent fifteen years residing in Cacheu and had worked as a servant in the house of a Portuguese captain. There, Pedro had seen Martín living with his parents – both free

---

[121] "Francisco Martín," AGN, SC, NE 43, legajo 13, doc. 9, fols. 39^{r-v}.
[122] "Francisco de Segura, mulato," AGN, SC, NE 43, legajo 10, doc. 9.
[123] "Francisco Martín," AGN, SC, NE 43, legajo 13, doc. 9, fols. 7^v–16^r.
[124] Ibid., fols. 17^r–26^v, and all further quotations in next two paragraphs.

Christians – and described how he saw them "have and possess their liberty." He explained that Martín had labored on ships in Tierra de Zoala and in Tierra de Cape, serving "white masters" who treated and paid him as a "free person born to free parents." A fifty-six-year-old free *mulato* named Domingo Morrera, a resident of Cartagena who was born in Tavira (Portugal), recalled that when he was laboring as a ship pilot in Guinea some twelve or thirteen years earlier, he had worked alongside Martín on a ship in Cacheu. Morrera recounted that he had seen Martín laboring for a wage as a *grumete* and that the entire crew considered Martín to be a free person. Another witness named Francisco, who was from Cabo Verde and enslaved to a ship captain in Cartagena, explained that he knew both Martín and the slave trader Bautista Pérez. Francisco described how he had been enslaved and forcibly displaced from Guinea to Cartagena eight years earlier and testified that he had known Martín for six or seven years during the time he lived in Cacheu. He stated that he had been brought up in those lands, and thus had known Martín since he was very young and living in the captain's house, "always seeing that he [Martín] lived and was reputed as a free man." Francisco added that he would have heard if Martín had been enslaved because "the land of Cacheu is very short," implying perhaps that news of residents' lives traveled fast.

A key question regarding this illegitimate enslavement concerned when and where Martín had been subjected to the physical branding of his body, thus marking his status as a slave. According to Martín, it was only upon arriving in Cartagena and hearing that he might litigate for his freedom that Bautista Pérez had branded his initials on Martín's chest with a hot iron. Three of Martín's witnesses attested that the branding occurred in Cartagena and not in Guinea. Barroso stated that Martín had not been branded when he disembarked from the ship, but that a few days later he saw him with a "mark of fire on his chest." Martín's seven witnesses attested to the common practice of branding captives in Guinea prior to their embarkation on ships, and assured the court that slave traders were prohibited in Guinea from branding free Black Christians as slaves. Another witness named Manuel, who had testified that he had been brought as a slave from Cacheu to Guinea some years earlier, explained that he knew that slaves were branded in Guinea because this had happened to him before he was displaced to Cartagena, and that he knew "they did not brand free people there [Guinea]."

Bautista Pérez refuted Martín's claim that he had been illegitimately enslaved. He explained that Martín had previously been enslaved to many other Portuguese traders in Guinea, and that he had purchased him from a Portuguese slave trader based in Cacheu named Juan Méndez Mezquita to settle the 150 pesos that Méndez Mezquita owed Bautista Pérez.[125] Bautista Pérez argued that Martín's litigation in Cartagena was calculated. Sufficient structures of justice existed in Cacheu, argued the irate slave owner, for Martín to have pursued his freedom there had he believed that his former owners had illegitimately enslaved him. The slave trader's witnesses confirmed that courts where enslaved people could seek justice did indeed exist in Cacheu, and reported that other free Black individuals in the Guinean port litigated there if they were illegitimately enslaved. Bautista Pérez also denied that Martín had been branded in Cartagena, instead asserting that this had taken place "with the rest of his Blacks" in Cacheu. The slave trader's witnesses confirmed this assertion.

Bautista Pérez also questioned the legitimacy and credibility of Martín's Black witnesses. On September 29, 1614 – one month after Martín had presented his witnesses – Bautista Pérez argued that his case was stronger because his witnesses were honorable men of great faith and credit who had resided in Cacheu for many years. In contrast, he argued, Martín had not proved anything because his Black and *mulato* witnesses "have no faith or credit." He alluded to widespread knowledge in Cartagena that because these Black people were of the same nation, "they say untruths and they are ignorant people who do not understand their oaths because of their incapacity." Finally, Bautista Pérez suggested that a conspiracy existed among Black dwellers of Cartagena to help each other obtain freedom by providing false witness testimonies.

After the court ruled in Martín's favor in November 1614, pronouncing him as a free man who had been illegitimately enslaved, Bautista Pérez presented an appeal in which he transformed the legal argument from a debate about the legitimacy of enslavement on the basis of Christianity or lack thereof to a juridical argument concerning just war.[126] On appeal, in November 1614, he recalled that two and a half years earlier, Martín had labored as a *grumete* on a ship owned by a Cacheu-based captain named Juan Méndez Mezquita. The crew comprised Black and white laborers who were tasked with recovering Black slaves who had been captured by "*negros de guerra* (Black people of war)," defined by Bautista Pérez as groups of Black people who "spend

---

[125] Ibid., fols. 27^r–36^v, and all further quotations in this and the next paragraph.
[126] Ibid., fols. 41^r–54^r, and all further quotations in this paragraph.

their time waylaying and robbing ships" on the coasts of Guinea to steal merchandise and ransom any enslaved Africans and crew on the ships to European merchants. Bautista Pérez explained that during the expedition, the *negros de guerra* overpowered Méndez Mezquita's ship, killing the captain and pilot and imprisoning the white and Black sailors, and enslaving the Black slaves and free men alike. It was at this moment, he argued, that Martín became enslaved – during a just war at the hands of the *negros de guerra*. According to Bautista Pérez, a Portuguese Cacheu resident named Enriquez Hernández recovered the captured ship and crew and negotiated ransom prices that would ensure the release of the captives. He posited that Martín was thus legitimately enslaved as he had been captured in a just war. Further, it was Martín's previous employer, Méndez Mezquita, who had provided Hernández with the 150 pesos for Martín's release, meaning that ownership of Martín was transferred to Méndez Mezquita. Thereafter, Bautista Pérez explained, Martín served as a slave in Méndez Mezquita's household in Cacheu, that is, until he was sold to Bautista Pérez.

The legal arguments presented in the case were therefore transformed from a discussion of the illegitimate enslavement of free Black Christians to the legitimacy of slavery through just war. All the while, Martín and his witnesses stood their ground, and argued that as a free Black Christian he could not be enslaved under Castilian laws of slavery, nor legitimately purchased as a slave. Responding to the appeal on February 20, 1615, Martín agreed that he had indeed labored as a *grumete* for Méndez Mezquita, but noted that he had done so as a free man who earned a salary "like the other free people."[127] He also agreed that one day some *negros de guerra* had captured the entire ship. Martín explained that they killed the captain and the pilot and tied up the remaining enslaved cargo and the free Black and white laborers onboard the vessel. However, he refuted the notion that the capture of the Portuguese ship meant that a just war had taken place. Martín agreed that Hernández had paid a ransom for him and the crew, but denied that he had been enslaved. Instead, he explained how upon returning to Cacheu, he and Méndez Mezquita signed a contract specifying that Martín would labor for him as a wage-earning *grumete* for two more years. Martín explained how later, while traveling toward Gambia, he managed to escape an English raid in a town where he was based and had returned to Méndez Mezquita's abode in Cacheu. Thus, even though Martín acknowledged that he had been

[127] Ibid., fols. 54ʳ–56ʳ.

captured by *negros de guerra* and was subsequently freed through a ransom paid by a Portuguese merchant, he positioned such an event in terms of his capture and rescue alongside other free white wage-earning sailors. He subsequently agreed to continue laboring for Méndez Mezquita, but with a time-specified labor contract as a wage-earning *grumete*.

The ruling by Luis de Coronado in Cartagena on November 22, 1614, that Martín was "free and not subject to captivity or servitude," along with the order that Bautista Pérez allow Martín "to enjoy (*gozar*) his liberty" without imposing any impediments, is especially surprising because of the weight that it gave to Martín's Black witnesses over those presented by Bautista Pérez.[128] In Cartagena, as in Guinea, Bautista Pérez interacted with trading associates who were part of his extended network belonging to the New Christian Portuguese diaspora.[129] Indeed, the witnesses who attested to Bautista's ownership of Martín on July 7, 1614 were slave traders ready to depart from Cartagena to Spain.[130] All six were *vecinos* of Portugal. They testified that they had spent time in the port of Cacheu during the previous decade and knew Martín there, while agreeing that Bautista Pérez was an honorable man of Christian faith who would never purchase or illegitimately enslave a free man.

Coronado's ruling and his favoring of the testimonies provided by enslaved and free Black people in Cartagena suggests that debates and doubts regarding the legitimacy of the enslavement of some Black people existed among royal deputies in Cartagena de Indias. His decision also paralleled the legal precedents described by the procurator, Francisco Gómez, who had stated that many similar legal cases regarding illegitimate enslavements had been previously heard in Cartagena courts and had resulted in the courts setting litigants free.[131] The ruling also dismissed Bautista Pérez's request to present evidence that Martín's witnesses were unreliable, untrustworthy, reputed as drunks, and were engaged in a conspiracy in Cartagena to free enslaved Black Africans. Similarly, his appeal based on just war and his legitimate purchase of an already enslaved person also failed. On March 17, 1615, Luis de Coronado decreed that his initial ruling, in which he had freed Martín, was final.[132] He referred the case to the Real Audiencia in Santa Fé for final sentencing and ordered

---

[128] Ibid., fols. 40r.
[129] Newson and Minchin, *From Capture*, 1–17, 32–71.
[130] "Francisco Martín," AGN, SC, NE 43, legajo 13, doc. 9, fols. 27r–36v.
[131] Sandoval, *Naturaleza*, BnF, LR, 4-O3C-6, fols. 65r–70v.
[132] "Francisco Martín," AGN, SC, NE 43, legajo 13, doc. 9, fol. 56r.

Reclaiming Freedom 223

both parties or their representatives to appear in that court four months later. The Real Audiencia considered the case on July 7, 1615, and by November 13, 1615, the court had reiterated Luis de Coronado's ruling of November 28, 1614, with the added clause that Martín should serve the person who paid his ransom for one year, thereby confirming his freedom while potentially subjecting him to another year of servitude to Bautista Pérez (although the ruling is ambiguous as to whether Martín had already served the year).[133] By May 10, 1616 – nearly two years after Martín initiated his petition in July 1614 – the Real Audiencia asked for both parties to be notified of the final decision.

A disjunction emerged between Martín's lived experience of partial, fractional, or inexistent freedom and the legal freedom specified by the court, at least in the months following the Cartagena court's ruling. He did not obtain any semblance of liberty in the first few months after the ruling, despite legally being liberated from slavery. When Martín was interviewed in early March 1615 for Bautista Pérez's appeal – three months after the ruling that supposedly freed him from slavery – Martín was languishing in the public jail.[134] By March 26, 1615, he had been transferred to Bautista Pérez's residence. On that date, Martín's procurator and a court scribe certified in sworn statements that Bautista Pérez had imprisoned Martín in chains. Thus, the legal pronouncement of Martín's freedom in November 1614 did not translate to a lived experience of liberty, at least not initially. Further, Martín's transfer between the public jail and Bautista Pérez's home in March 1615 suggests an extralegal corruption in due process, since the court had ordered that Martín be given his liberty. The final decision by the court in Santa Fé supposedly guaranteed that Martín would become free within a year; but, after the Real Audiencia's ruling – if Martín did indeed have to serve Bautista Pérez for another year – it is possible that he might have attempted to sell Martín, whom he perceived as his disobedient slave. In such a scenario, Martín would likely have endured another arduous and violent process of litigation for his freedom in a different court, wherever his new owner happened to be located.

The stakes were high: Martín suffered horrific violence and imprisonment at the hands of his owner in retribution for seeking his freedom in the courts. On July 5, 1614, the day after Martín's initial appeal, Gómez complained that upon hearing that Martín had submitted a petition to

[133] Ibid., fols. 57^r–60^r.
[134] Ibid., fols. 54^r–56^r.

the court for his liberty, Bautista Pérez had grabbed Martín and, "giving him many beatings (*porrazos*)," had taken Martín to the jail, and later that afternoon transferred him to his house and locked him in chains, giving "him many bad treatments."[135] A month later, Gómez complained that Bautista Pérez had violently and loudly whipped Martín late into the nights in retribution for his litigation. Enslaved Black neighbors who resided on the same street as Bautista Pérez testified that they heard sounds of whipping and shouting late into the evenings and Martín's cries in the mornings, while also seeing injuries on Martín's body on the days following the torture. Bautista Pérez also imprisoned Martín by locking him in chains in the house, apparently to prevent him from engaging with the Black population of Cartagena to locate witnesses. Martín's procurator complained to the courts that the imprisonment of Martín – with cuffs (*grillos*) chained to his feet – rendered the litigator unable to show the procurator his witnesses, and asked the court to order that Martín be permitted to freely conduct his business for his litigation. However, it was not until July 28, 1614, three weeks after the initial petition, that the court ordered for Martín to be forcibly removed from Bautista Pérez and placed in protective custody.

The reprise from the violence was short lived, though. Bautista Pérez's rebuttal led the court to order that Martín be returned to his owner three days later. Bautista Pérez attested that the whipping served as a punishment, not for Martín's litigation, but for Martín committing a robbery and disobeying his owner. He posited that Martín had stolen some corn from him on behalf of Agustin *Moreno*, who was known as the "captain of the Black people in Cartagena." By August 3, 1614, a month after legal proceedings had commenced, Gómez explained that Bautista Pérez had whipped Martín so harshly that the litigant was bedridden and could not leave the house. Martín therefore suffered severe physical violence in the month after he initiated litigation for his freedom. Considering the threat of violence and reprisals that participation in such a trial might entail, especially for those who were enslaved, and also for free Black city dwellers and those involved – even if only peripherally – in the slave trade (such as, for example, the free *mulato* trader Sebastián Barroso and the free *mulato* ship pilot Domingo Morrera), the testimonies that Martín's witnesses provided are striking, especially their reflections on what constituted a legitimate and an illegitimate enslavement.

---

[135] Ibid., fols. 7^v–16^r, and all further quotations in this and the next paragraph.

Francisco Martín's fate remains unclear; he disappears from the archival record after the May 1616 pronouncement in Real Audiencia of Santa Fé of his one-year-delayed liberty. Had he remained in Bautista Pérez's power for another year, there is little doubt that he would have been subjected to continued violence. He might also have found himself embarking on another voyage to Guinea, as Bautista Pérez left Cartagena for Portugal soon after the ruling – or perhaps earlier – to prepare for a second journey to Cacheu. In 1615, Bautista purchased 280 slave licenses at the House of Trade in Sevilla to prepare for his next slave-trading expedition to Guinea.[136] By November 25, 1616, Bautista – or someone whom he empowered – signed a contract with his uncle and mentor, Diogo Rodrigues, in Lisbon to specify upcoming slave purchases, goods to be sold in Cacheu, and shares of profits.

Over the next decade, Bautista Peréz became one of the wealthiest merchants in the Spanish Americas. After his second trip to Cacheu, he returned to Cartagena and thereafter established himself in Lima in 1619. While there, he organized yearly shipments of slaves from Cartagena. As Linda Newson and Susie Minchin describe, Bautista Pérez "traveled to Cartagena personally to acquire slaves [until 1623], but thereafter relied on agents who were based there, notably Sebastián Duarte," his brother in law.[137] During the 1620s and 1630s, Bautista "was shipping between 150 and 500 slaves a year from Cartagena to Peru."[138] Irene Silverblatt describes how Bautista Pérez dominated the slave trade by the 1630s, becoming one of the colony's wealthiest subjects and a powerful merchant in international commerce.[139] Toby Green has also uncovered that Bautista Pérez maintained familial ties in Cacheu while residing in Lima; he wrote letters to his daughter in Cacheu, who was born to a West African mother, and sent her money.[140] Bautista Pérez's downfall came at the height of his wealth and influence, when Inquisitors, who were investigating the lives of New Christian residents of Lima, focused their attention on one of the most prosperous of the Portuguese New Christian merchants in the city, Manuel Bautista Pérez. In 1635, the Inquisition of Lima arrested

---

[136] Newson and Minchin, *From Capture*, 16–22.
[137] Ibid.
[138] Ibid.
[139] Silverblatt, *Modern Inquisitions*, 29–54.
[140] Green, *A Fistful of Shells*, 51. For Bautista Peréz's brother (João Bautista Peréz), see Newson, "Africans and Luso-Africans."

him, accusing him of being the leader of a secret community of believers in the Jewish faith, and sentenced him to death in 1639.[141]

Martín's case is therefore an important reminder of the ambiguities of justice in this period. While he conversed with other enslaved and free Black people in Cacheu and Cartagena about Castilian laws of slavery and freedom, and was able to present a case for freedom in a royal court in Cartagena and successfully litigate against his illegitimate enslavement based on the illegality of enslaving Christians, winning the case in the first instance, as well as on appeal and again in the Real Audiencia of Santa Fé, he suffered severe violent reprisals for his litigation at the hands of his owner. Importantly, it remains unclear whether he ever lived as a free man after his successful litigation for freedom.

CONCLUSION

These freedom-for-litigation suits reveal how enslaved and free Black people discussed freedom and the laws concerning legitimate enslavement and privileges of liberty across the Atlantic in the sixteenth and early seventeenth centuries. These cases are exceptional as most enslaved people in the Spanish empire were unable to access royal or ecclesiastical courts for various reasons, including their geographical distance from a royal court or authority, the indifference of judges in local courts, corruption in judicial processes, threats of violence from their enslaver, a lack of interest from a court appointed procurator for the poor, a lack of Spanish language skills, and insufficient proof of their freedom, either in the form of paperwork or witness testimony. Yet these Black litigants' access to royal courts was the culmination of their participation in transoceanic relays of knowledge and information between Black communities and their accumulation of knowledge of the imperial realms that they were forced to inhabit, particularly the workings of the Spanish empire and the rule of law. This was a world in which individuals could gather witness testimonies in Santo Domingo in Isla Española regarding events that occurred on the other side of the Atlantic in Cabo Verde, or where witnesses at the Council of the Indies in Castilla could attest to events that took place in Honduras, or where a recently liberated Black woman in early sixteenth-century Cabo Verde could draw on a trusted network of traders operating between the archipelago near West Africa

---

[141] Silverblatt, *Modern Inquisitions*, 47–48; Schwartz, *Blood*.

and the Spanish Caribbean to send physical copies of her brother's freedom papers across the Atlantic to Puerto Rico in support of his struggle for liberation from illegitimate enslavement on that island.[142] This was also a world in which individuals who moved through urban metropolises and the trading entrepôts of the Spanish empire, such as Sevilla and Santo Domingo, gathered important knowledge about how to access royal justice and the array of legal arguments that enslaved Black people might deploy to pursue a case for freedom from illegitimate enslavement. Their lives reveal a world on the move in which knowledge and information about empire, access to justice, and legal strategies were constantly exchanged through word of mouth and epistles between Black populations, especially in the key trading entrepôts of the early Atlantic world.

These petitions for freedom from illegitimate enslavement reveal a fragmentary discourse and legal debates between the crown and enslaved subjects in the long sixteenth century on the question of the legitimacy of enslavement of Black people, the limits on how to define a legitimate or illegitimate enslavement, and the protections afforded to a legal status of liberty in Castilian law. These cases show that debates about the legitimacy and illegitimacy of slavery and the meanings of freedom in Black thought emerged among enslaved Black people in tandem with the earliest decades of the transatlantic trade. In this era, enslaved Black people shared ideas, knowledge, and debates about Castilian rules of law and legal customs in other polities in the Atlantic world, and this Black legal consciousness sometimes spurred enslaved people to litigate for their freedom on the basis that their enslavement was illegitimate.

---

[142] "Domingo Gelofe," AGI, Indiferente, 1205, no. 21; "Rodrigo López," AGI, Justicia, 11, no. 4; "Pedro de Carmona," AGI, Justicia, 978, no. 2, ramo 1.

6

Practicing Freedom

Documenting Capital

An important facet of the laws of slavery and freedom in the Spanish empire was that liberty granted a free person the right to own and accrue capital at their own discretion. Documenting one's actions as an economic actor therefore served as an important marker of freedom within a local community. Akin to Black *horros*' understanding of how freedom papers (*cartas de alhorría*) could protect their freedom, liberated and freeborn people understood that generating paperwork to record commercial transactions could protect and assure their liberty in the Spanish empire. For example, contracting the services of public notaries to document commercial transactions with other parties not only formalized agreements and protected economic interests, but also served to publicly display the exercising of the rights and privileges of freedom. Participating in such acts also ensured that those present could later be called on to testify about how they had witnessed a person use their liberty. As explored in Chapter 1, witnesses who testified about the liberty of free and liberated Black people in late sixteenth-century Sevilla often used phrases such as "because of the great trades/dealings that he had with her" to explain how they knew that a person was free. In addition, documentation of notarial *escrituras* in which a free person was recognized as someone who possessed liberty by their community might prevent a slave trader or enslaver from attempting to steal the free person's liberty and subjecting them to an illegitimate enslavement. Records of commercial transactions and property ownership therefore reveal the lives and ideas about freedom of people who may never have pressed for justice or grace in royal courts, but who practiced freedom by eking out a living in early modern economies.

This chapter explores how free Black women often documented their capital as a way of practicing and protecting their freedom. The analysis emerges in conversation with scholarship that has traced how free and liberated Black women in the principal towns of the Carrera de Indias in the late sixteenth and early seventeenth centuries (namely Sevilla, Cartagena de Indias, Nombre de Dios, Portobelo, Veracruz, and Havana) and in towns along the Caminos Reales (such as Jalapa and Puebla de los Ángeles in New Spain) and in the viceregal capitals (such as Lima and Mexico City) sometimes accumulated significant capital and invested resources to document their capital.[1] In particular, historian Terrazas Williams has traced how Afro-descended women of means in seventeenth-century Jalapa documented their capital and commercial transactions before public notaries in order to generate a trail of documents that assured their capital.[2] These pages study the life of Ana Gómez (see Chapter 2), a free Black woman who accumulated significant capital over the course of her lifetime and who documented her economic ties in order to practice and protect her freedom. The records relating to her life offer unique details about a free Black woman who occupied a position as a wealthy trader in late sixteenth-century Nombre de Dios. Gómez carefully documented her various economic ties across the Atlantic through paperwork, and astutely measured her trust and social capital with associates when determining whether to record a commercial transaction in writing or whether to rely on verbal agreements, which she usually only excercised for her credit lines to Black residents of Nombre de Dios and close trading associates. The records of her life reveal how free Black women invested significant resources to document their capital in order to assure and protect freedom.

ANA GÓMEZ: A LIFE BETWEEN ATLANTIC SITES

Ana Gómez was born sometime in the 1530s in a *condado* of the Duke of Medina Sidonia called Niebla, a small port town on the southwest Atlantic coast of Castilla along the Rio Tinto, east of the city of Huelva.[3] In the various documents and testimonies about Gómez's life, she was described interchangeably as *negra* or *morena*, but never as a *mulata*. In

---

[1] Graubart, "Los Lazos" and "The Bonds"; O'Toole, *Bound Lives* and "The Bonds of Kinship"; Silva Luna, "Fragile Fortunes"; Smith, "African-Descended Women"; Terrazas Williams, "My Conscience" and *The Capital of Free Women*; von Germeten, *Violent Delights*; Walker, *Exquisite Slaves*; Wheat, *Atlantic Africa* and "Catalina."
[2] Terrazas Williams, *The Capital of Free Women*.
[3] "Ana Gómez," AGI, Contratación 257A, no. 3, ramo 12.

her place of birth in Niebla, most dwellers in the mid sixteenth century were descended from enslaved Black West Africans as a result of local merchants' illicit slave-trading activities in Guinea in the late fifteenth and early sixteenth centuries.[4] In her early adulthood, Gómez moved from Niebla to Sevilla. In that city, she married Juan Pérez – but was subsequently widowed. This status likely gave her the independence to manage her own economic affairs. While residing in Sevilla, Gómez traded in clothing and precious stones. She also purchased four pairs of houses located in central neighborhoods: two houses in the San Gil parish on Calle Parras; two plots with four houses in the Magdalena parish; and two houses in the San Salvador parish on the corner of Calle Torneros (known today as Calle Álvarez Quintero) and the historic carpentry workshops (see Figure C.1.1, C1–3).[5] Gómez later estimated that she earned 1,500 *ducados* of annual income in rent from these properties.[6]

In the late 1570s, Gómez prepared to depart to the Spanish Americas. She sought a loan of 600 *ducats* from a well-known *converso* merchant of Sevilla named Juan de la Barrera to fund her journey to the Panama region in 1579.[7] She also conversed with a wealthy Sevilla noblewoman named Doña Mencia de Zuñiga about her plans to sail to the Caribbean, as Gómez traveled to the Indies with merchandise to sell on Zuñiga's behalf.[8] Gómez likely petitioned for a passenger license at the Council of the Indies and latterly for an embarkation license at the House of Trade in Sevilla, although I have not located either of these documents. There is also a possibility that in 1577 she traveled as a wage-earning servant with Juan Gutiérrez de la Sal, as a passenger list record matches her name, region of birth, and date of travel. It states "Ana Gómez, Black, *horra*, natural of Huelva, daughter of Amador de Cáceres and Francisca García, to Tierra Firme as the servant of Juan Gutiérrez de la Sal. – October 15."[9] Juan Gutiérrez de la Sal was traveling to the Panama region with his wife Elvira and their young child as he had been appointed to a minor administrative post in the area.[10]

---

[4] Izquierdo Labrado, "La esclavitud"; Cortés Alonso, "La población."
[5] "Ana Gómez," AGI, Contratación 257A, no. 3, ramo 12, fols. 89^r–116^r (Testamentos) fols. 116^v–126^r (and Inventario de Bienes en Tierra Firme).
[6] Ibid.
[7] Ibid.
[8] Ibid. It is possible that she is Doña Mencia de Zuniga, wife of Hernando de Guzman, in Franco Idígoras, *Catálogo*, 42, no. 52.
[9] "Ana Gómez," AGI, Contratación, 5538, libro I, fol. 57. Romera Iruela and Galbis Díez, *Catálogo de Pasajeros*, vol 5, book 2, no. 5120.
[10] "Real Cédula, Juan Gutiérrez de la Sal," AGI, Indiferente, 1969, libro 22, fols. 26^r-26^v; "Juan Gutiérrez de la Sal," AGI, Indiferente, 2089, no. 87.

Although Gómez had the means to pay for her own journey – as well as owning her houses, she was able to raise a substantial loan from a local merchant for the passage, and also took Zuñiga's merchandise – she may have embarked on the journey as a wage-earning servant to avoid having to petition for a passenger license at the Council of the Indies. In other words, she may have tapped into the emerging market in Sevilla for wage-earning servants and employers, who were able to travel on the passenger license of someone who had been granted a royal decree and permission to take a servant.[11] Gómez's assertion in her 1585 will that she owed a *converso* merchant in Sevilla money that she had borrowed to cross the ocean casts some doubt on whether she was the same person who traveled as a servant, or perhaps this suggests that she borrowed money for the journey but then found a passenger who charged her a fee in return for her claiming the position as servant in his retinue.

Gómez likely arrived in Nombre de Dios in the late autumn of 1579 on a ship in the fleet of Tierra Firme that would have departed from Sevilla in August of that same year. Late sixteenth-century Nombre de Dios was a town at the crossroads for trade and travel in the Spanish Atlantic. It served as the port at which ships involved in the most lucrative trade in the Spanish empire of the late sixteenth century were loaded: the silver violently extracted with forced Indigenous and Black labor from the mines in the mountainous peaks of the silver-boomtown of Potosí (in present-day Bolivia) that was transported to Castilla.[12] Testimonies in this period point to passengers sailing on small *fragatas* from other ports, such as Cartagena, to join the large fleet that set sail from Nombre de Dios.[13] After 1596, the fleet for Tierra Firme anchored at Portobelo instead of Nombre de Dios.[14] These two towns were bustling ports where merchants and colonial officials loaded silver transported overland from Potosí onto fleets destined for Castilla, and offloaded cargo brought from Castilla and West Africa and West-Central Africa that was destined for Peru, including enslaved Africans.[15] Treacherous navigation through mountainous regions and across inland rivers caused Spanish colonial officials to rely on Black

---

[11] For a discussion of emerging wage-earning servant market for Atlantic crossings, see Chapter 1, notes 64–66.
[12] Castillero Calvo, *Portobelo*; Díaz Ceballos, *Poder compartido*; Lane, *Potosí*.
[13] "Juan de Pineda," AGI, Indiferente, 2094, no. 1.
[14] García-Montón, "The Rise."
[15] Castillero Calvo, *Portobelo*; García-Montón, "Trans-Imperial"; Lane, *Potosí*; O'Toole, *Bound Lives*.

and Indigenous people's labor and knowledge of the terrain to ensure the safe transportation of precious cargos.

Despite the sizeable population of passersby and its importance as a principal port in the Carrera de Indias, Nombre de Dios had a small permanent population. A report about port fortifications, penned by the principal engineer for the Spanish crown named Bautista Antonelli in the mid 1580s, described Nombre de Dios as a small town of thirty *vecinos*, a large proportion of whom were foreigners. By 1596, the *oidor* (senior judge) of the Real Audiencia of Panamá estimated that Nombre de Dios had a population of over 600 men and many free Black and Indigenous people who resided in the town.

The history of the Panama isthmus in the sixteenth century was marked by the Spanish crown's lengthy wars against communities of fugitive enslaved Black people who had escaped their owners and established *palenques* in the hinterlands of the key port towns; the most notable of these were the Bayano Wars (1549–1556 and 1579–1582).[16] Black fugitives wielded significant power in the mountainous and inland river regions through which the trade routes passed, regularly disrupting caravels and looting precious cargo. With intimate knowledge of the interior of the Panama region and often at war with the Spanish empire in the late sixteenth century, Black *palenques* allied with foreign invaders in the 1570s and played a significant role in determining the political and interimperial landscape of the late sixteenth-century Caribbean, most famously aiding English privateer Francis Drake during his sacking of the isthmus in 1572–1573 by providing expert knowledge of interior routes and how to navigate the tough terrain.[17] After decades of wars, and because of the threat of their alliances with foreign enemies, Spanish officials in the Panama region eventually negotiated peace with specific Black communities in the late 1570s and 1580s. The crown negotiated for some *palenques* to form politically autonomous Black towns in strategic locations in return for their residents' loyalty to the Spanish crown and their undertaking to offer military protection of the isthmus from foreign incursions. One such town was Santiago del Principe, located about a league

---

[16] Select scholarship on maroonage in sixteenth-century Panama region: Díaz Ceballos, "Cimarronaje"; Hidalgo Pérez, *Una historia* and "Volviendo"; Kauffman, *Black Tudors*; Landers, "The African" and "Cimarrón"; Laviña et al., "La localización"; Obando Andrade, *De objeto*; Sánchez Jiménez, "Raza"; Schwaller, *African Maroons*, "Contested," and *The Spanish Conquest*; Tardieu, *Cimarrones*; Wheat, *Atlantic Africa*, 1–4.

[17] Kauffman, *Black Tudors*, Kindle Loc. 958–1514; Tardieu, *Cimarrones*.

away from Nombre de Dios. In the early 1580s, the governors of Nombre de Dios attempted to establish greater political control over Santiago del Principe, while the Black soldiers wished to govern themselves, and other enslaved Black Africans such as Antón *Zape* petitioned the crown for freedom and land because of their loyalty to the crown during the wars and subsequent negotiations to establish the Black town.[18]

Ana Gómez arrived in Nombre de Dios five years after Francis Drake's first devastating raid on the town in 1572. She joined a small Black community of permanent residents who had ties and memories that stretched across the Atlantic world. At least two other free Black women who resided in the town were also from Castilla. One was Francisca de Soria, from Ciudad Rodrigo in Castilla, who had settled in Nombre de Dios in 1566 and profited from the town's position as a busy port by developing a cooking business that served passing travelers.[19] This enabled Soria to accumulate some capital, and she and her husband purchased a house in Nombre de Dios. The couple saved enough to be able to cross the Atlantic as independent passengers with their two children for unspecified business matters in Sevilla in the late 1570s, and they subsequently returned to Nombre de Dios in 1577, around the same time that Gómez arrived in the port town. Witness testimonies in Sevilla reveal significant elements about Soria's reputation in Nombre de Dios as a free Black *vecina*. The couple gathered four witnesses in Sevilla to support their petition for a passenger license to return to Nombre de Dios.[20] Two witnesses hailed from Ciudad Rodrigo and remembered Soria's birth and early years in her native city. They testified to having known her since she was a child and also to seeing her depart to the Indies some years earlier. Ship pilots who labored on fleets that crisscrossed the Atlantic also testified to knowing both husband and wife from the times that they had passed through Nombre de Dios, agreeing that she "resided in the city of Nombre de Dios with her house and worked/traded (*trató*) providing food to the passengers and soldiers."[21] Francisco Sánchez, a *vecino* of Ciudad Rodrigo, commented on Soria's reputation in Nombre de Dios as a free woman,

---

[18] "Real Cédula," AGI, Panama, 237, libro 12, fol. 21ᵛ. On Antón Zape, petitioning for freedom and land, see "Carta," AGI, Panama, 13, ramo 22, no. 150; "Libertad de Antón Zape," AGI, Panama, 237, libro 12, fols. 12ᵛ–13ʳ; "Real Cedula licencia de armas a Antón Zape," AGI, Panama, 237, libro 12, fol. 23ʳ.

[19] "Francisca de Soria," AGI, Contratación, 5537, libro 2, fol. 204ᵛ; "Francisca de Soria," AGI, Contratación, 5537, libro 3, 475; "Alonso Bautista, Francisca de Soria," AGI, Indiferente, 2089, no. 39.

[20] "Alonso Bautista, Francisca de Soria," AGI, Indiferente, 2089, no. 39, fols. 2ʳ–8ᵛ.

[21] Ibid.

noting that he had heard about her life there from numerous people who had come from the port to Sevilla, agreeing that she "always lived peacefully and as a peaceful women [and] all loved her well (*todos la querían bien*)."[22] While living in Nombre de Dios, Gómez might also have interacted with the previously mentioned wealthy free Black woman named Sebastiana de la Sal (see Chapter 2), who had accumulated sufficient capital to send letters and funds to her *mulata* daughter in Sevilla, offering to pay for her to cross the Atlantic to Nombre de Dios, and who was well known to merchants based in Sevilla who passed through that town.[23] These three Black women – Francisca de Soria, Ana Gómez, and Sebastiana de la Sal – lived as propertied *vecinas* in late sixteenth-century Nombre de Dios, despite previous attempts by town-officials to bar free Black men and women from residing there, which largely seems to have been ignored by the crown.[24]

Gómez may also have known Black women who resided in the nearby towns of Portobelo and Panamá (the port town facing the Pacific, where the seat of royal governance for the region was located). Various free property-owning Black women from her generation who resided in these towns specialized as wage-earning servants in Atlantic crossings, and regularly traveled between Panamá, Portobelo, Nombre de Dios, and Sevilla.[25] Gómez may also have become acquainted in the latter part of her life with Lucía Tenorio Palma (see Chapter 2), who perished in Portobelo in 1615. Tenorio had been previously enslaved in Sevilla and later settled in Portobelo, where she accumulated some wealth and married an enslaved Black man named Cristóbal de la Palma, to whom she lent 500 pesos so that he could liberate himself from slavery. She also traded in jewels and purchased at least six Black slaves and the houses where they lived in Portobelo, as well as a *buhío* (wooden hut).[26] After Tenorio Palma perished, an auction of her property in 1615 fetched 2,168 pesos and 6 reales.[27]

---

[22] Ibid.
[23] "Luisa de Valladolid," AGI, Indiferente, 2097, no. 197.
[24] "Real Cédula," AGI, Panama, 236, libro 9, fol. 44^v. For the population of the city of Panamá, see also Aram et al., "Aproximaciones."
[25] "Angelina Díaz," AGI, Contratación, 5251B, no. 2, ramo 42; "Felipa Pérez," AGI, Indiferente, 2105, no. 32; "Felipa Pérez," AGI, Contratación, 5266, no. 1, ramo 59; "Dominga Díaz," AGI, Indiferente, 2100, no. 3; "Dominga Díaz de Cea," AGI, Contratación, 5245, no. 1, ramo 41; "Dominga Díaz de Sea," AGI, Contratación, 5538, libro 3, fol. 207^v; Galbis Díez, *Catálogo de Pasajeros*, vol. VII, 3254.
[26] "Lucia Tenorio Palma," AGI, Contratación 526, No. 1, ramo 1, doc. 8, fol. 60^r.
[27] "Lucía Tenorio Palma," 1621, AGI, Contratación 526, no. 1, ramo 1.

DOCUMENTING ECONOMIC TIES: PAPERWORK AND INFORMAL AGREEMENTS

Ana Gómez's two-decade residency between 1579 and 1596 in Nombre de Dios coincided with the apex of the town's position as the principal Atlantic port for the region. While there, Gómez continued to trade in precious stones, jewels, and clothes. By the mid 1590s – when an inventory of her property was made – she owned at least eight slaves; her other property included bars of gold, gemstones, jewelry, trunks of clothes, and some houses in Nombre de Dios.[28]

Gómez also continued to foster her commercial ties in Sevilla while living across the Atlantic. In the first six years that she resided in Nombre de Dios, Gómez sent Juan de la Barrera a pair of emeralds for him to sell in Sevilla because she could not sell them for more than 100 *ducados* in Nombre de Dios, which she explained, was well below their value.[29] She sent Barrera the jewels via a factor named Miguel Ramírez, who presumably ensured the delivery of such precious cargo by hand. Another time, Gómez sent Barrera money to pay a debt. In Sevilla, Barrera also acted as Gómez's factor during her absence from the city, for example, receiving payment of 20 *ducados* from one of her Sevilla-based debtors.[30] Further, Barrera also repaired one of Gómez's properties in Sevilla in repayment of a debt that he owed Gómez.[31] Gómez's ties in Sevilla were strong enough that even though she spent twenty years living in Nombre de Dios, she continued to own four pairs of houses in the Castilian city and earned an income through rents collected by Sevilla-based factors; she had appointed two residents of Sevilla to look after her properties during her absence.[32] In Nombre de Dios, Gómez thus maintained ties with her former commercial associates, friends, and family in Sevilla and nearby Huelva.[33]

Gómez was aware of the importance of paperwork to track her various commercial agreements, and she generated credit notes throughout her life, while also keeping copies of letters and the outcomes of any litigation. An inventory of her possessions in 1596 listed at least thirty-seven separate documents that registered her most important trading credits

---

[28] "Ana Gómez," AGI, Contratación 257A, no. 3, ramo 12, fols. 89ʳ–116ʳ, 116ᵛ–126ʳ.
[29] Ibid., fols. 89ʳ–116ʳ.
[30] Ibid.
[31] Ibid.
[32] Ibid.
[33] Ibid.

and debits, at least five letters that different associates in nearby trading entrepôts and Sevilla had sent to her, a draft account book that Gómez had "written in her own hand" listing her credits and debts, and copies of a legal dispute between Gómez and the *mayordomo* of the church in Nombre de Dios.[34] Among her papers were also three wills, which included a final will dated from 1585, a *memoria* dated from January 1596 in Portobelo, and a third *codicilio* that she wrote in February 1596 in Nombre de Dios. The 1585 will and testament had been signed before a public notary in Nombre de Dios and was "closed and sealed" with threads and seals; it contained folios of the will in one handwriting and "many annotations in different handwritings" in the margins of each folio.[35] Each of these three documents was signed by Gómez, showing that she was able to read and write. She kept these papers in a box under lock and key.

In addition to the trading activities documented across the paperwork, Gómez also maintained trading and credit relationships based on trust that she did not usually record in writing. Alonso López, who claimed to be Gómez's nephew, explained that "against some [debtors] she [Gómez] has *vales* and written agreements, against others she has no collection/security at all."[36] An example of her decisions to extend credit and agreements to some people without any paperwork is recorded in the details of her financial relationships with other free Black people in Nombre de Dios. For instance, after Gómez's death, a *morena libre* named Leonor de Méndez requested that her estate return Méndez's horse, while a free Black woman named Isabel Suárez claimed that Gómez had promised to leave 50 pesos to her daughter, Dominga.[37] Neither of these agreements is noted in Gómez's copious paperwork.

In Nombre de Dios, Gómez also developed kinship ties with two men and extended informal credit agreements to both. A *mulato* named Pedro López resided with her in Nombre de Dios, served as her close confidante, and later claimed to be her nephew. In her will dated in 1596, Gómez explained that "I order for Pedro López of *mulato* color to be paid 20 pesos," while in a later document she noted, "I declare that I owe Pedro López of *mulato* color 40 patacones of the 50 that he lent me and I order that these be paid from my estate."[38] The other man

[34] Ibid., fols. 116ᵛ–126ʳ.
[35] Ibid.
[36] Ibid., 43ᵛ–88ᵛ (Testimonio de Alonso López).
[37] Ibid., fols. 315ᵛ–340ʳ.
[38] Ibid., fols. 89ʳ–116ʳ.

was the aforementioned Alonso López, who may perhaps have been the same person as Pedro López as he also claimed to be Gómez's nephew, although the scribe interviewing him did not describe him as a *mulato* and used a different first name. In an interview after Gómez's death, Alonso López described how he would stay at Gómez's houses in Nombre de Dios when he passed through the town.[39] He also detailed how he knew that Gómez's trading activities stretched across the Atlantic and were recorded in her trade accounts, but that she also had various trading ties that she did not record as these were based on trust. Alonso cited an example of this. He described how Gómez often received merchandise brought by a ship captain from Sevilla, and that she sometimes received such merchandise on credit (*"entiende este testigo que le traen a la dicha Ana Gómez algunas mercaderías en confianza"*).[40] She had written to him when he was in Cartagena, asking him to collect this merchandise from the ship captain and take it from Cartagena to Nombre de Dios.[41]

Gómez therefore had a clear understanding of the importance of paperwork to assure and practice her freedom in the Spanish empire. However, like many traders, she also operated on trust among those whom she knew well. In particular, she extended credit agreements to Black dwellers of Nombre de Dios and charged two men who served as her confidants (and were possibly her nephews) with responsibility for some of her affairs, without documenting such agreements in formal paperwork.

BI-LOCAL CATHOLIC GEOGRAPHIES; ATLANTIC ENDOWMENTS

Ana Gómez's three wills composed between 1585 and 1596 reflected her transatlantic life and ties, and the significant trading and religious relationships that she maintained in Sevilla during her two-decade absence.[42] During the twenty years that she lived in Nombre de Dios, she saw herself living between two cities on either side of the Atlantic.[43] For example, writing from Nombre de Dios in 1585 – six years after leaving Castilla – Gómez made provisions in her testament for her

---

[39] Ibid., 43^v–88^v and 315^v–340^r (Testimonio de Alonso López).
[40] Ibid., fol. 335^v.
[41] Ibid.
[42] Ibid., fols. 89^r–116^r.
[43] Ibid.

burial service whether she happened to die in Nombre de Dios or in Sevilla, noting "And if I died in Spain in Sevilla they should bury me in the Magdalena Church of Sevilla."[44]

In Sevilla, Gómez had developed a long-lasting relationship with the Magdalena Church, so much so that four of her properties were located within the parish: one on the San Pablo street near the city door to Triana, another two bordered the physical walls of the Magdalena monastery, and another stood in close proximity on the same street (Figure C.1.1, C1–3). While living in Nombre de Dios, she continued to maintain contact with the Magdalena Church. An inventory of her papers in 1596 included a copy of a letter that she had written and sent "to Castilla to Antonio López, *Clerigo*."[45] Further, in her 1585 will, she specified that if she perished in Spain, she should be buried in the Magdalena Church in "the tomb (*sepultura*) that there was given to me" and that she be buried dressed in the "habit of San Francisco" in the presence of twelve children.[46] She also specified that she wished her executors to dress twelve poor people with shirts and shoes and linen doublets or bodices (*jubon*), and that they sing a mass on the day of San Andrés in the church where she would be buried.[47] Gómez also arranged to establish a perpetual *capellanía* in the Magdalena Church to hold masses on her behalf and pray for the salvation of her soul – a costly enterprise for which she set aside 2,600 ducats of Castilian gold, as well as permitting the church to receive rental income in posterity from the properties that she owned in Sevilla.

That same 1585 testament highlights how Gómez participated in visions of Catholicism particular to the Castilian geopolitical landscape despite her long absence from Castille. She organized to send money to a dozen churches and four hospitals across Sevilla and to her native village of Niebla in Huelva, where she wished to endow two hospitals, and to the church in Nombre de Dios. Gómez also set money aside to pay for the ransoms of young boys aged between six and twelve who had been captured by North African pirates from her native Niebla.[48] In doing so, she participated in a particular mid sixteenth-century Castilian tradition, reflecting societal panic – to fund missions sponsored by the Mercedarian

---

[44] Ibid., fol. 97ʳ.
[45] Ibid., fols. 116ᵛ–126ʳ.
[46] Ibid., fols. 89ʳ–116ʳ.
[47] Ibid.
[48] Ibid.

Order (a Christian order established in 1218 for the redemption of Christian captives) to pay ransoms for captured Christians languishing in North Africa, fears that were also particularly prominent in theaters in cities such as Sevilla during her residency there.[49] Gómez's endowment to the Mercedarian Order highlights that she remained embedded in Castilian Catholic geopolitical concerns, and specifically in the localized relationship of such concerns with her hometown of Niebla, even from across the Atlantic when she was residing in Nombre de Dios.[50]

SIR FRANCIS DRAKE AND ANA GÓMEZ: GÓMEZ AS A SLAVE-OWNER

Gómez's fate became entangled in the interimperial wars of the late sixteenth century, in particular the final voyage of the English corsairs Francis Drake and Richard Hawkins, who attacked Nombre de Dios in 1596. Her experience of the events highlights her Black kinship ties within the town, commercial relationships with and obligations to the nearby town of Black soldiers, her reputation within the port where she dwelled, and, importantly, the lives and experiences of the eight Black men and women who were enslaved to her. Records of these events catalog the strategies that her slaves adopted in order to obtain their freedom after she perished and highlight their understanding of the importance of her paperwork. Their testimonies show that they were loyal to their owner and protected her treasured papers during a time of great insecurity and danger – the second sacking of Nombre de Dios by Francis Drake in 1596 – in order to argue for their freedom after her death.

The particularly devastating attack on Nombre de Dios in early January 1596 spelled the downfall of the town as a major port for the region.[51] Local officials were aware that the port was vulnerable to attacks owing to a weak harbor and previous English incursions in the town. Bautista Antonelli's report on the Panama region – which by the mid 1590s had fallen into the hands of the English collector and editor of narratives of voyages, Richard Hakluyt (1552–1616) and had been translated into English – detailed the terrible environmental conditions that rendered the Nombre de Dios harbor difficult for shipping: "it is a very bad harbour,

---

[49] For example, see Stackhouse, "Beyond Performance."
[50] "Ana Gómez," AGI, Contratación 257A, no. 3, ramo 12, fols. 89^r–116^r.
[51] "Carta de Miguel Ruíz de Elduayen," AGI, Panama, 44, no. 22, fols. 106^v–110^v. Except for note 68, I henceforth cite the 1972 English translation of this source: "32. Report by Miguel Ruiz Delduayen" in Andrews, *The Last Voyage*, Kindle Loc. 4948–5231.

neither is there any good water: and it is subject to Northerly winds and Easterly windes, which continually doe blow upon this coast."[52] Such conditions tested many ship captains when docking there:

> many of the great ships which doe come to this place doe unlade halfe their commodities betweene the two ledges of rockes, for that there is but little water in the harbor; and after that a ship hath unladen halfe of her goods, then shee goeth to the second rocke, as it doth appear by the platforme, but the small ships come neere unto another rocke on the West side.[53]

Stormy weather was a serious threat. As Antonelli explained:

> if the winde chance to come to the North and Northwest, and that it overblowe, then such great ships as then be in the roade must of force more themselves with sixe cables a head, especially in a storme, and yet nevertheless sometimes they are driven ashore and so cast away, and all because they dare not vier cable ynough, because of so many shelves and rockes which are in both those places.[54]

This problematic harbor rendered the town prone to attacks from foreign enemies.[55]

Drake and Hawkins had embarked on a pillaging voyage to the Spanish Indies in 1595 at the helm of twenty-seven ships and 2,500 men. Reportedly, Drake determined to take Panama or die in the attempt.[56] After sacking the city of Cádiz in Castilla, their fleet sailed to the Caribbean and attacked Cartagena and Santa Marta in the winter of 1595, taking some residents captive.[57] Manso de Contreras, the governor of Santa Marta, detailed how Drake captured "100 Negroes and Negresses from the pearl station [in Rio de la Hacha], who for the most part joined him voluntarily, and some citizens and other prisoners."[58] Contreras also reported that he had successfully delayed Drake in Santa Marta by frustrating negotiations about ransom payments so that he

---

[52] "Antonelli's report," in Andrews, *The Last Voyage*, Kindle Loc. 4827–4858.
[53] Ibid.
[54] Ibid.
[55] "30. Manso de Contreras to the king, January 15, 1596," in Andrews, *The Last Voyage*, Kindle Loc. 4706–4848.
[56] "37. Report on the return of the English to Porto Belo and subsequent events," Testimony of Gregorio Mendes, in Andrews, *The Last Voyage*, Kindle Loc. 5466–5510.
[57] "Carta de D. Francisco Manso de Contreras, Gobernador de Santa Marta," AGI, Santa Fe, 49, ramo 17, no. 120; "32. Report by Miguel Ruíz Delduayen" in Andrews, *The Last Voyage*, Kindle Loc. 4948–5231; "Cartas de Gobernadores," AGI, Santa Fe 49, ramo 17, no. 120.
[58] "30. Manso de Contreras to the king, January 15, 1596," in Andrews, *The Last Voyage*, Kindle Loc. 4706–4848.

could determine the scale of the English fleets and buy time to send news to Cartagena and Panama. As a result, in December 1595, officials in Nombre de Dios received word that Drake's and Hawkins' ships were sailing towards the port.[59]

After the news of impending English fleets reached the town, residents proceeded to retreat to the hinterlands. Free Black *vecina* Ana Gómez, who by then was sixty years old and had lived in Nombre de Dios for two decades, made provisions for her slaves, servants, and trusted confidants to hide her extensive property in a *buhio* that she had built in the countryside, and she retired to the hinterlands – as did most other residents of the town. Indeed, Gómez's slaves later provided testimonies describing how they had retreated to the hinterlands with her property.[60] One of her slaves, Gaspar *de tierra Bañol*, who was described as a Christian *ladino* (the term *ladino* usually meant individuals who grew up in Spanish-speaking regions and spoke Spanish fluently), explained that he received news that his owner had built a *buhio* in the mountains and that he and another slave named Juseph *Bran* had buried some of Gómez's boxes and other property near it.[61] Another of Gómez's slaves – an elderly *ladino* Christian named Juan *Jolofo* – later testified that Gómez had asked him to watch over her *buhio*.[62]

Arriving in late December 1595 to find a deserted town devoid of any treasures, for all *vecinos* had retreated to the hinterlands, Drake's and Hawkins' armies sacked Nombre de Dios. John Troughton described how "we sett saile for Nombre de Dios, to which we came the xxvijth daie, wher in like manner the people had acquitted the Towne."[63] Although the town was abandoned, they reported receiving help – or intelligence – from some Black people as to the location of "Sowes of silver, golde in Bullion, some Jwells, great store of plate and ryalls of plate, with much other Lugage."[64] Spanish officials described how the English were guided by a *mulato* cowherd whom they had reportedly brought with them.[65] In addition to sacking the town, the English destroyed a

---

[59] "32. Report by Miguel Ruíz Delduayen" in Andrews, *The Last Voyage*, Kindle Loc. 4948–5231.
[60] "Ana Gómez," AGI, Contratación, 257A, no. 3, ramo 12, fols. 43ᵛ–88ᵛ.
[61] Ibid.
[62] Ibid.
[63] "19. John Troughton's journal," in Andrews, *The Last Voyage*, Kindle Loc. 3102–3107.
[64] Ibid.
[65] "a *mulato* cowherd," in "32. Report by Miguel Ruíz Delduayen," in Andrews, *The Last Voyage*, Kindle Loc. 4948–5231.

pearl factory on the outskirts, stealing some of the enslaved Black people who labored there.

During the raid, the English captured residents of Nombre de Dios, adding to their coterie of *vecinos* who had been imprisoned aboard their ships since their previous attack on Santa Marta. Their hope was to ransom the *vecinos* back to the Spanish crown. Gómez's slave, Juseph *Bran*, who was keeping a watchful eye on her *buhio*, testified that he escaped when the English arrived, but had witnessed English soldiers entering the hut and stealing most of Gómez's belongings.[66] Gaspar, another of Gómez's slaves, described how the English came to the village and found the *buhio*; they also captured Gómez and stole her clothes and property, leaving only four boxes.[67] These testimonies match the descriptions of events by Spanish military commanders. Miguel Ruíz de Elduayen explained in a letter to the crown that an architect named Alberto Ojada had left with the English, taking with him a friend named Ana Gómez. He detailed that "they took some Black *horras*, especially Ana Gomes the rich trader," and Ojada "went away with the English and dined with Drake and was very friendly with him; and he took Ana Gómez with him."[68]

Although concerns that free Black *vecinos* might aid foreign enemies are frequently aired in correspondence between the Real Audiencia of Panamá and the crown in this period, and even though officials seemed unclear about whether Ana Gómez had left voluntarily with the English, there is no indication that they were concerned that Gómez had been disloyal. The testimonies of her slaves also specified that Gómez had been captured.[69] Some stated that they witnessed the English taking her, while others explained that they received news of her capture later, once she regained her liberty in Portobelo. The English captains seemed

---

[66] "Ana Gómez," AGI, Contratación, 257A, no. 3, ramo 12, fols. 55^r–58^v.
[67] Ibid., fols. 43^v–88^v.
[68] Ibid.; "Carta de Miguel Ruíz de Elduayen," AGI, Panama, 44, no. 22, fol. 107^v. My transcription of the letter is as follows:

> Tomaron algunas negras horras expecial Ana Gomes tratante rrica y algunos españoles pobres que algunos solto y otros se fueron y entre ellos Juan Ojeda arquitecto que tuvo a su cargo la obra de la fuerza de San Juan de Ulúa que se fue con el ingles y comía con Wag(*sic*) y era muy su amigo y tambien llevaron consigo a Ana Gomes.

See also "32. Report by Miguel Ruiz Delduayen," in Andrews, *The Last Voyage*, Kindle Loc. 4948–5231; Guasco, *Slaves and Englishmen*, 297.
[69] "Ana Gómez," AGI, Contratación, 257A, no. 3, ramo 12, fols. 43^v–88^v.

to recognize Gómez as a property-owning Black *vecina*, as Drake and Hawkins grouped her with other Spanish *vecinos* whom they attempted to ransom to Spanish officials in Nombre de Dios, rather than with the Black slaves whom they had also captured (some of whom belonged to Gómez).

For his part, Drake may have hoped that Gómez would be loyal to the English rather than the Spanish. An enslaved Black man from Nombre de Dios named Diego had aided Drake in his raid fifteen years earlier and had helped the English commander to form an alliance with Black *palenques* in the region.[70] Of course, by the 1590s, very few Black people were interested in helping the English. Black residents of the town of Santiago del Principe, who had professed loyalty to the Spanish crown in return for their freedom and autonomy, fought a fierce battle against the English in the 1596 raid, and killed numerous English commanders. If Drake did envision Gómez playing such a role, he chose an unlikely collaborator, for she was a well-established *vecina* who had much to lose from an English attack. In any case, Spanish commanders in Nombre de Dios refused to pay the ransoms that Drake demanded for the captive *vecinos*. In retribution, his armies sacked and burned the town before departing. Diego Mendes Torres, a *vecino* of Panama who served as a captain in Nombre de Dios at the time of the attack, reported:

> on the afternoon of Wednesday the 10th the enemy began to set fire to the city of Nombre de Dios and the next day in the afternoon he resumed and burned it all. On the same day, Thursday, they all withdrew to the launches, taking with them all those of our people who had fallen into their hands, whites as well as Blacks.[71]

Testimonies by Ana Gómez's slaves about this episode provide an unprecedented view into Gómez's position as a slave-owner and the views and experiences of her slaves. The records of these events also catalog the strategies employed by the enslaved people – whom she owned – to obtain their freedom after she perished and their understanding of the importance of her paperwork. Their testimonies highlight how they deployed the notion of loyalty to their owner and their protection of her treasured papers to argue for their freedom after her death. In Gómez's absence, four of her slaves attempted to secure her remaining property.[72] Gaspar of *tierra Bañol* described how another of Gómez's slaves, Lucía *Cocoli*,

---

[70] Kauffman, *Black Tudors*, Kindle Loc. 958–1514; Tardieu, *Cimarrones*.
[71] "32. Report by Miguel Ruíz Delduayen," in Andrews, *The Last Voyage*, Kindle Loc. 5226.
[72] "Ana Gómez," AGI, Contratación, 257A, no. 3, ramo 12, fols. 43ᵛ–88ᵛ.

took some of Gómez's property, including her surviving papers, to a house nestled in the mountains on the route to Panamá owned by Antón Castilla Arras, where the English would not find them.[73] Apparently, Lucía told Gaspar that she had abandoned the box of papers as she was afraid that the English would capture her.[74] Gaspar reported how he had subsequently traveled to the location and found the abandoned box, broken the lock, and retrieved the papers, then walked the route from Nombre de Dios to Panamá to the house where Lucía and Ana Gómez's remaining slaves were hiding.[75] He described how upon arriving in the house, he told Lucía that she must look after the papers and ensure that no one remove them from her possession.[76] When he eventually returned to Gómez's *buhio*, Gaspar discovered that the English had stolen everything, while some of Gómez's other slaves informed him that the English had burned Gómez's houses in Nombre de Dios.[77] These testimonies reveal that Gómez's slaves attempted to protect her property and understood the value of her paperwork.

In late January 1596, the English ships arrived in Portobelo, largely depleted of men and energy following various skirmishes and naval battles with Castilian armies in the islands between Nombre de Dios and Portobelo.[78] In a subsequent report, the Real Audiencia of Panamá explained that Spanish officials had not seen or heard of the English ships for twenty-four days since they left Nombre de Dios.[79] Drake perished in the bay of Portobelo, while infighting and mistrust of the commanders marred the surviving crew. As Thomas Maynarde described, "Our generalls beinge dead most mens hartes were bent to hasten for England, as soone as they might."[80] On the Spanish side, Ruíz de Elduayden described how "On the night of the twelfth the two soldiers, Pedro Cano and Tomé, who had been sent to Porto Belo, returned and reported that the enemy fleet was at anchor. There were twenty-one ships, but few launches or men were to be seen."[81]

---

[73] Ibid.
[74] Ibid.
[75] Ibid.
[76] Ibid.
[77] Ibid.
[78] "19. John Troughton's journal," in Andrews, *The Last Voyage*, Kindle Loc. 3114: "the xxviijth daie we came in with Porta la Bella."
[79] "Carta del oidor licenciado Salazar," AGI, Panama, 14, ramo 12, no. 68.
[80] "18. Thomas Maynarde's narrative, Sir Francis Drake his voyage 1595," in Andrews, *The Last Voyage*, Kindle Loc. 2801.
[81] "37. Report on the return of the English to Porto Belo and subsequent events," in Andrews, *The Last Voyage*, Kindle Loc. 5492.

Anchored at Portobelo, the English tried to ransom their captive Spanish *vecinos* from Santa Marta and Nombre de Dios one final time.[82] Ruíz de Elduayden explained that "there came another message from Captain Diego Mendes Torres at Nombre de Dios, reporting the arrival there of a man, apparently a mariner, bringing certain letters from Spanish prisoners in the English fleet and a safe-conduct from the general thereof to bring them to Panama."[83] He reported that the messenger was named "Gregorio Mendes, a Portuguese, and he had orders and authority to negotiate the ransom of Don Francisco Flores for 4,000 ducats, of two regidores of Río de la Hacha and Santa Marta for other sums, and of Ana Gómez, a free Negro of Nombre de Dios, for 2,000 ducats."[84] Mendes also informed his Spanish interlocutors that Drake had perished in the bay of Portobelo and described the alarming death rate among the remaining English crew.[85] Sensing the desperation among the English, Spanish officials refused to pay the ransoms for the captured *vecinos*. This failed attempt to ransom Gómez, first in Nombre de Dios and then in Portobelo, suggests that the English commanders also differentiated between her status as a free and propertied *vecina* and the Black slaves whom they captured and subsequently took to England.

Gómez's slave, Gaspar, recalled how news spread in Nombre de Dios that the English armada had arrived in Portobelo and had abandoned his owner in the bay of that port.[86] Indeed, upon failing to ransom their captives, the English abandoned the Spanish *vecinos* on the shores near Portobelo in late January 1596, and hastily made their way back to England, taking their captured Black slaves with them. A Spanish general reported that he rode towards Portobelo and

> arrived about nine in the morning [of Sunday the 18th], and on the way he received news that the enemy had put ashore all the Spaniards he had captured at Rio de la Hacha and in this kingdom, including Alberto de Ojeda, except two or three from Río de la Hacha who were to be ransomed and a number of Negroes and Negresses; and that he had set sail that very Sunday morning and was sailing away from the port, though still in sight of it.[87]

Ana Gómez was one of the captives whom the English abandoned.

---

[82] Ibid., Kindle Loc. 5492–5503.
[83] "32. Report by Miguel Ruíz Delduayen" in Andrews, *The Last Voyage*, Kindle Loc. 5495.
[84] Ibid.
[85] Ibid.
[86] Ibid., "Ana Gómez," fols. 43ᵛ–88ᵛ.
[87] "37. Report on the return of the English to Porto Belo and subsequent events," in Andrews, *The Last Voyage*, Kindle Loc. 5528.

Upon arriving in Portobelo, after surviving the ordeal onboard ship, Gómez had become very ill as a result of her captivity and knew that she would soon perish. She penned and sent a letter to her close confidant and nephew, Pedro López, in Nombre de Dios.[88] She explained her predicament and her great desire to die in Nombre de Dios, asking López to find twelve willing Black soldiers from the Black village of Santiago del Príncipe who would collect her from Portobelo and help her to return to Nombre de Dios for the sum of 100 *ducados*.[89]

Gómez was likely unaware that the Black soldiers of Santiago del Principe had also sustained heavy losses during Drake's and Hawkins' incursion in Nombre de Dios, and that many of them had played key defense roles in protecting the town and the Spanish crown. In a report to the crown, Ruíz de Elduayen later commended these soldiers, noting "that the Negroes of Santiago del Principe would not allow the enemy to take water at the river Fator and killed some of them, including a captain of some importance, whom they buried with lowered flags."[90] They had reportedly burned their own village to prevent the English from advancing, with Ruíz de Elduayden explaining that "the enemy sent ten manned launches against them and that the Negroes, who until then had stayed in their village, which is less than half a league from Nombre de Dios, now set fire to their huts and withdrew to the bush, from which they killed a number of Englishmen, about twenty-five altogether."[91] He commended their efforts, stating that "The subjugated Negroes of both factions at Santiago del Principe and Santa Cruz la Real have rallied to his majesty's service with loyalty, hard work and energy, and the freed Negroes came to serve in this war under the banner of their captain Juan de Rosales who is also one of them."[92] Further, he described that "more loyalty was found among the slaves than was expected, for it was their disloyalty which was feared here and which the enemy counted upon: he relied upon it to bring him quick success."[93]

After receiving the letter that Gómez had dispatched to Nombre de Dios, Pedro López arrived in Santiago del Principe to search for twelve

---

[88] "Ana Gómez," AGI, Contratación, 257A, no. 3, ramo 12, fols. 43ᵛ–88ᵛ.
[89] Ibid.
[90] "32. Report by Miguel Ruíz Delduayen" in Andrews, *The Last Voyage*, Kindle Loc. 5134.
[91] Ibid.
[92] Ibid.
[93] Ibid.

Black soldiers who would accompany him to Portobelo. Because of the damage sustained by the village, he had to make great efforts to do so. Lacking liquid capital to pay the soldiers, López offered to pawn one of Gómez's slaves, a Black woman named Juana.[94] Vicente Rodrigues, a *moreno horro vecino* of Santiago del Principe, later described how the *mulato* Pedro López had arrived with a Black slave who would serve as temporary payment for the work.[95] He further reported meager appetite for the task among the remaining Black soldiers of the village; they were unwilling to do it unless they were paid for their services upfront.[96] Eventually, after López had made various inquiries, including to the governor of the village, twelve Black soldiers agreed to accompany him to Portobelo to collect Gómez with a payment agreement in place and Juana left as a bond.[97] Another of Gómez's slaves, Gaspar *de tierra Bran*, testified to traveling to Portobelo with Pedro López and the Black soldiers.[98]

Meanwhile, in Portobelo, Gómez composed an addendum to her will.[99] In a few short pages, she made provisions to liberate two of her slaves, Dominga and Ysavellilla, *mulata*, who were the daughters of her slaves Lucía and Catalina *Bran*. She also listed the seven other slaves she owned, "Lucía *Cocoli*, and Juana *de tierra Bañol*, and Jussepe *Bran*, and Catalina *Bran*, and Juan *Jolofo*, and Juana *Biafara*, and Gasparillo *Bañon*," in addition to enumerating her silver, pearls, emeralds, crucifixes of silver and pearls, and a few outstanding debts.[100] She also named a new executor and arranged to send 100 *ducados* to Sevilla to the daughter of an associate named Juan Rivera, and noted the money that she owed Pedro López for collecting her from Portobelo on her deathbed.

With the help of López and the Black soldiers, Gómez arrived in Nombre de Dios in early February 1596. There, she surveyed her staggering losses and made a third addendum to her will.[101] Adjusting how much she owed López, she calculated the value of her property after the losses: approximately 7,000 pesos in gold. Juan *Jolofe* later testified that although the English had captured many of Gómez's slaves, eight remained: Lucía *Cocoli*, Juana *Biafara* (who was pawned in Santiago del

---

[94] "Ana Gómez," AGI, Contratación, 257A, no. 3, ramo 12, fols. 43^v–88^v.
[95] Ibid., fols. 192^r–202^v.
[96] Ibid.
[97] Ibid.
[98] Ibid., fols. 43^v–88^v.
[99] Ibid., fols. 89^r–116^r.
[100] Ibid.
[101] Ibid.

Principe to the Black soldiers for 100 pesos), Gaspar *Bran*, Juseppe *Bran*, Juana Viga *Casaga* (likely *Casanga*), and the witness himself, although Juan noted that Gómez kept him as a "free slave," two other young slaves, Dominga and Isabel, who Gómez had freed in her last testament, written in Portobelo.[102]

Ana Gómez's desire to return from Portobelo to Nombre de Dios before her death reveals her life as an Atlantic trader and her ties with Black residents of the port and nearby towns. Her ties to Pedro Lopez, her slaves, and her commercial transaction with the Black soldiers from the village of Santiago del Principe all indicate that she was also embedded among diverse Black communities in the region.

Gómez perished a few days after arriving in Nombre de Dios, in February 1596. After her death, Simon de Torres, the judge who was tasked to administer the probate for her estate and who had been dispatched to Nombre de Dios from Panamá, treated her property as he would that of any other property-owning *vecina* and *natural* of Castilla, attending to her credits and debts, and to executing her will.[103] Because a great proportion of Gómez's property in Nombre de Dios had been destroyed in the English attack, she was etched into the historical archive at the moment of her greatest poverty. On her deathbed, she owned eight enslaved Black people, some houses in Nombre de Dios, bars of gold, jewelry, trunks of fine clothes, and four pairs of houses on the other side of the Atlantic in the city of Sevilla.[104] For their part, the Black soldiers of Santiago del Principe successfully petitioned the judge for the 100 pesos that Gómez owed them for collecting her from Portobelo.[105]

To determine the extent of Gómez's property and the events that had transpired, Torres interviewed her slaves, describing most as "very *ladino* Christian," although at least one was not interviewed for being "very *bozal*," a description that implies he did not speak Spanish.[106] These testimonies reveal their strategy to position themselves as loyal to their owner and as taking heroic actions and risks during the attack on Nombre de Dios, possibly with the aim of making a later claim to freedom owing to their loyalty and bravery. Certainly, they would have been aware of discussions among other enslaved people in the town about

[102] Ibid., fols. 43^v–88^v.
[103] Ibid., fols. 366^r–367^v.
[104] Ibid.
[105] Ibid., fols. 192^r–202^v.
[106] Ibid., fols. 43^v–88^v.

the possibility of petitioning the crown for freedom based on these reasons.[107] For example, Pedro *Zape Yalonga* would go on to successfully petition the crown for freedom from slavery following his loyalty to the Spanish crown during this episode.[108] Gómez's slaves provided detailed testimony of their labors to protect their owner's property and to defend Nombre de Dios during a time of great insecurity. These testimonies suggest that she had trusted relationships with at least some of her slaves, and, like many urban slave-owners, permitted them to operate semiautonomously. While none of these enslaved people made an explicit claim for their freedom during these interviews, Juan *Jolofe* positioned himself as a "free slave" who was treated by Ana Gómez as a free person.

After sifting through Gómez's various commercial obligations, establishing a timeline of events leading to her death, and ascertaining the contents of her three wills dating from 1585, January 1596, and February 1596, Simon de Torres ordered a public auction of her remaining property in Nombre de Dios. A Black *criollo* crier named Francisco auctioned her belongings, including her remaining slaves.[109] The auction took weeks to complete. Nombre de Dios residents were reeling from their losses and rebuilding the town and their houses: No one seemed interested in purchasing Gómez's slaves and other property. The crier sent detailed reports of the many days that he spent marching a couple of the slaves around every street and public square of the town, announcing the forthcoming sales. Even members of a passing ship crew who sojourned in Nombre de Dios did not seem interested. After various auctions, Francisco eventually sold half of Gómez's slaves at well below their expected value. As explored in Chapter 3, public auctions could become spaces in which enslaved people could negotiate the terms of their purchase with prospective buyers. While any such ephemeral conversations in this instance are lost to the historical record, it is possible that Gómez's slaves spoke with potential buyers during the long days of auctions. In particular, Juan *Jolofo* may have told potential buyers about his self-perception as a free person. Simon de Torres eventually took Gómez's remaining three slaves to Panama, including one whom he described as "an elderly and ill Black man of eighty years old named Juan *Jolofo* who says that he is free."

---

[107] See note 104.
[108] "Pedro Zape Yalonga," AGI, Panama, 44, no. 56⁽²⁾. See also Pedro Yalonga, in Wheat, *Atlantic Africa*, 1–4.
[109] "Ana Gómez," AGI, Contratación, 257A, no. 3, ramo 12, fols. 152ᵛ–170ᵛ.

In Sevilla, word spread quickly among residents about Gómez's death in Nombre de Dios and news of the value of her estate arriving in Castilla. In 1599, Simón Torres had sent the value that he had managed to collect of Gómez's estate, which amounted to 694 pesos, along with extensive paperwork detailing his investigations into her assets, copies of her three wills, and an inventory of her papers on the *galeón* of Nuestra Señora del Rosario. In Sevilla, Gómez's cousins named Ana and Leonor de Pineda heard news that around 694 pesos of Gómez's estate had arrived on the *galeón*. They also heard that Gómez had perished intestate. They petitioned the House of Trade to inherit the estate on the basis that they were Gómez's cousins and that she had no other heirs for she was widowed. At this stage, they seemed unaware that Gómez had made a will. In fact, Gómez listed a woman named Leonor de Pineda as her daughter in her 1585 will.[110] However, Gómez's 1585 will also described her great desire to found a perpetual *capellanía* in the Magdalena Church to hold masses on her behalf and pray for the salvation of her soul. Gómez had set aside an ambitious 2,600 ducats of Castilian gold (this is likely to be *moneda de oro* (*escudo*), worth approximately 32,890 *maravadíes*) and the rental incomes from her four pairs of houses in Sevilla.[111] The 694 pesos that comprised Gómez's estate fell well below her intended endowment of 2,600 ducats of Castilian gold. As a result, the Magdalena Church petitioned the House of Trade for permission to sell Gómez's property in Sevilla and use the proceeds to establish the perpetual *capellanía*. The sale of these houses raised 31,000 *maravadíes* (see Chapter 2), and the Magdalena Church used the proceeds to establish the *capellanía* in Gómez's name. In subsequent correspondence about the accounts for the *capellanía* between administrators of the Madgalena Church and the Archbishop's Palace over the next two centuries, the *capellanía* was described as belonging to "Ana Gómez, *la morena*."[112]

CONCLUSION

Gómez's detailed imprint in the historical archive provides some of the clearest details to date of how free Black women understood and

---

[110] Ibid., fols. 2ʳ–2ᵛ.
[111] "Ana Gómez." AGI, Contratación 257A, no. 3, ramo 12, 89ʳ–116ʳ. I have calculated the approximate values of these sums with Muñoz Serrulla, *La Moneda*, xxix, Table 6.
[112] "Libro de Capellanías de Santa María de Magdalena," AGAS, sección 2, Libros del Capellanías 2043, no. 5, leg. 03448, fol. 236.

participated in cultures of paperwork to practice and protect their freedom in the late sixteenth-century Atlantic world, and is a rare insight into the life of a Black woman who documented financial transactions in her own account books. The three wills that Gómez composed over a twenty-year period and her astute choices in documenting her credits and debts reveal her maneuverings as an economic actor in the early modern period, and the significance of her relationships with other Black women of Nombre de Dios with whom she did not use paperwork to record transactions, instead relying on trust and her word for agreements. Her astute use of paperwork shows how she envisioned her freedom in expansive terms, as a free subject of the Spanish crown who could and did engage in trade and accumulation of property, and was fully aware of the significance of the act of generating and archiving paperwork and building community ties for evidentiary thresholds when attempting to seek justice in the Spanish empire. Gómez may never have petitioned in a royal court to defend or expand the political meanings of freedom, and yet she shaped the meanings of Black freedom in the sites where she resided and among those with whom she interacted, including Spanish royal officials, through her daily practice of engaging in cultures of paperwork. Ana Gómez made astute choices throughout her life to document her capital to practice and protect her freedom.

Coda

Felipa de la Cruz's World and Letters

This study has traced how numerous enslaved and free Black people kept in touch with associates, friends, and kin from afar, through word of mouth and letter writing, and the myriad ways that they shared ideas and knowledge about freedom and slavery. Such conversations shaped ideas and epistemologies about slavery and freedom in the Spanish empire, whether from the perspective of political discourse of how individuals and communities pressed for expansive views of political belonging and Black freedom or through economic prisms of daily practices of freedom, or through legal maneuverings for royal justice through different legal jurisdictions. Conversations and exchanges about freedom between Black people in the Spanish Atlantic and the bourgeoning Black public spheres that they created in particular sites and across the Spanish empire shaped the meanings of slavery and freedom in this period.

Although the existence of such Black public spheres where slavery and freedom were debated and contested are apparent throughout this book, as enslaved people sought credit from lenders to purchase their freedom, or discussed the meanings and laws of slavery to develop a legal strategy for their litigation for freedom, there are scant archival documents that catalog the contents of these ephemeral conversations. The existence of this communication appears haphazardly across carefully crafted witness testimonies in particular legal processes, including among witnesses in litigation for freedom suits, among testimonies presented for petitions for embarkation and passenger licenses, and among testimonies in Inquisition trials. However, one example of the contents of communication between Black kin across the vast Atlantic emerges through the documentation preserved as part of Antón Segarra's estate.

Coda

As explored in Chapter 2, at the turn of the seventeenth century, an enslaved Black woman named Felipa de la Cruz penned two letters to her freed husband in New Spain.[1] In her letters, she reminded her husband of her expectation that he would send funds from Veracruz to Sevilla to pay for her liberation from slavery and that of their children. These letters include extended discussions about Cruz's commitment to securing liberty for herself and their children, and she reminded her husband not to forget her desire for freedom in her 1608 letter: "You already know my [enslaved] condition and that it does not spare anyone, and so for your life's sake keep this ahead of anything else and see that your children are captive, and suffering grief and spite. You already know how much we desire freedom."[2] This line reveals Cruz's expectation that her husband would gather funds in Veracruz through his labor as a free man and send them to Sevilla to liberate her and their children from slavery.

Felipa de la Cruz's letters hold immense historical value. These rare surviving epistles constitute the earliest known private letters written by an enslaved Black woman in the Atlantic world. Reading the private correspondence between Cruz and her absent husband also reveals the day-to-day lives of enslaved people in an urban environment, details of which are beyond the scope of this study. For this reason, both of Felipa de la Cruz's letters appear here in Spanish and in English translation.[3] To complement them, I include a map of the places of residence in Sevilla of twelve free Black men and women who resided near Cruz and who petitioned for embarkation or passenger licenses between 1569 and 1621 (the approximate era when Cruz was alive), as well as the places of residence of seven free Black men and women who resided near Cruz, who perished in the Americas between 1589 and 1626, and whose estates were administered by the courts of the assets of the deceased at the House of Trade (Figures C.1.1–C.1.2). The map allows readers to trace the community ties of a select group of Black residents of late sixteenth-century Sevilla, some of whom were Felipa de la Cruz's neighbors and all of whom were alive during her lifetime, and to explore her letters with reference to the community of people whom she may have known or been acquainted with in Sevilla.

---

[1] "Antonio Segarra," AGI, Contratación, 303, no. 2, fols. 10^r, 18^v–20^v.
[2] Ibid.
[3] These letters also appear alongside a transcription of Antón Segarra's freedom papers in Spanish and with a brief introduction in Ireton and Álvarez Hernández, "Epístolas de amor," 15–28.

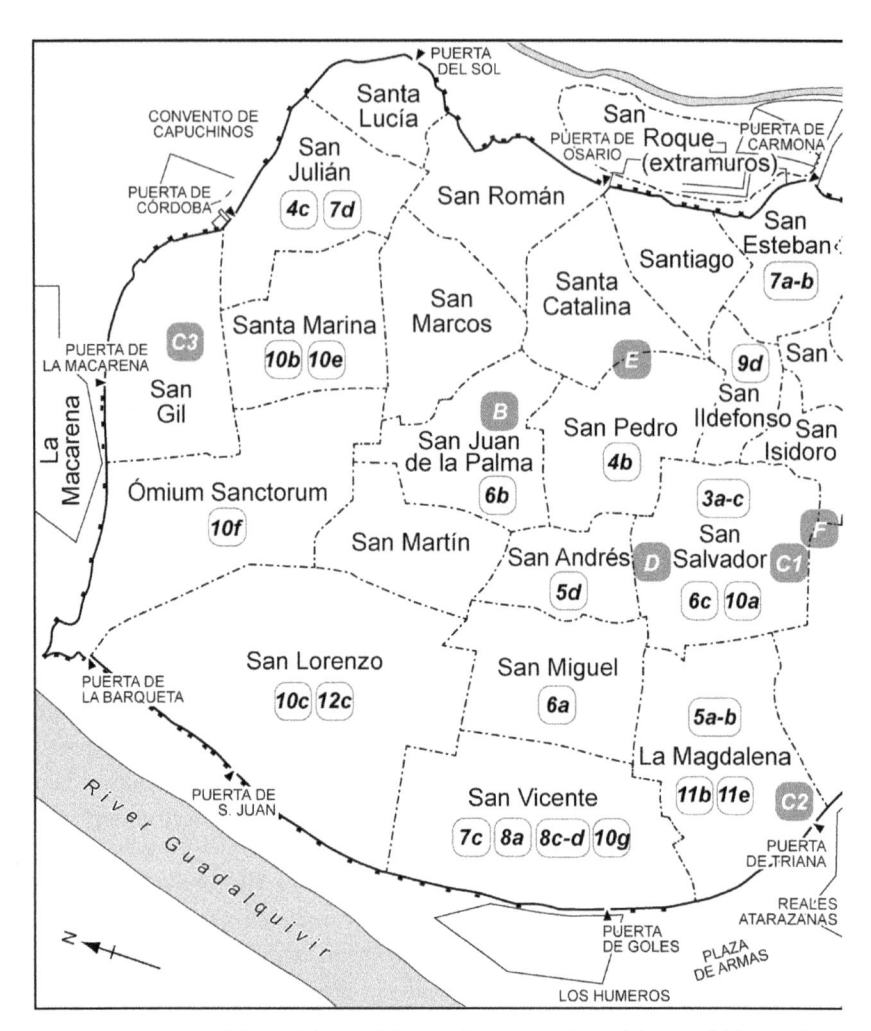

254   Slavery and Freedom in the Early Spanish Atlantic

FIGURE C.I.I Map of the social ties of a generation of free and liberated Black Sevillians in the late sixteenth century (c. 1569–1626). Map drawn by Cath D'Alton, Drawing Office, University College London. With thanks to Antonio Collantes de Terán Sánchez and Víctor Pérez de Escolano for granting me permission to redraw a map of Sevilla based on the maps that they each published in the following publications: Víctor de Pérez Escolano and Fernando Villanueva Sandino, eds., *Ordenanzas de Sevilla, facsímil de la edición de 1632, impresa en Sevilla por Andrés Grande.* Sevilla: OTAISA, 1975; Antonio Collantes de Terán Sánchez, *Sevilla en la baja Edad Media: La ciudad y sus hombres.* Sevilla: Sección de Publicaciones del Excmo. Ayuntamiento, 1977. Please note that the parish lines in the redrawn map are based on research by Antonio Collantes de Terán Sánchez into parish boundaries in sixteenth-century Sevilla and published in the above-mentioned publication.

Coda 255

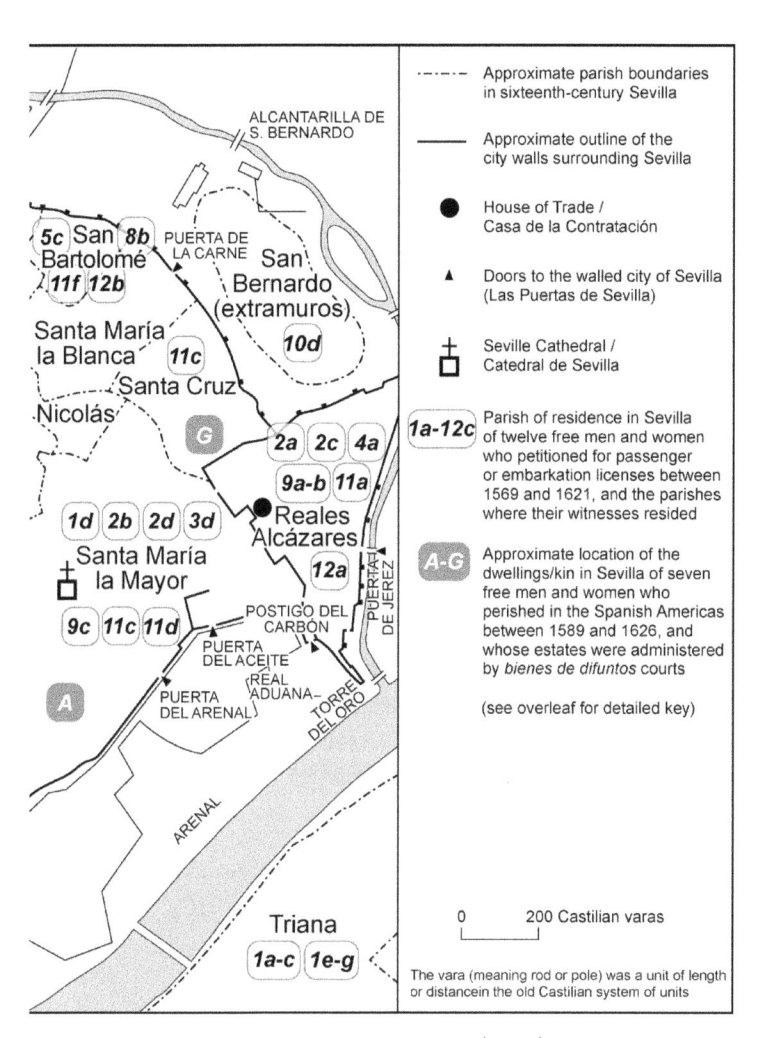

FIGURE C.1.1 (cont.)

Extended key A–E: Approximate location of the dwellings/kin in Sevilla of seven free men and women who perished in the Spanish Americas between 1589 and 1626 and whose estates were administered by *bienes de difuntos* **courts.**

A. Diego Suárez, free, *mulato*, actor, soldier, and alms collector. Suárez resided on Calle de la Pajeria (present-day C/ Zaragoza) in the parish of Santa María la Mayor (perished in 1589, Arequipa, Peru).
B. Pedro de Montedeosca, free, *mulato*, sailor and soldier. Montedeosca resided in the parish of San Juan de la Palma (perished in 1591, at sea).
C1–3. Ana Gómez, free, Black/*morena*, widow. Gómez owned houses in Sevilla in the parishes of San Salvador (C1), La Magdalena (C2), and San Gil (C3) (perished in 1596, in Nombre de Dios, Tierra Firme).
D. Antón Segarra, *horro*, Black, wage-earning servant. Segarra's enslaved Black wife resided in Calle Carpinterías (present-day C/ Cuna), parish of San Salvador (perished in 1609, Veracruz, New Spain).
E. Luis Pinelo, free, *mulato*, sailor. Pinelo resided in Plazuela de Santa Catalina, parish of San Pedro (perished in 1610, in Havana, Cuba).
F. Lucía Tenorio Palma, *horra*, Black. Tenorio Palma resided in Sevilla as an enslaved woman in the house of her enslaver in San Leandro in the parish of San Salvador (perished in 1615, in Portobelo, Tierra Firme).
G. Alonso de Castro, *horro*, Black, drummer (*atambaor*). Castro resided in the parish of Santa Cruz (perished in 1626, at sea).

Extended key, 1a–12c. Parish of residence in Sevilla of twelve free men and women who petitioned for passenger or embarkation licenses between 1569 and 1621, and the parishes where their witnesses resided.

NB Parenthetical information includes *profession or biographical details*, and parish of residence, if known. If the parish of residence is not specified, the number appears in the map near the House of Trade.

1a–g. Francisco González and Juana Gutiérrez, 1569 and 1577:
Petitioners: 1a, Francisco González, free, Black (*sailor and diver*, Triana), and Juana Gutiérrez, free, Black (*wife of Francisco González*, Triana).
Witnesses in 1569: 1b, Tomas Luys (*sailor*, Triana); 1c Andrés de Film [sic] (*sailor*, Triana); 1d, Brian de Caritate [sic] (*unknown*, Santa María [la Mayor]).
Witnesses in 1577: 1e, Miguel Fardel [sic] (*ship pilot of the navigation of the Indies*, Triana); 1f, Bernardo Fiano [sic] (*man of the sea*, Triana); 1g, Domingo Alonso Auguero (*ship pilot*, Triana).

2a–d. Jerónima, 1570.
Petitioner: 2a, Jerónima, *horra*, Black (*formerly enslaved to Doña María de Caña*, unknown parish).
Witnesses: 2b, Ivan [sic] Doria [sic] (*licenciado [university educated] and brother of Jerónima's former owner*, Santa María de la Mayor); 2c, Felipe Ramos, enslaved Black man (*enslaved to Mateo [sic] Ramos*, unknown parish); 2d, Francisco de Espinosa (*servant of Ivan [sic] Doria [sic]*, 2b, Santa María de la Mayor).

3a–d. Ana de Carvajal, 1576.
Petitioner: 3a, Ana de Carvajal, free, *mulata* (*daughter of a mulato named Francisco de Caravajal and an enslaved Black woman from Guinea named Francisca*, unknown parish, but likely in San Salvador).

FIGURE C.1.2 Extended key for Figure C.1.1.

Coda

Witnesses: 3b, María de Josefa (*wife of Diego [sic], vecino*, San Salvador); 3c, María de la Barrera (*vecina*, San Salvador); 3d, Juan López (*vecino*, Santa María la Mayor).

4a–c. María Gómez, 1577.
Petitioner: 4a, María Gómez, free, Black (*born in Cabo Verde and travelled to Sevilla as a free woman*, unknown parish).
Witnesses: 4b, Domingo López (*blacksmith*, San Pedro); 4c Antón de Vega, free, Black (*unknown trade*, San Julián).

5a–d. Juan de Pineda, 1583.
Petitioner: 5a, Juan de Pineda, *horro, mulato* (*born enslaved in Lima, Peru, and later liberated by his owner, Pedro de Ribera*, La Magdalena).
Witnesses: 5b Gaspar de Ribera (*brother of Pedro de Ribera*, La Magdalena); 5c, Juan Martínez de Herrera (*consul of the University of the House of Trade*, San Bartolomé); 5d, Alonso Álvarez (*merchant*, San Andrés).

6a–c. Juana Bautista, 1592.
Petitioner: 6a, Juana Bautista, *horra*, Black (*daughter of Pedro Martín and Elena Hernández, who were enslaved people from Guinea; in 1592 Bautista was travelling as a wage-earning servant [criada] of Simón López*, San Miguel).
Witnesses: 6b, María de Flores, free, Black (*possibly a servant to Don Francisco de Alcazar*, San Juan de la Palma); 6c, Leonor de Alarcon, free, *mulata* (*lived on Calle Carpinterías*, San Salvador).

7a–d. Lucía de Mendoza, 1592.
Petitioner: 7a, Lucía de Mendoza, *horra*, Black (*daughter of Antón and Paula, who were enslaved people from Guinea, and Mendoza was formerly enslaved to Juan Fernández de Mendoza*, San Esteban).
Witnesses: 7b, Doña Leonor Porras (*widow of Gonzalo de León, vecina*, San Esteban); 7c, Gabriel Barajona (*treasurer of the Sevilla Cabildo*, San Vicente); 7d, Barbola de Gallegos (*vecina*, San Julián).

8a–d. Agustina de Jesús, 1593.
Petitioner: 8a, Agustina de Jesús, *horra*, Black (*daughter of enslaved people from Guinea, and formerly enslaved to Gonzalo de Armental; upon liberation from slavery, she was described as a vecina*, San Vicente).
Witnesses: 8b, Juana de Armental (*sister of Gonzalo de Armental, who previously owned Agustina de Jesús*, San Bartolomé); 8c, [indiscipherable name] (San Vicente); 8d, Alonso de Herrera (*son of Gonzalo de Armental, who previously owned Agustina de Jesús*, San Vicente).

9a–d. Magdalena, 1596.
Petitioner: 9a Magdalena, *horra*, Black (*formerly enslaved to Elvira Martín*, unknown parish).
Witnesses: 9b, Ana Pérez (*widow*, unknown parish); 9c, Inés de Aguilar (*vecina*, Santa María de la Iglesia Mayor); 9d, Alonso García de Lazaros (*royal notary [escribano de su magestad]*, San Ildefonso).

10a–g. María de la O, 1600.
Petitioner: 10a, María de la O, *horra*, Black (*daughter of Ana Pinto and Sebastián de Torres, and born enslaved in Sevilla, and she was later liberated*

FIGURE C.1.2 (cont.)

from slavery, and in 1600 travelled to the Indies with her husband, Francisco Hernández, San Salvador).

Witnesses: 10b, Gaspar de los Reyes (*shoemaker*, Santa Marina); 10c, Juan Borseguinero [sic] (*unknown trade*, San Lorenzo); 10d, Alonso María [sic] de la Barrera (gardener [*hortelano*], San Bernardo); 10e, Diego de Morales (laborer [*travallador*], Santa Marina); 10f, Beatriz de Barrientos (*widow of Juan González*, Ómium Sanctorum); 10g, Doña Isabel Xuárez (*doncella*, San Vicente).

11a–b. Francisca de Figueroa, 1600 and 1601.

Petitioner: 11a Francisca de Figueroa, free, *mulata* (*claimed to be poverty-stricken*, unknown parish).

Witnesses in 1600: 11b, Francisca de Mendoza (*wife of Sevastian de Saavedra, who labored as messenger for distribution of royal mail [he was a "correo a la caballo del rey"]*, La Magdalena); 11c, Juan López (*shopkeeper [tendero]*, Santa María la Mayor); 11d, María de Aguilar (*wife of Francisco Aparicio, lived on Calle San Gregorio*, Santa María la Mayor).

Witnesses in 1601: 11e Elvira de Medina (*widow*, La Magdalena). 11f, Felipe de Selpuldes [sic] (*messenger for distribution of mail [correo]*, San Bartolomé); 11b. Francisca de Mendoza (*wife of Sevastian de Saavedra, who labored in the royal mail [he was a "correo a la caballo del rey"]*, La Magdalena).

12a–12c. Catalina de Tapia, 1621.

Petitioner: 12a, Catalina de Tapia, *horra*, Black (*born enslaved in Santo Domingo, and lived in Santo Domingo, Cartagena de Indias, and in Sevilla before being liberated from slavery*, unknown parish).

Witnesses: 12b, Barbola Ybarra, Black, free (*wife of Diego de Santial (laborer) and sister of María Ybarrra (12c)*, San Bartolomé); 12c, María Ybarra, free, Black (*wife of Antón Gallegos, and sister of Barbola Ybarrra (12b); resided in the corral del Narajuelo*, San Lorenzo).

Archival material consulted for 1a–12c and A–E:

AGI, Contratación: 255, no. 1, ramo 5; 257A, no. 3, ramo 12; 296A, no. 2, ramo 3; 303, no. 2; 485, no. 4, ramo 5; 526, no. 1, ramo 1; 5225A, no. 1, ramo 35; 5226, no. 2, ramo 28; 5237, no. 2, ramo 47; 5240, no. 1, ramo 31; 5243, no. 2, ramo 40; 5252, no. 1, ramo 11; 5261, no. 2, ramo 33; 5262A, no. 55; 5268, no. 2, ramo 68; 5380, no. 41.

AGI, Indiferente: 2052, no. 14; 2058, no. 6; 2084, no. 98; 2094, no. 1.

FIGURE C.1.2 (cont.)

LETTER 1, FROM FELIPA DE LA CRUZ TO ANTÓN SEGARRA, 1604[4]

Spanish Transcription
Chloe L. Ireton and José María Álvarez Hernández.

------

24 junio 1604 – Sevilla a Veracruz

Carta V

Hermano mío y deseado de mi alma:

Su carta recibí con mucho contento en saber tenía bnid [buena] salud y de la buena navegación que tuviste y me holgué mucho y plega a Dios de se la dar dar entera como yo deseo. Yo estoy buena. El pago que me han dado estos señores ha sido como yo merecí que es en lugar de echarme a la cocina porque vendieron a Ana porque se casó.

Vuestra hija María está buena y tenéis un hijo que se llama Andrés porque nació víspera de San Andrés. Vuestro padrino Julián González que no está en casa porque lo despidió don Francisco mi señor que tuvo cierta pesadumbre con él. Tenéis por un padre a Luis de Aguilar que sacó a Andrés de pila.[5] Todos estos señores están buenos. Bendito Dios. María la negra está casada, y mi señora parió por navidad un niño que se dice don Alonso de Santillán. La señora Velasco y la Señora María de Paz y Beatriz Gómez y su sobrina y Valderrama y toda su gente os besan todos las manos. Andrea os besa las manos y está ya muy grande.

Y por no ser para más, Dios os guarde como puede y dé.

Sevilla a 24 de junio de 1604 años

    Vuestra mujer, Felipa de la Cruz.

English Translation
Chloe L. Ireton, with many thanks to John Beusterein and Baltasar-Fra Molinero for offering suggestions and critiques.

------

[4] "Antón Segarra," AGI, Contratación, 303, no. 2, fols. 18^v–19^r.
[5] "Andrés Segarra, baptism record," AGAS, Parroquia del Salvador, 3.I.1.1, Libro de Bautismos, libro 11, 1597–1605, December 11, 1602, fol. 330.

June 24, 1604. Sevilla to Veracruz

Letter V

Brother of mine, and my soul's desire.

I received your letter with much happiness to learn that you are in good health and that you had a successful crossing [of the Atlantic], and I rejoiced greatly, and I plead to God that he give you [good health], and that he gives it to you entirely, which is what I wish. I am well. These noble people have rewarded me as I deserved, instead of throwing me in the kitchen when they sold Ana because she married.

Your daughter María is well, and you have a son named Andrés because he was born on the eve of San Andrés. Your godfather Julián González is not in the house because my *señor* Don Francisco dismissed him because they quarreled. You have Luis de Aguilar as a godfather, who lifted Andres out of the baptismal font. All of these noble people are in good health. God Bless. María the Black got married, and my *señora* gave birth to a child last Christmas, a boy called don Alonso de Santillán.[6] *Señora* Velasco and *señora* María de Paz and Beatriz Gómez and her niece and Valderrama and all of their families kiss your hands. Andrea kisses your hands, and she is already very grown.

And as there is no more to say, may God protect you, as he can and will.

Sevilla on 24th June of 1604 years.

Your wife, Felipa de la Cruz

LETTER II, FROM FELIPA DE LA CRUZ TO ANTÓN SEGARRA, 1608[7]

Spanish Transcription
Chloe L. Ireton and José María Álvarez Hernández.

---

[6] Felipa uses the phrase "mi señora" and "mi señor" to refer to her owners/enslavers and never refers to them as her owners. In the translation, I have retained the words that she uses in Spanish to refer to these people.

[7] "Antón Segarra," AGI, Contratación, 303, no. 2, fols. 19^r–20^r.

15 de marzo de 1608

Otra carta.

A mi marido, Antón Segarra, que nuestro señor guarde en el convento de Santo Domingo en San Juan de Ulúa.

Hermano mío: por la presente os hago saber cómo quedo buena y de salud yo y vuestros hijos y deseosa de saber de la vuestra. Dios os la dé como yo deseo para mí.

Muy quejosa estoy del gran descuido que habéis tenido en escribirme tanto tiempo ha y no sé a qué atribuirme el grande olvido vuestro, pero debe de ser el poco amor que me tenéis a mí y a vuestros hijos;– no es firme como el mío porque cada hora y momento me acuerdo de vos y ninguna vez voy a misa y en casa que no os encomiendo a Dios que os guarde y os traiga ante mis ojos y de nuestros hijos para que se cumpla el gran deseo que tienen de veros.

Vuestra hija María está buena, aunque en días pasados la tuve muy malita y todo es preguntar por vos y que cuándo habéis de venir y tienen mucho cuidado de encomendaros a Dios cada noche cuando se acuesta. Vuestro hijo Andrés Segarra también está bonito: todo es jugar con estas señoras y de esta suerte se entretienen ambos hermanos y todo piando por su padre. Y no me espanto que no tienen otro bien ni otro remedio después de Dios si no es el que vos le habéis de dar.

Don Francisco, mi señor, está bueno, aunque antes de ahora tuvo una grande enfermedad que apenas quedara ciego. Tiene otro hijo más. Mi señora está buena. Solamente entiende en parir y empreñar a apriesa. Don Antonio de Aguilar está aquí en Sevilla en esta casa que se vino a curar de una grande enfermedad. Tiene casada su hija con un caballero de Écija. Doña Beatriz y doña Luisa están muy bonitas. Alonso López no está ya en casa, que todo lo dio Andrés Adame. Beatriz Gómes casó su sobrina con un gorrero y está preñada. María de Paz está buena y su hijo Juan Ramírez. Y os besan las manos. Casilda de Velasco también está buena. Ya habéis sabido cómo murió su hija Francisca de Velasco y cómo casó su nieta con un zapatero de Montilla. María Jiménez casó su hija Elvira con un platero. Y dio en casamiento cuatrocientos ducados de mil que le habían dado por la muerte de Julián González. Todos los demás conocidos os besan las manos con mucho deseo de veros.

Hermano mío de mi alma, acordaos de la suerte que estoy y cómo estoy en casa ajena, aunque estos señores me han criado y me hacen merced en efecto. Ya sabéis la condición de mí y que no la perdona a nadie y ansí por vida vuestra que se os ponga esto por delante y ver que vuestros hijos están cautivos y recibiendo pesadumbre y malas razones. Ya sabéis lo que se desea la libertad. Avísame de vuestra salud.

Muy largo pues. El mensajero es cierto que es el señor Juan García. Y con esto no tengo más que decir, sino que Dios os dé la salud que yo deseo y os traiga a ojos de quien bien os quiere.

Fecho en Sevilla, a 15 marzo de mil y seiscientos y ocho años.

Vuestra mujer, Felipa de la Cruz.

English Translation
Chloe L. Ireton, with many thanks to John Beusterein and Baltasar-Fra Molinero for offering suggestions and critiques.

March 15, 1608

Another letter

To my husband, Antón Segarra, who may our Lord protect in the convent of Santo Domingo in San Juan de Ulúa.

Brother of mine: with this letter, I relay to you that I am doing well, and in good health, as are your children. I am anxious to know about your health. May God be giving you good health as I wish for myself.

I am very upset for the great neglect that you have shown in not writing to me for so long, and I do not know what I can attribute to your great forgetfulness, except that it must be for to the little love that you have for me and your children; it [your love] is not steadfast like mine because every hour and every moment I remember you and there is never a time that I attend mass or that I am in the house that I do not entrust you to God that he protect you and bring you before my eyes and those of our children so that their great wish to see you can be fulfilled.

Your daughter María is healthy, although in past days the poor creature was very unwell, and all she does is ask after you and when you will return, and they take great care to entrust you to God every night when they go to sleep. Your son Andrés Segarra is also pretty: all he does is play with these ladies, and in this way, fortunately, both siblings entertain themselves, and they are always chirping for their father. And I am not surprised, because they do not have any other source of goodness or relief other than God, if it is not the one you will have to provide them.

Don Francisco, my *señor*, is well, although before now he had a great illness that almost left him blind. He has had another son. My *señora* is well. She only cares about giving birth and getting pregnant soon after. Don Antonio de Aguilar is here in Sevilla in this house as he came to get cured from a serious illness. He has married his daughter to a gentleman from Écija. Doña Beatriz and doña Luisa are very pretty. Alonso López is no longer in the house, because Andrés Adame gave [him] everything. Beatriz Gómes married her niece to a capmaker, and she is pregnant. María de Paz is well and so is her son, Juan Ramírez. And they both kiss your hands. Casilda de Velasco is also well. You have already heard that her daughter Francisca de Velasco died, and how she married her granddaughter to a shoemaker from Montilla. María Jiménez married her daughter, Elvira, to a silversmith. As a dowry for the marriage, she gave 400 ducats of the 1,000 that she had been given for the death of Julián González. All our other acquaintances kiss your hands with a great desire to see you.

Dear brother of my soul, remember my predicament and how I am not in my house, even though it is true that these people raised me and treat me well. You already know my [enslaved] condition and that it does not spare anyone, and so for your life's sake keep this ahead of anything else and see that your children are captive, and suffering grief and spite. You already know how much we desire freedom. Let me know about your health.

This is rather long. The messenger is trustworthy as it is *señor* Juan García. And with this I do not have any more to say except that God may give you the health that I wish for myself and that he may bring you before the eyes of the one who loves you well.

Dated in Sevilla on March 15, 1608

Your wife, Felipa de la Cruz

Bibliography

ARCHIVAL MATERIAL

Archivo del Museo Canario, Las Palmas de Gran Canaria, Las Palmas, Spain

AMC, Tribunal del Santo Oficio de la Inquisición de Canarias
Inquisición de Canarias, INQ-142.001, Causas de fe, Libros de penitenciados, Vol. 146, Libro 34 de penitenciados.

Archivo General del Arzobispado de Sevilla (Cited as AGAS), Spain

AGAS, Gobierno
"Libro de Capellanías de Santa María de Magdalena," AGAS, sección 2, Libros del Capellanías 2043, no. 5, leg. 03448, fols. 236.

AGAS, Justicia, Cofradias y Hermandades
"Pleito entre la Hdad de Ntra Sra de la Antigua y la de los Ángeles III.1.6," L.9883, Expte 2.
"Pleito, Nuestra Señora de los Angeles," 1.III.1.6, L.9885, no. 1.

AGAS, Parroquia de San Salvador
Libro de Bautismos, Parroquia del San Salvador, 3.I.2.1, libros 9–11.
Libro de Matrimonios, Parroquia del San Salvador, 3.I.2.1, Libros 2–6.

Archivo General de Indias (Cited as AGI), Spain

AGI Contaduría
241, nos. 74, 117.
1072, no. 1, ramo 3, fols. 381^r–91^v.

AGI Contratación

255, no. 1, ramo 5.
257A, no. 3, ramo 12.
273, no. 22.
293A, no. 1, ramo 6.
296A, no. 2, R.3.
303, no. 2.
324B, no. 1, ramo 9.
476, no. 1, ramo 5.
485, no. 4, ramo 5.
488, no. 3, ramo 2.
515, no. 1, ramo 5.
526, no. 1, ramo 1, docs. 8, 12.
938A, no. 10.
941B, no. 32.
962A, no. 3.
963, no. 2, ramo 11.
5218, no. 88.
5222, no. 4, ramo 70.
5225A, no. 1, ramo 35.
5225B, no. 33.
5226, no. 2, ramos 27–30.
5227, no. 2, ramos 25 and 36.
5232, no. 25.
5237, no. 2, ramo 47.
5238, no. 1, ramo 38.
5240, no. 1, ramo 31.
5241, no. 2, ramo 63.
5243, no. 2, ramo 40.
5245, no. 1, ramo 41.
5248, no. 1, ramos 1, 17.
5251B, no. 2, ramo 42.
5252, no. 1, ramos 11, 75.
5258, no. 1, ramo 45.
5260B, no. 1, ramo 44.
5261, no. 2, ramos 33, 65.
5262A, nos. 55, 73.
5266, no. 1, ramo 59.
5266, no. 2, ramo 72.
5268, no. 2, ramo 68.
5280, no. 11.
5282, no. 83.
5283, no. 82bis.
5289, no. 36.
5301, no. 2, ramo 6.
5313, no. 13.
5323, nos. 53, 54.

5324, no. 30.
5326, no. 49.
5327, no. 83.
5536, libro 5, fols. 156$^{r(1)}$.
5338, no. 24.
5340, no. 4.
5343. no. 8.
5352, no. 33.
5355, no. 42.
5357, no. 18.
5360, no. 75.
5361, no. 14.
5370, no. 30.
5375, no. 25.
5380, no. 41.
5406, no. 1.
5420, no. 70.
5536, libros 1–5.
5537, libros 1–3.
5538, libros 1, 3.
5577, no. 65.
5578, no. 51.
5581, no. 72.
5709, no. 7.
5709, no. 211, ramo 24.
5709, no. 218, ramos 21, 23, 27.
5792, libro 2, fols. 61^v–62.
5792, libro 1, fols. 198–199.

AGI Escribanía
48A, libro 13, no. 2.
974.
1012A, años 1601–1603.

AGI, Indiferente
416, libro 3, fols. 19^v, 23^v, 34^v–35^r.
422, libro 17, fols. 114^r–115^r.
424, libro 21, fols. 124^r–124^v.
424, libro 22, fols. 147^r–147^v.
427, libro 30, fols. 248^r–249^r.
427, libro 31, fols. 184^v–185^v.
449, libro A2, fols. 101–101^v.
449, libro A3, fols. 103^v–104^v.
450, libro A4, fols. 44–44^v, 148–148^v.
450, libro A5, fols. 1–1^v, 28^v–29, 202^v–203, 253^v–254^v.
1205, no. 21.

1207, no. 60, fols. 1.
1227.
1233, "Juan Baptista de Cárdenas."
1257.
1258.
1259.
1260.
1434.
1435.
1438.
1439.
1440.
1952, libro 2, fols. $4^{r(2)}$, 208.
1952, libro 3, fols. 195.
1961, libro 3, fols. 324^r–324^v.
1964, libro 10, fols. 88, 351^v–352, 354^v.
1965, libro 13, fols. 432^v.
1967, libro 16, fols. 251–251^v.
1968, libro 19, fols. 214^v.
1968, libro 20, fols. 255^v, 259.
1968, libro 21, fols. 1, 131^v, 183^v.
1969, libro 22, fols. 26^r–26^v, 248^v, 130, 195^v.
1978, fol. 16.
2048, no. 4.
2049, no. 54.
2052, no. 14.
2053, no. 43.
2054, no. 43.
2058, no. 6.
2058, no. 51.
2059, no. 97.
2059, no. 108.
2058, no. 6.
2058, no. 51.
2059, no. 108.
2060, no. 10.
2061, no. 134.
2064, no. 135.
2065, no. 60.
2066, no. 92.
2067, no. 24.
2074, nos. 50, 67.
2075, no. 140.
2076, no. 87.
2084, nos. 52, 98.
2089, no. 29, 39, and 87.
2091, no. 24.
2093, nos. 23, 181.

2094, nos. 1, 144.
2095, no. 14.
2097, no. 197.
2098, no. 18.
2100, no. 3.
2102, no. 166.
2105, no. 32.

AGI, Justicia
11, no. 4.
712, no. 1.
940, no. 10.
978, no. 2, ramo 1.
1177, no. 1.

AGI Panamá
13, ramo 22, no. 150.
14, ramo 12, no. 68.
44, nos. 22, 56.
229, Libro 2, fols. 74^v–75^{BIS-r}.
235, libro 7, fols. 121^v–122^r.
235, libro 8, fols. 347^v–348^v.
236, libro 9, fols. 44^v, and 369^r–369^v.
236, libro 10, fols. 210^V–214^r.
237, libro 11, fols. 38^V–39^V, 47^{r}47^V.
237, libro 12.

AGI Patronato
252, ramo 11.

AGI Mexico
1092, libro 12, fols. 53^v–54^v.

AGI Santa Fe
49, Ramo 17, no. 120.

Archivo General de la Nación de Colombia, (Cited as AGN, Colombia)

AGN, Colombia, Sección Colonial (Cited as SC), Negros y esclavos (Cited as NE)
SC, NE 43, legajo 9, doc. 1.
SC, NE, 43, legajo 9, doc. 13.

SC, NE 43, legajo 10, doc. 9.
SC, NE, 43, legajo 13, doc. 9.

Archivo General de la Nación, Mexico, (Cited as AGN, Mexico)

GD61 Inquisición
vol. 102. exp. 3.
vol. 103, exp. 6.
vol. 107, exp. 4.
vol. 131, exp. 2.
vol. 207, exp. 1.
vol. 208, exp.3.
vol. 310, exp. 7.
vol. 341, exp. 1.
vol. 435, exp. 248.
vol. 466, exp. 3.

Indiferente Virreinal
caja-exp.: 4156-039, Real Audiencia. Año: 1612–1613, fols. 1–12.
caja-exp.: 6455-053. Real Audiencia. Año: 1616, fs. 1.

Archivo General de la Nación, Peru (Cited as AGN, Peru)

"Concurso de Acreedores de Manuel Bautista Pérez," AGN, Peru, Tribunal de la Inquisición, legajo 35, fols. 153–154, 165–166, 173–174, 179–182.

AGN, Peru, Protocolos Notariales de Lima, (Cited as PNL)
PNL, N 1 Alonso de la Cueva, Protocolo, 29,264, fols. 7^v-9 (9/1/1580).
PNL, N 1 AYH1: 10,39, fols. 246-246^v; 10,291, fols. 317-317^v.
PNL, N 1 AYH1: 11,305, fols. 84-84^v; 11,319, fols. 105-105^v.
PNL, Bartolomé Gascón, Protocolo, 42.1, 19, fols. 23-25 (07/01/1554).
PNL, N 1 CAM1 3,786, fols. 1193-1193^v.
PNL, N 1 CAM1: 5,730, fols. 1232-1232^v; 7,151, fols. 281^v-282.
PNL, Cristóbal De Aguilar Mendieta, Protocolo, 4,177, fols. 367^v-368 (01/04/1597).
PNL, Notarias, 1 CYH1, 28,70, fols. 103-106.
PNL, Notarias 1 CYH1, 28,402, 188^v-189.
PNL, N 1, CYH1: 29,74, fols. 102^v-103^v; 29,397, fols. 261-261^v.
PNL, Notarias, no. 1 DCM1 23,75, & 23,76 fols. 109^v-112 (21/11/1591).
PNL, N 1 JBE1 12,679, fols. 1075-1075^v.
PNL, Juan Gutiérrez y Nicolás de Grado, Protocolo, 69,827, fols. 1018-1019 (24/11/1567).
PNL, Juan Gutiérrez, Protocolo, 71,205, fols. 422-424^v (16/04/1573).
PNL, N 1 RGB1 43,61 fols. 105^v-106.

Archivo General de Simancas, Spain

AGS, Patronato (Cited as PTR)
PTR, 87, 38.
PTR, 87, 39.

Archivo Histórico Nacional, España (Cited as AHN, España), Spain

AHN, España, Inquisición
Inquisición, 2075, expedientes 1–29.
Inquisición, 4672, exp. 8.
Inquisición, 4673, exp. 6.
Inquisición, 4822, exp. 2.

AHN, España, Consejos
Inventario de consultas de Gracia, 1571–1621, Consejos, Libro 2754.
Inventario de decretos de Gracia, 1571–1621, Consejos, Libro 2752.

Archivo Histórico Provincial de Sevilla, (Cited as AHPS), Spain

AHPS, Protocolos Notariales
signatura P-53.
signatura P-152.
signatura P-1518.
signatura P-2163.
signatura P-2182.
signatura P-2183.
signatura P-2195.
signatura P-3276.
signatura P-5856.

Biblioteca de la Universidad de Sevilla, Spain

USB, Fondo Antiguo
*Origen y Descendencia de la Casa y familia de Santillán de la Ciudad de Sevilla, con otras varias noticias de los linages de ella por el enlace que tienen con la referida casa.*16??, Biblioteca de la Universidad de Sevilla, A 331/214, fol 42^v.
Morgado, Alonso. *Historia de Sevilla: en la qval se contienen svs antigvedades, grandezas, y cosas memorables en ella acontecidas, desde su fundacion hasta nuestros tiempos* ... En Sevilla: En la Imprenta de Andrea Pescioni y Iuan de Leon, 1587 (Fondo Antiguo de la Universidad de Sevilla, Escuela Técnica Superior de Arquitectura, Biblioteca, ABREV.946.0), Accessed via Biblioteca Virtual Miguel de Cervantes.

Biblioteca Nacional de España (Cited as BNE), Spain

BNE, Manuscritos
"Relacion del alçamiento que negros y mulatos libres," MSS 2010, fols. 158–164.

Bibliotèque Nacionale de France (Cited as BNF), Paris, France

BNF, Livres Raires (LR)
Sandoval, Alonso de. *Naturaleza, policia sagrada i profana, costumbres i ritos, disciplina i catechismo evangelico de todos Etiopes*, por el P. Alonso de Sandoval. Seville: F. de Lira, 1627. BNF, Paris, département réserve des livres rares (LR), 4-O3C-6.

Huntington Library, San Marino, California, USA (Cited as HLSM)

HL, Huntington Manuscripts (Cited as HM)
HM, 35165.
HM, 35130, Volume 36, 1650–1684.

John Carter Brown (Cited as JCB) Library, Providence, Rhode Island, USA

JCB Library, Rare Books (Cited as RB)
"Auto Publico de Fe Celebrado en la Ciudad de Sevilla, 1648," en *Sermon que predico en el Convento de Religiosas de Sa[n]cta Maria de Gracia à la festiuidad de el Sanctissimo Sacramento,* En Mexico: Por la Viuda de Bernardo Calderon, 1646, JCB Library, Rare Books (Cited as RB), BA646.A446s, fols. 158ʳ.

Unidad de Servicios Bibliotecarios y de Información, Jalapa (Cited as USBI, Xalapa), Mexico

USBI, Xalapa, Protocolos Notariales Jalapa
Clave del acta: 21, 1574, 182.
Clave del acta: 22, 1578, 196.
Clave del acta: 27, 1578, 446.
Clave del acta: 27, 1600, 1217, no. 3.
Clave del acta: 27, 1600, 1126.
Clave del acta: 27, 1600, 1127.
Clave del acta: 27, 1600, 1187.
Clave del acta 27, 1600, 1461.
Clave del acta: 27, 1600, 1658, no. 3.
Clave del acta: 27, 1617, 2644.
Clave del acta: 27, 1617, 2761, no. 5.
Clave del acta: 27, 1617, 2766.

Clave del acta: 27, 1617, 2769.
Clave del acta: 27, 1617, 2774, no. 5.
Clave del acta: 27, 1617, 2775.
Clave del acta: 27, 1632, 3297.
Clave del acta: 27, 1632, 3298.
Clave del acta: 85, 1632, 3818.
Clave del acta: 27, 1632, 3822, no. 6.
Clave del acta: 27, 1645, 4033.

USBI, Xalapa, Protocolos Notariales de Orizaba
Clave del acta: 220, 1583, 21290.

USBI, Xalapa, Protocolos Notariales de Veracruz Vieja
Clave del acta: 19, 1645, 4037.

USBI, Xalapa, Protocolos Notariales San Antonio Huatusco
Clave del acta: 220, 1583, 21317.
Clave del acta: 223, 1583, 21289.

USBI, Xalapa, Potocolos Notariales de México
Clave del acta: 36, 1617, 2996.

USBI, Xalapa, Protocolos Notariales Puebla de los Ángeles
Clave del acta: 53, 1578, 489.
Clave del acta: 53, 1578, 490.

PRINTED SOURCES

Cervantes Saavedra, Miguel de. *Cuatro Entremeses Atribuidos a Miguel de Cervantes,* edited by Adolfo de Catrol. Barcelona, 1957. *"Entremes de los Mirones"* 25–26.
de Salas Barbadillo, Alonso Jeronimo, *The Gawkers/Los Mirones,* edited by Alexander Samson and John Beusterien. Liverpool: Liverpool University Press, forthcoming.
Índice de la colección de don Luis de Salazar y Castro. Tomo XVII. Madrid: Real Academia de la Historia, 1956.
Las Casas, Bartolomé de. *Brevísima relación de la destrucción de África; preludio de la destrucción de Indias: primera defensa de los guanches y negros contra su esclavización,* edited by Isacio Pérez Fernández. Salamanca: Editorial San Esteban, 1989.
Las Siete partidas del Sabio Rey don Alfonso el nono por las quales son derimidas las questiones è pleytos que en España ocurren ... [Partidas 4ª, 5ª, 6ª y 7ª]... Salamanca, Lyon Solarrona: Alonso Gómez and Henrrique Toti, 1550. Consulted online via Biblioteca Virtual Miguel de Cervantes, 2009.

Latino, Juan. "*The Song of John of Austria.*" In *The Battle of Lepanto*, edited and translated by Elizabeth R. Wright, Sarah Spence, and Andrew Lemons. Cambridge: Harvard University Press, 2014.

Navarro Antolín, Carlos. "Una empresa cordobesa figura ya como titular del Palacio de la Motilla," *Diario de Sevilla*, Sevilla, 12 November, 2022. Online version of the article: www.diariodesevilla.es/sevilla/empresa-cordobesa-titular-Palacio-Motilla_0_1737428456.html

Ordenanças de Seuilla ... : recopilacion de las ordenanças de la muy noble y muy leal cibdad de Seuilla ..., [Sevilla] : por Andres Grande, 1632. Biblioteca de la Universidad de Sevilla, Fondo Antiguo de la Universidad de Sevilla, A 132/161. Accessed digitally: https://archive.org/details/A132161

Ordenanzas de Sevilla; Ed. facsímil de la Ed. de 1632 impresa en Sevilla por Andrés Grande, edited by Víctor Pérez Escolano and Fernando Villanueva Sandino. Sevilla: OTAISA, 1975.

Ramírez de Guzmán, Juan. *Libro de algunos ricoshombres* (manuscript circa 1652), edited by Juan Cartaya Baños and Real Maestranza de Ronda, 2015.

Recopilacion de las ordena[n]ças de la muy noble [y] muy leal cibdad de Seuilla... Impressas... en la dicha cibdad de Seuilla: por Juan Varela de Salamanca... 1527. Universidad de Valladolid, Repositorio Documental, Incunables e Impresos Raros [528], U/Bc IyR 164 http://uvadoc.uva.es/handle/10324/29072

Sandoval, Alonso de. *Treatise on Slavery: Selections from De Instauranda Aethiopum Salute*, edited and translated by Nicole von Germeten. Indianapolis, IN: Hackett, 2008.

WORKS CITED

Acree Jr, William G. "Jacinto Ventura De Molina: A Black *Letrado* in a White World of Letters, 1766–1841," *Latin American Research Review*, 44:2, 2009, 37–58.

Acree, William G. and Alex Borucki. eds. *Los caminos de la escritura negra en el Río de la Plata*. Madrid: Iberoamericana-Verbuet, 2010.

Adorno, Rolena and Ivan Boserup. *Unlocking the Doors to the Worlds of Guaman Poma and His Nueva corónica*. Chicago: The University of Chicago Press, 2015.

Almorza Hidalgo, Amelia. *"No se hace pueblo sin ellas." Mujeres españolas en el virreinato del Perú: emigración y movilidad social (siglos XVI–XVII)*. Madrid: Consejo Superior de Investigaciones Científicas, and Universidad de Sevilla, and Diputación de Sevilla, 2018.

Altman, Ida. *Emigrants and Society: Extremadura and Spanish America in the Sixteenth Century*. Berkeley and Los Angeles: University of California Press, 1989.

al-Musawi, Muhsin J. *The Medieval Islamic Republic of Letters: Arabic Knowledge Construction*. Notre Dame: University of Notre Dame Press, 2015.

Andrews, Kenneth R., ed. *The Last Voyage of Drake and Hawkins*. London: Routledge, Hakluyt Society, 2017.

Apodaca Valdez, Manuel. *Cofradías Afrohispánicas: Celebración, resistencia furtiva y transformación cultural*. Leiden: Brill, 2022.

Aram, Bethany, Juan Guillermo Martín, and Iosvany Hernández Mora. "Aproximaciones a la población de Panamá Viejo a partir de la arqueología funerariay la documentación histórica, 1519–1671," *Anuario de Estudios Americanos*, 77:2, 2020, 485–512.

Araujo, Ana Lucia. *Reparations for Slavery and the Slave Trade; A Transnational and Comparative History*, 2nd edn. London and New York: Bloomsbury, 2023.

Araujo, Ana Lucia. *Slavery in the Age of Memory; Engaging the Past*. London and New York: Bloomsbury, 2020.

Ares Queija, Berta. "'Un borracho de chicha y vino': La construcción social del mestizo (Perú, siglo XVI)." In *Mezclado y sospechoso: Movilidad e identidades, España y América (siglos XVI–XVIII)*, edited by Gregorio Salinero, 121–144. Madrid: Casa de Velázquez, 2005.

Ares Queija, Berta. "La cuestión del bautismo de los negros en el siglo XVII: La proyección de un debate americano." In *Mirando las dos orillas: intercambios mercantiles, sociales y culturales entre Andalucía y América*, edited by Enriqueta Vila Vilar and Jaime J. Lacueva Muñoz, 469–485. Sevilla: Fundación Buenas Letras, 2012.

Ares Queija, Berta and Alessandro Stella. eds. *Negros, Mulatos, Zambaigos: Derroteros africanos en los mundos ibericos*. Sevilla: Editions EEHA, 2000.

Baldwin, Davarian L. "Foreword." In *Ideas in Unexpected Places: Reimagining Black Intellectual History*, edited by Brandon R. Byrd, Leslie M. Alexander, and Russell Rickford, xi–xviii. Chicago: Northwestern University Press, 2022.

Ball, Erica, Tatiana Seijas, and Terri Snyder. eds. *As If She Were Free: A Collective Biography of Women and Emancipation in the Americas*. Cambridge: Cambridge University Press, 2020.

Barragan, Yesenia. *Freedom's Captives: Slavery and Gradual Emancipation on the Colombian Black Pacific*. Cambridge: Cambridge University Press, 2021.

Baskes, Jeremy. "The Colonial Economy of New Spain." Oxford Research Encyclopedia of Latin American History. February 26, 2018; Accessed January 23, 2024. https://oxfordre.com/latinamericanhistory/view/10.1093/acrefore/9780199366439.001.0001/acrefore-9780199366439-e-493.

Bauer, Ralph and Marcy Norton. "Introduction: Entangled Trajectories: Indigenous and European Histories," *Colonial Latin American Review*, 26:1, 2017, 1–17.

Bay, Mia E., Farah J. Griffin, Martha S. Jones, and Barbara D. Savage. *Toward an Intellectual History of Black Women*. Chapel Hill: The University of North Carolina Press, 2015.

Belmonte Postigo, José Luis. "La vida improbable de Juana Escobar. Esclavitud, intimidad y libertad en Ponce, Puerto Rico, 1815–1830," *Anuario De Estudios Americanos*, 80:2, 2023, 657–686. https://doi.org/10.3989/aeamer.2023.2.10.

Bennett, Herman L. *Africans in Colonial México: Absolutism, Christianity, and Afro-Creole Consciousness, 1570–1640*. Bloomington: Indiana University Press, 2003.

Bennett, Herman L. *Colonial Blackness: A History of Afro-México*. Bloomington: Indiana University Press, 2009.

Bennett, Herman L. *African Kings and Black Slaves: Sovereignty and Dispossession in the Early Modern Atlantic*. Philadelphia: University of Pennsylvania Press, 2019.

Benton, Bradley. *The Lords of Tetzcoco: The Transformation of Indigenous Rule in Postconquest Central Mexico*. New York: Cambridge University Press, 2017.
Benton, Lauren. *Law and Colonial Cultures: Legal Regimes in World History, 1400–1900*. New York: Cambridge University Press, 2002.
Berruezo-Sánchez, Diana. "'Negro poeta debió de ser el que tan negro romance hizo': ¿poetas negros en el Siglo de Oro?" *Hipogrifo*, 9:1, 2021, 131–142.
Berruezo-Sánchez, Diana. *Black Voices in Early Modern Spanish Literature (1500–1750)*. Oxford: Oxford University Press, 2024.
Berruezo-Sanchez, Diana, Manuel Olmedo Gobante, and Cornesha Tweede. *Iberia negra: Textos para otra historia de la diaspora africana (siglos XVI y XVII)*. London: Routledge, 2024.
Berry, Daina Ramey, and Leslie M. Harris, eds. *Sexuality and Slavery: Reclaiming Intimate Histories in the Americas*. Athens: University of Georgia Press, 2018.
Beusterein, John. *An Eye on Race: Perspectives from Theater in Imperial Spain*. Lewisburg: Bucknell University Press, 2006.
Beusterien, John, Chloe L. Ireton, and Sara Pink. "Callejeando Sevilla histórica: Una caminata antirracista por la ciudad," *Hispania*, 104:3, 2021, 332–339.
Bird, Jonathan Bartholomew. *For Better or Worse: Divorce and Annulment Lawsuits in Colonial Mexico (1544–1799)*. PhD Dissertation, Duke University, 2013. Retrieved from: https://hdl.handle.net/10161/7094
Blain, Keisha N., Christopher Cameron, and Ashley D. Farmer, eds. *New Perspectives on the Black Intellectual Tradition*. Chicago: Northwestern University Press, 2018.
Blanchet, Didier, and Jean-Noël Biraben. "Essay on the Population of Paris and Its Vicinity Since the Sixteenth Century (Population, 1–2, 1998)," *Population*, 54:HS1, 1999, 155–188.
Blumenthal, Deborah, *Enemies and Familiars; Slavery and Mastery in Fifteenth-Century Valencia*. Ithaca: Cornell University Press, 2009.
Bonil-Gómez, Katherine. "Free People of African Descent and Jurisdictional Politics in Eighteenth-Century New Granada: The *Bogas* of the Magdalena River," *Journal of Iberian and Latin American Studies*, 24:2, 2018, 183–194.
Bonil-Gómez, Katherine. "Las movilidades esclavizadas del río Grande de la Magdalena, Nuevo Reino de Granada, s. XVIII," *Revista Fronteras de la Historia*, 27:2, 2022, 11–39.
Borucki, Alex. *From Shipmates to Soldiers Emerging Black Identities in the Río de la Plata*. Alburquerque: University of New Mexico Press, 2015.
Borucki, Alex, David Eltis, and David Wheat. "Atlantic History and the Slave Trade to Spanish America," The American Historical Review, 120:2, 2015, 433–461.
Böttcher, Nikolaus, Bernd Hausberger, and Max S. Hering Torres, eds. *El peso de la sangre: Limpios, mestizos y nobles en el mundo hispánico*. Mexico City: El Colegio de México, 2011.
Boyd-Bowman, Peter. *Índice geobiográfico de más de cuarenta mil pobladores*. Volumen I. Bogotá: Instituto Caro y Cuervo, 1964.
Boyd-Bowman, Peter. *Indice geobiográfico de más de 56 mil pobladores de la América hispánica: 1493–1519*. Volume 1. Mexico City: Fondo de Cultura Económica, Instituto de Investigaciones Históricas, Universidad Nacional Autónoma de México, 1985.

Brading, David A., and Harry E. Cross. "Colonial Silver Mining: México and Peru," *Hispanic American Historical Review*, 52:4, 1972, 545–579.
Branche, Jerome C, ed. *Trajectories of Empire: Transhispanic Reflections on the African Diaspora*. Nashville: Vanderbilt University Press, 2022.
Brendecke, Arndt. *Imperio e información: Funciones del saber en el dominio colonial español*, translated by Griselda Mársico. Madrid: Iberoamericana, 2012.
Bretones Lane, Fernanda. "Free to Bury Their Dead: Baptism and the Meanings of Freedom in the Eighteenth-Century Caribbean," *Slavery & Abolition*, 42:3, 2021, 449–465.
Brewer-García, Larissa. *Beyond Babel: Translations of Blackness in Colonial Peru and New Granada*. Cambridge: Cambridge University Press, 2020.
Bristol, Joan C. "'Although I am black, I am beautiful': Juana Esperanza de San Alberto, Black Carmelite of Puebla." In *Gender, Race and Religion in the Colonization of the Americas*, edited by Nora E. Jaffary, 67–80. Burlington: Ashgate, 2007.
Bristol, Joan C. *Christians, Blasphemers, and Witches: Afro-Mexican Ritual Practice in the Seventeenth Century*. Albuquerque: University of New Mexico Press, 2007.
Bromley, Juan, ed. *Libros de Cabildos de Lima*, Volume 13. Lima: Torres Aguirre, 1944.
Brown, Vincent. *The Reaper's Garden; Death and Power in the World of Atlantic Slavery*. Cambridge: Harvard University Press, 2010.
Brown, Vincent. "Mapping a Slave Revolt: Visualizing Spatial History through the Archives of Slavery," *Social Text*, 33:(125), 2015, 134–141.
Brown, Vincent. *Tacky's Revolt; The Story of an Atlantic Slave War*. Cambridge: Harvard University Press, 2020.
Brunstetter, Daniel. "Bartolomé de Las Casas." In *Just War Thinkers: From Cicero to the 21st Century*, edited by Daniel Brunstetter, and Cian O'Driscoll, 92–104. London: Routledge, 2017.
Bryant, Sherwin K. *Rivers of Gold, Lives of Bondage; Governing through Slavery in Colonial Quito*. Chapel Hill: The University of North Carolina Press, 2014.
Byrd, Brandon R. "The Rise of African American Intellectual History," *Modern Intellectual History*, 18:3, 2021, 833–864.
Byrd, Brandon R., Leslie M. Alexander, and Russell Rickford, eds. *Ideas in Unexpected Places: Reimagining Black Intellectual History*. Chicago: Northwestern University Press, 2022.
Camacho Martínez, Ignacio. *La Hermandad de los Mulatos de Sevilla; antecedentes históricos de la Hermandad del Calvario*. Sevilla: Area de Cultura del Ayuntamiento de Sevilla, 1998.
Camba Ludlow, Ursula. *Imaginarios ambiguos, realidades contradictorias: conductas y representaciones de los negros y mulatos novohispanos, siglos XVI–XVII*. Mexico City: El Colegio de Mexico, 2008.
Camplani, Clara. "La defensa de los Negros en Bartolomé de Las Casas." In *Bartolomé de Las Casas: Face à l'esclavage des Noir-e-s en Amériques/Caraïbes. L'aberration du Onzième Remède (1516)*, edited by Victorien Lavou Zoungbo, 89–98. Perpignan: Presses Universitaires de Perpignan, 2011.

Campos, Fernández de Sevilla, Javier F. ed. *Catálogo de Cofradías del Archivo del Arzobispado de Lima*. Madrid: Estudios Superiores del Escorial San Lorenzo del Escorial, 2014. https://javiercampos.com/fls/dwn/catalogo-cofradias-archivo-arzobispado-lima.pdf

Candido, Mariana P. "African Freedom Suits and Portuguese Vassal Status: Legal Mechanisms for Fighting Enslavement in Benguela, Angola, 1800–1830," *Slavery and Abolition*, 32.3, 2011, 447–459.

Candido, Mariana P. *An African Slaving Port and the Atlantic World: Benguela and Its Hinterland*. Cambridge: Cambridge University Press, 2013.

Candido, Mariana P. *Wealth, Land, and Property in Angola: A History of Dispossession, Slavery, and Inequality*. New York: Cambridge University Press, 2022.

Candido, Mariana P., and Adam Jones. *African Women in the Atlantic World; Property, Vulnerability & Mobility, 1660–1880*. Rochester: Boydell & Brewer, 2020.

Cañizares-Esguerra, Jorge. "Entangled Histories: Borderland Historiographies in New Clothes," *American Historical Review*, 112.3, 2007, 787–799.

Cañizares-Esguerra, Jorge, ed. *Entangled Empires: The Anglo-Iberian Atlantic, 1500–1830*. Philadelphia: University of Pennsylvania Press, 2018.

Cañizares-Esguerra, Jorge. "The Imperial, Global (Cosmopolitan) Dimensions of Nonelite Colonial Scribal Cultures in the Early Modern Iberian Atlantic." In *Cosmopolitanism and the Enlightenment*, edited by Joan-Pau Rubiés, and Neil Safier, 144–176. Cambridge: Cambridge University Press, 2023.

Cañizares-Esguerra, Jorge, Matt D. Childs, and James Sidbury, eds. *The Black Urban Atlantic in the Age of the Slave Trade*. Philadelphia: University of Pennsylvania Press, 2013.

Cárdenas, Eduardo. "La ética cristiana y la esclavitud de los negros: Elementos históricos para el planteamiento de un problema," *Theologica Xaveriana*, 55, April–June 1980, 227–257.

Cardim, Pedro. "'Portugal unido, y separado'. Propaganda and the discourse of identity between the Habsburgs and the Braganza." In *Catalonia and Portugal: The Iberian Peninsula from the Periphery*, edited by Flocel Sabaté and Luís Adão da Fonseca, 395–418. Bern: Peter Lang, 2015.

Cardim, Pedro. "Reassessing the Portuguese Imperial Past: Scholarly Perspectives and Civic Engagement," *Journal of Lusophone Studies*, 8:1, 2023, 176–205.

Cardim, Pedro, Tamar Herzog, José Javier Ruiz Ibáñez, and Gaetano Sabatini, eds. *Polycentric Monarchies: How Did Early Modern Spain and Portugal Achieve and Maintain a Global Hegemony?* Eastbourne: Sussex Academic Press, 2012.

Carroll, Patrick J. *Blacks in Colonial Veracruz: Race, Ethnicity, and Regional Development*. Austin: University of Texas Press, 1991.

Cartaya Baños, Juan. "Un listado inédito de veinticuatros de Sevilla (1494–1590)," *Historia. Instituciones. Documentos*, 49, 2022, 83–116.

Castañeda García, Rafael. "Santos negros, devotos de color. Las cofradías de San Benito de Palermo en Nueva España. Identidades étnicas y religiosas, siglos XVII–XVIII." In *Devoción y paisanaje: las cofradías, congregaciones y hospitales de naturales en España y América*, edited by Óscar Álvarez Gila,

Alberto Angulo Morales, and Jon Ander Ramos Martínez, 145–164. Vitoria: Universidad del País Vasco, 2014.

Castañeda García, Rafael. "La devoción a Santa Ifigenia entre los negros y mulatos de Nueva España. Siglos XVII y XVIII." In *Esclavitud, Meztizaje, y Abolicionismo en los mundos Hispánicos*, edited by Aurelia Martín Casares, 151–172. Granada: Editorial Universidad de Granada, 2015.

Castañeda García, Rafael. "Modelos de santidad: devocionarios y hagiografías a San Benito de palermo en Nueva España," *Historia Moderna*, 38:1, 2016, 39–64.

Castañeda García, Rafael. "Piedad y participación femenina en la cofradía de negros y mulatos de San Benito de Palermo en el Bajío novohispano, siglo XVIII," *Nuevo Mundo -Mundos Nuevos,* Debate, posted online on 5th December, 2012 (Accessed March 2018). http://nuevomundo.revues.org/64478

Castañeda García, Rafael. *Esclavitud africana en la fundación de la Nueva España*, vol. 12. Mexico City: Instituto de Investigaciones Históricas, Dirección General de Publicaciones y Fomento Editorial, 2021.

Castañeda García, Rafael, and Juan Carlos Ruíz Guadalajara, eds. *Africanos y afrodescendientesen la América hispánica septentrional; Espacios de convivencia, sociabilidad y conflicto*. Vol I–II. San Luis Potosí: El Colegio de San Luis, A.C, 2020.

Castañeda García, Rafael, and María Elisa Velázquez. "Introducción," *Nuevo Mundo Mundos Nuevos [En línea], Debates,* posted online on 5th December, 2012, (Accessed March 2018). http://nuevomundo.revues.org/64475

Castillero Calvo, Alfredo. *Portobelo y el San Lorenzo del Chagres: Perspectivas Imperiales. siglos XVI–XIX* (tomo 1). Panamá: Editora Novo Art, 2016.

Castro, Daniel. *Another Face of Empire: Bartolomé de Las Casas, Indigenous Rights, and Ecclesiastical Imperialism*. Durham: Duke University Press, 2007.

Cavanaugh, Stephanie. "Litigating for Liberty: Enslaved Morisco Children in Sixteenth-Century Valladolid," *Renaissance Quarterly* 70:4, 2017, 1282–1320.

Cerquera Hurtado, Miguel Ángel. "El Pleito entre la Hermandad de la Inmaculada Concepción de la Parroquia de San Sebastián y la de Santiago de Alcalá de Guadaíra de 1613," *Amargura, (Boletín de la Hermandad Sacramental Armargura)*, ÉPOCA I, Año XXVI, Cuaresma, 2021, Boletín no. 33, 22–25.

Chamberlain, Robert S. "The Founding of the City of Gracias a Dios, First Seat of the Audiencia de los Confines," *The Hispanic American Historical Review*, 26:1, 1946, 2–18.

Chira, Adriana. "Affective Debts: Manumission by Grace and the Making of Gradual Emancipation Laws in Cuba, 1817–68," *Law and History Review*, 36:1, 2018, 1–33.

Chira, Adriana. "Freedom with Local Bonds: Custom and Manumission in the Age of Emancipation," *The American Historical Review*, 126:3, 2021, 949–977.

Chira, Adriana. *Patchwork Freedoms: Law, Slavery, and Race beyond Cuba's Plantations*. New York: Cambridge University Press, 2022.

Clark, Joseph M. H. "Environment and the Politics of Relocation in the Caribbean Port of Veracruz, 1519–1599." In *The Spanish Caribbean and the Atlantic World in the Long Sixteenth Century*, edited by Ida Altman, and David Wheat, 189–210. Lincoln: University of Nebraska Press, 2019.

Clark, Joseph M. H. *Veracruz and the Caribbean in the Seventeenth Century.* New York: Cambridge University Press, 2023.

Clayton, Lawrence A. *Bartolomé de Las Casas: A Biography.* Cambridge: Cambridge University Press, 2012.

Clendinnen, Inga. *Ambivalent Conquests: Maya and Spaniard in Yucatan, 1517–1570.* Cambridge: Cambridge University Press, 1987.

Collantes de Terán Sánchez, Antonio. *Sevilla en la baja Edad Media: La ciudad y sus hombres.* Sevilla: Sección de Publicaciones del Excmo. Ayuntamiento, 1977.

Collantes de Terán Sánchez, Antonio. "Los Mercados De Abastos En Sevilla," *Historia. Instituciones. Documentos,* ISSN 0210-7716, N° 18, 1991, 57–70.

Collantes de Terán Sánchez, Antonio, Josefina Cruz Villalon, Rogelio Reyes Cano, and Salvador Rodriguez Becerra. *Diccionario Histórico de las Calles de Sevilla.* Vols. I, II, and III. Sevilla: Consejeria de Obras Publicas y Transportes, Ayuntamiento de Sevilla, 1993.

Coleman, David. *Creating Christian Granada: Society and Religious Culture in an Old-World Frontier City, 1492–1600.* Ithaca: Cornell University Press, 2003.

Cook, Karoline P. *Forbidden Passages, Forbidden Passages: Muslims and Moriscos in Colonial Spanish America.* Philadelphia: The University of Pennsylvania Press, 2016.

Córdova Aguilar, Maira Cristina. "Cimarrones en el sur de la Nueva España: rutas y estrategias de fuga de los africanos esclavos del obispado de Oaxaca (1591–1769)," *Fronteras De La Historia,* 27:2, 2022, 211–231.

Corona Pérez, Eduardo. "Aproximación a la mortalidad infantil de los esclavos en Sevilla, (1620–1650)," *Revista De Demografía Histórica-Journal of Iberoamerican Population Studies,* 38:2, 2020, 83–105.

Corona Pérez, Eduardo. *Trata Atlántica y esclavitud en Sevilla, (ca. 1500–1650).* Sevilla: Editorial de Universidad de Sevilla, 2022.

Cortés Alonso, Vicenta. *La esclavitud en Valencia durante el reinado de los Reyes católicos (1479–1515),* Valencia: Publicaciones del Archivo Municipal, 1964.

Cortés Alonso, Vicenta. "La población negra de Palos de la Frontera," *Actas y Memorias del XXXVI Congreso Internacional de Americanistas,* 3, 1964, 609–618. Sevilla.

Cortés Alonso, Vicenta. "La Liberación Del Esclavo," *Anuario De Estudios Americanos,* 22, 1965, 533–568.

Cossar, Roisin, Filippo de Vivo, and Christina Neilson, "Introduction to 'Shared Spaces and Knowledge'," *Transactions in the Italian Renaissance City, Tatti Studies in the Italian Renaissance,* 19:1, 2016, 5–22.

Cuartero y Huerta, Baltasar, Antonio Vargas Zúñiga, and Marqués de Siete Iglesias, eds. *Índice de la Colección de don Luis de Salazar y Castro.* Vol. XVII. Madrid: Real Academia de la Historia, 1956.

Cunill, Caroline. "La negociación indígena en el Imperio Ibérico: aportes a su discusión metodológica," *Colonial Latin American Review,* 21:3, 2012, 391–412.

Cunill, Caroline. *Los defensores de indios de Yucatán y el acceso de los mayas a la justicia colonial, 1540–1600.* Mérida: Centro Peninsular en Humanidades y Ciencias Sociales, Universidad Nacional Autónoma de México, 2012.

Cunill, Caroline. "Los intérpretes de Yucatán y la Corona española: negociación e iniciativas privadas en la fragua del Imperio ibérico, siglo XVI," *Colonial Latin American Historical Review,* 18:4, 2013, 361–380.

Cunill, Caroline. "El uso indígena del discurso jurídico colonial: estudio de las probanzas de méritos y servicios de algunos mayas de Yucatán (siglo XVI)," *Signos Históricos*, 16:32, 2014, 14–47.

Cunill, Caroline. "Etnicidad en clave histórica: categorías jurídicas coloniales y cultura maya en el siglo XVI," *Trace*, 65, 2014, 7–22.

Cunill, Caroline. "Justicia e interpretación en sociedades plurilingües: el caso de Yucatán en el siglo XVI," *Estudios de Historia Novohispana*, 52, 2015, 18–28.

Cunill, Caroline. "Philip II and Indigenous Access to Royal Justice: Considering the Process of Decision-Making in the Spanish Empire," *Colonial Latin American Review*, 24(4), 2015, 505–524.

Cunill, Caroline. "Pobres, esclavos, indígenas y personas miserables: reflexiones en torno a sus abogados en el Consejo de Indias y en la Audiencia de México, siglo XVI," *Fronteras de la Historia*, 28:1, 2023, 15–37.

Cunill, Caroline, and Luis Miguel Glave Testino, eds. *Las lenguas indígenas en los tribunales de América Latina: intérpretes, mediación y justicia (siglos XVI–XXI)*. Bogotá: Instituto Colombiano de Antropología e Historia ICANH, 2019.

Cunill, Caroline, Dolores Estruch, and Alejandra Ramos, eds. *Actores, redes y prácticas dialógicas en la construcción y uso de los archivos en América Latina (siglos XVI–XXI)*. Ciudad de México: Universidad Nacional Autónoma de México, 2021.

Curto, José C. "The Story of Nbena, 1817–1820: Unlawful Enslavement and the Concept of 'Original Freedom' in Angola." In *Trans-Atlantic Dimensions of Ethnicity in the African Diaspora*, edited by Paul E. Lovejoy, and David V. Trotman, 42–64. London: Continuum, 2003.

Curto, José C. "Struggling against Enslavement: The Case of José Manuel in Benguela, 1816–20." *Canadian Journal of African Studies*, 39:1, 2005, 96–122.

Curto, José C. "Experiences of Enslavement in West-Central Africa," *Histoire sociale / Social History*, 41:82, 2008, 381–415.

Dawson, Kevin. "The Cultural Geography of Enslaved Ship Pilots." In *The Black Urban Atlantic in the Age of the Slave Trade*, edited by Jorge Cañizares-Esguerra, Matt D. Childs, and James Sidbury, 163–184. Philadelphia: University of Pennsylvania Press, 2013.

Dawson, Kevin. *Undercurrents of Power: Aquatic Culture in the African Diaspora*. Philadelphia: University of Pennsylvania Press, 2018.

Dawson, Kevin. "A Sea of Caribbean Islands: Maritime Maroons in the Greater Caribbean," *Slavery & Abolition*, 42:3, 2021, 428–448.

Deardorff, Max. *A Tale of Two Granadas: Custom, Community, and Citizenship in the Spanish Empire, 1568–1668*. New York: Cambridge University Press, 2023.

de Ataíde Vilhena Cabral, Iva Maria. *A primeira elite colonial atlântica: dos "homens honrados brancos" de Santiago à "nobreza da terra": finais do séc. XV – início do séc. XVII*. Cabo Verde: Pedro Cardoso Livraria, 2015.

de Avilez Rocha, Gabriel. "Maroons in the Montes: Toward a Political Ecology of Marronage in the Sixteenth-Century Caribbean." In *Early Modern Black Diaspora Studies: A Critical Anthology*, edited by Cassander L. Smith, Nicholas R. Jones, and Miles Grier, 15–35. Cham, Switzerland: Palgrave Macmillan, 2018.

de Carvalho Soares, Mariza. *People of Faith: Slavery and African Catholics in Eighteenth-Century Rio de Janeiro*, translated by Jerry Dennis Metz. Durham: Duke University Press October 2011.

de Carvalho Soares, Mariza. "African Barbeiros in Brazilian Slave Ports." In *The Black Urban Atlantic in the Age of the Slave Trade*, edited by Jorge Cañizares-Esguerra, Matt D. Childs, and James Sidbury, 207–230. Philadelphia: University of Pennsylvania Press, 2013.

de la Fuente, Alejandro. "Slave Law and Claims-Making in Cuba: The Tannenbaum Debate Revisited," *Law and History Review*, 22:2, 2004, 339–369.

de la Fuente, Alejandro. *Havana and the Atlantic in the Sixteenth Century*. Chapel Hill: University of North Carolina Press, 2011.

de la Fuente, Alejandro, and Ariela J. Gross. *Becoming Free, Becoming Black: Race, Freedom, and Law in Cuba, Virginia, and Louisiana*. Cambridge: Cambridge University Press, 2020.

de la Puente Luna, José Carlos. "That Which Belongs to All: Khipus, Community, and Indigenous Legal Activism in the Early Colonial Andes," *The Americas*, 72:1, 2015, 19–54.

de la Puente Luna, José Carlos. "En lengua de indios y en lengua española: escribanos indígenas, cabildos de naturales y escritura alfabética en el Perú colonial." In *Desafíos metodológicos para la historia de los pueblos indígenas*, edited by Ana Luisa Izquierdo de la Cueva, 51–113. Mexico City: Universidad Nacional Autónoma de México, 2016.

de la Puente Luna, José Carlos. *Andean Cosmopolitans: Seeking Justice and Reward at the Spanish Royal Court*. Austin: University of Texas Press, 2018.

de la Puente Luna, José Carlos, and Renzo Honores. "Guardianes de la real justicia: alcaldes de indios y justicia local en los Andes," *Histórica*, 40:2, 2016, 11–48.

de la Serna, Juan Manuel. "Los cimarrones en la sociedad novohispana." In *De la libertad y la abolición: Africanos y afrodescendientes in Iberoamérica*, edited by Juan Manuel de la Serna, 83–109. Mexico City: Centro de estudios mexicanos y centroamericanos, 2010.

de la Torre, Oscar. *The People of the River: Nature and Identity in Black Amazonia, 1835–1945*. Chapel Hill: The University of North Carolina Press, 2018.

de Vito, Christian G. "History Without Scale: The Micro-Spatial Perspective," *Past & Present*, 242:14, 2019, 348–372.

de Vivo, Filipo, *Information and Communication in Venice: Rethinking Early Modern Politics*. Oxford: Oxford University Press, 2007.

de Vivo, Filipo. "Walking in Sixteenth-Century Venice: Mobilizing the Early Modern City," *Transactions in the Italian Renaissance City, Tatti Studies in the Italian Renaissance*, 19:1, 2016, 115–141.

de Vivo, Filipo. "Microhistories of Long-Distance Information: Space, Movement and Agency in the Early Modern News," *Past & Present*, 242:14, 2019, 179–214.

del Valle Pavon, Guillermina. *El camino México-Puebla-Veracruz: Comercio poblano y pugnas entre mercaderes a fines de la época colonial*. México City: Gobierno del Estado de Puebla, Secretaría de Gobernación, Archivo General de la Nación, 1992.

del Valle Pavon, Guillermina. "Desarrollo de la economía mercantil y construcción de los caminos México-Veracruz en el siglo XVI," *América Latina en la Historia Económica*, 27, 2007, 5–49.
Delmas, Adrien. "Introduction." In *Written Culture in a Colonial Context; Africa and the Americas 1500–1900*, edited by Adrien Delmas, and Nigel Penn, xvii-xxx. Leiden: Brill, 2012.
Dias Paes, Mariana Armond. "Shared Atlantic Legal Culture: The Case of a Freedom Suit in Benguela," *Atlantic Studies: Global Currents*, 17:3, 2020, 419–440.
Dias Paes, Mariana Armond. *Esclavos y tierras entre posesión y títulos; La construcción social del derecho de propiedad en Brasil (siglo XIX)*. Frankfurt: Max Planck Institute for Legal History and Legal Theory, 2021.
Díaz, María Elena. *The Virgin, the King, and the Royal Slaves of El Cobre: Negotiating Freedom in Colonial Cuba, 1670–1780*. Stanford: Stanford University Press, 2000.
Díaz Ceballos, Jorge. "Cimarronaje, jurisdicción y lealtades híbridas en la Monarquía Hispánica." In *Dimensiones del Conflicto: resistencia, violencia y policía en el mundo urbano*, edited by Tomás A. Mantecón, Susana Truchuelo, and Marina Torres Arce, 79–102. Cantabria: Editorial de la Universidad de Cantabria, 2020.
Díaz Ceballos, Jorge. *Poder compartido: Repúblicas urbanas, monarquía y conversación en Castilla del Oro, 1508–1573*. Madrid: Marcial Pons, 2020.
Díaz Rementería, Carlos. "La formación y el concepto del derecho indiano." In *Historia del derecho indiano*, edited by Ismail Sánchez Bella, Alberto de la Hera, and Carlos Díaz Rementería, 36–87. Madrid: Editorial MAPFRE, 1992.
Di-Capua, Yoav. *No Exit: Arab Existentialism, Jean-Paul Sartre, and Decolonization*. Chicago: The University of Chicago Press, 2018.
DiFranco, Ralph A., and José Julián Labrador Herraiz. "Villancicos de negros y otros testimonios al caso en manuscritos del Siglo de Oro." In *De la canción de amor medieval a las soleares. Profesor Manuel Alvar "in memorian,"* edited by Pedro Manuel Piñero Ramírez, and Antonio José Pérez Castellano, 163–188. Sevilla: Editorial Universidad de Sevilla, 2004.
Domingues, Ângela, Maria Leônia Chaves de Resende, and Pedro Cardim, eds. *Os indígenas e as justiças no mundo ibero-americano (sécs. XVI–XIX)*. Lisbon: Centro de História da Universidade de Lisboa, CHAM, 2019.
Domínguez Domínguez, Citlalli. "Entre resistencia y colaboración: Los negros y mulatos en la sociedad colonial veracruzana, 1570–1650," *E-Spania*, 25, posted online on 1st October, 2016, http://journals.openedition.org/e-spania/25936
Domínguez Domínguez, Citlalli. "Circulaciones imperiales de Negros Libres en el Atlántico ibérico, siglos XVI–XVII." In *L'invention de la ville dans le monde hispanique (IXe-XVIIIe siècle)*, edited by Louise Bénat-Tachot, Mercedes Blanco, Araceli Guillaume-Alonso, and Hélène Thieulin-Pardo, 377–398. Paris: éditions hispaniques, Lettres Sorbonne Université, CLEA, 2019.
Domínguez Domínguez, Citlalli. "Veracruz: port, ville, carrefour des mondes. Les Afro-ibériques et les Luso-africains dans la construction de la ville de Veracruz (1570–1650)," PhD Thesis, Sorbonne Université, 2021.
Domínguez Ortíz, Antonio. *La población de Sevilla en la baja Edad Media y en los tiempos modernos*. Madrid: Publicaciones de la Real Sociedad Geográfica, 1941.

Domínguez Ortíz, Antonio. "La población de Sevilla a mediados del siglo XVII," *Archivo hispalense: Revista histórica, literaria y artística*, 72:221, 1989, 7–16.
Domínguez Ortíz, Antonio. *Orto y ocaso de Sevilla*, 4th ed. Sevilla: Universidad de Sevilla, 1991.
Domínguez Ortíz, Antonio. *La esclavitud en Castilla durante la edad moderna, otros estudios marginados*. Granada: Editorial Comares, 2003.
Durán López, Gonzalo. "Pasajes a Indias a principios del siglo XVIII, precios y condiciones." In *La emigración española a Ultramar: 1492–1914*, edited by Antonio Eiras Roel, 199–214. Madrid: Asociación de Historia Moderna, Tabapress, 1991.
Dussel, Enrique. *Política de la liberación. Historia mundial y crítica*. Madrid: Editorial Trotta, 2007.
Eltis, David. "A Brief Overview of the Trans-Atlantic Slave Trade," *Slave Voyages: The Trans-Atlantic Slave Trade Database*, www.slavevoyages.org/voyage/about (Accessed April 27, 2018).
Eller, Anne. "Rumors of Slavery: Defending Emancipation in a Hostile Caribbean," *The American Historical Review*, 122:3, 2017, 653–679.
Escudero, José Antonio. *Felipe II: El rey en el despacho*. Madrid: Real Academia de la Historia, 2002.
Farnsworth, Cacey B., and Pedro Cardim. "Mulheres negras protestam em Lisboa em 1717." In *Resistências. Insubmissão e revolta no Império Português*, edited by Mafalda Soares da Cunha, 217–225. Lisbon: Casa das Letras / LeYa Leya, 2021.
Fernández Chaves, and Manuel Francisco. "Amas, Esclavas y Libertad en Sevilla, 1512–1600," *OHM: Obradoiro de Historia Moderna*, 32, 2023, 1–25.
Fernández Chaves, Manuel Francisco, and Rafael Mauricio Pérez García, eds. *Tratas atlánticas y esclavitudes en América. Siglos XVI–XIX*. Sevilla: Editorial Universidad de Sevilla, 2021.
Fernández López, Francisco. *La Casa de la Contratación: una oficina de expedición documental para el gobierno de las Indias (1503-1717)*. Sevilla and Zamora: Universidad de Sevilla; Colegio de Michoacán, 2018.
Fernández Martín, Javier. "La esclavitud ante la justicia del rey: el caso de la Chancillería de Granada (ca. 1577–1700)." In *Tratas, esclavitudes y mestizajes: una historia conectada, siglos XV–XVIII*, edited by Rafael Mauricio Pérez García, Manuel Francisco Fernández Chaves, and Eduardo França Paiva, 277–288. Sevilla: Editorial Universidad de Sevilla, 2020.
Ferreira, Roquinaldo. *Cross-Cultural Exchange in the Atlantic World: Angola and Brazil during the Era of the Slave Trade*. Cambridge: Cambridge University Press, 2012.
Fisk, Bethan. "Black Knowledge on the Move: African Diasporic Healing in Caribbean and Pacific New Granada," *Atlantic Studies*, 18:2, 2021, 244–270.
Fisk, Bethan. "Transimperial Mobilities, Slavery, and Becoming Catholic in Eighteenth-Century Cartagena de Indias," *Journal of Iberian and Latin American Studies*, 28:3, 2022, 345–370.
Flannery, Kristie. "Can the Devil Cross the Deep Blue Sea? Imagining the Spanish Pacific and Vast Early America from Below," *The William and Mary Quarterly*, 79:1, 2022, 31–60.
Fracchia, Carmen. *"Black but Human": Slavery and Visual Arts in Hapsburg Spain, 1480–1700*. Oxford: Oxford University Press, 2019.

Fra-Molinero, Baltasar. *La imagen de los negros en el teatro del Siglo de Oro*. Madrid: Siglo Veintiuno, 1995.
Fra-Molinero, Baltasar. "A Postcard from Wakanda to the King of Spain: The Portrait of the Mulatos de Esmeraldas (1599)." In *Trajectories of Empire: Transhispanic Reflections on the African Diaspora*, edited by Jerome C. Branche, 142–160. Nashville: Vanderbilt University Press, 2022.
Fra-Molinero, Baltasar. "Black Pride, Honor, and Sex: Dramatis Personae in *El valiente negro en Flandes*." In *The Valiant Black Man in Flanders / El valiente negro en Flandes*, edited by Andrés de Claramonte, 255–302. Liverpool: Liverpool University Press, 2023.
Fra-Molinero, Baltasar. "'Mis padres vinieron de Guinea negros esclavos': Catalina Déniz, la Inquisición, magia y medicina." In *Iberia negra: Textos para otra historia de la diaspora africana (siglos XVI y XVII)*, edited by Diana Berruezo-Sanchez, Manuel Olmedo Gobante, and Cornesha Tweede, 29–40. London: Routledge, 2024.
Fra-Molinero, Baltasar, Nelson López, and Manuel Olmedo Gobante, "Antón's Linguistic Blackface and Freedom." In *The Valiant Black Man in Flanders / El valiente negro en Flandes*, edited by Andrés de Claramonte, 335–354. Liverpool: Liverpool University Press, 2023.
Franco Idígoras, Inmaculada. *Catálogo de la colección nobiliaria del Archivo Municipal de Sevilla, El archivo familiar de los Ortiz de Zúñiga*. Sevilla: Ayuntamiento de Sevilla, 2000.
Franco Silva, Alfonso. "La esclavitud en Sevilla entre 1526 y 1550," *Archivo hispalense: Revista histórica, literaria y artística*, 61:188, 1978, 77–91.
Franco Silva, Alfonso. *La esclavitud en Sevilla y su tierra a fines de la Edad Media*. Sevilla: Diputación Provincial, 1979.
Fromont, Cécile. *The Art of Conversion; Christian Visual Culture in the Kingdom of Kongo*. Chapel Hill: The University of North Carolina Press, 2014.
Fromont, Cécile, ed. *Afro-Catholic Festivals in the Americas: Performance, Representation, and the Making of Black Atlantic Tradition*. University Park, PA: Penn State University Press, 2019.
Fuentes, Marisa J. *Dispossessed Lives: Enslaved Women, Violence, and the Archive*. Philadelphia: University of Pennsylvania Press, 2016.
Gaglo Dagbovie, Pero. "African American Intellectual History: The Past as a Porthole into the Present and Future of the Field." In *The Black Intellectual Tradition: African American Thought in the Twentieth Century*, edited by Derrick P. Alridge, Cornelius L. Bynum, and James B. Stewart, 17–39. Champaign: University of Illinois Press, 2021.
Galbis Díez, María del Carmen. *Catálogo de Pasajeros a Indias durante los siglos xvi, xvii y xviii*, Vols. VI and VII. Sevilla: S.G. Archivos Estatales, 1986.
Gallup-Díaz, Ignacio, "A Legacy of Strife: Rebellious Slaves in Sixteenth-Century Panamá," *Colonial Latin American Review*, 19:3, 2010, 417–435.
García, Guadalupe. *Beyond the Walled City: Colonial Exclusion in Havana*. Berkeley: University of California Press, 2015.
García de León, Antonio. *Tierra adentro, mar en fuera: el puerto de Veracruz y su litoral a Sotavento, 1519–1821*. "Ciudad de México: Fondo de Cultura Económica, Gobierno del Estado de Veracruz, Universidad Veracruzana," 2011.

García-Montón, Alejandro. "The Rise of Portobelo and the Transformation of the Spanish American Slave Trade, 1640s–1730s: Transimperial Connections and Intra-American Shipping," *Hispanic American Historical Review*, 99:3, 2019, 399–429.

García-Montón, Alejandro. "Trans-Imperial, Transnational and Decentralized: The Traffic of African Slaves to Spanish America and Across the Isthmus of Panama, 1508–1651." In *American Globalization, 1492–1850; Trans-Cultural Consumption in Spanish Latin America*, edited by Bartolomé Yun-Casalilla, Ilaria Berti, and Omar Svriz-Wucherer, 13–31. New York and London: Routledge, 2021.

García Quintana, Josefina, and Víctor M. Castillo Farreas, eds. *Tratado curioso y docto de las grandezas de la Nueva España. Relación breve y verdadera de algunas cosas de las muchas que sucedieron al padre fray Alonso Ponce en las provincias de la Nueva España siendo comisario general de aquellas partes*. Tomo II, Tercera edición. Ciudad de México: Universidad Nacional Autónoma de México, Instituto de Investigaciones Históricas, 1993.

Garnham, Nicholas. "Habermas and the Public Sphere," *Global Media and Communication*, 3:2, 2007, 201–214.

Garofalo, Leo J. "Afro-Iberian Subjects; Petitioning the Crown at Home, Serving the Crown Abroad, 1590s–1630s." In *Afro-Latino Voices: Narratives from the Early Modern Ibero-Atlantic World, 1550–1812*, edited by Kathryn Joy McKnight, and Leo Garofalo, 52–63. Indianapolis: Hackett Publishing, 2009.

Garofalo, Leo J. "The Shape of a Diaspora: The Movement of Afro-Iberians to Colonial Spanish America." In *Africans to Spanish America: Expanding the Diaspora*, edited by Sherwin Bryant, Rachel O'Toole, and Ben Vinson III, 27–49. Champaign: University of Illinois Press, 2012.

Garofalo, Leo J. "Afro-Iberians in the Early Spanish Empire, ca. 1550–1600." In *Global Africa: Into the Twenty-First Century*, edited by Dorothy L. Hodgson, and Judith A. Byfield, 39–48. Berkeley: University of California Press, 2017.

Gharala, Norah L. A. *Taxing Blackness: Free Afromexican Tribute in Bourbon New Spain*. Tuscaloosa: University of Alabama Press, 2019.

Gharala, Norah L. A. "Black Tribute in the Spanish Americas." In *Oxford Research Encyclopedia of Latin American History*, edited by Ángela Vergara, 1–27. New York: Oxford University Press, 2014. Published online December 22, 2021.

Gharala, Norah L. A. "'This Woman's Resistance to Her Son's Paying Tribute': Afrodescendant Women, Family, and Royal Tribute in New Spain," *Mexican Studies/Estudios Mexicanos*, 38:1, 2022, 10–34.

Ghobrial, John-Paul A. "Introduction: Seeing the World Like a Microhistorian," *Past & Present*, 242: Supplement 14, November 2019, 1–22.

Ghobrial, John-Paul A. "Moving Stories and What They Tell Us: Early Modern Mobility Between Microhistory and Global History," *Past & Present*, 242: Supplement 14, November 2019, 243–280.

Ghobrial, John-Paul A. *The Whispers of Cities; Information Flows in Istanbul, London, and Paris in the Age of William Trumbull*. Oxford: Oxford University Press, 2013.

Gil-Bermejo García, Juana. "Pasajeros a Indias," *Anuario de Estudios Americanos*, 31, 1974, 323–384.

Gómez, Alejandro E. "El estigma africano en los mundos hispano-atlánticos, (siglos XIV al XIX)," *Revista de Historia*, 153, 2005, 139–179.

Gómez, Michael A. *Black Crescent: African Muslims in the Americas*. Cambridge: Cambridge University Press, 2005.
Gómez, Pablo F. *The Experiential Caribbean: Creating Knowledge and Healing in the Early Modern Atlantic*. Chapel Hill: University of North Carolina Press, 2017.
Gómez Gómez, Margarita. "Libros de gestión para el gobierno de América: El caso del Consejo de Indias." In *La escritura de la memoria: Libros para la administración*, edited by José Antonio Munita Loinaz, and José Angel Lema Pueyo, 259–269. Bilbao, Spain: Universidad del País Vasco, 2012.
Gonzalbo Aizpuru, Pilar. "Afectos e intereses en los matrimonios en la ciudad de México a fines de la colonia," *Historia Mexicana*, 56:4, 2007, 1117–1161.
Gonzalbo Aizpuru, Pilar. "La trampa de las castas." In *La sociedad novohispana: Estereotipos y realidades*, edited by Solange Alberro, and Pilar Gonzalbo Aizpuru, 17–191. Mexico City: Colegio de Mexico, 2013.
González de Caldas, Victoria. *Judíos o cristianos?: el proceso de fe Sancta Inquisitio*. Sevilla: Universidad de Sevilla, 2000.
González Martínez, Nelson Fernando. "Comunicarse a pesar de la distancia: La instalación de los Correos Mayores y los flujos de correspondencia en el mundo hispanoamericano (1501–1640)," *Nuevo Mundo, Mundos Nuevos* [En línea], "Debates," posted online on 11 December, 2017, http://journals.openedition.org/nuevomundo/71527
González Martínez, Nelson Fernando. "Communicating an Empire and Its Many Worlds: Spanish American Mail, Logistics, and Postal Agents, 1492–1620," *Hispanic American Historical Review*, 101:4, 2021, 567–596.
González Sánchez, Carlos Alberto. *Dineros de ventura: La varia fortuna de la emigración a Indias (siglos XVI–XVII)*. Sevilla: Universidad de Sevilla, 1995.
Goodman, Dena. *The Republic of Letters: A Cultural History of the French Enlightenment*. Ithaca: Cornell University Press, 1996.
Gould, Eliga. "Entangled Histories, Entangled Worlds: The English-Speaking Atlantic as a Spanish Periphery," *American Historical Review*, 112:3, 2007, 764–786.
Graubart, Karen B. *With Our Labor and Sweat: Indigenous Women and the Formation of Colonial Society in Peru, 1550–1700*. Stanford: Stanford University Press, 2007.
Graubart, Karen B. "'So color de una cofradía': Catholic Confraternities and the Development of Afro-Peruvian Ethnicities in Early Colonial Peru," *Slavery & Abolition*, 33:1, 2012, 43–64.
Graubart, Karen B. "Los lazos que unen: Dueñas negras de esclavos negros en Lima, ss. XVI–XVII," *Revista Nueva Corónica*, 2, 2013, 625–640.
Graubart, Karen B. "The Bonds of Inheritance: Afro-Peruvian Women's Legacies in a Slave-holding World." In *Uncovering the Colonial Archive: Women's Textual Agency in Spanish America 1500–1800*, edited by Mónica Díaz, and Rocío Quispe-Agnoli, 130–150. New York: Routledge, 2017.
Graubart, Karen B. "Shifting Landscapes. Heterogeneous Conceptions of Land Use and Tenure in the Lima Valley," *Colonial Latin American Review*, 26:1, 2017, 62–84.
Graubart, Karen B. "*Pesa más la libertad*: Slavery, Legal Claims, and the History of Afro-Latin American Ideas," *The William and Mary Quarterly*, 78:3, 2021, 427–458.

Graubart, Karen B. *Republics of Difference; Religious and Racial Self-Governance in the Spanish Atlantic World*. New York: Oxford University Press, 2022.
Green, Toby. *The Rise of the Trans-Atlantic Slave Trade in Western Africa, 1300–1589*. Cambridge: Cambridge University Press, 2012.
Green, Toby. "Beyond an Imperial Atlantic: Trajectories of Africans from Upper Guinea and West-Central Africa in the Early Atlantic World," *Past & Present*, 230:1, 2016, 91–122.
Green, Toby. "Baculamento or Encomienda? Legal Pluralisms and the Contestation of Power in the Pan-Atlantic World of the Sixteenth and Seventeenth Centuries," *Journal of Global Slavery*, 2:3, 2017, 310–336.
Green, Toby. "Pluralism, Violence and Empire: The Portuguese New Christians in the Atlantic World." In *Cosmopolitanism in the Portuguese-Speaking World*, edited by Francisco Bethencourt, 40–58. Leiden: Brill, 2018.
Green, Toby. *A Fistful of Shells; West Africa from the Rise of the Slave Trade to the Age of Revolution*. Chicago: The University of Chicago Press, 2019.
Grove Gordillo, María. "Una aproximación a la población esclava: la collación de Santa Ana de Sevilla (1620–1634)." In *Tratas, esclavitudes y mestizajes. Una historia conectada, siglos XV–XVIII*, edited by Rafael Mauricio Pérez García, Manuel Francisco Fernández Chaves, and Eduardo França Paiva, 289–302. Sevilla. Editorial Universidad de Sevilla, 2020.
Guasco, Michael. *Slaves and Englishmen: Human Bondage in the Early Modern Atlantic World*. Philadelphia: University of Pennsylvania Press, 2014.
Guerrero Mosquera, Andrea. "Alonso de Sandoval: Un tratadista en Cartagena de Indias." In *Cuaderno de Bitácora III. Cartagena: Epicentro De La América Bicentenaria*, edited by Fundación Carolina Colombia, 13–21. Colombia: Fundación Carolina Colombia, 2012.
Guerrero Mosquera, Andrea. "Misiones, misioneros y bautizos a través del atlántico: evangelización en Cartagena de Indias y en los reinos del Kongo y Ngola. Siglo XVII," *Revista Memoria y Sociedad*, 18:37, 2014, 14–32.
Guerrero Mosquera, Andrea. "Los jesuitas en Cartagena de Indias y la evangelización de africanos. Una aproximación," *Revista Montalbán*, 52, 2018, 4–27.
Guerrero Mosquera, Andrea. "Bolsas mandingas en Cartagena de Indias durante el siglo XVII," *Revista Memorias, Memorias: Revista Digital de Historia y Arqueología desde el Caribe colombiano*, 43, 2021, 69–93.
Guerrero Mosquera, Andrea. "De esclavizados a traductores. La catequización de africanos en el Colegio jesuita de Cartagena de Indias." In *Inmigración, trabajo, movilización y sociabilidad laboral. México y América Latina siglos XVI al XX*, edited by Sonia Pérez Toledo, 29–62. Ciudad de México: Universidad Autónoma Metropolitana, 2022.
Guerrero Mosquera, Andrea. "African Diaspora Protection: Amulets in New Spain, New Granada and the Caribbean," *Anuario Colombiano de Historia Social y de la Cultura*, 50:2, 2023, 285–319.
Guerrero Quintero, Saúl José. "The Environmental History of Silver Refining in New Spain and Mexico, 16c to 19c: A Shift of Paradigm," PhD Thesis, McGill University, 2015. Retrieved from: https://escholarship.mcgill.ca/concern/theses/zs25xc58s

Habermas, Jürgen. *The Structural Transformation of the Public Sphere: An Inquiry into a Category of Bourgeois Society*, translated by Thomas Burger. Cambridge: MIT Press, 1989, 1991.

Hampe Martínez, Teodoro. "Esbozo de una transferencia política: asistentes de Sevilla en el gobierno virreinal de México y Perú," *Historia Mexicana*, 41:1, 1991, 49–81.

Hanke, Lewis. *All Mankind Is One: A Study of the Disputation between Bartolomé de Las Casas and Juan Ginés de Sepúlveda in 1550 on the Intellectual and Religious Capacity of the American Indians*. DeKalb: Northern Illinois University Press, 1994.

Harding, Vanessa. "The Population of London, 1550–1700: A Review of the Published Evidence," *The London Journal*, 15:2, 111–128.

Harris, Katie. *From Muslim to Christian Granada: Inventing a City's Past in Early Modern Spain*. Baltimore: Johns Hopkins University Press, 2007.

Hartman, Saidiya. "Venus in Two Acts," *Small Axe; A Caribbean Journal of Criticism*, 12:2, 2008, 1–14.

Havik, Philip J. "Walking the Tightrope: Female Agency, Religious Practice and the Portuguese Inquisition on the Upper Guinea Coast." In *Bridging the Early Modern Atlantic World: People, Products and Practices on the Move*, edited by Caroline A. Williams, 173–202. Farnham: Ashgate, 2009.

Havik, Philip J. "Gendering the Black Atlantic: Women's Agency in Coastal Trade Settlements in the Guinea Bissau Region." In *Women in Port, Gendering Communities, Economies, and Social Networks in Atlantic Port Cities, 1500–1800*, edited by Douglas Catterall, and Jodi Campbell, 315–356. Leiden: Brill, 2012.

Hayes, Marcella. "'They Have Been United as Sisters': Women Leaders and Political Power in Black Lay Confraternities of Colonial Lima," *The Americas*, 79:4, 2022, 559–586.

Hébrard, Jean. "L'esclavage au Brésil : le débat historiographique et ses racines." In *Brésil: quatre siècles d'esclavage. Nouvelles questions, nouvelles recherches*, edited by Jean Hébrard, 7–61. Paris: Karthala & CIRESC, 2012.

Helg, Aline. *Slave No More: Self-Liberation before Abolitionism in the Americas*, translated from the French by Lara Vergnaud. Chapel Hill: University of North Carolina Press, 2019.

Helton, Laura, Justin Leroy, Max A. Mishler, Samantha Seeley, and Shauna Sweeney. "The Question of Recovery: An Introduction," *Social Text*, 33:4 (125), 2015, 1–18.

Hering Torres, Max S. "Purity of Blood: Problems of Interpretation." In *Race and Blood in the Iberian World*, edited by Max S. Hering Torres, María Elena Martínez, and David Nirenberg, 11–38. Zurich: LIT Verlag, 2012.

Hering Torres, Max S., María Elena Martínez, and David Nirenberg, eds. *Race and Blood in the Iberian World*. Zurich: LIT Verlag, 2012.

Hernández González, Salvador. "Ronda y la Emigración Americana en la Edad Moderna (I) Pasajeros a Indias del Siglo XVI," *takurunna*, 2, 2012, 293–336.

Hershenzon, Daniel. *The Captive Sea: Slavery, Communication, and Commerce in Early Modern Spain and the Mediterranean*. Philadelphia: University of Pennsylvania Press, 2018.

Herzog, Tamara. *Defining Nations: Immigrants and Citizens in Early Modern Spain and Spanish America*. New Haven: Yale University Press, 2003.

Herzog, Tamara. *Frontiers of Possession: Spain and Portugal in Europe and the Americas*. Cambridge, MA: Harvard University Press, 2015.

Heywood, Linda M. *Njinga of Angola: Africa's Warrior Queen*. Cambridge, MA: Harvard University Press, 2017.

Heywood, Linda M., and John K. Thornton. *Central Africans, Atlantic Creoles, and the foundation of the Americas, 1585–1660*. New York: Cambridge University Press, 2007.

Hidalgo Pérez, Marta. "Una historia atlántica en el Panamá del siglo XVI: los 'Negros de Portobelo' y la villa de Santiago del Príncipe." PhD Thesis, Universitat de Barcelona, 2019.

Hidalgo Pérez, Marta. "'Volviendo a los valientes cimarrones': Visiones e historia del cimarronaje en Panamá a través de los versos de la Dragontea de Lope de Vega," *Boletín americanista*, 79, 2019, 113–130.

Hoexter, Miriam, Shmuel N. Eisenstadt, and Nehemia Levtzion, eds. *The Public Sphere in Muslim Societies*. Albany: SUNY Press, 2002.

Hoonhout, Bram, and Thomas Mareite. "Freedom at the Fringes? Slave Flight and Empire-Building in the Early Modern Spanish Borderlands of Essequibo–Venezuela and Louisiana–Texas," *Slavery & Abolition*, 40:1, 2019, 61–86.

Ireton, Chloe L. "'They Are Blacks of the Caste of Black Christians': Old Christian Black Blood in the Sixteenth- and Early Seventeenth-Century Iberian Atlantic," *Hispanic American Historical Review* 97:4, 2017, 579–612.

Ireton, Chloe L. "Black Africans' Freedom Litigation Suits to Define Just War and Just Slavery in the Early Spanish Empire," *Renaissance Quarterly*, 73:4, 2020, 1277–1319.

Ireton, Chloe L. "Margarita de Sossa, Sixteenth-Century Puebla de los Ángeles, New Spain (Mexico)." In *As If She Were Free: A Collective Biography of Women and Emancipation in the Americas*, edited by Erica Ball, Tatiana Seijas, and Terri Snyder, 27–42. Cambridge: Cambridge University Press 2020.

Ireton, Chloe L. "L'imaginaire éthiopien dans le premier monde hispanique : esclavage et baptême dans le *Catéchisme évangélique* de Sandoval," *Revue d'histoire moderne & contemporaine*, 68:2, 2021/2, 104–130.

Ireton, Chloe L. "The Life and Legacy of Francisco Carreño: Practicing and Protecting Freedom between the Canary Islands and New Spain." In *Constructing Racial Slavery in the Atlantic World*, edited by Paul J. Polgar, Marc H. Lerner, and Jesse Cromwell, 87–103. Philadelphia: University of Pennsylvania Press, 2023.

Ireton, Chloe L. and José María Álvarez Hernández. "Epístolas de amor y Cartas de libertad: Felipa de la Cruz y Antón Segarra." In *Iberia negra: Textos para otra historia de la diaspora africana (siglos XVI y XVII)*, edited by Diana Berruezo-Sanchez, Manuel Olmedo Gobante, and Cornesha Tweede, 15–28. London: Routledge, 2024.

Israel, Yanay. "The Politics of Records: Petitions and Depositions in the Legal Struggle of a Fifteenth-Century Converso," *Viator*, 48:2, 2017, 279–303.

Israel, Yanay. "The Requerimiento in the Old World: Making Demands and Keeping Records in the Legal Culture of Late Medieval Castile," *Law and History Review*, 40:1, 2022, 37–62.

Israel, Yanay. "Petition and Response as Social Process: Royal Power, Justice, and the People in Late Medieval Castile (c.1474–1504)," *Past & Present*, 261:1, 2023, 1–43.

Izquierdo Labrado, Julio. "La esclavitud en Huelva y Palos a finales del siglo XVI," *Huelva en su historia*, 6, 1997, 47–74.

Jacobs, Auke P. *Los movimientos migratorios entre Castilla e Hispanoamérica durante el reinado de Felipe III, 1598–1621*. Amsterdam and Atlanta: Rodopi, 1995.

Jaque Hidalgo, Javiera, and Miguel A. Valerio, eds. *Indigenous and Black Confraternities in Colonial Latin America: Negotiating Status through Religious Practices*. Amsterdam: Amsterdam University Press, 2022.

Jarana Vidal, Sara. "Lebrija en la primera mitad del siglo XVI demografía y esclavitud." In *Tratas, esclavitudes y mestizajes. Una historia conectada, siglos XV–XVIII*, edited by Rafael Mauricio Pérez García, Manuel Francisco Fernández Chaves, and Eduardo França Paiva, 303–328. Sevilla: Editorial Universidad de Sevilla, 2020.

Jiménez Jiménez, Ismael. "A mayor culto de Nuestra Señora de Consolación de Utrera. Las celebraciones de la cofradía de indios del convento limeño de la Merced en los siglos XVII y XVIII," *Temas Americanistas*, 46, 2021, 349–371.

Johnson, Jessica Marie. *Wicked Flesh; Black Women, Intimacy, and Freedom in the Atlantic World*. Philadelphia: University of Pennsylvania Press, 2020.

Jones, Nicholas R. *Staging Habla de Negros; Radical Performances of the African Diaspora in Early Modern Spain*. University Park: Penn State University Press, 2019.

Jouve Martín, José R. *Esclavos de la ciudad letrada: esclavitud, escritura y colonialismo en Lima (1650–1700)*. Lima: Instituto de Estudios Peruanos, 2005.

Jouve Martín, José R. "Public Ceremonies and Mulatto Identity in Viceregal Lima: A Colonial Reenactment of the Fall of Troy (1631)," *Colonial Latin American Review*, 16:2, 2007, 179–201.

Kagan, Richard L. "Contando Vecinos: El Censo Toledano De 1569," *Studia Historica: Historia Moderna*, 12:1, 1994, 115–135.

Kars, Marjoleine. *Blood on the River: A Chronicle of Mutiny and Freedom on the Wild Coast*. New York: The New Press, 2020.

Kauffman, Miranda. *Black Tudors: The Untold Story*. London: Oneworld Publications, 2017.

Kazanjian, David. *The Brink of Freedom: Improvising Life in the Nineteenth-Century Atlantic World*. Durham: Duke University Press, 2016.

Kelley, Sean M., and Paul E. Lovejoy. "Oldendorp's 'Amina': Ethnonyms, History, and Identity in the African Diaspora," *Journal of Global Slavery*, 8:2–3, 2023, 303–330.

Konadu, Kwasi. *Many Black Women of this Fortress. Graça, Mónica and Adwoa, Three Enslaved Women of Portugal's African Empire*. London: Hurst and Company, 2022.

Lampe, Armando. "Las Casas and African Slavery in the Caribbean: A Third Conversion." In *Bartolomé de las Casas, O.P. History, Philosophy, and Theology in the Age of European Expansion*, edited by David Thomas Orique, and Rady Roldán-Figueroa, 421–436. Leiden: Brill, 2019.

Landers, Jane. "Spanish Sanctuary: Fugitives in Florida, 1687–1790," *The Florida Historical Quarterly*, 6:3, 1984, 296–313.

Landers, Jane. *Black Society in Spanish Florida*. Urbana: University of Illinois Press, 1999.
Landers, Jane. "Cimarrón and Citizen; African Ethnicity, Corporate Identity and the Evolution of Free Black Towns in the Spanish Circum-Caribbean." In *Slaves, Subjects, and Subversives: Blacks in Colonial Latin America*, edited by Jane G. Landers, and Barry M. Robinson, 111–145. Alburquerque: University of New Mexico Press, 2006.
Landers, Jane. *Atlantic Creoles in the Age of Revolutions*. Cambridge: Harvard University Press, 2011.
Landers, Jane. "The African Landscape of 17th Century Cartagena and Its Hinterlands." In *The Black Urban Atlantic in the Age of the Slave Trade*, edited by Jorge Cañizares-Ezguerra, James Sidbury, and Matt D. Childs, 147–162. Philadelphia: University of Pennsylvania Press, 2013.
Lane, Kris. *Potosi: The Silver City that Changed the World*. Berkeley: The University of California Press.
Laviña, Javier, Tomás Mendizábal, Ricardo Piqueras Céspedes, Guillermina-Itzel de Gracia, Marta Hidalgo Pérez, Meritxell Tous, Rubén López, and Jordi Juan i Tresserras. "La localización de la villa de Santiago del Príncipe, Panamá," *Canto Rodado: Revista especializada en patrimonio*, 10, 2015, 125–148.
Law, Robin. *Ouidah: The Social History of a West African Slaving "port," 1727–1892*. Athens, OH: Ohio University Press, 2004.
Lazzari, Matteo. "'A Bad Race of Infected Blood' The Atlantic Profile of Gaspar Riveros Vasconcelos and the Question of Race in 1650 New Spain," *Journal of Early American History*, 11:1, 2021, 3–25.
Lewis, Laura A. "Between 'Casta' and 'Raza': The Example of Colonial Mexico." In *Race and Blood in the Iberian World*, edited by Max S. Hering Torres, María Elena Martínez, and David Nirenberg, 99–123. Zurich: LIT Verlag, 2012.
Liberato, Carlos, Mariana P. Candido, Paul Lovejoy, and Renée Soulodre-La France, eds. *Laços Atlânticos: África e africanos durante a era do comércio transatlântico de escravos*. Luanda: Museu Nacional da Escravatura, 2017.
Liddell, Abraham L. "Social Networks and the Formation of an African Atlantic: The Upper Guinea Coast, Cape Verde, and the Spanish Caribbean, 1450–1600," PhD Dissertation, Vanderbilt University, 2021. Retrieved from: https://ir.vanderbilt.edu/handle/1803/16891
Lingna Nafafé, José. *Lourenço da Silva Mendonça and the Black Atlantic Abolitionist Movement in the 17th Century*. New York: Cambridge University Press, 2022.
Lobo Cabrera, Manuel. *Los libertos en la sociedad canaria del siglo XVI*. Madrid: "Consejo Superior de Investigaciones Científicas," 1983.
Lobo Cabrera, Manuel. "Los libertos y la emigración a América en el siglo XVI a través de las licencias de pasajeros," *Anuario de Estudios Atlánticos*, 68, 2022, 1–11.
Lofkrantz, Jennifer, and Olatunji Ojo. "Slavery, Freedom, and Failed Ransom Negotiations in West Africa, 1730-1900," *Journal of African History*, 53:1, 2012, 25–44.

Lowe, Kate. "Visible Lives: Black Gondoliers and Other Black Africans in Renaissance Venice," *Renaissance Quarterly*, 66:2, 2013, 412–452.
Lowe, Kate, and Thomas F. Earle, eds. *Black Africans in Renaissance Europe*. Cambridge: Cambridge University Press, 2005.
Lucena Salmoral, Manuel, ed. *Regulación de la esclavitud negra en las colonias de América Española (1503–1886): Documentos para su estudio*. Alcalá: University of Alcalá de Henares, 2005.
Luque Talaván, Miguel. *Un universo de opiniones: La literatura juridical indiana*. Madrid: Consejo Superior de Investigaciones Científicas, 2003.
Mangan, Jane E. *Transatlantic Obligations: Creating the Bonds of Family in Conquest-Era Peru and Spain*. Oxford: Oxford University Press, 2016.
Manzorro Guerrero, Irene. "Prácticas documentales y de escritura de Juan de Ledesma, escribano de cámara del Consejo de Indias: Los 'libros de peticiones' (1571–1594)." In *Funciones y prácticas de la escritura*, edited by Juan Carlos Galende Díaz, 129–133. Madrid: Universidad Complutense de Madrid, 2013.
Marcocci, Giuseppe. "Too Much to Rule: States and Empires across the Early Modern World," *Journal of Early Modern History*, 20:6, 2016, 511–525.
Marcocci, Giuseppe. "Portuguese Mercenary Networks in Seventeenth-Century India: An Experiment in Global Microhistory and its Archive," *Journal of Early Modern History*, 27:1–2, 2023, 59–82.
Marcocci, Giuseppe, and Arjuna Keshvani, "Contested legacies Portugal," Digital Project: https://contestedlegaciesportugal.org/About
Mark, Peter, and José da Silva Horta. *The Forgotten Diaspora: Jewish Communities in West Africa and the Making of the Atlantic World*. Cambridge: Cambridge University Press, 2011.
Martín Casares, Aurelia. *La esclavitud en la Granada del siglo XVI: Género, raza y religión*. Granada: Universidad de Granada, 2000.
Martín Casares, Aurelia. *Juan Latino: Talento y Destino; Un Afroespañol en Tiempos de Carlos V y Felipe II*. Granada: Universidad de Granada, 2016.
Martín Casares, Aurelia, and Margarita García Barranco, eds. *La Esclavitud Negroafricana en la Historia de España (Siglos XVI–XVII)*. Albolote: Comares, 2011.
Martín Casares, Aurelia, and Rocío Periáñez Gómez, eds. *Mujeres esclavas y abolicionistas en la España de los siglos XVI al XIX*. Madrid: Iberoamericana Editorial Vervuert, 2015.
Martins Marcos, Pátricia. "Blackness Out of Place: Black Countervisuality in Portugal and Its Former Empire," *Radical History Review*, 144, 2022, 106–130.
Martins Marcos, Pátricia. "White Innocence, Black Erasure: Reviewing Alcindo (2020) Against the Fictions of Portuguese Colonial Bonhomie," *Práticas da História*, 16, 2023, 151–171.
Martínez, María Elena. "The Black Blood of New Spain: Limpieza de Sangre, Racial Violence, and Gendered Power in Early Colonial México," *The William and Mary Quarterly*, 61:3, 2004, 479–520.
Martínez, María Elena. *Genealogical Fictions; Limpieza de Sangre, Religion, and Gender in Colonial Mexico*. Stanford: Stanford University Press, 2008.

Martínez, José Luis. *Pasajeros de Indias: Viajes Trasatlánticos en el Siglo XVI*. Madrid: Alianza Editorial, 1983.

Martínez López-Cano, María Del Pilar, and Guillermina del Valle Pavón, eds. *El crédito en Nueva España*. Ciudad de México: El Colegio de México, 1998.

Martínez Shaw, Carlos. *La emigración española a América, 1492–1824*. Colombres: Fundación Archivo de Indianos, 1994.

Masferrer León, Cristina Verónica. *Muleke, negritas y mulatillos. Niñez, familia y redes sociales de los esclavos de origen africano de la Ciudad de México, siglo XVII*. Ciudad de México: INAH, 2013.

Masferrer León, Cristina Verónica. "Confraternities of People of African Descent in Seventeenth-Century Mexico City." In *Indigenous and Black Confraternities in Colonial Latin America: Negotiating Status through Religious Practices*, edited by Javiera Jaque Hidalgo, and Miguel A. Valerio, 63–90. Amsterdam University Press, 2022.

Masters, Adrian. "A Thousand Invisible Architects: Vassals, the Petition and Response System, and the Creation of Spanish Imperial Caste Legislation," *Hispanic American Historical Review*, 98:3, 2018, 377–406.

Masters, Adrian. *We, the King: Creating Royal Legislation in the Sixteenth-Century Spanish New World*. Cambridge: Cambridge University Press, 2023.

Matilla Tascón, Antonio. *Americanos en la documentación notarial de Madrid*. Madrid: Fundación Matritense del Notariado, D.L., 1990.

McClure, Julia. "Worlds Within Worlds: The Institutional Locations of Global Connections in Early-Modern Seville," *Bulletin for Spanish and Portuguese Historical Studies*, 44:1, 2019, 33–51.

McKinley, Michelle A. *Fractional Freedoms: Slavery, Intimacy, and Legal Mobilization in Colonial Lima, 1600–1700*. Cambridge: Cambridge University Press, 2016.

McKnight, Kathryn J. "Confronted Rituals: Spanish Colonial and Angolan 'Maroon' Executions in Cartagena de Indias (1634)," *Journal of Colonialism and Colonial History*, 5:3, 2004, 1–19.

Méndez Maín, Silvia María, and Luis J. Abejez. "Apuntes para la historia de una migración forzada: las mujeres angolas en Veracruz, Nueva España (1588–1677)." In *Migraciones y movilidades humanas a lo largo del tiempo: perspectivas transdisciplinarias*, edited by Claudia Contente, and Isabelle Séguy, 141-169. Barcelona: Bellaterra Editions, 2023.

Mierau, Konstantin. "El discurso del destierro pre-nacional: el caso del Madrid del Siglo de Oro." In *Españoles en Europa; Identidad y Exilio desde la Edad Moderna hasta nuestros días*, edited by Yolanda Rodríguez Pérez and Pablo Valdivia, 9–22. Leiden: BRILL, 2018.

Mierau, Konstantin. "Transient Marginal Identities and Networks in Early Modern Madrid: The 1614 Case of the 'Armenian', 'Greek' and 'Turkish' Counterfeiters," *Urban History*, 49:1, 2022, 28–43.

Mijares, Ivonne, ed. *Catálogo de Protocolos del Archivo General de Notarías de la Ciudad de México, Fondo Siglo XVI*, En línea (cited as CPAGNXVI), Seminario de Documentación e Historia Novohispana, México, UNAM-Instituto de Investigaciones Históricas, 2014. http://cpagncmxvi.historicas.unam.mx/catalogo.jsp

Mijares, Ivonne, ed. *Catálogo de Protocolos del Archivo General de Notarías de la Ciudad de México, Fondo Siglo XVII,* En línea (cited as CPAGNXVII). Seminario de Documentación e Historia Novohispana, México, UNAM-Instituto de Investigaciones Históricas, 2016. http://cpagncmxvi.historicas.unam.mx/catalogo.jsp

Miller, Mary Ellen, and Barbara Munday, eds. *Painting a Map of Sixteenth-Century Mexico City: Land, Writing, and Native Rule.* New Haven: Yale University Press, 2012.

Milton, Cynthia, and Ben Vinson III. "Counting Heads: Race and Non-Native Tribute Policy in Colonial Spanish America," *Journal of Colonialism and Colonial History,* 3:3, 2002. https://doi.org/10.1353/cch.2002.0056

Mondragón Barrios, Lourdes. *Esclavos africanos en la Ciudad de México: el servicio doméstico durante el siglo XVI.* Mexico City: Ediciones Euroamericanas, 1999.

Morales Padrón, Francisco. "La Historia de Sevilla de Luis de Peraza," *Boletín de la Real Academia Sevillana de Buenas Letras: Minervae Baeticae,* 6, 1978, 75–173.

Moreno, Isidoro. *La antigua hermandad de los negros de Sevilla: etnicidad, poder y sociedad en 600 años de historia.* Sevilla: Editorial de la Universidad de Sevilla, 1997.

Morgado García, Arturo Jesús. "Los libertos en el Cádiz de la Edad Moderna," *Studia historica. Historia moderna,* 32, 2010, 399–436.

Morgado García, Arturo Jesús. *Una metrópoli esclavista: El Cádiz de la Modernidad.* Granada: Editorial Universidad de Granada, 2013.

Morgan, Jennifer L. "Accounting for 'The Most Excruciating Torment': Gender, Slavery, and Trans-Atlantic Passages," *History of the Present,* 6:2, 2016, 184–207.

Morgan, Jennifer L. *Reckoning with Slavery Gender, Kinship, and Capitalism in the Early Black Atlantic.* Durham: Duke University Press, 2021.

Mörner, Magnus, and Harold Sims. *Aventureros y proletarios: los emigrantes en Hispanoamérica.* Madrid: Editorial MAPFRE, 1992.

Mumford, Jeremy. "Litigation as Ethnography in Sixteenth-Century Peru: Polo de Ondegardo and the Mitimaes," *Hispanic American Historical Review,* 88:1, 2008, 5–40.

Mumford, Jeremy. "Aristocracy on the Auction Block: Race, Lords, and the Perpetuity." In *Imperial Subjects: Race and Identity in Colonial Latin America,* edited by Andrew D. Fisher, and Matthew O'Hara, 39–60. Durham: Duke University Press, 2009.

Munday, Barbara E. "Indigenous Civilization." In *Mapping Latin America: A Cartographic Reader,* edited by Jordana Dym, and Karl Offen, 42–60. Chicago: University of Chicago Press, 2011.

Muñoz Serrulla, María Teresa. *La moneda castellana en los reinos de Indias durante la Edad Moderna.* Madrid: Universidad Nacional de Educación a Distancia, 2015.

Navarrete Peláez, María Cristina. Esclavitud negra e Inquisición: los negros en Colombia (1600–1725). PhD Thesis, Universidad Complutense de Madrid, 1971.

Navarrete Peláez, María Cristina. "Los artesanos negros en la sociedad cartagenera del siglo XVII," *Historia y espacio,* 15, 1994, 7–25.

Navarrete Peláez, María Cristina. *Cimarrones y Palenques en el Siglo XVII*. Cali: Universidad del Valle, 2003.
Navarrete Peláez, María Cristina. *Génesis y desarrollo de la esclavitud en Colombia siglos XVI y XVII*. Cali: Universidad del Valle, 2005.
Navarrete Peláez, María Cristina. "'Por haber todos concebido ser general la libertad para los de su color': construyendo el pasado del palenque de Matudere," *Historia Caribe*, 13, 2008, 7–44.
Navarrete Peláez, María Cristina. "Las cartas Annuas jesuitas; Y la representación de los etíopes en el siglo XVII." In *Genealogías de la diferencia: tecnologías de la salvación y representación de los africanos esclavizados en Iberoamérica colonial*, edited by María Eugenia Chaves Maldonado, 22–57. Bogotá: Editorial de la Pontificia Universidad Javeriana, Instituto de Estudios Sociales y Culturales Pensar; Abya-Yala, 2009.
Navarrete Peláez, María Cristina. "De reyes, reinas y capitanes: los dirigentes de los palenques de las sierras de María, siglos XVI y XVII," *Fronteras de la historia: revista de historia colonial latinoamericana*, 20:2, 2015, 44–63.
Navarrete Peláez, María Cristina. "Consideraciones en Torno a la Esclavitud de los Etíopes y la operatividad de la Ley, Siglos XVI y XVII," *Historia y espacio*, 2:27, 2017, 1–23.
Naveda Chávez-Hita, Adriana. *Esclavos negros en las haciendas azucareras de Córdoba, Veracruz. 1690–1830*. Xalapa: Universidad Veracruzana, 1987.
Naveda Chávez-Hita, Adriana. "De San Lorenzo de los negros a los morenos de Amapa: cimarrones veracruzanos, 1609–1735." In *Rutas de la esclavitud en Africa y América Latina*, edited by Rina Cáceres Gómez, 157–174. San José: Universidad de Costa Rica, 2001.
Nemser, Daniel. *Infrastructures of Race: Concentration and Biopolitics in Colonial Mexico*. Austin: University of Texas Press, 2017.
Nemser, Daniel. "Triangulating Blackness: Mexico City, 1612," *Mexican Studies/Estudios Mexicanos*, 33:3, 2017, 344–366.
Newson, Linda A. "Africans and Luso-Africans in the Portuguese Slave Trade on the Upper Guinea Coast in the Early Seventeenth Century," *Journal of African History*, 53:1, 2012, 1–24.
Newson, Linda A., and Susie Minchin. *From Capture to Sale: The Portuguese Slave Trade to Spanish South America in the Early Seventeenth Century*. Leiden: Brill, 2007.
Newton, Gill, and Richard Smith. "Convergence or Divergence? Mortality in London, Its Suburbs and Its Hinterland between 1550 and 1700," *Annales de démographie historique*, 126:2, 2013, 17–49.
Northrup, David. *Africa's Discovery of Europe: 1450–1850*. New York: Oxford University Press, 2002.
Norton, Marcy. "The Chicken or the Iegue: Human-Animal Relationships and the Columbian Exchange," *The American Historical Review*, 120:1, 2015, 28–60.
Norton, Marcy. "Subaltern Technologies and Early Modernity in the Atlantic World," *Colonial Latin American Review*, 26:1, 2017, 18–38.
Norton, Marcy. *The Tame and the Wild; People and Animals after 1492*. Cambridge: Harvard University Press, 2024.

Núñez González, María. *La casa sevillana del siglo XVI en la collación de San Salvador: dibujo y estudio de tipologías*. Sevilla: Universidad de Sevilla, Secretariado de Publicaciones, 2012.

Núñez González, María. "Las áreas de mercado y negocios en la Sevilla del siglo XVI: análisis urbano y arquitectónico de las Gradas y las alcaicerías de Santa María la Mayor y San Salvador," *Arte y Ciudad – Revista de Investigación*, 17, 2020, 7–36.

Núñez González, María. *Arquitectura, dibujo y léxico de alarifes en la Sevilla del siglo XVI: casas, corrales, mesones y tiendas*. Sevilla: Editorial de la Universidad de Sevilla, 2021.

Obando Andrade, Rafael. *De objeto a sujeto. Los esclavos ante la legislación y el poder colonial en Centroamérica, 1532–1600*. San Salvador, El Salvador: UCA editores, 2019.

Ogborn, Miles. *The Freedom of Speech: Talk and Slavery in the Anglo-Caribbean World*. Chicago: University of Chicago Press, 2019.

Oliveira, Vanessa S. *Slave Trade and Abolition Gender, Commerce, and Economic Transition in Luanda*. Madison: University of Wisconsin Press, 2020.

Orique, David T. "A Comparison of Bartolomé de Las Casas and Fernão Oliveira: Just War and Slavery," *E-Journal of Portuguese History* 12.1, 2014, 87–118.

Orique, David T., and Rady Roldán-Figueroa, eds. *Bartolomé de Las Casas, O.P.: History, Philosophy, and Theology in the Age of European Expansion*. Leiden: Brill, 2018.

Ortega y Sagrista, Rafael. "La Cofradía de los Negros en el Jaén del Siglo XVII," *Boletín del Instituto de Estudios Giennenses*, 12, 1957, 125–134.

Ostos-Salcedo, Pilar. "Un pleito, una encrucijada de escrituras." In *Cervantes en Sevilla un documento cervantino en la Biblioteca Universitaria*, edited by Luis Rafael Méndez Rodríguez, and José Beltrán Fortes, 107–134. Sevilla: Editorial de la Universidad de Sevilla, 2017.

O'Toole, Rachel Sarah. *Bound Lives: Africans, Indians, and the Making of Race in Colonial Peru*. Pittsburgh, PA: University of Pittsburgh Press, 2012.

O'Toole, Rachel Sarah. "The Bonds of Kinship, the Ties of Freedom in Colonial Peru," *Journal of Family History*, 42:1, 2017, 3–21.

O'Toole, Rachel Sarah. "(Un)Making Christianity: The African Diaspora in Slavery and Freedom." In *The Oxford Handbook of Latin American Christianity*, edited by David Orique, Susan Fitzpatrick-Behrens, and Virginia Garrard, 101–119. New York: Oxford University Press, 2020.

Otte, Enrique. *Cartas privadas de emigrantes a Indias, 1540–1616*. Sevilla: Consejería de Cultura, Junta de Andalucía/Escuela de Estudios Hispanoamericanos, 1988.

Owensby, Brian P. "How Juan and Leonor Won Their Freedom: Litigation and Liberty in Seventeenth-Century Mexico," *Hispanic American Historical Review*, 85:1, 2005, 39–79.

Owensby, Brian P. *Empire of Law and Indian Justice in Colonial México*. Stanford: Stanford University Press, 2008.

Owensby, Brian P. "Pacto entre rey lejano y súbditos indígenas: Justicia, legalidad y política en Nueva España, siglo XVII," *Historia Mexicana*, 61:1, 2011, 59–106.

Owensby, Brian P. "The Theater of Conscience in the 'Living Law' of the Indies." In *New Horizons of Spanish Colonial Law: Contributions to Transnational Early Modern Legal History*, edited by Thomas Duve, and Heikki Pihlajamäki, 125–159. Frankfurt: Max Plank Institute for European Legal History, 2015.

Owensby, Brian P., and Richard J. Ross, eds. *Justice in a New World: Negotiating Legal Intelligibility in British Iberian, and Indigenous America*. New York: New York University Press, 2018.

Palmié, Stephan. *The Cooking of History; How Not to Study Afro-Cuban Religion*. Chicago: The University of Chicago Press, 2013.

Patterson, Orlando. *Slavery and Social Death: A Comparative Study, with a New Preface*. Cambridge: Harvard University Press, 2018.

Pérez Fernández, Isacio. "Bartolomé de las Casas y los esclavos negros." In *Afroamericanos y V Centenario ponencias*, edited by José Luis Cortés, 39–61. Madrid: Mundo Negro, 1992.

Pérez Fernández, Isacio. *Fray Bartolomé de Las Casas. De Defensor de Los Indios A Defensor de los Negros*. Salamanca: Editorial San Esteban, 1995.

Pérez García, Rafael Mauricio. "Metodología para el análisis y cuantificación de la trata de esclavos hacia la América española en el siglo XVI." In *Los vestidos de Clío: Métodos y tendencias recientes de la historiografía modernista española (1973–2013). VII Coloquio de Metodología Histórica Aplicada*, edited by Ofelia Rey Castelao and Fernando Suárez Golán, 823–840. Santiago: Universidad de Santiago, 2015.

Pérez García, Rafael Mauricio. "Christian Freedom and Natural Freedom. An Introduction to an Archaeology of Catholic Controversies over Slavery." In *Rethinking Catholicism in Renaissance Spain*, edited by Xavier Tubau, 182–210. New York: Routledge, 2022.

Pérez García, Rafael Mauricio. "Matrimonio, Vida Familiar y Trabajo de Esclavas y Libertas en la Sevilla de los Siglos XVI y XVII," *OHM: Obradoiro de Historia Moderna*, 32, 2023, 1–22.

Pérez García, Rafael Mauricio, and Manuel F. Fernández Chaves. "La cuantificación de la población esclava en la Andalucía moderna. Una revisión metodológica," *Varia Historia*, 31:57, 2015, 711–740.

Pérez García, Rafael Mauricio, Manuel Francisco Fernández Chaves, and Eduardo França Paiva, eds. *Tratas, esclavitudes y mestizajes: Una historia conectada, siglos XV–XVIII*. Sevilla: Editorial Universidad de Sevilla. 2020.

Pérez González, María Luisa. "Los caminos reales de América en la legislación y en la historia," *Anuario De Estudios Americanos*, 58:1, 2001, 33–60.

Pérez-Mallaína Bueno, Pablo Emilio. *Spain's Men of the Sea; Daily Life on the Indies Fleets in the Sixteenth Century*. Translated by Carla Rahn Phillips. Baltimore: Johns Hopkins University Press, 2005.

Phillips, William D. *Slavery in Medieval and Early Modern Iberia*. Philadelphia: University of Pennsylvania Press, 2014.

Pike, Ruth. "Sevillian Society in the Sixteenth Century: Slaves and Freedmen," *Hispanic American Historical Review*, 47:3, 1967, 344–359.

Pollack, Aaron, "Hacia una historia social del tributo de indios y castas en Hispanoamérica. Notas en torno a su creación, desarrollo y abolición," *Historia mexicana*, 66:1, 2016, 65–160.

Ponce Vázquez, Juan José. *Islanders and Empire: Smuggling and Political Defiance in Hispaniola, 1580–1690*. New York: Cambridge University Press, 2020.
Porro Girardi, Nelly R. "Criados en Indias: presencia y significado (siglo XVI)," In *Memoria del X Congreso del Instituto Internacional de Historia del Derecho Indiano*, vol. II, edited by Escuela Libre de Derecho, México, 1221–1253. Mexico City: Universidad Nacional Autónoma de México, 1995.
Premo, Bianca. "Custom Today: Temporality, Law, and Indigenous Enlightenment," *Hispanic American Historical Review*, 94:3, 2014, 355–379.
Premo, Bianca. *The Enlightenment on Trial: Ordinary Litigants and Colonialism in the Spanish Empire*. New York: Oxford University Press, 2017.
Proctor III, Frank (Trey). "Slave Rebellion and Liberty in Colonial Mexico." In *Black Mexico: Race and Society from Colonial to Modern Times*, edited by Ben Vinson III and Matthew Restall, 21–50. Albuquerque: University of New Mexico Press, 2009.
Proctor III, Frank (Trey). *Damned Notions of Liberty: Slavery, Culture, and Power in Colonial Mexico, 1640–1769*. Albuquerque: University of New Mexico Press, 2010.
Pujol i Coll, Josep. "Els vilancets 'de negre' al segle XVII," PhD Thesis, Universitat Autònoma de Barcelona, Spain, 2016.
Rahn Phillips, Carla. *El tesoro del "San José."* Madrid: Marcial Pons, 2010.
Ramey Berry, Daina, and Leslie M. Harris, eds. *Sexuality and Slavery: Reclaiming Intimate Histories in the Americas*. Athens: University of Georgia Press, 2018.
Ramos, Gabriela, and Yanna Yannakakis. *Indigenous Intellectuals; Knowledge, Power, and Colonial Culture in Mexico and the Andes*. Durham: Duke University Press, 2014.
Rappaport, Joanne. *The Disappearing Mestizo: Configuring Difference in the Colonial New Kingdom of Granada*. Durham: Duke University Press, 2014.
Rappaport, Joanne, and Tom Cummins. *Beyond the Lettered City: Indigenous Literacies in the Andes*. Durham: Duke University Press, 2011.
Rediker, Marcus. *The Slave Ship: A Human History*. New York: Penguin Books, 2008.
Reis, João José. *Slave Rebellion in Brazil: The Muslim Uprising of 1835 in Bahia*, translated by Arthur Brakel. Baltimore: The Johns Hopkins University Press, 1993.
Reis, João José. "African Nations in Nineteenth-Century Salvador, Bahia." In *The Black Urban Atlantic in the Age of the Slave Trade*, edited by Jorge Cañizares-Esguerra, Matt D. Childs, and James Sidbury, 63–82. Philadelphia: University of Pennsylvania Press, 2013.
Reis, João José. *Divining Slavery and Freedom: The Story of Domingos Sodré, an African Priest in Nineteenth-Century Brazil*. Cambridge: Cambridge University Press, 2015.
Reis, João José, Flávio dos Santos Gomes, and Marcus de Carvalho. *Oalufá Rufino: Tráfico, escravidão e liberdade no Atlântico Negro (c. 1822–c. 1853)*. São Paulo: Companhia das Letras, 2010.
Restall, Matthew. *The Black Middle: Africans, Mayas, and Spaniards in Colonial Yucatan*. Stanford: Stanford University Press, 2009.

Rey Castelao, Ofelia. *El vuelo corto. Mujeres y migraciones en la Edad Moderna.* Santiago de Compostela: Universidad de Santiago de Compostela, 2021.

Rivarola y Pineda, and Juan Félix Francisco. *Descripcion historica, chronologica y genealogica, civil, politica y militar.* Madrid: Diego Martínez Abad, 1729.

Rodríguez Lorenzo, Sergio M. "El mar se mueve: la experiencia del viaje trasatlántico entre los pasajeros de la carrera de Indias (siglos XVI y XVII)," *Communication and Culture Online,* Special Issue 1, 2013, 67–78.

Rodríguez Lorenzo, Sergio M. *La Carrera de Indias, la ruta, los hombres, las mercancías.* Madrid: Editorial La Huerta Grande, S.L. 2ª ed. 2015.

Rodríguez Lorenzo, Sergio M. "Sevilla y la carrera de Indias: las compraventas de naos (1560–1622)," *Anuario de estudios americanos,* 73:1, 2016, 65–97.

Rodríguez Lorenzo, Sergio M. "El contrato de pasaje en la carrera de Indias (1561–1622)," *Historia mexicana,* 66:3, 2017, 1479–1571.

Romera Iruela, Luis, and María del Carmen Galbis Díez. *Catálogo de Pasajeros a Indias durante los siglos xvi, xvii y xviii.* Vol. V, tomo 1 and 2. Sevilla: S.G. Archivos Estatales, 1980.

Roselló Soberón, Estela. "Relevancia y función de las cofradías en el fenómeno de la evangelización de los negros y los mulatos: el caso de San Benito de Palermo en el puerto de Veracruz, siglo XVII." In *Africanos y afrodescendientes en la América hispánica septentrional; Espacios de convivencia, sociabilidad y conflicto.* Vol I, edited by Rafael Castañeda García, and Juan Carlos Ruiz Guadalajara, 337–358. San Luis Potosí: El Colegio de San Luis, A.C, 2020.

Rosenmüller, Christoph, ed. *Corruption in the Iberian Empires: Greed, Custom, and Colonial Networks.* Albuquerque: University of New Mexico Press, 2017.

Rossi, Benedetta. "Beyond the Atlantic Paradigm: Slavery and Abolitionism in the Nigérien Sahel," *Journal of Global Slavery,* 5:2, 2020, 238–269.

Rossi, Benedetta. "Global Abolitionist Movements." *Oxford Research Encyclopedia of African History.* July 19, 2023; Accessed January 19, 2024. https://oxfordre.com/africanhistory/view/10.1093/acrefore/9780190277734.001.0001/acrefore-9780190277734-e-945

Rowe, Erin. *Black Saints in Early Modern Global Catholicism.* New York: Cambridge University Press, 2019.

Ruan, Felipe E. "The *Probanza* and Shaping a Contesting *Mestizo* Record in Early Colonial Peru," *Bulletin of Spanish Studies,* 94:5, 2017, 843–869.

Rubiales Torrejón, Javier, ed. *La Real Audiencia y la plaza de San Francisco de Sevilla.* Sevilla: Editorial Universidad de Sevilla, 2022.

Rupert, Linda. *Creolization and Contraband: Curaçao in the Early Modern Atlantic World.* Athens: University of Georgia Press, 2012.

Rupert, Linda. "'Seeking the Water of Baptism': Fugitive Slaves and Imperial Jurisdiction in the Early Modern Caribbean." In *Legal Pluralism and Empires, 1500–1850,* edited by Lauren Benton and Richard J. Ross, 199–232. New York: New York University Press, 2013.

Rupert, Linda. "Curaçaoan Maroons in Venezuela." In *Sociétés marronnes des Amériques,* edited by Jean Moomou, 139–151. Guadaloupe: Ibis Rouge, 2015.

Rupprecht, Anita. "Middle Passage." *Oxford Research Encyclopedia of African History.* June 21, 2023; Accessed January 25, 2024. https://oxfordre.com/africanhistory/view/10.1093/acrefore/9780190277734.001.0001/acrefore-9780190277734-e-901

Sainz Varela, José Antonio. "Los pasajeros a Indias," *Tabula: revista de archivos de Castilla y León*, 9, 2006, 11–72.
Salazar Rey, Ricardo Raúl. *Mastering the Law: Slavery and Freedom in the Legal Ecology of the Spanish Empire*. Tuscaloosa: University of Alabama Press, 2020.
Salvadore, Matteo. *The African Prester John and the Birth of Ethiopian-European Relations, 1402–1555*. London and New York: Routledge, 2016.
Salvadore, Matteo. "African Cosmopolitanism in the Early Modern Mediterranean: The Diasporic Life of Yohannes, the Ethiopian Pilgrim Who Became a Counter-Reformation Bishop," *The Journal of African History*, 58:1, 2017, 61–83.
Sánchez-Godoy, Rubén A. "Bartolomé de Las Casas crítico de las esclavizaciones portuguesas en las islas Canarias y la costa occidental de África." In *Bartolomé de Las Casas: Face à l'esclavage des Noir-e-s en Amériques/Caraïbes. L'aberration du Onzième Remède (1516)*, edited by Victorien Lavou Zoungbo, 135–155. Perpignan: Presses Universitaires de Perpignan, 2011.
Sánchez-Godoy, Rubén A. *El peor de los remedios: Bartolomé de Las Casas y la crítica temprana a la esclavitud africana en el Atlántico ibérico*. Pittsburgh, PA: Instituto Internacional deLiteratura Iberoamericana, 2016.
Sánchez Jiménez, Antonio. "Raza, identidad y rebelión en los confines del Imperio hispánico: los cimarrones de Santiago del Principe y La Dragontea (1598) de Lope de Vega," *Hispanic Review*, 75:2, 2007, 113–333.
Sancho de Sopranis, Hipólito. *Las cofradías de morenos en Cádiz*. Madrid: Consejo Superior de Investigaciones Científicas, 1958.
Santos Morillo, Antonio. *"Quién te lo vezó a dezir" El habla de negro en la literatura del XVI, imitación de una realidad lingüística*. Madrid and Frankfurt: Iberoamericana Vervuert, 2020.
Sartorius, David. *Ever Faithful; Race, Loyalty, and the Ends of Empire in Spanish Cuba*. Durham: Duke University Press, 2014.
Schäfer, Ernst. *Las rúbricas del consejo real y supremo de las Indias: Desde la fundación del Consejo en 1524 hasta la terminación del reinado de los Austrias*. Sevilla: Universidad de Sevilla, 1934.
Schneider, Elena A. "A Narrative of Escape: Self Liberation by Sea and the Mental Worlds of the Enslaved," *Slavery & Abolition*, 42:3, 2021, 484–501.
Schwaller, Robert C. *Géneros de Gente in Early Colonial México: Defining Racial Difference*. Norman: University of Oklahoma Press, 2016.
Schwaller, Robert C. "Contested Conquests: African Maroons and the Incomplete Conquest of Hispaniola, 1519–1620," *The Americas*, 75:4, 2018, 609–638.
Schwaller, Robert C. *African Maroons in Sixteenth-Century Panama: A History in Documents*. Norman: University of Oklahoma Press, 2021.
Schwaller, Robert C. "The Spanish Conquest of Panama and the Creation of Maroon Landscapes, 1513–1590." In *Overlooked Places and Peoples; Indigenous and African Resistance in Colonial Spanish America, 1500–1800*, edited by Dana Velasco Murillo, and Robert C. Schwaller, 19–46. Routledge, 2024.
Schwartz Stuart B. *Sea of Storms: A History of Hurricanes in the Greater Caribbean from Columbus to Katrina*. Princeton: Princeton University Press, 2015.
Schwartz, Stuart B. *Blood and Boundaries; The Limits of Religious and Racial Exclusion in Early Modern Latin America*. The Menahem Stern Jerusalem Lectures. Brandeis University Press, 2020.

Scott, Julius S. *The Common Wind: Afro-American Currents in the Age of the Haitian Revolution*. London and New York, Verso, 2018.

Scott, Rebecca J., and Jean M. Hébrard. *Freedom Papers: An Atlantic Odyssey in the Age of Emancipation*. Cambridge: Harvard University Press, 2012.

Scott, Rebecca J., and Carlos Venegas Fornias, "María Coleta and the Capuchin Friar: Slavery, Salvation, and the Adjudication of Status," *The William and Mary Quarterly*, 76:4, 2019, 727–762.

Scott, Samuel Parsons. "Freedom." In *Las Siete Partidas, Volume 4: Family, Commerce, and the Sea: The Worlds of Women and Merchants (Partidas IV and V)*, edited by Robert I. Burns, 981–986. Philadelphia: University of Pennsylvania Press, 2001.

Seijas, Tatiana, and Pablo Miguel Sierra Silva. "The Persistence of the Slave Market in Seventeenth-Century Central México," *Slavery & Abolition: A Journal of Slave and Post-Slave Studies*, 37:2, 2016, 307–333.

Sellers-García, Sylvia. *Distance and Documents at the Spanish Empire's Periphery*. Stanford: Stanford University Press, 2013.

Shami, Seteney. "Introduction." In *Publics, Politics and Participation Locating the Public Sphere in the Middle East and North Africa*, edited by Seteney Shami, 13–44. New York: Social Science Research Council, 2009.

Sierra Silva, Pablo Miguel. *Urban Slavery in Colonial Mexico: Puebla de los Ángeles, 1531–1706*. New York: Cambridge University Press, 2018.

Sierra Silva, Pablo Miguel. "Afro-Mexican Women in Saint-Domingue: Piracy, Captivity and Community in the 1680s and 1690s," *Hispanic American Historical Review*, 100:1, 2020, 3–34.

Sierra Silva, Pablo Miguel. "The Slave Trade to Colonial Mexico: Revising from Puebla de los Ángeles, 1590–1640." In *From the Galleons to the Highlands; Slave Trade Routes in the Spanish Americas*, edited by Alex Borucki, David Eltis, and David Wheat, 73–102. Albuquerque: The University of New Mexico Press, 2020.

Sierra Silva, Pablo Miguel. *Mexico, Slavery, Freedom: A Bilingual Documentary History, 1520–1829*. Indianapolis: Hackett Publishing Company, 2024.

Silva Campo, Ana María. "Through the Gate of the Media Luna: Slavery and the Geographies of Legal Status in Colonial Cartagena de Indias," *Hispanic American Historical Review*, 100:3, 2020, 391–421.

Silva Campo, Ana María. "Fragile Fortunes: Afrodescendent Women, Witchcraft, and the Remaking of Urban Cartagena," *Colonial Latin American Review*, 30:2, 2021, 197–213.

Silverblatt, Irene. *Modern Inquisitions: Peru and the Colonial Origins of the Civilized World*. Durham: Duke University Press, 2004.

Singleton, Theresa A., and Jane Landers. "Maritime Marronage: Archaeological, Anthropological, and Historical Approaches," *Slavery & Abolition*, 42:3, 2021, 419–427.

Slave Voyages. Trans-Atlantic Slave Trade Database, voyage id 28143, accessed May 2024. www.slavevoyages.org/voyages/lY8z

Smallwood, Stephanie. *Saltwater Slavery: A Middle Passage from Africa to American Diaspora*. Cambridge: Harvard University Press, 2007.

Smith, Cassander L., Nicholas R. Jones, and Miles Grier. "Introduction: The Contours of a Field." In *Early Modern Black Diaspora Studies: A Critical*

Anthology, edited by Cassander L. Smith, Nicholas R. Jones, and Miles Grier, 1–14. Cham, Switzerland: Palgrave Macmillan, 2018.

Smith, Matthew J. *Liberty, Fraternity, Exile: Haiti and Jamaica after Emancipation*. Chapel Hill: The University of North Carolina Press, 2014.

Smith, Sabrina. "Juana Ramírez, Eighteenth-Century Oaxaca, New Spain (Mexico)." In *As If She Were Free: A Collective Biography of Women and Emancipation in the Americas*, edited by Erica L. Ball, Tatiana Seijas, and Terri L. Snyder, 207–217. Cambridge: Cambridge University Press, 2020.

Smith, Sabrina. "African-Descended Women: Power and Social Status in Colonial Oaxaca, 1660–1680," *The Americas*, 80:4, 2023, 569–598.

Sobel, Michal. *The World They Made Together: Black and White Values in Eighteenth-Century Virginia*. Princeton: Princeton University Press, 1988.

Splendiani, Anna María, José Enrique Sánchez Bohórquez, and Emma Cecilia Luque de Salazar, eds. *Cincuenta años de inquisición en el Tribunal de Cartagena de Indias, 1610–1660*, 4 vols. Bogotá: Pontificia Universidad Javeriana, 1997.

Splendiani, Anna María, and Tulio Aristizábal Giraldo, eds. *Proceso de beatificación y canonización de san Pedro Claver*. Bogotá: Pontifica Universidad Javeriana, 2002.

Stackhouse, Kenneth A. "Beyond Performance: Cervantes's Algerian Plays, El trato de Argel and Los baños de Argel," *Bulletin of the Comediantes*, 52:2, 2000, 7–30.

Starr-LeBeau, Gretchen D. *In the Shadow of the Virgin: Inquisitors, Friars, and Conversos in Guadalupe, Spain*. Princeton: Princeton University Press, 2008.

Stella, Alessandro. *Histoires d'esclaves dans la péninsule ibérique*. Paris: Editions de l'EHESS, 2000.

Stella, Alessandro. *Ser esclavo y negro en Andalucia (siglos XVII y XVIII)*. Madrid: MAPFRE-Tavera, 2005.

Stella, Alessandro. *Amours et désamours à Cadix aux XVIIe et XVIIIe siècles*. Toulouse: Presses Universitaires du Mirail, 2008.

Subrayaman, Sanjay. "Holding the World in Balance: The Connected Histories of the Iberian Overseas Empires, 1500–1640," *The American Historical Review*, 112:5, 2007, 1359–1385.

Sued Badillo, Jalil. "El pleito de Pedro Carmona sobre su libertad," *Revista del Instituto de Cultura Puertorriqueña*, 86, 1984, 10–12.

Sweeney, Shauna J. "Market Marronage: Fugitive Women and the Internal Marketing System in Jamaica, 1781–1834," *The William and Mary Quarterly* 76:2, 2019, 197–222.

Sweeney, Shauna J. "Black Women in Slavery and Freedom: Gendering the History of Racial Capitalism," *American Quarterly*, 72:1, 2020, 277–289.

Sweet, James H. "The Iberian Roots of American Racist Thought," *William and Mary Quarterly*, 54:1, 1997, 143–166.

Sweet, James H. *Recreating Africa: Culture, Kinship, and Religion in the African-Portuguese World, 1441–1770*. Chapel Hill: University of North Carolina Press, 2003.

Tardieu, Jean Pierre. *Cimarrones de Panamá: la forja de una identidad afroamericana en el siglo XVI*. Madrid: Iberoamericana Vervuert, 2009.

Tau Anzoátegui, Víctor. *La ley en América hispana: Del descubrimiento a la emancipación*. Buenos Aires: Academia Nacional de la Historia, 1992.

Tau Anzoátegui, Víctor. *El poder de la costumbre: Estudios sobre el derecho consuetudinario en América hispana hasta la emancipación*. Buenos Aires: Instituto de Investigaciones de Historia del Derecho, 2001.

Tempère, Delphine. *Vivre et mourir sur les navires du Siècle d'Or*. Paris: Presses de l'Université Paris-Sorbonne, 2009.

Terraciano, Kevin, "Three Views of the Conquest of Mexico from the Other Mexica." In *Conquest All Over Again: Nahuas & Zapotecs Thinking, Writing & Painting Spanish Colonialism*, edited by Susan Schroeder, 15–40. London: Sussex Academic Press, 2010.

Terrazas Williams, Danielle. "'My Conscience Is Free and Clear': African-Descended Women, Status, and Slave Owning in Mid-Colonial Mexico," *The Americas*, 75:3, 2018, 525–554.

Terrazas Williams, Danielle. *The Capital of Free Women; Race, Legitimacy, and Liberty in Colonial México*. New Haven: Yale University Press, 2022.

Thiébaut, Virginie "San Juan de Ulúa y Veracruz: miradas cruzadas desde la historia y la antropología," *Ulúa*, 36, 2020, 11–16.

Thornton, John K. "The Development of an African Catholic Church in the Kingdom of Kongo, 1491–1750," *The Journal of African History*, 25:2, 1984, 147–167.

Thornton, John K. *Africa and Africans in the Making of the Atlantic World, 1400–1800*. Cambridge: Cambridge University Press, 1988.

Thornton, John K. "African Political Ethics and the Slave Trade: Central African Dimensions." In *Abolitionism and Imperialism in Britain, Africa, and the Atlantic*, edited by Derek R. Peterson, 38–62. Athens: Ohio University Press, 2010.

Turits, Richard Lee. "Slavery and the Pursuit of Freedom in 16th-Century Santo Domingo." *Oxford Research Encyclopedia of Latin American History*. September 30, 2019; Accessed January 25, 2024. https://oxfordre.com/latinamericanhistory/view/10.1093/acrefore/9780199366439.001.0001/acrefore-9780199366439-e-344

Valerio, Miguel A. "The Spanish Petition System, Hospital/ity, and the Formation of a Mulato Community in Sixteenth-Century Mexico," *The Americas*, 78:3, 2021, 415–437.

Valerio, Miguel A. "'That There Be No Black Brotherhood': The Failed Suppression of Afro-Mexican Confraternities, 1568–1612," *Slavery & Abolition*, 42:2, 2021, 293–314.

Valerio, Miguel A. *Sovereign Joy; Afro-Mexican Kings and Queens, 1539–1640*. New York: Cambridge University Press, 2022.

Valverde Barneto, Paula. "La esclavitud en Sevilla durante el siglo XVI a través de las partidas de bautismo de la parroquia del Salvador." In *Los negocios de la esclavitud. Tratantes y mercaderes de esclavos en el Atlántico Ibérico, siglos XVI-XVIII*, edited by Rafael Mauricio Pérez García, Manuel Francisco Fernández Chaves, and José Luis Belmonte Postigo, 263–280. Sevilla: Editorial Universidad de Sevilla, 2018.

van Deusen, Nancy E, ed. *The Souls of Purgatory: The Spiritual Diary of a Seventeenth-Century Afro-Peruvian Mystic, Ursula de Jesús*. Albuquerque: University of New Mexico Press, 2004.

van Deusen, Nancy E. *Global Indios: The Indigenous Struggle for Justice in Sixteenth-Century Spain*. Durham: Duke University Press, 2015.

Vargas Matías, Sergio Arturo. "El Camino Real de Veracruz: Pasado, Presente y Futuro," *Folios, Revista De La Facultad De Comunicaciones Y Filología*, 27, 2012, 101–102.

Vaseur Gamez, Jorge, Rafael Mauricio Pérez García, and Manuel Francisco Fernández Chaves, eds. *La esclavitud en el sur de la península Ibérica, siglos XV-XVII. Demografía e Historia Social*. Madrid: Los Libros de la Catarata, 2021.

Velázquez Gutiérrez, María Elisa. *Mujeres de orígen africano en la capital Novohispana: siglos XVII y XVIII*. Mexico City: Universidad Naciónal Autónoma, INAH, 2006.

Velázquez Gutiérrez, María Elisa, and Ethel Correa Duró, eds. *Poblaciónes y culturas de origen africano en México*. Mexico City: INAH, 2005.

Vidal Ortega, Antonino. *Cartagena y la región histórica del Caribe: 1580–1640*. Sevilla: Escuela de Estudios Hispanoamericanos, Universidad de Sevilla, and Diputación de Sevilla, 2002.

Vignaux, Hélène. *L'Église et les Noirs dans l'audience du Nouveau Royaume de Grenade*. Montpellier: Presses universitaires de la Méditerranée, 2009.

Villacañas Berlanga, José Luis. *Imperiofilia y el Populismo Nacional-Católico; Otra Historia Del Imperio Español*. Madrid: Lengua De Trapo, 2019.

Vincent, Bernard. "L'esclavage dans la Péninsule ibérique à l'époque moderne." In *Les traites et les esclavages. Perspectives historiques et contemporaines*, edited by Myriam Cottias, Elisabeth Cunin, and António de Almeida Mendes, 67–75. Paris: Karthala, 2010.

Vincent, Bernard. "San Benito de Palermo en España," *Studia Historica: Historia Moderna*, 38:1, 2016, 23–38.

Vinson III, Ben. *Bearing Arms for His Majesty: The Free-Colored Militia in Colonial Mexico*. Stanford: Stanford University Press, 2001.

Vinson III, Ben. *Before Mestizaje: The Frontiers of Race and Caste in Colonial México*. New York: Cambridge University Press, 2018.

Vinson III, Ben, and Matthew Restall, eds. *Black Mexico: Race and Society from Colonial to Modern Times*. Albuquerque: University of New Mexico Press, 2009.

von Germeten, Nicole. *Black Blood Brothers: Confraternities and Social Mobility for Afro-Mexicans*. Gainesville: University Press of Florida, 2006.

von Germeten, Nicole. "African Women's Possessions: Inquisition Inventories in Cartagena de Indias." In *Documenting Latin America: Gender, Race, and Empire*, edited by Erin E. O'Connor, and Leo J. Garofalo, 101–100. New York: Pearson, 2011.

von Germeten, Nicole. *Violent Delights, Violent Ends: Sex, Race, and Honor in Colonial Cartagena de Indias*. Albuquerque: University of New México Press, 2013.

Walker, Tamara. *Exquisite Slaves: Race, Clothing, and Status in Colonial Lima.* New York: Cambridge University Press, 2017.
Walleit, Lisa. "El oficio de pregonero municipal en la Castilla bajomedieval." In *Governar a cidade na Europa medieval. The Governance of Medieval European Towns*, edited by A. Aguiar Andrade, and G. Melo da Silva, 83–97. Lisbon: IEM – Instituto de Estudos Medievais, 2021.
Wheat, David. "The First Great Waves: African Provenance Zones for the Transatlantic Slave Trade to Cartagena De Indias, 1570–1640," *Journal of African History*, 52:1, 2011, 1–22.
Wheat, David. "Global Transit Points and Travel in the Iberian Maritime World, 1580–1640." In *Governing the Sea in the Early Modern Era: Essays in Honor of Robert C. Ritchie*, edited by Peter C. Mancal, and Carole Shammas, 253–274. San Marino: Huntington Library Press, 2015.
Wheat, David. *Atlantic Africa and the Spanish Caribbean, 1570–1640.* Chapel Hill: University of North Carolina Press, 2016.
Wheat, David. "Catalina de los Santos, femme libre de couleur et son navire (Santo Domingo, 1593)," *Clio. Femmes, Genre, Histoire*, 50, 2019, 139–154.
Wheat, David. "Tangomãos en Tenerife y Sierra Leona a mediados del siglo XVI," *Cliocanarias*, 2, 2020, 545–569.
Wheat, David. "Otros pasajes. Movilidades africanas y la polifuncionalidadde los navíos negreros en el Atlántico ibérico, siglos XVI–XVII." In *Sometidos a esclavitud: los africanos y sus descendientes en el Caribe Hispano*, edited by Consuelo Naranjo Orovio, 89–116. Santa Marta: Unimagdalena, 2021.
Wheat, David, and Marc Eagle. "The Early Iberian Slave Trade to the Spanish Caribbean, 1500–1580," In *From the Galleons to the Highlands; Slave Trade Routes in the Spanish Americas*, edited by Alex Borucki, David Eltis, and David Wheat, 47–72. Albuquerque: University of New México Press, 2020.
Wheeler, Eva Michellem. "(Re)Framing *Raza*: Language as a Lens for Examining Race and Skin Color Categories in the Dominican Republic," PhD Dissertation, University of California Santa Barbara, 2015.
Wisnoski, Alexander L. "Intimate Knowledge and the Making of Witnesses in Lima's Seventeenth-Century Divorce Court," Colonial Latin American Review, 29:2, 2020, 239–55.
Withers, Charles W. J. "Place and the 'Spatial Turn' in Geography and in History," *Journal of the History of Ideas*, 70:4, 2009, 637–658.
Wright, Elizabeth R. *The Epic of Juan Latino; Dilemmas of Race and Religion in Renaissance Spain.* Toronto: University of Toronto Press, 2016.
Yannakakis, Yanna. *The Art of Being In-Between: Native Intermediaries, Indian Identity, and Local Rule in Colonial Oaxaca.* Durham: Duke University Press, 2008.
Yannakakis, Yanna. "Allies or Servants? The Journey of Indian Conquistadors in the Lienzo of Analco," *Ethnohistory*, 58:4, 2011, 653–682.
Yannakakis, Yanna. "Indigenous People and Legal Culture in Spanish America," *History Compass*, 11:11, 2013, 931–947.

Yannakakis, Yanna. *Since Time Immemorial; Native Custom and Law in Colonial Mexico*. Durham: Duke University Press, 2023.

Yannakakis, Yanna, and Martina Schrader-Kniffki. "Between the 'Old Law' and the New: Christian Translation, Indian Jurisdiction, and Criminal Justice in Colonial Oaxaca," *Hispanic American Historical Review*, 96:3, 2016, 517–548.

Index

Note: Page numbers in *italic* refers to table. Endnotes are indicated by the page number followed by "n" and the endnote number e.g., 20 n1 refers to endnote 1 on page 20.

Abrego, Luisa de, 94
Agustin *Moreno*, 224
Alarcon, Leonor de, 89, 257
Alaves, Melchor, 159
Albornoz, Barbola de, 29
Alegre
    Francisco de Alegre, 199
    Hernando Alegre, 199
Almodóvar, Juan de, 198
Álvarez, Antonio, 129, 141–150. *See also* Margarita de Sossa
Ana Zavala, 134
Andrea (no second name listed), 138
Angeles, Hipólita de los, 163n42
Antón *Jolofe*, 139
Antón *Zape*, 233
Antonelli, Bautista, 232, 240
Antonia (no second name listed), 163n42
Arellano, Juan de, 181–186
Arenas, Antonio de, 94
Arriaga, Beatriz de, 128
Arriaga, Lacayo de (*cofrade*), 169
Azuaga, Francisca de, 101–102

baptism, debates about the validity of
    baptisms in Middle Passage, 210–212
Barrera, Juan de la, 230, 235
Barroso, Sebastián, 215

Bartolomé (Black *criollo*), 181–186
Bautista de Cárdenas, Juan, 156–157, 164
Bautista Pérez, Manuel, 207–226
Bautista, Juan (*fiscal*), 169
Bautista, Juana, 46, 89, 257
Bautista, María, 101–102
Bayano Wars [Panama], 155
    first Bayano War 1549–1556, 154
    second Bayano War 1579–1582, 154
Bolivia (present-day country)
    Potosí, 55
Bustos, Isabel de, 163n42

Cabrera, Clara Ruíz de, 140
Cáceres, Juan de, 119
Camacho, Francisco de, 130
Cañete, Mateo, 42
Carmona, Pedro de, 28, 190, 198–207
Carreño
    Francisco Carreño, 140, 159
    Juan de Carreño, 141
Carrera de Indias, 4
    impact on daily life in
        Nombre de Dios and Portobelo (Panama), 231–239
        Sevilla (Spain), 82–90
        towns between Veracruz and Mexico City (Mexico), 119–129
Carvajal, Ana de, 89, 256

Casas, Bartolomé de Las (bishop of
    Chiapas, Dominican friar), 20,
    191, 198–207
Castro, Alonso de, 256
Castroverde, Cristóbal de, 44, 94, 96–97
Catalina (no second name listed), 30, 56
  Balthasar Bonifico, 30
  Juan Bonifico, 30
Catalina *Zape*, 137
  Juana, 137
  María, 137
Catholicism
  Black Catholics, 165–175, 189–227
    Kriston community, Cacheu, 213
  confraternities and brotherhoods,
    165–175
  discourse of Catholicism as historically
    inclusive of Black people,
    165–175
  in West Africa, 192–198, 207–226
Celada, Bartolomé de (procurator),
    168–172, 174
Cerda, Alonso de, 135
Chichimeca Wars (1550–1590), [Mexico],
    159, 179
Cisna, Señora Lucrecia de, 119
citizenship. *See also* political discourses
    deployed by Black petitioners
    before royal courts
  naturaleza, 37–39
  requests for local authorities to issue
    confirmations of *vecindad* and
    freedom, 58–60
  vecindad, 37–39, 154–156, 179
    attempts by city leaders to exclude
    Black people, 154–156
Claver, Pedro de (Jesuit, 1580–1654),
    210–211
Colombia (present-day country)
  Cartagena de Indias, 4, 29, 45, 47, 63,
    100, 162, 207–226
  Santa Fé de Bogotá, 30, 223
communication
  across spaces
    in cities
      discussions about Black people's
      status as enslaved, free-
      born or *horro* among urban
      communities, 45–51
    proving ties with Spanish Americas
      in Sevilla, 104
    Sevilla, 65–115

  oceanic trading routes
    Carrera de Indias, 65–115
    navío de aviso (a ship within the
      annual fleet that transported
      royal mail), 98
    poderes (legal powers) sent across the
      Spanish Atlantic world, 103
    speed of, 6
  terrestrial trading routes
    caminos (New Spain), 119–141
  modes
    letter writing, 4–5, 54, 65–115,
      238, 246
    Felipa de la Cruz's letters to Antón
      Segarra, 252–255
    public discussions about private
      letters, 99–102
    word-of-mouth, 4–5, 65–115
      about Castilian laws of slavery and
      freedom, 189–227
    royal petitioning, 156–165,
      175–186
  professions or trades
    correo (messenger by trade for
      both official and private
      correspondence), 101
    escribiente (offers services in reading
      and writing for a fee), 102
    particulares (messengers), 98
  public sphere (concept), 6–7
confraternities and brotherhoods, 6–7
  Lima (Peru)
    Cofradía de Nuestra Señora de la
      Antigua (Lima Cathedral), 109
    Mexico City (Mexico), 175–186
    mutual aid practices among Black
      confraternities and
      brotherhoods for *rescate*
      (including gifts and loans),
      138–140
    Mexico City (Mexico), 137–138
    Portobelo (Panama), 137–138
  Sevilla (Spain)
    Brotherhood of Mulatos of
      Ildelfonso, 165
    Our Lady of Antiquity, 167
    Our Lady of the Angels, 9–10, 76–77,
      165–175
      leadership roles and membership in
      1604, 168
      leadership roles and membership in
      1606, 168

Index 311

patronage ties, 165–175
Our Lady of the Rosary, 167
San Buenaventura and Ánimas in the Casa Grande (San Francisco convent), 79
Contreras, Manso de (*gobernador* of Santa Marta), 240
Contresas, Luisa de, 139
conversos, 20, 36
Cordera, Lucía, 88
Coronado, Luis (*moreno*), 140
Coronado, Luis de (*teniente general* of the *gobernador* of Cartagena de Indias), 215, 222–223
Coronado, Magdalena de, 59, 163
Corza, Angelina, 163n42
Cosme (no second name listed), 139
Cota, María de, 57n129
criers
  employed by an institution (by royal appointment)
    House of Trade criers, Sevilla, 91–92, 116
  municipal
    Black and *mulato* criers, 138, 134–138, 249
    San Miguel de Allende, 179
    Sevilla, 74, 81
Cruz, Felipa de la, 26, 65–115, 164
  map of the social ties of a generation of free and liberated Black Sevillanos in Felipa de la Cruz's generation (approximately, 1569–1626), 252–255
  transcription and translation of Felipa de la Cruz's letters, 252–255
Cruz, Juana de la, 132
Cruz, Jusephe de la, 132
Cruz, Pedro de la, 131
Cuba (present-day country)
  Havana, 4, 101, 162, 203

de Gongora, Francisco (*mayordomo*), 169
Déniz, Catalina, 97
Dias, Ambrosio, 216
Díaz de Cea, Dominga, 163n42
Díaz, Ana, 62, 63
Díaz, Angelina, 45, 162
Díaz, Inés, 61
divorce (ecclesiastical). *See* marriage
Domingo *Gelofe*, 38, 192–198
Domínguez, Luissa, 29

Dominican Republic (present-day country)
  Isla Española
    1522 uprising led by enslaved *Jolofs*, 193
    Santo Domingo, 28, 47, 63, 198–207
Drake, Sir Francis (1540–1596), 228–251

ecclesiastical courts
  Juzgados del Palacio Arzobispal (courts of the Archbishopric Palace), Sevilla, 165–175
  tribunal eclesiástico, Puebla de los Ángeles
    petition for ecclesiastical divorce, 141–150
  papal courts, Vatican, 168, 173, 175
Ecuador (present-day country)
  Quito, 161
Elena (*Zape* nation), 216
England (present-day country)
  London, population estimate, 34
English piracy, 228–251
enslavement
  branding
    enslavers' practice of burning initials or symbols on enslaved people's skin with scorching irons to brand their property, 49–51, 120, 149, 216, 219–220
  debates on the legitimacy of enslavement under Castilian law
    conditions for a just war that permitted legitimate enslavement, 220–222
    enslaved people's petitions to royal courts for their liberty on the basis of their illegitimate enslavement, 189–227
    general, conditions that permitted legitimate enslavement under Castilian law, 189–227
    on the enslavement of Black Africans, 189–227
      Bartolomé de las Casas, 205–206
    on the enslavement of fellow Christians, 192–198, 216, 207–226
    on the enslavement of Indigenous Americans, 192–198
  transatlantic trade in enslaved Africans, 1–3
Espinosa, Leonor de, 56n125

Ethiopian Church, 215
ethnonyms
  West Africa
    Bañol, 18, 241, 244, 247
    Bañon, 247
    Biafara, 18, 129, 247
    Bran, 18, 215, 218, 241, 247
    Cocoli, 18, 244, 247
    Jolofo/Jolofe, 18, 241, 247
    Mandinga, 18, 131
    Yalonga, 18
    Zape, 18, 131, 213–216, 233, 249
  West-Central Africa
    Angola, 18, 128, 129
    Congo, 18
exile sentences
  petitions for pardons, 175–186

Faustina (no second name listed), 57n129
Felipa (*Mandinga*), 131
Fernández de Córdoba y López de las Roelas, Diego (viceroy of New Spain, 1612–1621), 177, 180
Fernández de Santillán, 67
  family palace known as
    Casa Palacio Francisco Fernández de Santillán, 1500?–1679, 67, 105
    Palacio del Marqués de la Motilla, 1679–2023, 114
    sale of palace in 2023, 114
  members of the family
    Don Alonso Fernández de Santillán, (b. 1604), 114
    Don Francisco Fernández de Santillán, (b. 1565) (*veinticuatro de Sevilla*), 67, 113–115
    Don Francisco Fernández de Santillán, (b. 1629) (*Marqués de la Motilla*, 1679–), 114
    Doña Beatriz Gómez [Fernández de Santillán], 113
Fernández, Vasco, 61
Figueroa
  Francisca de Figueroa, 100–101, 258
  Juana de Figueroa, 100
  María de Figueroa, 100
Flandes, Isabel de, 54–55
Flores, María de, 257
France (present-day country)
  Paris, population estimate, 34
Francisco (Black *criollo* crier), 249

Francisco (enslaved, and no second name listed), 219
Francisco (*natural* of Sevilla), 42
freedom
  freedom (general)
    discussions about Black people's status as enslaved, free-born or *horro* among urban communities, 45–51
    freedom within discourses of political belonging, 165–186
    protections of freedom under Castilian law, debates, 189–227
    the stealing or looting of someone's liberty (discourse), 191
    visual and aural markers of freedom, 49–51
    vulnerability of freedom, 189–227
  freedom papers, and practices of protection and possession, 28–29
    autos or royal decrees confirming an individual's freedom following their petition for liberty in a royal court, 189–227
    carta de alhorría, 22, 129–141
    discussions about freedom papers among urban communities, 104–105
    documenting capital as a means of practising and protecting freedom, 228–251
    enslavers' practice of stealing or illegitimately withholding a liberated person's freedom papers, 198–207
    implications of misplacing freedom papers, 60–62, 106
    importance of possession of freedom papers to prove liberty before a royal court, 198–207, 209
    practice of requesting supplementary confirmations of liberty with additional notaries or municipal authorities, 22, 30, 51–64
    protection and possession, 51–64, 141
  liberation from slavery (*alhorría*–legal act of liberating an enslaved person from captivity, per Castilian legal codes)
    act of, 25–27

Index 313

liberation clauses in enslavers' testaments, 22, 24, 28, 40, 55, 57, 140, 199, 247
  practice of heirs or executors withholding the testament to prevent liberation, 198–207
rescate (the purchase of one's own or another person's liberty from slavery)
  at auctions
    negotiating terms of enslavement with prospective owners, 134–138
    negotiating terms of loans with prospective creditors, 134–138
  average price that enslaved Black people paid to purchase their liberty, 112, 129
  mutual aid practices among kin for *rescate* (including gifts and loans), 106–110, 129–141, 234
  mutual aid practices in Black confraternities and brotherhoods for *rescate* (including gifts and loans), 137–140
  practises of *rescate* in Sevilla, 106–110
  self-purchase, 129–141
    access to credit, 129–141
    paying for liberty in instalments, 129–141
  petitions for freedom in royal courts due to illegitimate enslavement, 189–227
Fuentes, Gaspar de, 132, 133
fuero [municipal legislation], 154

Gallardo, Francisco, 149
Gamarra
  Ana (no second name listed), 108–109
  Francisco de Gamarra, 7, 108–109
Gasco, Amar O (*mayordomo*), 169, 174
Gaspar (no second name listed), 242
Gaspar *de tierra Bañol*, 241, 243, 245, 247
Gerónima, María, 96
Gómez, Ana, 88, 91–92, 97, 134, 137, 228–251, 256
  founding of a perpetual *capellanía* in the Magdalena Church, Sevilla (Spain), 238

  ties with Black residents of Santiago del Principe, Nombre de Dios (Panama), 246–247
Gómez, Francisco (procurator), 216–217, 222
Gómez, María, 60–62, 106–107, 163, 257
González, Francisco, 256
González, Jerónimo, 161
González, Julián, 105
Gutiérrez de la Sal, Juan, 230
Gutiérrez, Elvira, 138
Gutiérrez, Juana, 256

Hakluyt, Richard (1553–1616), 232
Hernández [Portilla], Sebastián, 140
Hernández de Santiago, Alonso (*canónigo*, and commissary to the Inquisition in Puebla de los Ángeles), 126, 129, 147–148
Hernández, Ana, 130, 140
Hernández, Enriquez, 221
Hernández, Gabriel (*cofrade*), 169
Hernández, Hipólito, 127
Hernández, Isabel, 97, 198–199, 207
Hernández, Josefe (*cofrade*), 169
Hernández, Luis, 155
Hernández, Pero, 58, 125
Hernández, Sofía, 103
Herrera, Crispina de, 100n117
Herrera, Pedro de, 182, 185
Honduras (present-day country), 200
  Gracias a Dios, 201
  San Juan de Puerto de Caballos (present-day Puerto Cortés), 201
Hortiz de Espinosa, Pedro, 155

Iberian ideas about race and difference
  municipal authorities' attempts to exclude Black people from *vecindad*, 154–156
  municipal authorities' attempts to link Blackness to fugitivity and disloyalty to the Spanish crown, 154–156
  racialised terms to describe people
    atezado, 19
    bozal, 19, 128
    explanation of usage, 18–19
    lora, 19
    morena, 19

Index

Iberian ideas (cont.)
   mulata, 19
   negra, 19
   visual or aural markers of slavery or freedom beyond racialization, 49–51
Iberian Union (1580–1640), 21
Inquisitorial courts
   general, 29, 36
   Holy Office of the Inquisition, Cartagena de Indias, 29, 212, 214
   Holy Office of the Inquisition, Lima, 225
   Holy Office of the Inquisition, Lisbon, 214
   Holy Office of the Inquisition, México (Mexico City), 119, 125, 141–150
      commissary in Puebla de los Ángeles, 126
   Holy Office of the Inquisition, Sevilla, 77, 78
   Inquisitorial investigations in West Africa
      Cacheu, 214
inter-imperial warfare, 228–251
Isabel (*tierra Zape*), 131
Isabel de Bustos, 45
Isla Española. *See* Dominican Republic (present-day country)
Isla, Leonor de la, 96–98
Italy (present-day country)
   Venice, population estimate, 34

Jalapa, Juana, 125
Jamaica (present-day country), 3, 24
Jerónima (no second name listed), 48, 53, 103, 256
Jesús, Agustina de, 89, 257
Jesús, Ana de, 55
Jesús, Inés de, 87
Juan (no second name listed), born in Triana, 135
Juan *Biafara*, 138
Juan III, King of Portugal and the Algarves (reigned, 1521–1557), 206
Juan *Jolofo*, 241, 247, 249
Juan, Gaspar, 90
   litigation for freedom from illegitimate enslavement in Real Audiencia de Sevilla (Spain), 57–58
Juana (no second name listed), 103n130, 132–133, 139

Juanillo (no second name listed), 201
Juseph *Bran*, 241–242

labor, free people (selected examples)
   enslaved people
      labor-for-hire agreements between enslaved and their enslavers, 117, 124, 131, 150
   maritime, 42
      diver (*buzo*), 42, 51
      grumete (in Spanish context–ship laborer), 42
      grumete (in West Africa, Cacheu context–Kristo rowers, pilots, interpreters, petty traders, and brokers), 213–214, 216, 220–221
      mariner, 42
      page (*paje de nao*), 42
      wage-earning servants (*criados*) to passengers on ships, 30, 43–46, 53–54, 58–62, 65, 89, 107, 127, 152, 162–163, 197, 204, 230, 234
   military
      soldier, 42, 79, 87, 157, 160–161, 239, 246
   rural
      administer plantations, 159
      leaseholders of agricultural land, 179
      master of sugar, 141
      owner of small-scale livestock, 54
      tenant of small parcel of land, 54
      wage-earning plantation workers, (mentioned in the *discurso de vida* in Juana Jalapa's Inquisitorial trial), 125
   urban
      builder (*albañil*), 108
      chocolate producers, 124
      clothes-washers, 124
      cook, 124, 130, 233
      healer, 124, 127
      hospital workers, 124
      innkeeper, 127, 149
      merchant (*tratante*), 215, 228–251
      pastry chef, 178
      seamstress, 124
      street sweepers, 124
      tailor, 156
      wage-earning servants to private employers, 75, 184, 218

Index

Landa, Beatriz de, 100n117
Latino, Juan, 97, 172
Leonor (no second name listed), 138
Limón, Juan, 29
López, Alonso, 236, 237
López, Pedro, 236, 245–247
López, Rodrigo, 28, 198
Lorenzo, Francisco (*diputado*), 169
Loya
    Antón de Loya, 178, 181–186
    Francisco de Loya, 177, 181–186
Lucía *Cocoli*, 244
Lucrecia "*bozal Angola*", 128
Lugones, Juan de (*escribiente* / writer), 95
Luis, Antonio (*alcalde*, 1604, and *prioste*, 1606), 169, 174
Luisa (no second name listed), 139
Lumbreras, Agustina de, 163n42
Luna, Pedro de, 181–186
Lunares, Pedro de, 103

Magdalena (no second name listed), 52, 257
Manuel (enslaved, and no second name listed)
    testimony about experience of enslavement and displacement across Middle Passage, 219
Marqués de la Motilla. *See* Fernández de Santillán
marriage
    abandonment, 94, 125, 141–150
    bigamy, 94, 125
    expectations of marital duties, 141–150
    petitions for annulments of a marriage, 94, 125
    petitions for divorce (ecclesiastical), 141–150
    depósito, 145, 146
    public perceptions of a marriage, 141–150
    violence between spouses, 141–150
marronage, 3–4, 24–25
    fugitivity from enslavers in Castilian laws of slavery, *Siete Partidas*, 25
    New Kingdom of Granada, 212
        Black *palenques* in the hinterlands of Cartagena de Indias, 217
            Matudere Palenque, 217
            Palenque del Limón, 217
    New Spain
        establishment of powerful Black *palenque* in Córdoba, led by Yanga, 176
    Panama, Isthmus, 154
        alliance between Black maroons and English privateer Francis Drake, 1572–3, 232–233
        Bayano Wars (1549–1556, and 1579–1582), 232–33
        negotiations for peace and maroons agreements to, 232–233
Marta (*Zape*), 131
Martín, Antón, 216
Martín, Bartolomé, 127–128. *See also* Ana de Tapia
Martín, Francisco, 207–226
Martín, Lucas, 140
Maynarde, Thomas, 244
Mendes Torres, Diego, 243
Méndez Mezquita, Juan, 220–121
Méndez, Leonor de, 236
Mendoza, Francisca, 101
Mendoza, Lucía de, 46, 257
Mendoza, Luis de (*alcalde*), 169, 174
Mendoza, Sebastián de (*prioste*), 169
Merlo, Dionosio de, 132
Mexico (present-day country)
    Jalapa, 103, 119–141
    León, 159, 156–165
    Mérida, 160
    Metepec, 159
    México (Mexico City), 4, 94, 103, 119–141, 156–165, 175–186
        1612 suspected Black conspiracy
        Black *vecinos*' petitions to be exempt from prohibitions on Black *vecindad*, 175–186
        effects on Black *vecinos* in San Miguel de Allende, 175–186
        Real Audiencia de México attempts to prohibit Black *vecindad* in cities, 175–186
        Real Audiencia de México issues capital punishments and permanent exile sentences to Black *vecinos* suspected as perpetrators, 175–186
    confraternities and brotherhoods, 153
    Orizaba, 119–141
    Huatusco, 140
    Puebla de los Ángeles, 118–150

Mexico (present-day country) (cont.)
  roads between San Juan de Ulúa and
      Mexico City
    Camino de Veracruz, 119–141
    Camino Nuevo, 119–141
    San Juan de Ulúa, 119–141
    San Miguel de Allende, 175–186
    Sierra Madre Oriental, 121
    Toluca, 159
    Veracruz, 4, 43, 60, 94, 119–141
      New Veracruz, 119–141
      Old Veracruz, 119–141
  viceroyalty of New Spain (general), 62
  wars
    Chichimeca Wars (1550–1590), 159, 179
    Mixtón War (1540–1542), 126
  Yucatán, 160
    Mérida, 58
Middle Passage, 1–3, 207–226
  arrival of slave ships at San Juan de
      Ulúa, New Spain, 121
Miguel, Juan, 88, 182, 185
Mixtón Wars (1540–42), [Mexico], 126
Montedeosca
  Juan de Montedeosca, 87
  Pedro de Montedeosca, 87, 91, 256
Monterrey, Melchiora de, 177
Morales, Diego de, 49
Morales, María de, 139
moriscos, 20, 36
  expulsion from Castilla in 1610, 34
Moronta, Juan, 139
Morrera, Domingo, 219
municipal officers and chiefs of justice
  alcalde, 52–55, 155, 159–160
  alcalde mayor, 159
  alcalde ordinario
    Lima, 55
    San Miguel de Allende, 179
  asistente, 155
    asistente de Sevilla, 53
    teniente of the *asistente de Sevilla*, 53
  corregidor, 155
  gobernador, 155
  teniente general (chief legal counsel to
      the *gobernador*), 207–226
Muñoz, Pedro, 139

naturaleza. *See* citizenship
New Laws of the Indies, the, 1542 (Las
      Leyes Nuevas de Indias, 1542)
  prohibition by Castilian crown of the
      enslavement of Indigenous
      Americans, except for just war,
      20, 192–198
Nicaragua (present-day country), 61
Niño de Guevara, Fernando (Archbishop
      of Sevilla) (b. 1541–1609),
      165–175

O, María de la, 48, 89, 106, 257
Ojada, Alberto, 242
Ordás, Diego de (*conquistador*), 192
Ortiz, Isabel, 163n42

palenques. *See* marronage
Palma, Cristóbal de la, 234. *See also* Lucía
      Tenorio Palma
Panama (present-day country)
  attack by Francis Drake and Richard
      Hawkins, 1595–6, 239–246
  Gulf of Panama, 29
  impact of Carrera de Indias on daily
      life in Nombre de Dios and
      Portobelo, 231–239
  Nombre de Dios, 4, 88, 99, 156–165,
      228–251
  Panamá (Panama City), 45,
      156–165, 234
    cabildo, 154
  Portobelo, 4, 130, 137, 228–251
  Santiago del Principe, 243
    experiences of 1595 attack, and links
      with Ana Gómez, 246–247
  Veragua, 29
papal ambassador, 173
papal bull, 173
Pedro *de Tierra Bran*, 215, 218
Pedro *Zape Yalonga*, 249
Peres de Tudela, Licenciado Clemente,
      163
Pérez, Domingo, 177, 181–186
Pérez, Felipa, 163n42
Pérez, Juan, 230
Peru (present-day country), 197
  Lima, 4, 29, 55, 95, 108–109, 225
Philippines, Republic of (present-day
      country)
  Manila, 119
Pineda (Lima)
  Juan de Pineda, 95, 257
  María de Pineda, 95

Index

Pineda (Sevilla)
  Ana (*lora*), 40
  Juan de Pineda, 40
  Pedro de Pineda, 40
Pinelo, Luis, 91, 256
piracy, 228–251
Pisana, Beltran (*cofrade*), 169
poderes (legal powers), 85–87, 168, 186
political discourses deployed by Black petitioners before royal courts
  belonging, 7–9, 154–188
  Catholicism as historically inclusive of Black people, 165–175
  freedom, 154–188
    practicing freedom in expansive terms, 228–251
  good governance, 165–175
  loyalty, 154–188
  petitions for exemptions to tribute tax, 156–165
  vassalage, 154–188
  vecindad, 154–188
    against exclusion and expulsion of Black *vecinos*, 154–156
Porras, Francisca de, 139
Portugal (present-day country), 20–21
  colonial entrepôts and settlements. *See also* West Africa; West-Central Africa
  Azores, 21
  Madeira, 21
  Lisbon, 203
  Mora, 160
  Porto, 119
  Tavira, 60, 219
Prado, Francisco del (friar), 173
Priego, Hernan, 135
procurators, 207–226
  Black petitioners in Sevilla for the Council of the Indies (Madrid), 175–186
  in freedom litigation suits, 200, 207–226
  Our Lady of the Angels (Sevilla), 165–175
  Sebastián Rodríguez (Panamá), 155
  specialist in confraternity disputes in Sevilla, 168
Puerto Rico (present-day country), 28, 198–207
  San Juan, 199

Ramírez, Catalina, 87
Ramírez, Diego, 179–180
Ramírez, Pedro (*moreno*), 169
Ramos, Felipe, 48
Rebenga, Inés de, 28
Reyes, Baltasar de los, 184
Reyes, Melchora de los, 58–59, 163
Ribas, Alonso de, 129
Ribera, María de, 92
Robles, Sebastián de, 181–186
Rodrigues, Vicente, 247
Rodríguez, Antonio, 214, 216
Rodríguez, Sebastián, 42
Rodríguez, Sebastián (procurator), 155
Romero, Mateo (procurator of assets), 169
royal courts
  Casa de la Contratación (House of Trade), (Sevilla, Spain), 36, 156–165, 193, 206
  bienes de difuntos (probate courts / assets of the deceased), 91–92, 110–115, 228–251
  licencias de embarque (embarkation licenses), 22–64, 175–186
  interviews with petitioners and their witnesses, 41
  Consejo de Indias (Council of the Indies), (itinerant across Castilla between 1526 and 1561, and located in Madrid from 1561 onwards, 27, 35, 40, 111–112, 156–165, 175–186, 192–207
  licencias de pasaje (passenger licenses), 22–64, 175–186
  royal decrees, 156–165, 175–186
  matters heard by royal courts (general)
  grace (explanation), 155
  justice (explanation), 155
  Real Audiencia de Guatemala (Gracias a Dios, Honduras), 198–207
  Real Audiencia de México (Mexico City, Mexico), 141, 156–165, 175–186
  1612 suspected Black conspiracy
  Real Audiencia de México issues capital punishments and permanent exile sentences to Black *vecinos* suspected as perpetrators, 153

royal courts (cont.)
  Real Audiencia de Panamá (Panama City, Panama), 156–165, 242
  Real Audiencia de Santa Fé (Bogotá, Colombia), 30, 207–226
  Real Audiencia de Santo Domingo (Santo Domingo, Dominican Republic), 198–207
  Real Audiencia de Sevilla (Sevilla, Spain), 57, 76, 77, 165–175
  Real Audiencias (general), 29
  teniente general (chief legal counsel to the governor) in Cartagena de Indias (Cartagena, Colombia), 207–226
royal decrees
  circulation of royal decrees among Black communities, 156–165, 175–186
Ruíz [Díaz], Juana, 59
Ruíz de Elduayen, Miguel, 242, 244
Ruíz, Baltasar, 59
Ruíz, Catalina, 102
Ruíz, Isabel, 131

Saenz, Martín, 132
Sal, Sebastiana de la, 98–100, 234
Salas Barbadillo, Alonso Jerónimo de (1581–1635), 165
San Miguel, Francisca de, 138
Sánchez Coello, Alonso (1531–1588), 83
Sánchez, Ana, 85
Sánchez, Constanza, 103n130
Sánchez, Cristóbal, 138
sanctuary laws (Spanish crown, 1680s), 4
Sandoval, Alonso de (Jesuit priest), 208–214
Santiago, Felipa de, 103n130
Sebastián (no second name listed), 135
Segarra
  Antón Segarra, 22, 26, 54, 65, 67, 98, 104–105, 256
    deceased, 111
  Doña Juana Segarra de Saavedra, 22, 67
  Francisco Segarra, 22
Selpuldes, Felipe de, 101
Siete Partidas, Las, 23, 25
  on freedom, 24–25, 154–156
    limited conditions when a liberated person could be returned to captivity, 25
  on slavery, 118, 189
  on the illegitimacy of enslaving fellow Christians, 196
  punishments for fugitivity from an enslaver, 25
Silva, Pedro de, 179
silver
  silver mining (New Spain)
    effects on economy, 123
    engineering projects for more efficient transport, 123
    surplus of money, 134
  silver mining (Peru)
    Potosí, 55
    significance of the port of Nombre de Dios, and later Portobelo (present-day Panama), 231–232
  silver mining (Spanish Americas)
    transportation to Castilla, 82, 232
    importation of silver to Sevilla, and effects on city life, 80, 85
slavery. *See* enslavement
Soria, Francisca de, 233–234
Sosa, Ginesa de, 108
Sossa, Margarita de, 88, 117–131, 141–150
Soto, Pedro de (priest), 137
Spain (present-day country)
  Aranda, 204, 198–207
  Baena, 37
  Cádiz, 34, 103
  Canary Islands, 42, 130, 141, 159
    Tenerife, 97, 192
  Ciudad Rodrigo, 233
  Córdoba, 37
  Écija, 22, 53, 105
  Huelva, 127
    Lepe, 54
    Niebla (condado of the Duke of Medina Sidonia), 229
  Jérez de la Frontera, 37, 94
  la Torre, 37
  Madrid, 63, 156–165
  Málaga, 164
  Montemolin, 37
  San Lucar de Barrameda, 192
  Sevilla, 4, 31–116, 120, 175–186, 192–207, 228–251
    arrival of petitioners from Spanish Americas *en route* to the Council of the Indies, 156–165, 175–186

Index

Black religious brotherhoods, 165–175
churches, convents, and monasteries
  Convento Nuestra Señora de la Merced (Convent of Mercy), 173
  Magdalena Church, 238
  Salvador Church, 74–77
parishes and neighborhoods
  La Magdalena, 101, 112, 238, 256
  Ómium Sanctorum, 258
  San Andrés, 257
  San Bartolomé, 101, 257
  San Bernardo, 49, 258
  San Esteban, 257
  San Gil, 230, 256
  San Ildefonso, 165, 257
  San Juan de la Palma, 87, 107, 256
  San Julián, 257
  San Lorenzo, 258
  San Miguel, 257
  San Pedro, 107, 256–257
  San Roque, 165, 168
  San Salvador, 67–81, 230, 256
  San Vicente, 257
  Santa Cruz, 256
  Santa María la Blanca, 165
  Santa María la Mayor, 256
  Santa Marina, 258
  Triana, 167, 256
population in long sixteenth century
  expulsion of *moriscos* in 1610, 34
  free and enslaved Black people, 34–35
  growth, 31–34
  plagues
    1599–1601, 34
    1647–1652, 34
street names
  Calle Conde Negro, 165
  Calle de los Mulatos, 165
  Plaza de los Mulatos, 165
  Plazuela del Atambor, 167
Sevilla (province)
  Carmona, 96
  Sanlucar la Mayor, 37
Talavera, 38
Úbeda, 38
Valencia, 156, 164
Valencia de Alcantara, 38
Zafra, 38, 39
Suárez, Alonso, 42
Suárez, Ana, 29
Suárez, Diego, 79, 91, 97, 256
Suárez, Isabel, 236
sumptuary legislation, 154, 178

Tamayo, Francisco de, 181–186
Tapia y Cáceres, Alonso de, 63
Tapia, Ana de, 127–129. *See also* Bartolomé Martín
Tapia, Catalina de, 47, 62–64, 258
Tenorio
  Gregorio Tenorio, 90
  Juana Tenorio, 90
  Lucía Tenorio Palma, 90, 130, 234, 256
Toral, María del, 136
Toral, Sebastián de, 58, 160
Torre, Antón de la (*cofrade*), 169
Torre, María de la, 113
Torres
  Francisco de Torres, 43
  José Vásquez, 43
Torres, Melchor de, 199–204
Torres, Simon de (judge of *bienes de difuntos* in Panamá), 248–249
travel licenses
  attempts by Spanish crown to prevent certain people from travelling to the Americas, and the establishment of travel licensing
  prohibited people, 36
  practice of falsification of passenger licenses, and evasion of embarkation licenses, 41–42
  types
    asientos de pasajeros (passenger lists), 31–45, 197
    licencias de embarque (embarkation licenses), 31–45, 175–186
    proving family ties or American *naturaleza*, 92–104
    licencias de pasaje (passenger licenses), 31–45, 175–186
    circumvention of requirement for a passenger license by obtaining employment as a *criado*, 43–45
    proving family ties or American *naturaleza*, 92–104
tribute tax
  introduction of tax liability for free Black men and woman in the Indies, 1574, 156–165

tribute tax (cont.)
    petitions for exemptions from tribute tax liability, 156–165. *See also* political discourses deployed by Black petitioners before royal courts
    Spanish crown's justifications for the introduction, 157
Troughton, John, 241

Valladolid, Lorenza de, 56–57
Valladolid, Luisa de, 98–99
Vargas, Isabel de, 90
Vasconcelos, Gaspar de, 97
Vatican. *See* ecclesiastical courts
vecindad. *See* citizenship
Vega, Lope de (playwright, 1562–1635), 77
Velasco y Castilla, Luis de (viceroy of New Spain, 1590–1595, 1607–1611, and president of Council of the Indies, 1611–1617), 176–178, 183–184
Velázquez, Beatriz, 163n42
Venezuela (present-day country)
    Gulf of Paría, 193
Venta de los Naranjos. *See* Bartolomé Martín
viceroys (New Spain)
    Diego Fernández de Córdoba y López de las Roelas (viceroy of New Spain, 1612–1621), 177, 180
    Juan de Mendoza y Luna (viceroy of New Spain, 1603–1607), 183
    Lorenzo Suárez de Mendoza Jiménez (viceroy of New Spain, 1580–1583), 183
    Luis de Velasco y Castilla (viceroy of New Spain, 1590–1595, 1607–1611, and president of Council of the Indies, 1611–1617, 123, 176
Viegas, Jorge, 61
Villalobos, Antonio de (*escribano*), 96, 168–170

Villancicos de Negros, 77
Villegas, Pedro de, 179
Vitoria, Isabel de, 100n146, 108

West Africa
    general, 198
    Gold Coast
        São Jorge da Mina, 21
    islands and archipelagos, near coast
        Cape Verde, 21, 28, 106, 198, 213, 219
        Santiago, 61
    Senegambia
        Gambia, 213
        Jolof Empire, 192–198
        Petite Côte
            New Christian–Sephardic–Senegambian communities, 192–198
    Sierra Leone, 212–213
    Upper Guinea
        Cacheu, 21, 207–226
        grumetes and *tungumás*, 213
        Kriston, 213
West-Central Africa
    Angola (present-day country)
        Benguela, 21
        Luanda, 21, 209
    islands
        São Tomé and Principe (present-day country)
            São Tomé, 21, 209

Xuárez, Doña Isabel, 49

Ybarra
    Barbola, 47, 64, 258
    María, 47, 64, 258

Zafra, Antón de, 38
Zafra, Isabel de, 38–39
Zuñiga, Doña Mencia de, 230